Microsoft®

Microsoft® Office Visio® 2003 Step by Step

Judy Lemke and Resources Online

PUBLISHED BY
Microsoft Press
A Division of Microsoft Corporation
One Microsoft Way
Redmond, Washington 98052-6399

Library of Congress Cataloging-in-Publication Data pending.

ISBN 0-7356-2125-X

Printed and bound in the United States of America.

4 5 6 7 8 9 QWT 9 8 7 6

Distributed in Canada by H.B. Fenn and Company Ltd.

A CIP catalogue record for this book is available from the British Library.

Microsoft Press books are available through booksellers and distributors worldwide. For further information about international editions, contact your local Microsoft Corporation office or contact Microsoft Press International directly at fax (425) 936-7329. Visit our Web site at www.microsoft.com/learning/. Send comments to *mspinput@microsoft.com.*

Acquisitions Editors: Juliana Aldous and Hilary Long
Project Editor: Kristine Haugseth
Editorial and Production: Online Training Solutions, Inc.

Body Part No. X10-82958

Contents

What's New in Visio 2003

You'll notice some changes as soon as you start Microsoft Office Visio 2003. The toolbars and menu bar have a new look, and there are several more task panes available on the right side of the drawing page. For example, when you start Visio you can use task panes to get task and diagram-specific information while you work, review diagrams, search the Web, collaborate, and so on. But the features that are new or improved in this version of Visio go beyond just changes in appearance. Some changes won't be apparent until you start using Visio.

New in Visio 2003

To help you quickly identify features that are new or enhanced in this version of Visio, this book uses the New icon in the margin whenever those features are discussed or shown.

The following table lists the new features that you might be interested in, as well as the chapters in which those features are discussed.

To learn how to	See
Download templates that come with shapes already on the drawing page	Chapter 1, page 3
Get task and diagram-specific information while you work	Chapter 1, page 7
See sample diagrams for every diagram type in Visio and find ideas about who could use the diagrams and how	Chapter 1, page 19
Find an answer to a Visio question on the Internet using the Visio Help task pane	Chapter 1, page 20
Find specific information about how to use a template	Chapter 1, page 20
Find product tours, templates, sample diagrams, tutorials, tips and tricks, in-depth articles about using Visio, answers to frequently asked questions, and links to Knowledge Base articles	Chapter 1, page 20
Locate a shape using the Search for Shapes box	Chapter 2, page 48
Rotate a shape using the new rotation handle	Chapter 2, page 29
Select multiple shapes using the selection tools on the Pointer Tool menu	Chapter 2, page 40
Resize more than one shape at a time	Chapter 2, page 41
Insert clip art into diagrams using the new Clip Art task pane	Chapter 2, page 50
Automatically reroute and connect shapes in a flowchart when you add a shape between two shapes that are already connected	Chapter 4, page 85
Use new and improved timeline shapes	Chapter 5, page 103

To learn how to	See
Insert expanded timelines into a diagram that are synchronized with the primary timeline	Chapter 5, page 102
Use new and improved organization chart shapes	Chapter 6, page 129
Specify the employee information you want to show in organization chart shapes	Chapter 6, page 130
Experiment with different organization chart layouts	Chapter 6, page 142
Use new and improved office layout shapes	Chapter 7, page 156
Use new and improved network equipment shapes	Chapter 8, page 179
Create reports based on data stored in network diagrams	Chapter 8, page 190
Easily access drawing tools on the new Drawing toolbar	Chapter 10, page 222
Change the behavior of groups and shapes within groups	Chapter 10, page 228
Use the Pointer tool to modify custom shapes	Chapter 10, page 233
Organize shapes on the new Favorites stencil	Chapter 10, page 236

Some new features are beyond the scope of this book. However, you can easily find out more about them. In Visio, type the name of the feature in the Type a question for help box in the upper right corner of the Visio window, and then press the Enter key.

Feature	Description
Brainstorming Diagram template	Capture and arrange ideas with the new Brainstorming Diagram template. Export the diagram to a Microsoft Office Word outline to see the information in a linear view.
Business Process category	The new Business Process category includes templates you can use to create audit diagrams, basic flowcharts, cause and effect (fishbone) diagrams, cross-functional flowcharts, EPC diagrams, fault tree analysis diagrams, total quality management (TQM) diagrams, and workflow diagrams.
Calendar template	Import schedule information from Microsoft Office Outlook into the improved Calendar template, and then easily customize the information to suit your needs.
Ink tool	Sketch freely as you would on paper or whiteboards on your Tablet PC by using the new Ink tool.
Reviewing task pane	Mark up Visio diagrams with shapes and annotations using the new Reviewing task pane.

Feature	Description
Shared Workspace task pane	Easily collaborate on and share documents by using the Microsoft Office SharePoint integration in Visio 2003 incorporated into the Shared Workspace task pane.
Research task pane	Quickly find and refer to information online and on your computer without leaving Visio by using the Research task pane.

For more information about Visio products, visit the Microsoft Office Online Web site (*www.office.microsoft.com/*) or in Visio, on the Help menu, click Microsoft Office Online.

Getting Help

Every effort has been made to ensure the accuracy of this book and the contents of its CD. If you do run into problems, please contact the appropriate source for help and assistance.

Getting Help with This Book and Its CD

If your question or issue concerns the content of this book or its companion CD, please first search the online Microsoft Knowledge Base, which provides support information for known errors in or corrections to this book, at the following Web site:

www.microsoft.com/mspress/support/search.asp

If you do not find your answer at the online Knowledge Base, send your comments or questions to Microsoft Press Technical Support at:

mspinput@microsoft.com

Getting Help with Microsoft Office Visio 2003

If your question is about Microsoft Office Visio 2003, and not about the content of this Microsoft Press book, your first recourse is the Visio Help system. This system is a combination of help tools and files stored on your computer when you installed Visio 2003 and, if your computer is connected to the Internet, help files available from Microsoft Office Online. When you have a question about using Visio, you can type it in the Type a question for help box at the right end of the Visio menu bar, and then press Enter to display a list of Help topics from which you can select the one that most closely relates to your question.

If you want to practice getting help, you can work through this exercise, which demonstrates two ways to get help.

1. Start Visio. At the right end of the Visio menu bar, in the **Type a question for help** box, type **Getting Help**, and press Enter.

   A list of topics that relate to your question appears in the Search Results task pane in the right side of the Visio window.

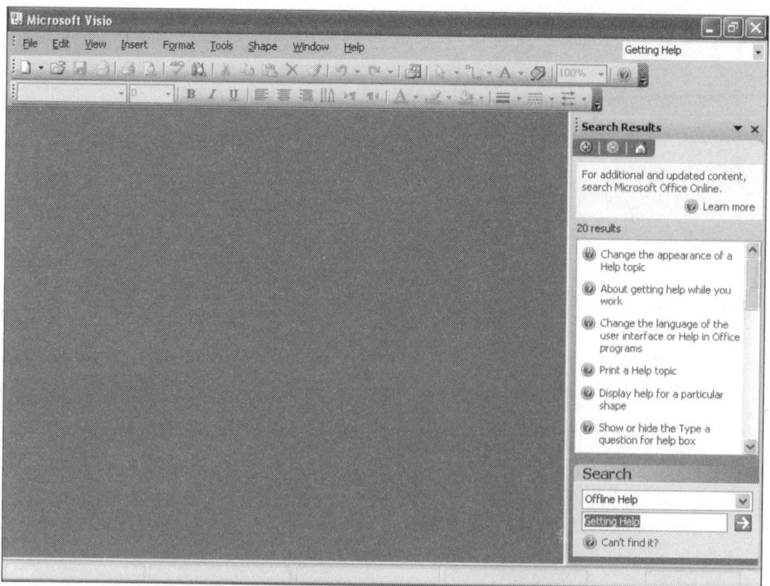

2 In the **Search Results** task pane, scroll down the results list, and click **About getting help while you work**.

The Microsoft Office Visio Help window opens and displays the Visio Help topic.

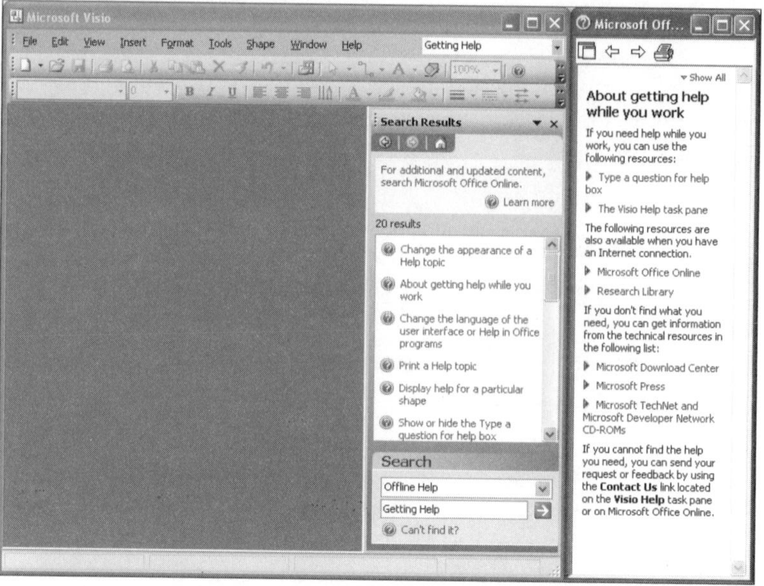

Close

3 On the **Microsoft Office Visio Help** title bar, click the **Close** button to close the window.

4 On the **Help** menu, click **Microsoft Office Visio Help**.

The Visio Help task pane appears in the right side of the Visio window. Notice the categories of information that are available from the Microsoft Office Online Web site. You can also reach this Web site by clicking Microsoft Office Online on the Help menu.

5 In the **Visio Help** task pane, click **Table of Contents**.

The Table of Contents appears in the Visio Help task pane.

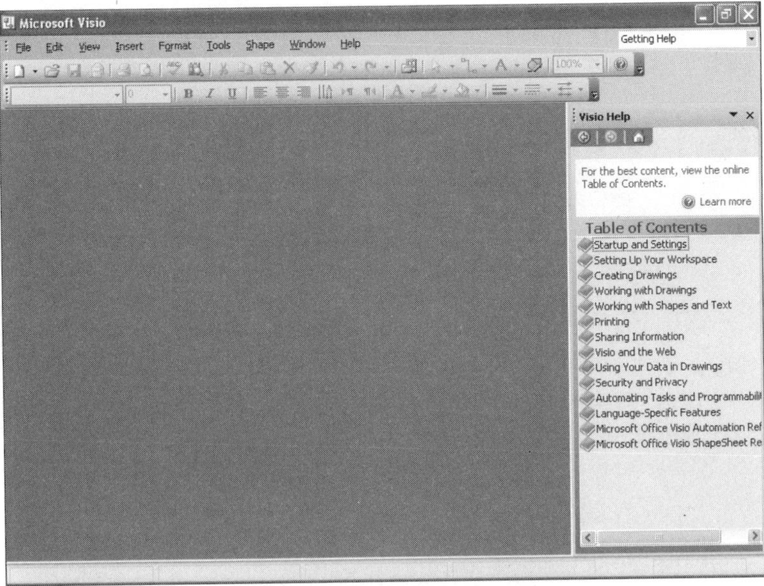

6 Under **Table of Contents**, click **Startup and Settings**.

The section opens and displays Visio Help topics.

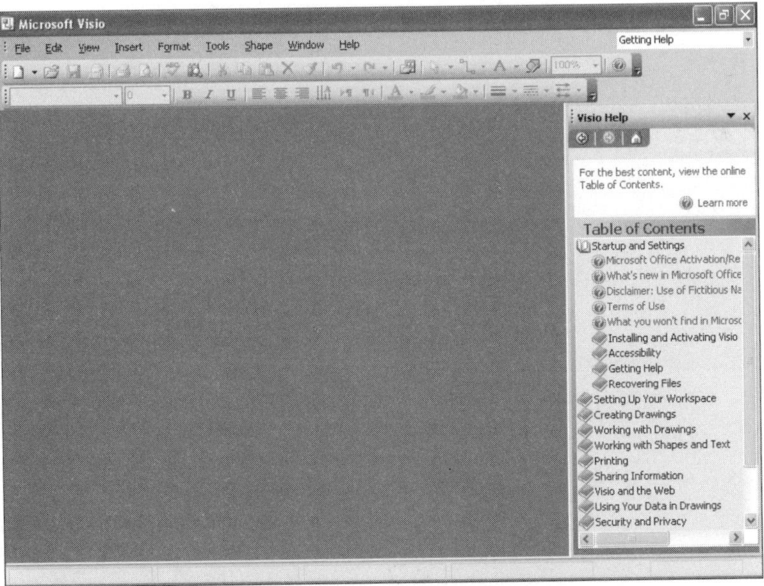

7. In the **Startup and Settings** section, click **Getting Help**.

   The section opens and displays various Visio Help topics.

8. In the **Getting Help** section, click **About getting help while you work**.

   The Microsoft Office Visio Help window opens and displays the Visio Help topic.

9. On the **Microsoft Office Visio Help** title bar, click the **Close** button to close the window.

10. On the **File** menu, click **Exit** to exit Visio.

More Information

If your question is about a Microsoft software product, including Visio 2003, and not about the content of this Microsoft Press book, please search the appropriate product support center or the Microsoft Knowledge Base at:

support.microsoft.com

In the United States, Microsoft software product support issues not covered by the Microsoft Knowledge Base are addressed by Microsoft Product Support Services. The Microsoft software support options available from Microsoft Product Support Services are listed at:

support.microsoft.com

Outside the United States, for support information specific to your location, please refer to the Worldwide Support menu on the Microsoft Product Support Services Web site for the site specific to your country:

support.microsoft.com

Using the Book's CD

The CD inside the back cover of this book contains the following files and software:

- Electronic version of the book (eBook)
- Setup to install the practice files
- Microsoft Office System Reference Pack eBooks:
  - Introducing the Tablet PC eBook
  - Microsoft Computer Dictionary, Fifth Edition eBook
  - Insider's Guide to Microsoft Office OneNote 2003 eBook
  - Microsoft Office System Quick Reference eBook
- Link to Microsoft Learning Technical Support

Important You must install the trial or full version of Microsoft Office Visio 2003 before doing the book's practices. To find information about Visio 2003 trial software availability in your country or region, visit the Microsoft Office System Worldwide Web site: *www.microsoft.com/office/worldwide.mspx*. If you want to order a 30-day trial of Visio Professional 2003, visit the Visio 2003 Trial Software Web site: *www.microsoft.com/office/visio/prodinfo/trial.mspx*.

For further information about using the CD, consult the Readme (Readme.txt) on the book's CD.

Minimum System Requirements

To use this book, you will need:

- Computer/Processor

  Computer with a Pentium 233-megahertz (MHz) or higher processor; Pentium III recommended
- Operating System

  Microsoft Windows 2000 with Service Pack 3 (SP3) or later, or Microsoft Windows XP or later
- Memory

  128 megabytes (MB) of RAM

- Hard Disk

  Hard disk space requirements vary depending on configuration; custom installation choices may require more or less hard disk space; 5 MB of hard disk space is required for installing the practice files
- Drive

  CD-ROM drive
- Display

  Super VGA (800 × 600) or higher-resolution monitor
- Peripherals

  Microsoft Mouse, Microsoft IntelliMouse, or compatible pointing device
- Programs

  Microsoft Office Visio 2003, and Microsoft Office Word 2003 and Microsoft Office Project are recommended
- Microsoft Internet Explorer 5.5 or later browser
- Internet access recommended

Installing the Practice Files

You must install the practice files before you can use them in the exercises in this book. Follow these steps to prepare the CD's files for your use:

1. Insert the CD into the CD drive of your computer.

   A menu screen appears.

   Important If the menu screen does not appear, start Windows Explorer. In the left pane, locate the icon for your CD and click this icon. In the right pane, double-click the StartCD file.

2. Click **Install Practice Files.**
3. Click **Next** on the first screen, and then click **Yes** to accept the license agreement on the next screen.
4. If you want to install the practice files to a location other than the default folder (My Documents\Microsoft Press\Visio 2003 SBS), click the **Browse** button, select the new drive and path, and then click **OK**.

   Important If you install the practice files to a location other than the default folder, go to that location when an exercise in this book instructs you to open a practice file instead of the default location.

5. Click **Next** on the **Choose Destination Location** screen, click **Next** on the **Select Features** screen, and then click **Next** on the **Start Copying Files** screen to install the selected practice files.
6. After the practice files have been installed, click **Finish**.

   Within the installation folder are subfolders for each chapter in the book.

Using the Practice Files

Each exercise in this book is preceded by a paragraph that lists the files needed for the exercise. The following table lists each chapter's practice files.

Chapter	Folder	Files
Chapter 1: Starting Diagrams	StartingDiagrams	Starting
Chapter 2: Adding Shapes to Diagrams	AddingShapes	BasicSaving BlockAddingText BlockFinding BlockMoving BlockPictures Logo
Chapter 3: Formatting Shapes and Diagrams	FormattingShapes	FormatDecorate FormatPrint FormatScheme FormatShapes
Chapter 4: Connecting Shapes	ConnectingShapes	ConnectFlowchart ConnectLayout ConnectModify
Chapter 5: Creating Project Schedules	CreatingSchedules	GanttChart NewGantt Timeline TimelineData
Chapter 6: Creating Organization Charts	CreatingCharts	OrgChart OrgChartLayout OrgChartWeb TGC Employees
Chapter 7: Laying Out Office Spaces	LayingOutSpaces	OfficeFurnished OfficeWalls
Chapter 8: Creating Network Diagrams	CreatingNetworks	NetworkReport NetworkStore

Chapter	Folder	Files
Chapter 9: Using Visio Diagrams with the Microsoft Office System	UsingDrawings	PlanPhase Proposal
Chapter 10: Creating Shapes, Stencils, and Templates	CreatingShapes	CreateStencil Garden Perennials GroupShapes ModifyShapes Perennial Garden Plan Perennials

Uninstalling the Practice Files

After you finish the exercises in this book, you can uninstall the practice files to free up hard disk space.

1 On the Windows taskbar, click the **Start** button, and then click **Control Panel**.

2 In Control Panel, click **Add or Remove Programs**.

3 In the list of installed programs, click **Microsoft Office Visio 2003 Step by Step**, and then click the **Remove** button.

   The Uninstall dialog box appears.

4 In the **Uninstall** dialog box, click **OK**.

5 After the files are uninstalled, click **Finish**, and then close the Add or Remove Programs window and Control Panel.

Important If you need additional help installing or uninstalling the practice files, please see the "Getting Help" section earlier in this book. Microsoft product support does not provide support for this book or CD.

Conventions and Features

You can save time when you use this book by understanding how the *Step by Step* series shows special instructions, keys to press, buttons to click, and so on.

Convention	Meaning
(CD icon)	This icon indicates a reference to the book's companion CD.
OPEN	This word is found at the beginning of paragraphs preceding step-by-step exercises. It draws your attention to practice files you need to open to begin the exercise.
CLOSE	This word is found at the end of the step-by-step exercises. It draws your attention to practice files you need to close to complete the exercise.
1 **2**	Numbered steps guide you through hands-on exercises in each topic.
●	A round bullet indicates an exercise that has only one step.
New in Visio 2003	This icon indicates a new or greatly improved feature in this version of Microsoft Office Visio.
Tip	These paragraphs provide a helpful hint or shortcut that makes working through a task easier.
Important	These paragraphs point out information that you need to know to complete the procedure.
Troubleshooting	These paragraphs tell you how to fix a common problem.
Save	The first time a button is referenced in a topic, a picture of the button and its name appear in the margin.
Ctrl+Shift	A plus sign (+) between two key names means that you must press those keys at the same time. For example, "Press Ctrl+Shift" means that you hold down the Ctrl key while you press Shift.
Black bold characters	The names of program elements, such as buttons, commands, and dialog boxes, are shown in black bold characters in the steps.
Blue italic characters	Terms that are explained in the glossary at the end of the book are shown in blue italic characters.
Blue bold characters	Text that you are supposed to type appears in blue boldface characters in the steps.

About the Author

Judy Lemke is an award-winning writer with more than ten years of experience writing, editing, and designing everything from developer documentation and tutorials to product manuals and marketing collateral. Ms. Lemke specializes in documentation and training for Microsoft Office Visio products.

Resources Online (*www.ronline.com*) has been creating and delivering content for companies and organizations via electronic and print media for more than fifteen years. The company provides content architecture and management services; Web and application development; and content development including writing, editing, and media production. In addition to creating books and training materials about Microsoft Visio, we use Visio extensively to model and build protocols for our health care products.

Quick Reference

Chapter 1 Starting Diagrams

Page 4 **To start a new diagram using a template**

1. On the **File** menu, point to **New**, and then click **Choose Drawing Type**.
2. In the **Category** list, click a diagram type, and then in the **Template** area, click the template you want to open.

8 **To move a shape**

- With the **Pointer Tool**, drag the shape.

8 **To display the task pane**

- On the **View** menu, click **Task Pane**.

8 **To show the shapes on a stencil in the Shapes window**

- Click the stencil's title bar.

8 **To add a shape to the drawing page**

- Drag a shape from a stencil onto the drawing page.

8 **To zoom in or out of the drawing page**

- On the **Standard** toolbar, click the **Zoom** down arrow, and then click a zoom percentage.

8 **To zoom in to the drawing page using a keyboard shortcut**

- Hold down Shift+Ctrl while you left-click once.

8 **To zoom out of the drawing page using a keyboard shortcut**

- Hold down Shift+Ctrl while you right-click once.

8 **To zoom in to a selected area on the drawing page using a keyboard shortcut**

- Hold down Shift+Ctrl while you drag a selection net around the area you want to zoom in to.

8 **To zoom out of the drawing page to view the whole page using a keyboard shortcut**

- Press Ctrl+W.

8 **To pan the drawing page**

- Hold down Shift+Ctrl while you drag with the right mouse button.

8 **To view a page in a drawing file**

- Click the page tab at the bottom of the drawing window.

8 **To insert a page in a drawing file**

- Right-click a page tab at the bottom of the drawing window, and then click **Insert Page** on the shortcut menu.

12 **To float a window**

- Right-click the window's title bar, and then click **Float Window**.

13 **To open a Visio drawing file**

- On the **File** menu, click **Open**, find the diagram you want to open, and then click **OK**.

13 **To hide or show the rulers**

- On the **View** menu, click **Rulers**.

13 **To hide or show the grid on the drawing page**

- On the **View** menu, click **Grid**.

13 **To display expanded menus**

1. On the **Tools** menu, click **Customize**, and then click the **Options** tab.
2. On the **Options** tab, select the **Always show full menus** check box, and then click **Close**.

13 **To display the Pan & Zoom window**

- On the **View** menu, click **Pan & Zoom Window**.

13 **To merge windows**

- Drag a window into another window or the **Shapes** window.

13 **To open a stencil**

- On the **Standard** toolbar, click the **Shapes** button, click a category, and then click the stencil you want to open.

13 **To change how shapes appear on a stencil**

1. On the stencil title bar, click the stencil icon in the upper left corner.
2. Point to **View**, and then click **Icons and Names**, **Icons Only**, **Names Only**, or **Icons and Details**.

13 **To move a stencil**

- Drag the stencil to another area of the Visio window.

13 **To close a stencil**

- On the stencil title bar, click the stencil icon in the upper left corner, and then click **Close**.

19 **To find an answer to a Visio question using keywords**

1. Type a keyword in the **Type a question for help** box to the right of the menu bar, and then press the Enter key.
2. In the list of topics that appears, click a topic.

19 **To display a Help topic about a particular drawing type or template**

1. On the **Help** menu, click **Microsoft Office Visio Help**.
2. In the Visio Help task pane that appears to the right of the drawing page, in the **Search for** box, type the name of the template or drawing type, and then click the topic you want.

19 **To display the Table of Contents in Visio Help**

1. On the **Help** menu, click **Microsoft Office Visio Help**.
2. In the Visio Help task pane that appears to the right of the drawing page, click **Table of Contents**.

19 **To view the Diagram Gallery**

- On the **Help** menu, click **Diagram Gallery**.

19 **To view the Getting Started Tutorial**

- On the **Help** menu, click **Getting Started Tutorial**.

Chapter 2 Adding Shapes to Diagrams

Page 28 **To select a shape**

- Click the shape.

28 **To deselect a shape**

- Click a blank area of the drawing page or pasteboard, or press the Esc key.

28 **To delete a shape**

- Click the shape, and then press the Del key.

30 **To determine what a control handle does**

- Pause the pointer over the control handle until its ScreenTip appears.

34 **To add text to a shape**

- Select the shape, and then type.

34 **To add a text-only shape to the drawing page**

- On the **Standard** toolbar, click the **Text Tool** button, click in the location on the drawing page where you want the text, and then type.

35 **To format text**

1. Select the shape that contains the text you want to format.
2. On the **Format** menu, click **Text**.
3. Choose the formatting you want, and then click **OK**.

40 **To select more than one shape at once**

- Hold down the Shift key while you click the shapes you want to select.

40 **To select multiple shapes that are close together**

- With the **Pointer Tool**, drag a selection net around the shapes you want to select.

41 **To size a shape**

- Select the shape, and then drag one of its selection handles.

41 **To nudge a shape**

- Select the shape, and then use the arrows on the keyboard to move the shape horizontally or vertically.

41 **To rotate a shape**

- Select the shape, and then drag its rotation handle in either direction.

41 **To copy a shape and position the copy in one action**

- Hold down the Ctrl key while you drag the shape.

41 **To duplicate a shape**

- Select the shape, and then press Ctrl+D.

46 **To subselect a shape in a group**

- Select the group, and then click the shape within the group.

48 **To find a shape for a diagram by using a keyword**

1. In the **Shapes** window, in the **Search for Shapes** box, type the keyword, and then click the arrow to the right of the **Search for Shapes** box.
2. From the new stencil that appears in the **Shapes** window, drag the shape onto the drawing page.

51 **To insert a picture created in a different program into a diagram**

1. On the **Insert** menu, point to **Picture**, and then click **From File**.
2. Find the picture you want to insert, and then click **Insert**.

51 **To insert clip art into a diagram**

1. On the **View** menu, click **Task Pane**.
2. Click the down arrow on the task pane title bar, and then click **Clip Art**.
3. In the **Search for** box, type a keyword, and then click the **Go** button to the right of the **Search for** box.
4. From the **Search Results** task pane, drag the clip art onto the drawing page.

55 **To save a drawing file for the first time**

1. On the **Standard** toolbar, click the **Save** button.
2. In the **File name** box, type a name for the drawing file.
3. Click **Save**.

55 **To save changes to a drawing file**

- On the **Standard** toolbar, click the **Save** button.

55 **To enter properties about a drawing file**

1. On the **File** menu, click **Properties**.
2. Enter the information you want, and then click **OK**.

Chapter 3 Formatting Shapes and Diagrams

Page 61 To change a shape's line color, thickness, or line ends

1. Select the shape.
2. On the **Format** menu, click **Line**.
3. Change the line attributes, and then click **OK**.

61 To change a shape's fill color

1. Select the shape.
2. On the **Format** menu, click **Fill**.
3. Change the shape's fill color, and then click **OK**.

61 To copy one shape's formatting to another shape

1. Select the shape that has the formatting you want to copy.
2. On the **Standard** toolbar, click the **Format Painter** button.
3. Click the shape to which you want to copy the formatting.

61 To copy one shape's formatting to multiple shapes

1. Select the shape that has the formatting you want to copy.
2. On the **Standard** toolbar, double-click the **Format Painter** button.
3. Click each shape—one at a time—to which you want to copy the formatting.
4. When you are finished, press the Esc key.

61 To change a shape's text attributes

1. Select the shape.
2. On the **Format** menu, click **Text**.
3. Change the shape's text attributes, and then click **OK**.

67 To add a border to a diagram

- From the **Borders and Titles** stencil, drag a border shape onto the drawing page.

67 To add a background to a diagram

- From the **Backgrounds** stencil, drag a background shape onto the drawing page.

70 **To format a diagram with a color scheme**

1. Right-click the drawing page, and then click **Color Schemes** on the shortcut menu. If **Color Schemes** doesn't appear on the shortcut menu, the drawing type doesn't support color schemes.
2. In the **Choose a color scheme** list, click the scheme you want, and then click **OK**.

74 **To change the drawing page size**

1. On the **File** menu, click **Page Setup**.
2. On the **Page Size** tab, click **Pre-defined size**, and then select an option. Or click **Custom size**, and then type the size you want.
3. Click **OK**.

74 **To change the drawing page orientation**

1. On the **File** menu, click **Page Setup**.
2. On the **Print Setup** tab, click **Portrait** or **Landscape**.
3. On the **Page Size** tab, make sure **Same as printer paper size** is selected.
4. If **Same as printer paper size** is not selected, click an option under **Page orientation** that matches the option you selected on the **Print Setup** tab.
5. Click **OK**.

74 **To preview a diagram before printing**

- On the **File** menu, click **Print Preview**.

74 **To display page breaks**

- On the **View** menu, click **Page Breaks**.

74 **To print the current drawing page**

- On the **Standard** toolbar, click the **Print Page** button.

74 **To print a diagram**

1. On the **File** menu, click **Print**.
2. Choose the options you want, and then click **OK**.

Chapter 4 Connecting Shapes

Page 81 **To draw a connector between two shapes**

1. On the **Standard** toolbar, click the **Connector Tool** button.

2. Drag from one shape to the other to draw a connector between the two shapes.

81 **To connect shapes as you drag them onto the drawing page**

1. On the **Standard** toolbar, click the **Connector Tool** button.
2. Drag the shapes onto the drawing page.

81 **To add text to a connector**

- Select the connector, and then type.

87 **To create a shape-to-shape connection**

- With the **Connector Tool**, point to the first shape, and when a red border appears around the entire shape, drag to the second shape until a red border appears around the second shape.

87 **To create a point-to-point connection**

- With the **Connector Tool**, point to a connection point on the first shape, and then when a red border appears around the connection point, drag to a connection point on the second shape.

87 **To insert a shape between two shapes that are already connected in a flowchart**

- Drag the new shape between the two shapes that are already connected.

87 **To delete a connector**

- Select the connector, and then press the Del key.

94 **To change the layout of a flowchart**

1. On the **Shape** menu, click **Lay Out Shapes**.
2. In the **Placement** area, click an option in the **Style** list.
3. Click an option in the **Direction** list.
4. Click **OK**.

94 **To distribute shapes evenly**

1. Select three or more shapes.
2. On the **Shape** menu, click **Distribute Shapes**.
3. In the **Distribute Shapes** dialog box, click the option you want.
4. Click **OK**.

94 **To align shapes**

1. Select two or more shapes, making sure the first shape you select is the one you want the others to align with.
2. On the **Shape** menu, click **Align Shapes**.
3. In the **Align Shapes** dialog box, click the option you want.
4. Click **OK**.

Chapter 5 Creating Project Schedules

Page 103 **To create a timeline**

1. On the **File** menu, point to **New**, point to **Project Schedule**, and then click **Timeline**.
2. Drag a timeline shape from the **Timeline Shapes** stencil onto the drawing page.
3. In the **Configure Timeline** dialog box, set the date range, scale, and format, and then click **OK**.
4. From the **Timeline Shapes** stencil, drag milestone and interval shapes onto the timeline.

103 **To add milestones to a timeline**

1. From the **Timeline Shapes** stencil, drag a milestone shape onto the timeline.
2. In the **Configure Milestone** dialog box, enter the milestone date and description, select a date format, and then click **OK**.

103 **To add interval markers to a timeline**

1. From the **Timeline Shapes** stencil, drag an interval shape onto the timeline.
2. In the **Configure Interval** dialog box, choose the interval start date, finish date, and date format, type the interval description, and then click **OK**.

103 **To change the milestone type**

1. Right-click the milestone, and then click **Set Milestone Type**.
2. In the **Milestone Shape** list, click an option, and then click **OK**.

103 **To add an expanded timeline to the drawing page**

1. From the **Timeline Shapes** stencil, drag the **Expanded timeline** shape onto the drawing page.
2. In the **Configure Timeline** dialog box, set the date range, scale, and format, and then click **OK**.

114 **To export a timeline**

1. Click the border of the timeline you want to export to select it.
2. On the **Timeline** menu, click **Export Timeline Data**.
3. Follow the instructions on the wizard pages to export the timeline.

114 **To create a Gantt chart**

1. On the **File** menu, point to **New**, point to **Project Schedule**, and then click **Gantt Chart**.
2. On the **Date** tab, type a number in the **Number of tasks** box.
3. Choose options for **Time units**, **Duration options**, and **Timescale range**, and then click **OK**.
4. Enter task names, start dates, finish dates, and durations in the chart.
5. Add tasks and milestones, and then link tasks.

119 **To modify duration information in a Gantt chart**

1. Click the cell that contains the duration you want to change.
2. Type the new duration using the following abbreviations: *m* for minutes, *h* for hours, *d* for days, and *w* for weeks.

119 **To add a column for resource names to a Gantt chart**

1. Right-click a column in the Gantt chart, and then click **Insert Column**.
2. In the **Column Type** list, click **Resource Names**.
3. Click **OK**.

119 **To add a new task to a Gantt chart**

- Right-click a cell in the row below the task you want to insert, and then click **New Task**.

119 **To change the milestone type for all the milestones in the Gantt chart**

1. On the **Gantt Chart** menu, click **Options**.
2. On the **Format** tab, click a milestone in the **Shapes** box, and then click **OK**.

Chapter 6 Creating Organization Charts

Page 129 **To create an organization chart**

1. On the **File** menu, point to **New**, point to **Organization Chart**, and then click **Organization Chart**.

2. From the **Organization Chart Shapes** stencil, drag the **Executive** shape onto the drawing page, and then type the name and title of the executive in the shape.
3. From the **Organization Chart Shapes** stencil, drag a **Manager** shape directly onto the **Executive** shape, and then type the name and title of the manager in the shape. Repeat this step until you've added all the managers.
4. From the **Organization Chart Shapes** stencil, drag a **Position** shape onto a manager shape, and then type the name and title of the employee in the shape. Repeat this step until you've added all the employees.

131 **To import organization data from a Microsoft Office Excel spreadsheet to create an organization chart**

1. On the **File** menu, point to **New**, point to **Organization Chart**, and then click **Organization Chart Wizard**.
2. Follow the instructions on the wizard pages to import the organization data and create an organization chart from the data.

131 **To add shapes to an organization chart**

1. From the **Organization Chart Shapes** stencil, drag a shape onto another shape, and then type the name and title of the employee.
2. Repeat the previous step until you've added all the employees you want.

131 **To enter names and titles in organization chart shapes**

1. Select an organization chart shape.
2. Type the person's name, press the Enter key, and then type the person's title.
3. Press the Esc key or click outside the shape.

131 **To add employee information to an organization chart**

1. Right-click the organization chart shape that represents the employee for which you want to add information, and then click **Properties** on the shortcut menu.
2. Type the information you want in the property fields, and then click **OK**.

131 **To change the information shown in organization chart shapes**

1. On the **Organization Chart** menu, click **Options**.
2. Click the **Fields** tab.
3. Choose the options you want to display in the various text blocks in organization chart shapes, and then click **OK**.

136 **To format the information shown in organization chart shapes**

1. On the **Organization Chart** menu, click **Options**.
2. Click the **Text** tab.
3. Choose the text formatting options for the various text fields in organization chart shapes, and then click **OK**.

136 **To display the Custom Properties window**

- On the **View** menu, click **Custom Properties Window**.

143 **To change the layout of organization chart shapes**

1. Select a top-level shape, such as a manager.
2. On the **Organization Chart** toolbar, click a layout option.

143 **To move a department to a new drawing page and keep it synchronized with the original page**

1. Right-click a manager shape, and then click **Create Synchronized Copy** on the shortcut menu.
2. In the **Create Synchronized Copy** dialog box, choose the page you want to move the shapes to, and then click **OK**.

143 **To add a hyperlink from a shape to another page in the same drawing file**

1. Select the shape, and then on the **Insert** menu, click **Hyperlinks**.
2. Click **Browse** next to the **Sub-address** box.
3. In the **Page** list, click a page, and then click **OK**.
4. In the **Description** box, type a name for the hyperlink, and then click **OK**.

143 **To apply a design theme to an organization chart**

1. On the **Organization Chart** menu, click **Options**.
2. On the **Options** tab, in the **Org chart theme** list, click a theme, and then click **OK**.

148 **To save a diagram as a Web page**

1. On the **File** menu, click **Save as Web Page**.
2. In the **File name** box, type a name for the Web page file.
3. Click **Change Title**, type a name for the Web page, and then click **OK**.
4. Click **Publish**.
5. Choose the options you want, and then click **OK**.

Chapter 7 Laying Out Office Spaces

Page 157 To create an office layout

1. On the **File** menu, point to **New**, point to **Building Plan**, and then click **Office Layout**.
2. From the **Walls, Doors and Windows** stencil, drag room or wall shapes onto the drawing page to create the office structure.
3. From the **Walls, Doors and Windows** stencil, drag door and window shapes onto wall shapes on the drawing page.
4. Add furniture and office equipment by dragging shapes from the stencils onto the drawing page.

157 To change the drawing scale

1. On the **File** menu, click **Page Setup**.
2. On the **Drawing Scale** tab, click options in the **Pre-defined scale** lists, and then click **OK**.

157 To create walls from space shapes

1. From the **Walls, Doors and Windows** stencil, drag **Space** shapes onto the drawing page.
2. With the **Space** shapes selected, on the **Plan** menu, click **Convert to Walls**.
3. Select the options you want, and then click **OK**.

165 To add a door to an office layout

- From the **Walls, Doors and Windows** stencil, drag a **Door** shape onto a wall shape on the drawing page.

165 To change the size of a door

1. Right-click the door shape, and then click **Properties**.
2. In the **Door Width** list, click a size, and then click **OK**.

165 To reverse the direction in which a door opens

- Right-click the door shape, and then click **Reverse In/Out Opening**.

165 To change the direction of the door swing

- Right-click the door shape, and then click **Reverse Left/Right Opening**.

165 **To add a window to an office layout**

- From the **Walls, Doors and Windows** stencil, drag a **Window** shape onto a wall shape on the drawing page.

171 **To determine which layers a shape is assigned to**

- Select the shape, and then on the **Format** menu, click **Layer**.

171 **To lock the shapes on a layer**

1. On the **View** menu, click **Layer Properties**.
2. Click the **Lock** column for the layers you want to lock, and then click **OK**.

171 **To change the color of shapes on a layer**

1. On the **View** menu, click **Layer Properties**.
2. Click the **Color** column for a layer.
3. In the **Layer Color** list, click a color, and then click **OK**.

171 **To hide the shapes on a layer**

1. On the **View** menu, click **Layer Properties**.
2. Click the **Visible** column for the layers you want to hide, and then click **OK**.

Chapter 8 Creating Network Diagrams

Page 180 **To create a network diagram**

1. On the **File** menu, point to **New**, point to **Network**, and then click **Basic Network Diagram**.
2. From the **Network and Peripherals** stencil, drag a **Ring network** or **Ethernet** shape onto the drawing page.
3. Drag computer, printer, and other shapes from the stencils onto the drawing page.
4. Drag the control handles on the **Ring network** or **Ethernet** shape to the network equipment shapes to connect them.

180 **To connect network equipment to an Ethernet shape**

- Drag a control handle from the **Ethernet** shape to a network equipment shape.

180 **To display the document stencil**

- On the **File** menu, point to **Shapes**, and then click **Show Document Stencil**.

186 **To create a custom property for a shape**

1. On the **View** menu, click **Custom Properties Window**.
2. Select the shape.
3. Right-click the **Custom Properties** window, and then click **Define Properties**.
4. Click **New**, type a name in the **Label** box, and then click **OK**.
5. In the **Define Custom Properties** dialog box, click **OK**.

186 **To create a custom property for a shape on the document stencil**

1. On the **View** menu, click **Custom Properties Window**.
2. On the **File** menu, point to **Shapes**, and then click **Show Document Stencil**.
3. Double-click the shape on the document stencil to open the shape editing window.
4. Select the shape in the shape editing window.
5. Right-click the **Custom Properties** window, and then click **Define Properties**.
6. Click **New**, type a name in the **Label** box, and then click **OK**.
7. In the **Define Custom Properties** dialog box, click **OK**.
8. In the shape editing window, click the **Close Window** button. When Visio prompts you to update all instances, click **Yes**.

190 **To run a report**

1. On the **Tools** menu, click **Reports**.
2. In the **Report** list, click a report, and then click **Run**.
3. Select the format you want, and then click **OK**.

190 **To create a new report definition**

1. On the **Tools** menu, click **Reports**.
2. Click **New**.
3. Follow the instructions on the wizard pages to create the report definition.
4. In the **Reports** dialog box, click **OK**.

Chapter 9 Using Visio Diagrams with the Microsoft Office System

Page 199 **To create a Visio diagram within an Office 2003 file**

1. On the **Insert** menu, click **Object**.
2. In the **Object type** list, click **Microsoft Visio Drawing**, and then click **OK**.

207 **To embed Visio shapes in an Office 2003 file**

1. In Visio, select the shapes you want to embed, and then on the **Edit** menu, click **Copy**.
2. In the Office 2003 file, on the **Edit** menu, click **Paste** to paste the shapes.

207 **To embed a Visio diagram in an Office 2003 file**

1. In Visio, make sure nothing is selected on the drawing page.
2. On the **Edit** menu, click **Copy Drawing**.
3. In the Office 2003 file, on the **Edit** menu, click **Paste** to paste the diagram.

207 **To modify a Visio diagram in an Office 2003 file**

1. Double-click the Visio diagram to start Visio and display Visio menus and toolbars.
2. Modify the diagram, and then click outside the Visio diagram to return to the Office 2003 file.

214 **To link a Visio diagram to an Office 2003 file**

1. In Visio, make sure nothing is selected on the drawing page.
2. On the **Edit** menu, click **Copy Drawing**.
3. In the Office 2003 file, on the **Edit** menu, click **Paste Special**.
4. Click **Paste Link**, and then click **OK**.

214 **To update a linked Visio diagram in an Office 2003 file**

1. Select the Visio diagram in the Office 2003 file.
2. On the **Edit** menu, click **Update Link**.

Chapter 10 Creating Shapes, Stencils, and Templates

Page 222 **To show the Visio drawing tools**

- On the **Standard** toolbar, click the **Drawing Tools** button.

223 **To draw a line**

1. On the **Drawing** toolbar, click the **Pencil Tool** button.
2. Point to where you want to start the line on the drawing page, and then drag horizontally, vertically, or diagonally.

223 **To draw an arc**

1. On the **Drawing** toolbar, click the **Pencil Tool** button.

2 Point to where you want to start the arc on the drawing page, and then drag in a circular motion.

223 **To draw a square**

1 On the **Drawing** toolbar, click the **Rectangle Tool** button.

2 Hold down the Shift key, and then drag.

223 **To draw a circle**

1 On the **Drawing** toolbar, click the **Ellipse Tool** button.

2 Hold down the Shift key, and then drag.

229 **To group shapes**

1 Select the shapes you want to group.

2 On the **Shape** menu, point to **Grouping**, and then click **Group**.

229 **To ungroup shapes**

1 Select a group.

2 On the **Shape** menu, point to **Grouping**, and then click **Ungroup**.

229 **To merge shapes**

1 Select two or more shapes.

2 On the **Shape** menu, point to **Operations**, and then click the operation you want to use.

233 **To modify a line or arc**

1 On the **Drawing** toolbar, click the **Pencil Tool** button.

2 Click the shape you want to modify, and then move or delete vertices, or drag control points to change the curve of an arc.

233 **To add a vertex to a line or arc**

1 On the **Drawing** toolbar, click the **Pencil Tool** button.

2 Click the shape you want to modify.

3 Hold down the Ctrl key, and then click where you want to add the vertex.

237 **To create a new stencil**

- On the **File** menu, point to **Shapes**, and then click **New Stencil**.

237 **To open the Favorites stencil**

- On the **File** menu, point to **Shapes**, point to **My Shapes**, and then click **Favorites**.

237 **To save a stencil**

1. Click the icon in the upper left corner of the stencil title bar, and then click **Save As**.
2. Type a file name, and then click **Save**.

237 **To add a shape to a stencil**

1. Drag the shape from the drawing page onto the stencil.
2. If Visio prompts you to open the stencil for editing, click **Yes**.

237 **To modify properties for a shape on a stencil**

1. Right-click a shape on a stencil that's open for editing, point to **Edit Master**, and then click **Master Properties**.
2. Make changes, and then click **OK**.

243 **To create a template**

1. On the **File** menu, point to **New**, click a category, and then click the template you want to modify to create your own template.
2. On the **Standard** toolbar, click the **Shapes** button, and then open the stencils you want to include with the template.
3. On the **File** menu, click **Page Setup**, select the page settings you want to use, and then click **OK**.
4. On the **File** menu, click **Save As**.
5. In the **Save as type** list, click **Template (*.vst)**. Type a file name, and then click **Save**.

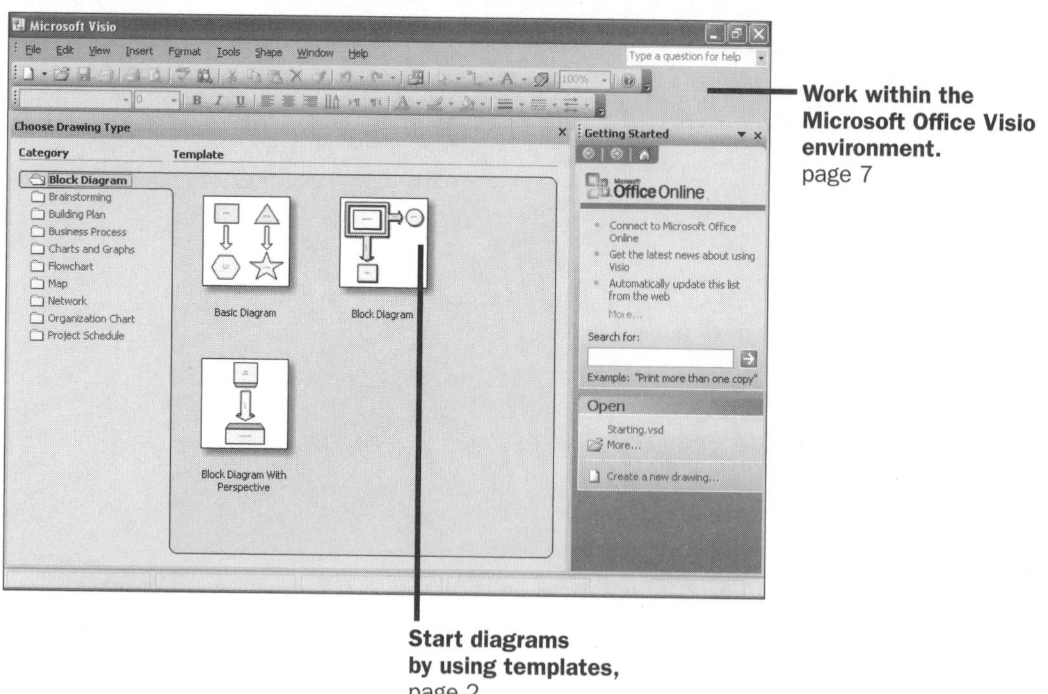

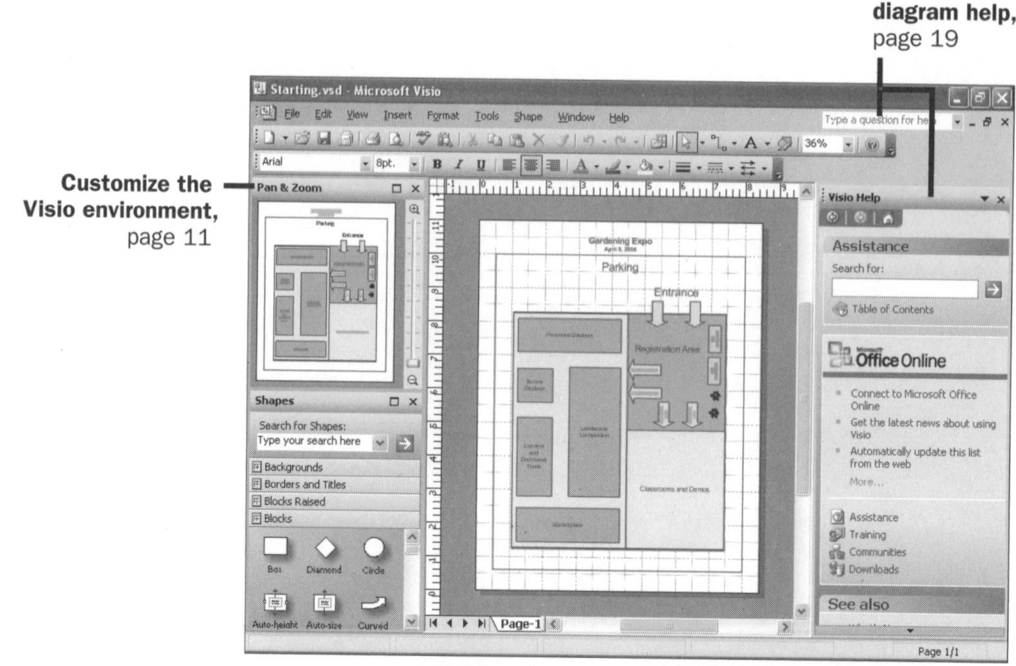

Chapter 1 at a Glance

1 Starting Diagrams

In this chapter you will learn to:

- ✔ Start diagrams by using templates.
- ✔ Work within the Microsoft Office Visio environment.
- ✔ Customize the Visio environment.
- ✔ Get Visio and diagram help.

Have you ever tried to explain a new team organization or a complex inter-departmental process in an e-mail message or a memo only to find that no one quite understood it? Have you ever given a presentation about critical project milestones, and then watched everyone walk away with a puzzled expression? Both of these situations are ideal times to use Microsoft Office Visio 2003–the business drawing and diagramming program that helps you communicate visually. *Visually* is the key word. When you can't effectively convey your message verbally, you need a diagram.

With Visio, you can *show* your audience what you mean using easy-to-understand diagrams, such as organization charts, flowcharts, and project timelines. Whether you need to analyze a new business process, visualize an office space, or create a map to a company picnic, you can create professional-looking diagrams quickly and easily using Visio–and no artistic talent is required.

This book helps you learn how to use Visio so that you can communicate visually using Visio drawings and diagrams. This chapter will first introduce you to Visio drawing and diagram types, and then show you how to start a Visio diagram by using a template. You will learn how to work within and customize the Visio drawing environment. Last, you will practice using Visio online Help so that you can easily find the answers to questions that might arise when you create your Visio diagrams.

See Also Do you need only a quick refresher on the topics in this chapter? See the Quick Reference entries on pages xxiii–xxv.

Important Before you can use the practice files in this chapter, you need to install them from the book's companion CD to their default location. See "Using the Book's CD" on page xv for more information.

Starting Diagrams by Using Templates

Regardless of your drawing abilities, Visio makes it easy for you to create all types of drawings and diagrams. *Shapes*—pre-drawn symbols included with Visio—are the key to quickly creating effective diagrams. For example, in an organization chart, you might use a Manager shape (a box with a name and job title) to represent a manager in a department, whereas in a flowchart, you might use a Decision shape (a diamond with a label) to indicate a decision someone must make in a process. By simply dragging shapes onto the drawing page, you can assemble a complete diagram.

The best way to start a diagram is by using a *template*—a file that includes all the tools, styles, settings, and shapes you need to assemble a particular type of drawing or diagram. For example, if you want to create a flowchart, use the Basic Flowchart template. It includes shapes that represent data, processes, decisions, and so on.

Templates also set up the drawing page and formatting styles for you. The Basic Flowchart template, for instance, sets up a letter-sized page suitable for printing on a desktop printer and lists text styles that are most often used in flowcharts. In addition, some templates include special-purpose commands or toolbars. For example, the Organization Chart template includes the Organization Chart toolbar, which makes it easy to rearrange employee shapes in a chart that you created with that template.

Visio makes it easy for you to find the appropriate template by organizing them into categories of related diagram types, as shown in the following table. Visio Professional 2003 includes all the templates available in Visio Standard 2003, in addition to special-purpose templates that you can use to create detailed network diagrams, database and software models, engineering schematics, process engineering diagrams, Web diagrams, and extensive building plans.

Template Category	Purpose
Block Diagram	Creating general-purpose diagrams using geometric shapes
New in Visio 2003 Brainstorming	Creating diagrams that help you formulate plans, solve problems, and make decisions
Building Plan	Arranging office space and furniture
Business Process	Diagramming business processes using audit diagrams, basic flowcharts, cause and effect (fishbone) diagrams, cross-functional flowcharts, Enterprise Process Center (EPC) diagrams, fault tree analysis diagrams, total quality management (TQM) diagrams, and workflow diagrams
Charts and Graphs	Designing charts, graphs, and diagrams for presentations, reports, and marketing documentation
Flowchart	Creating basic flowcharts and cross-functional flowcharts

Template Category	Purpose
Map	Assembling simple 2-D (two-dimensional) or 3-D (three-dimensional) directional maps
Network	Creating simple network designs using network and computer equipment shapes
Organization Chart	Showing hierarchical structures in organizations
Project Schedule	Tracking projects details in Program Evaluation and Review Technique (PERT) charts, Gantt charts, timelines, and calendars

New in Visio 2003

Tip If you don't want to start your diagrams by using a template that has a blank drawing page, there are now Visio 2003 templates that come with shapes already on the drawing page. Visit the Microsoft Office Online Web site at *http://www.office.microsoft.com*.

Just as templates are organized by categories, related shapes are organized on *stencils*. For example, when you open the Basic Diagram template, all the geometric shapes included with the template are organized on the Basic Shapes stencil. Likewise, all the border and title shapes for basic diagrams are organized on the Borders and Titles stencil, and so on. This makes finding shapes quick and easy. After you find the shape you want, just drag it onto the drawing page and you're on your way.

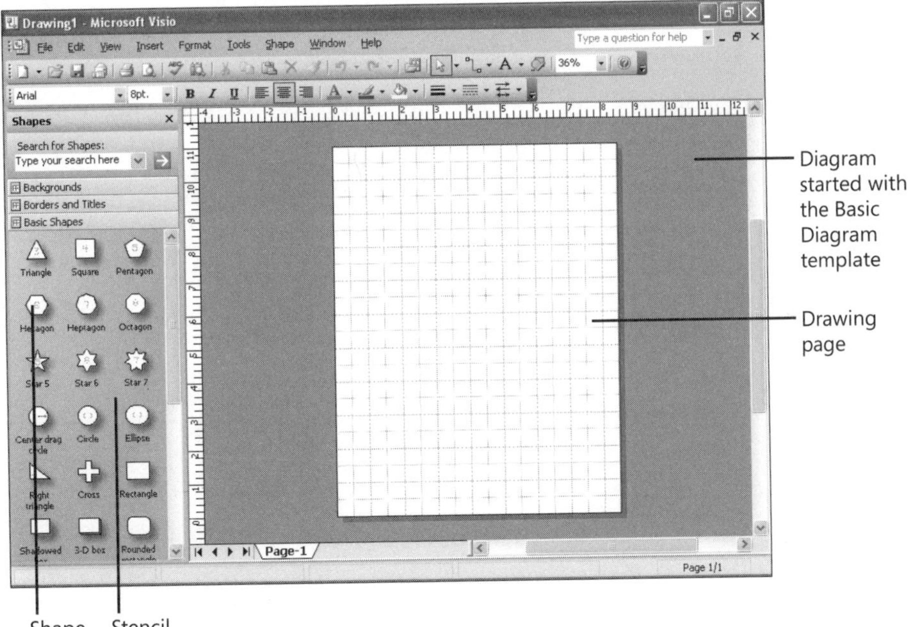

In this exercise, you start Visio, and then browse the Visio templates. You open a template, look at the shapes it includes, and then open another template to become acquainted with Visio templates and shapes.

start

1 On the taskbar, click the **Start** button, point to **All Programs**, point to **Microsoft Office**, and then click **Microsoft Office Visio 2003**.

Visio starts and opens the Choose Drawing Type window on the left and the Getting Started task pane on the right.

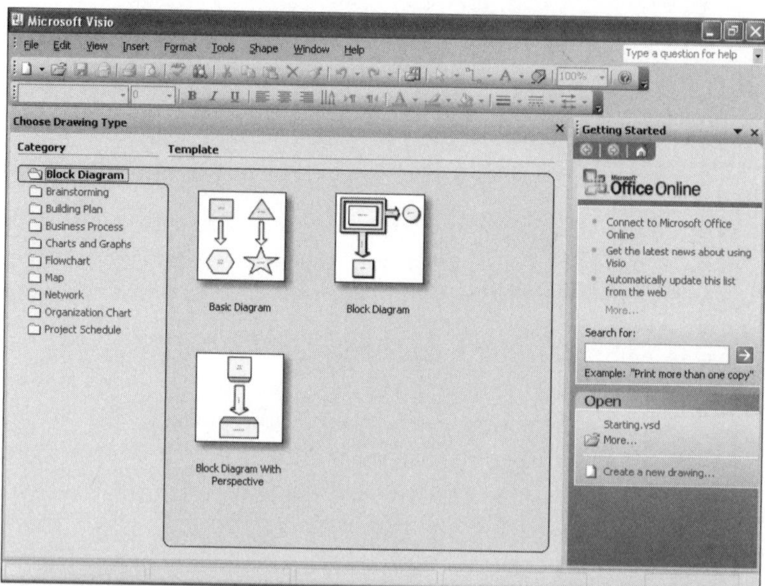

2 In the **Category** list, click **Flowchart**.

The Template area lists the templates included in this category and displays sample diagrams.

Tip If none of the templates are exactly what you are looking for, use a template with shapes that closely match what you need. For example, you can use the Basic Flowchart template to create a data flow diagram or the Basic Diagram template to create a diagram with a variety of geometric shapes. If the template doesn't include all the shapes you need, you can search for other shapes while you're creating your diagram.

See Also You'll learn more about searching for shapes in Chapter 2, "Adding Shapes to Diagrams."

---

3 Point to **Basic Flowchart** to display a description of the template in the lower-left corner of the window.

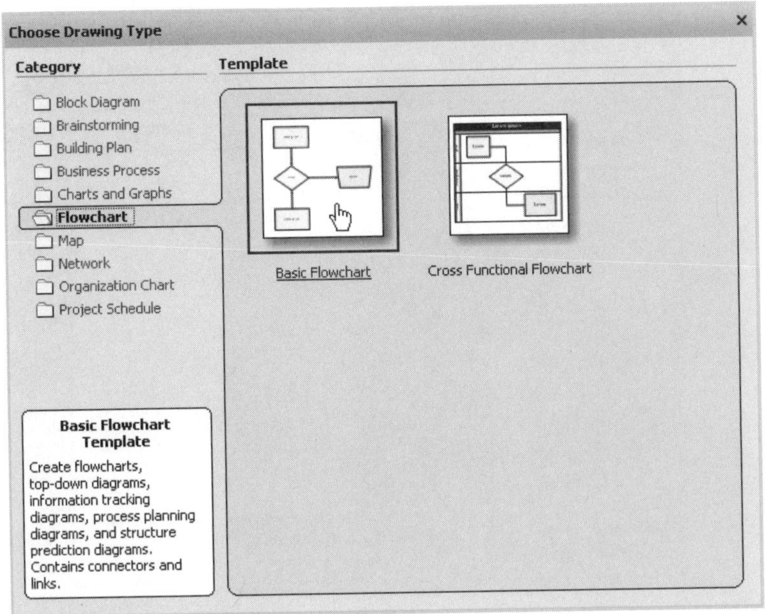

Troubleshooting If you see more template categories and names than are shown in the images in this book, it's probably because you're using Visio Professional 2003. This book includes images from Visio Standard 2003; however, the same drawing methods apply to both programs. To determine which Visio program you're using, on the Help menu, click About Microsoft Office Visio.

4 In the **Category** list, click **Block Diagram**.

In the Template area, the Basic Diagram, Block Diagram, and Block Diagram with Perspective template names appear with sample diagrams.

5 In the **Template** area, click **Basic Diagram**.

Visio opens a blank drawing page and the Basic Shapes, Borders and Titles, and Backgrounds stencils.

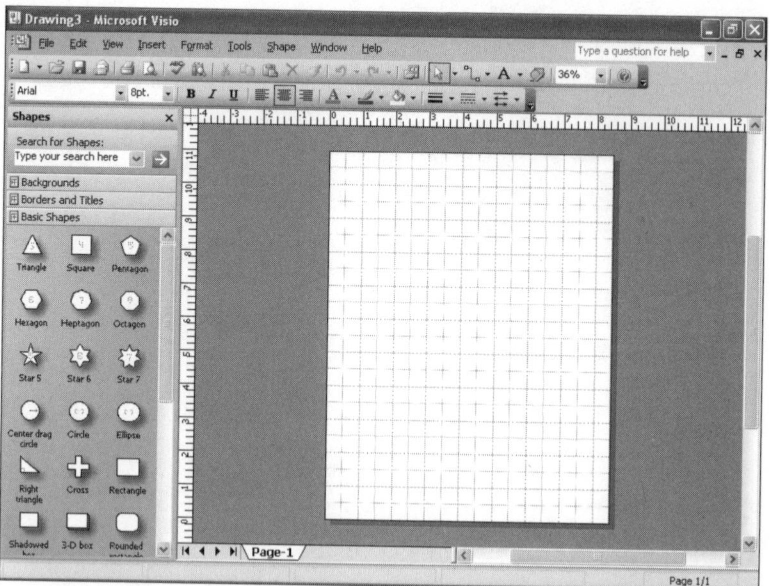

6 On the **File** menu, click **Close** to close the diagram and stencils.

7 On the **File** menu, point to **New**, and then click **Choose Drawing Type**.

The Choose Drawing Type window and New Drawing task pane appear.

New

Tip For quick access to Visio templates, on the Standard toolbar, click the New down arrow, point to the template category you want, and then click the name of the template you want to open. Or, on the File menu, point to New, point to the template category you want, and then click the name of the template you want to open.

8 In the **Template** area, click **Block Diagram**.

Troubleshooting If you don't see Block Diagram, in the Category list, click Block Diagram. Then, in the Template area, click Block Diagram.

Visio opens a blank drawing page and the Blocks, Blocks Raised, Borders and Titles, and Backgrounds stencils.

Close Window

9 In the gray area in the upper-right corner of the drawing page window, click the **Close Window** button.

Visio closes the new diagram without saving changes, but Visio remains open.

Troubleshooting The Close button on the right side of the Visio window's title bar is directly above the Close Window button on the drawing page window. Don't confuse the two. The Close button closes the drawing window *and* Visio. The Close Window button closes only the drawing window. In step 9, make sure you click the Close Window button so that Visio remains open.

Close

10 On the right side of the Visio window's title bar, click the **Close** button.

Visio closes.

Working Within the Microsoft Office Visio Environment

When you start a diagram, the Visio window, which contains the Visio menus and toolbars, opens. The Visio window also contains the Shapes window, drawing page, pasteboard, and rulers in a drawing window. The stencils that contain the shapes you need are located in the Shapes window to the left of the drawing page. Visio also includes special-purpose windows, menus, and toolbars for creating particular types of diagrams.

The Visio *drawing page* resembles graph paper with a *grid* that helps you position shapes. The horizontal and vertical *rulers* also help you position shapes and show you the size of the drawing page. Above the drawing page are the Visio menus and the Standard and Formatting toolbars (shown by default), which contain the most commonly used tools for creating, modifying, and formatting text, shapes, and diagrams. If you use other programs in the Microsoft Office System, many of the buttons on the toolbars should be familiar to you.

Many of the buttons on these toolbars have drop-down lists that include options or other tools you can select. To view the list for a specific button, click the down arrow on the button. If you are not familiar with a toolbar button, you can pause the pointer over it to display a *ScreenTip* that tells you which tool or command the button represents. Visio also includes easy access to frequently used commands on a *shortcut menu* that appears when you right-click an item. For example, right-click the drawing page, the toolbar area, a page tab, or a shape to see its shortcut menu.

New in Visio 2003

Below the drawing page, page tabs help you move between pages in multiple-page drawings, and the status bar displays information about shapes that are selected on the drawing page. To the right of the drawing page, you can display *task panes* from which you can quickly access task-specific and diagram-specific information. The light-blue area surrounding the drawing page is the *pasteboard*, which you can use as a temporary holding area for shapes and other drawing elements. Shapes on the pasteboard aren't printed.

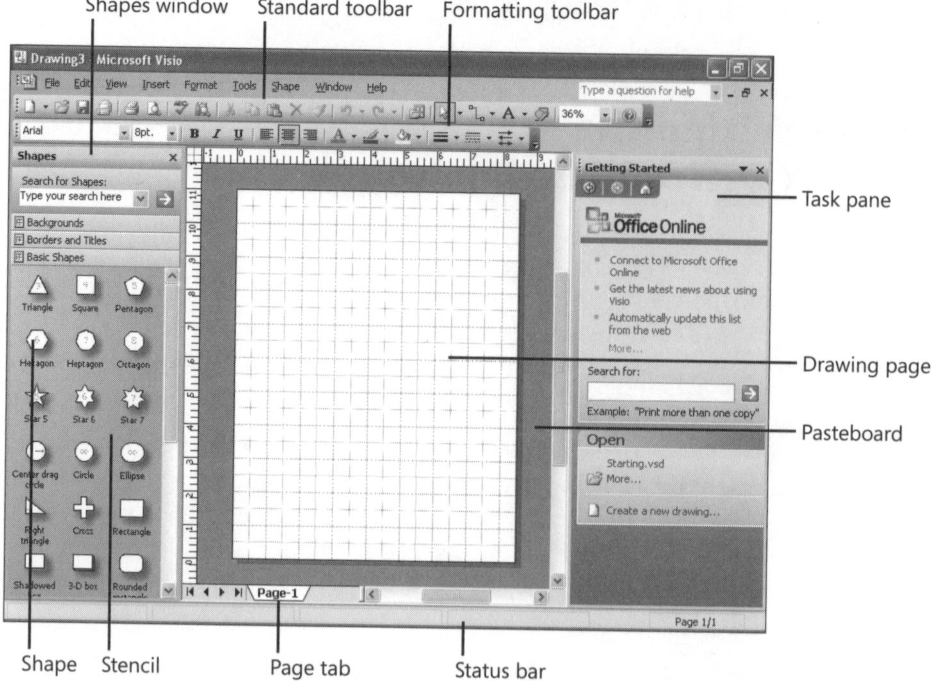

When you create a diagram from a template, Visio shows the entire drawing page. As you add shapes to the diagram, you can *zoom* in to an area for a closer view of that area or zoom out for a broader view of the diagram. Visio includes several ways to zoom in and out, including a toolbar button and keyboard shortcuts. One method isn't necessarily better than another–you can use the one that works best for you.

You can also *pan* large diagrams, which means that you can "grab" the drawing page with the pointer and move the page to see another area of it. Zooming and panning help you move quickly around the drawing page so that you can work efficiently in the Visio environment.

In this exercise, you explore the fundamental parts of the Visio drawing window. You display stencils in the Shapes window, and then zoom and pan the drawing page.

1. Start Visio. Click the down arrow on the **Getting Started** task pane's title bar, and then click **New Drawing**.

   Tip To show or hide the task pane, on the View menu, click Task Pane.

2. In the **New Drawing** task pane, in the **Recently used templates** list, click **Block Diagram**.

   Visio opens a blank drawing page and four stencils.

3 In the Shapes window, click the **Blocks Raised** stencil's title bar.

The Blocks Raised stencil is displayed on top of the other stencils, and the Blocks stencil is minimized at the bottom of the Shapes window.

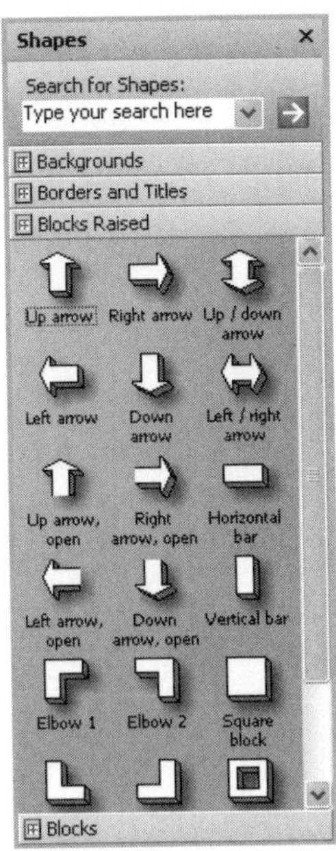

Troubleshooting When you click Blocks Raised, if Visio displays a stencil menu, you clicked the green icon on the stencil's title bar by mistake. Click the stencil name directly to display the stencil.

See Also You'll learn more about the stencil menu later in this chapter and in Chapter 10, "Creating Shapes, Stencils, and Templates."

---

4 Click the **Blocks** stencil's title bar to display the **Blocks** stencil.

5 Drag the scroll bar on the **Blocks** stencil down to see all the stencil's shapes.

Troubleshooting Your monitor's resolution and the size of your Visio window determine whether a scroll bar appears on the Blocks stencil. Because of these factors, your screen might not exactly match the images in this book. If you don't see a scroll bar on the stencil, all the shapes are already visible.

6 Scroll up to the top of the **Blocks** stencil.

7 Point to the **Box** shape in the upper-left corner of the **Blocks** stencil.

A ScreenTip appears describing the shape's purpose.

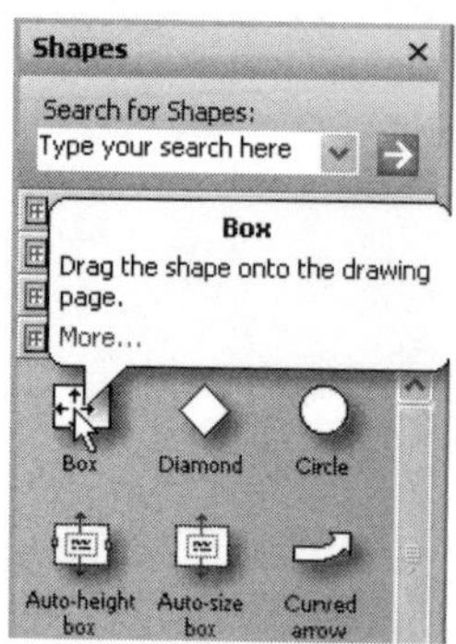

Tip All Visio shapes, toolbar buttons, window buttons, and even rulers have ScreenTips that explain what you can do with them. If you don't know how to use one of these elements, just pause the pointer over it to see a ScreenTip.

8 Drag the **Box** shape anywhere on the drawing page, and as you drag, watch the status bar at the bottom of the Visio window.

Visio determines the shape's position on the drawing page by using the horizontal and vertical rulers and displays the position in the status bar. Also, notice that the Box shape snaps to the grid as you move it around the drawing page.

9 Release the mouse button when you've positioned the shape where you want it.

The shape remains selected, and the status bar displays its width, height, and angle of rotation.

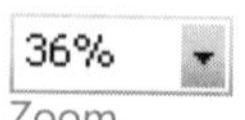

Zoom

10 On the Standard toolbar, click the **Zoom** down arrow to display a list of magnification levels, and then click **100%**.

Visio zooms in to 100 percent.

11 Hold down Shift+Ctrl while you right-click once.

Visio zooms out, and the zoom box displays the current zoom percentage.

12 Hold down Shift+Ctrl while you left-click once to zoom in to 100 percent again.

Tip When you press Shift+Ctrl, the pointer changes to a magnifying glass icon to indicate that left-clicking will zoom in and right-clicking will zoom out.

13 Hold down Shift+Ctrl while you drag a selection rectangle around the **Box** shape on the drawing page, and then release the mouse button.

Visio zooms in to the area you selected.

14 Press Ctrl+W to zoom out to the whole-page view.

15 Hold down Shift+Ctrl while you drag with the right mouse button.

The pointer changes to a hand icon as Visio pans, or moves, the drawing page.

16 Press Ctrl+W to zoom out to the whole-page view.

17 Right-click the **Page-1** page tab at the bottom of the drawing window.

Visio displays a shortcut menu for the page tab.

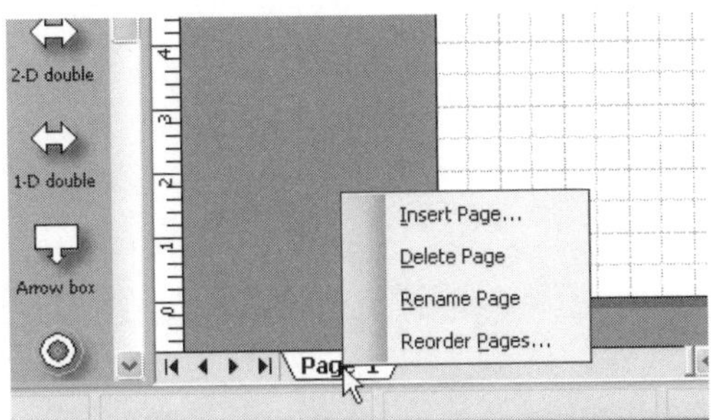

18 On the shortcut menu, click **Insert Page**, and then in the **Page Setup** dialog box, click **OK** to add a new drawing page to the diagram named **Page-2**.

Tip You can easily rename pages in your diagrams. First, double-click the page tab for the page you want to rename. Or, right-click the page tab and then click Rename Page. Both actions select the page name. Then, simply type the new page name to replace the old one.

19 Click the **Page-1** page tab to go back to the first page of the diagram.

Close

20 On the Visio window's title bar, click the **Close** button.

Visio displays a message asking if you want to save your changes to the drawing.

21 Click **No** to close Visio without saving the diagram.

Customizing the Visio Environment

Most of what you see in the Visio environment can be customized to suit the way that you like to work. For example, you can hide the grid if it makes the drawing page look too cluttered for your taste. You can also hide the rulers, as well as show or hide any toolbars. If you prefer to display all the Visio menu items immediately (without delay), instead of just the items that you use most frequently, you can.

Tip To display a list of the Visio toolbars that are available for the template that you have open, right-click the toolbar area to display the toolbar shortcut menu. Then click the name of the toolbar you want to appear. A check mark next to a toolbar's name indicates that it is currently shown.

If you're working with a low-resolution monitor and want more space on the screen, you can move, resize, or close the stencils. You can also *dock*, or snap, the Shapes window to a different part of the screen so that all the stencils are in a fixed position that's more convenient for you. You can also *float*, or detach, windows and stencils from the drawing window, so that you can quickly move them around as you work. If you don't want to have to scroll down a stencil to see all its shapes, you can make the list of shapes more compact by hiding the shape names and showing only the icons.

For quick access to related commands or drawing shortcuts, you can use the tools in various windows, such as the Pan & Zoom and Size & Position windows. The Pan & Zoom window displays a miniature version of your entire diagram, which you can use to quickly move to different parts of the drawing page. If you want to enter precise dimensions for the shapes in your diagrams rather than resizing shapes with the pointer, you can do that in the Size & Position window.

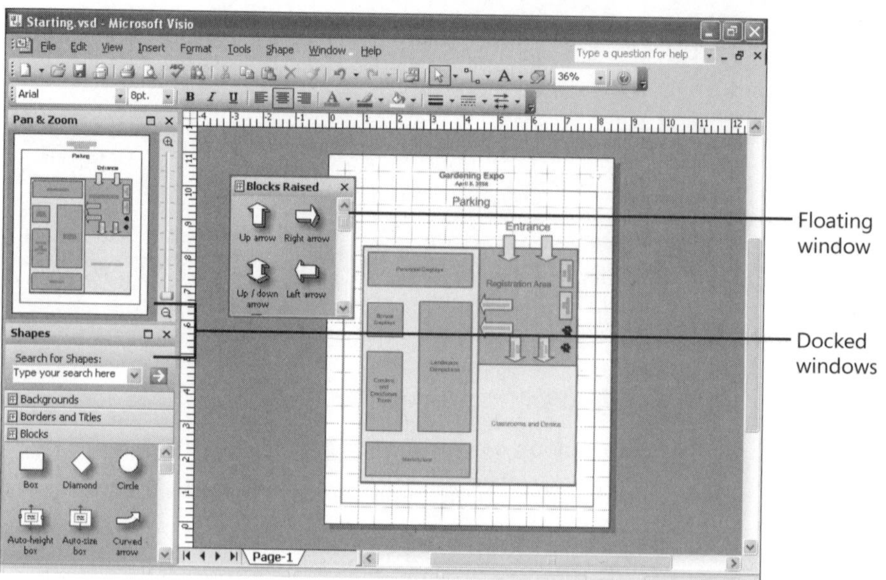

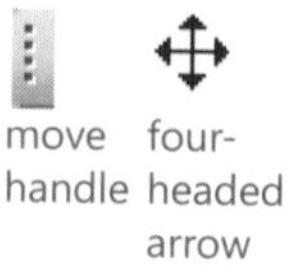

Tip By default, the Visio menu bar and toolbars are docked on the Visio window. However, you can float any toolbar or the entire menu bar, or dock them in a different location if it's more convenient for you. Position the pointer over the move handle on the menu bar or a toolbar, and when the pointer changes to a four-headed arrow, drag the bar to a new location. If you drag a floating menu bar or toolbar to an edge of the Visio window, Visio docks the item in that location.

In this exercise, you customize the Visio environment. You start by opening a diagram that shows the proposed layout for a gardening expo, hosted by The Garden Company, a fictitious company used throughout this book.

OPEN the *Starting* file in the My Documents\Microsoft Press\Visio 2003 SBS\StartingDiagrams folder.

Open

1 Start Visio. On the Standard toolbar, click the **Open** button to display the **Open** dialog box and then double-click the **Microsoft Press** folder.

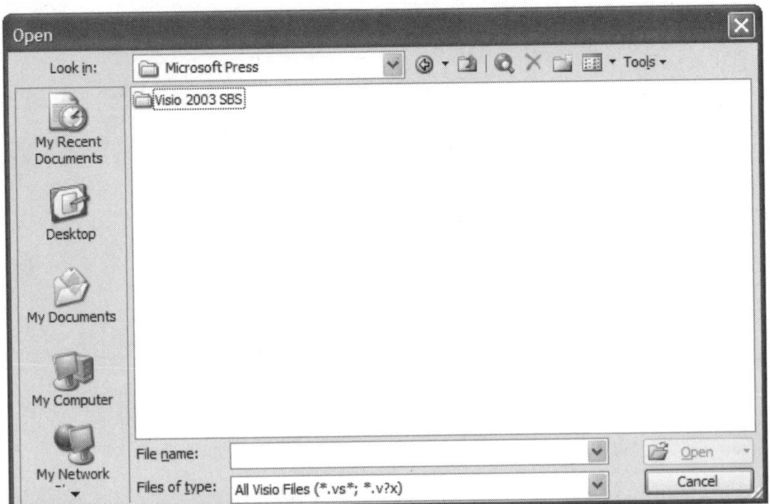

2 In the list of files and folder names, double-click the **Visio 2003 SBS** folder.

Troubleshooting By default, Visio opens the My Documents folder in the Open dialog box. Also, by default, all the practice files for this book are installed in the Microsoft Press\Visio 2003 SBS folder in My Documents. If you don't see the Visio 2003 SBS folder, navigate to the My Documents\Microsoft Press folder. If you installed the practice files for this book in a different location, when you use practice files throughout this book, you need to navigate to that location.

3 Double-click the **StartingDiagrams** folder, and then double-click **Starting**.

Tip If the file extensions on your computer aren't hidden, the file name you will see in the Open dialog box is Starting.vsd. The .vsd file extension stands for *Visio drawing*.

Visio opens a diagram showing the layout of a gardening expo and four stencils.

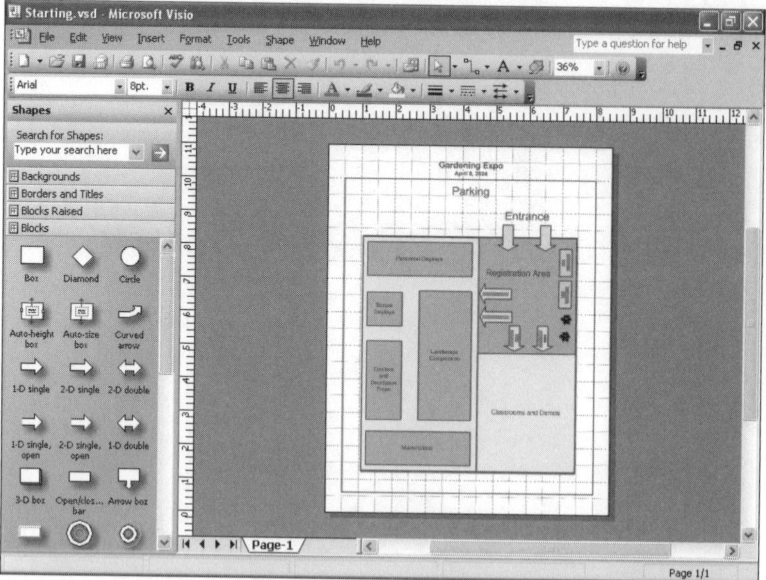

4 On the **View** menu, click **Rulers** to hide the horizontal and vertical rulers.

5 On the **View** menu, click **Grid** to hide the grid on the drawing page.

6 On the **Tools** menu, click **Customize**.

The Customize dialog box appears.

7 In the **Customize** dialog box, click the **Options** tab.

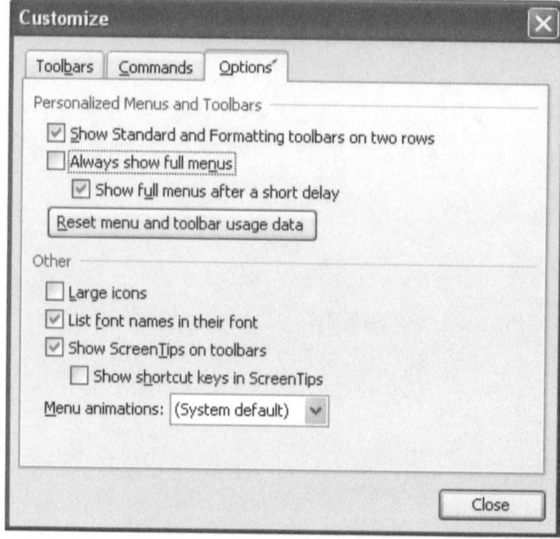

8 Select the **Always show full menus** check box, and then click **Close**.

From this point on, Visio will show all the items on its menus immediately, instead of only the ones that you use most frequently.

9 On the **View** menu, click **Pan & Zoom Window**.

Visio opens the Pan & Zoom window. If you have never opened it before, it is docked in the upper-right corner of the drawing window. If you have opened this window before, the window reappears in the location where it was last displayed.

10 In the Pan & Zoom window, drag to draw a selection rectangle around the green area in the upper-right corner of the window.

Visio zooms in to the diagram to show the selected area, which is highlighted with a red rectangle in the Pan & Zoom window. The Zoom box on the Standard toolbar displays the new zoom level.

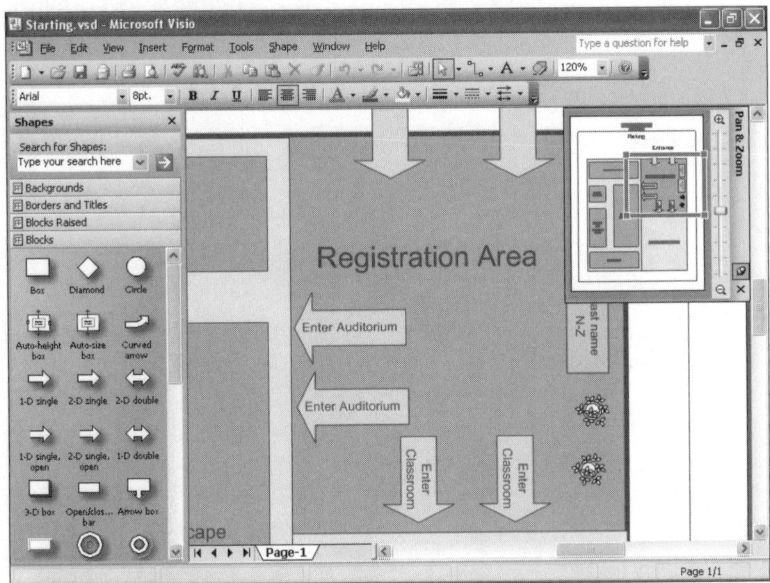

11 In the Pan & Zoom window, drag a corner of the red rectangle out to enlarge the selection.

Visio shows the new selected area and changes the level of zoom in the drawing window so that more of the page is visible.

AutoHide

12 On the title bar of the Pan & Zoom window, click the **AutoHide** button, and then move the pointer away from the window.

Visio slides the window out of sight until only the Pan & Zoom window's title bar is visible.

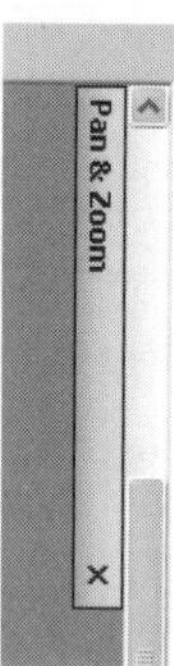

13 Point to the Pan & Zoom window's title bar.

Visio opens the window. As long as the pointer is over the window, it stays open.

14 Click the **AutoHide** button.

Visio turns off AutoHide so that the Pan & Zoom window stays open.

15 Drag the Pan & Zoom window by its title bar into the top of the Shapes window.

Visio docks the Pan & Zoom window above the Shapes window.

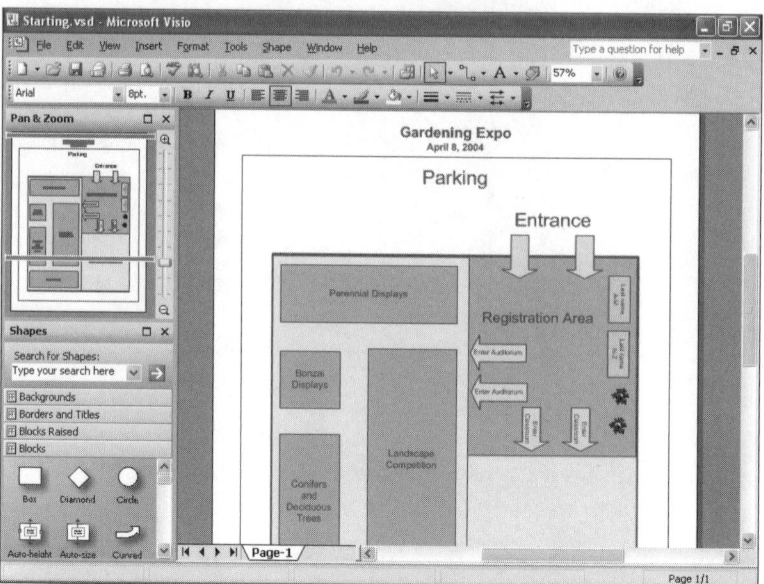

16 Point to the horizontal border between the Pan & Zoom window and the Shapes window.

The pointer changes to a two-headed arrow.

two-headed arrow

17 With the two-headed arrow pointer, drag the border up to make the Pan & Zoom window slightly smaller.

Close

18 Click the **Close** button in the upper-right corner of the Pan & Zoom window.

Visio closes the Pan & Zoom window and enlarges the Shapes window to fill the space.

Shapes

19 On the Standard toolbar, click the **Shapes** button.

Visio displays a menu of stencil categories.

20 Point to **Visio Extras**, and then click **Callouts**.

Visio opens the Callouts stencil, which contains annotation shapes, and displays it in the Shapes window on top of the other stencils.

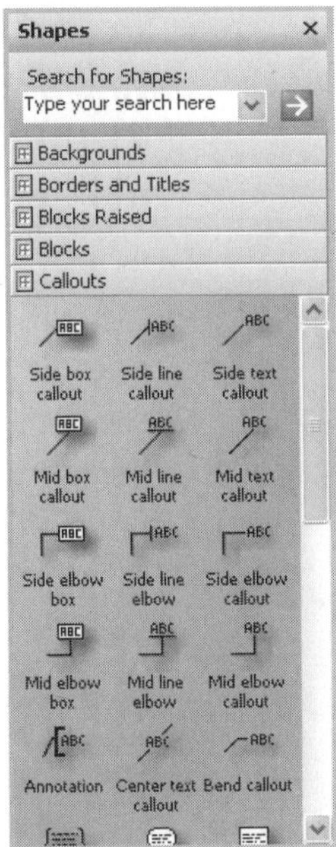

21 Point to the **Callouts** stencil's title bar, and then drag the stencil to the middle of the drawing page.

The stencil floats over the drawing page.

22 Point to the **Callouts** stencil's title bar, and then drag the stencil a little lower, but don't dock it to the bottom of the drawing page window.

Troubleshooting If you dock the Callouts stencil by mistake, just drag it away from the side of the window.

23 On the **Callouts** stencil, click the green stencil icon on the stencil's title bar.

Visio displays a menu for the stencil.

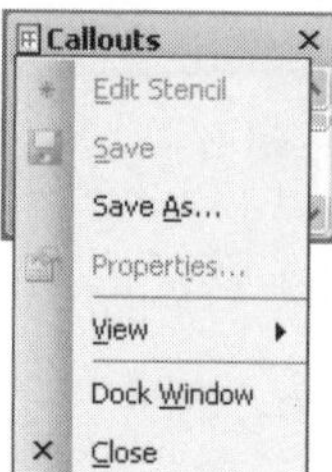

24 Point to **View**, and then click **Icons Only**.

Visio displays the shape icons without their names. Notice that Visio also changes the Blocks stencil view.

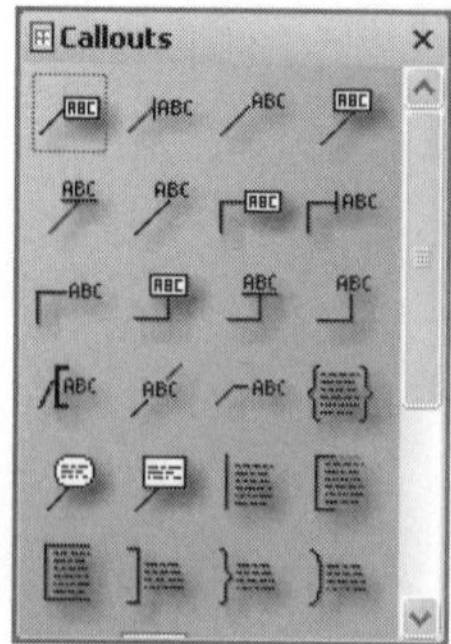

25 Click the green stencil icon on the stencil's title bar, point to **View**, and then click **Icons and Names**.

Visio displays both the shape icons and names on the stencil. Notice again that Visio also changes the Blocks stencil view.

26 Point to the **Callouts** stencil's title bar, and then drag the stencil back to the Shapes window.

Visio docks the stencil in the Shapes window.

27 On the **Callouts** stencil, click the green stencil icon on the stencil's title bar, and then click **Close**.

Visio closes the stencil.

28 On the **File** menu, click **Exit**.

Visio closes.

Customizing Colors and Other Options

You can customize many other aspects of the Visio environment by using the Options dialog box. For example, if you get tired of the green stencil window or the white drawing page, you can change those colors and others used by Visio. To choose different colors, on the Tools menu, click Options. In the Options dialog box, click the Advanced tab, and then click the Color Settings button.

Like other programs in the Microsoft Office System, Visio includes toolbars that you can customize. You can even create a new toolbar and add the commands that you use most often to it. On the Tools menu, click Customize to view the options for customizing toolbars.

Keep in mind that the more you customize Visio, the less your screen will match the images shown in this book.

Getting Visio and Diagram Help

Visio offers a variety of ways to get help while you're working, as shown in the following table.

Task	Action
New in Visio 2003 See sample diagrams for every diagram type in Visio and find ideas about who could use the diagrams and how	On the Help menu, click Diagram Gallery.
See animation for step-by-step procedures that teach you the basic skills that you need to create and share any Visio diagram	On the Help menu, click Getting Started Tutorial.
Quickly find answers to your questions by using keywords	Type a keyword in the "Type a question for help" box on the Visio menu bar, and then press the Enter key. Visio searches through its Help topics to find the ones related to the keyword.
New in Visio 2003 Peruse the list of Help topics included with Visio	On the Help menu, click Microsoft Office Visio Help to show the Visio Help task pane. Then in the Assistance area, click Table of Contents.

Task	Action
Find specific information about how to use a template	Type the name of the template followed by **template** in the "Type a question for help" box on the Visio menu bar, and then press the Enter key. For example, type **Basic Flowchart template**. ***New in Visio 2003*** If you are connected to the Internet, you can open the template, click the task pane's title bar, and then click Template Help. This task pane is available only if you're connected to the Internet.
Find specific information about how to use a shape	Right-click a shape, and then click Help.
New in Visio 2003 Find product tours, templates, sample diagrams, tutorials, tips and tricks, in-depth articles about using Visio, answers to frequently asked questions, and links to Microsoft Knowledge Base articles	On the Help menu, click Microsoft Office Online. Or, in the Visio Help task pane, click Microsoft Office Online.

New in Visio 2003

Tip To get the most recent Visio Help topics, make sure you're connected to the Internet when you use Visio Help. If you're not connected to the Internet, Visio will use the Help topics installed with the Visio program. To change Visio Help settings, on the Help menu, click Customer Feedback Options. Then in the Service Options dialog box, in the Category list, click Online Content.

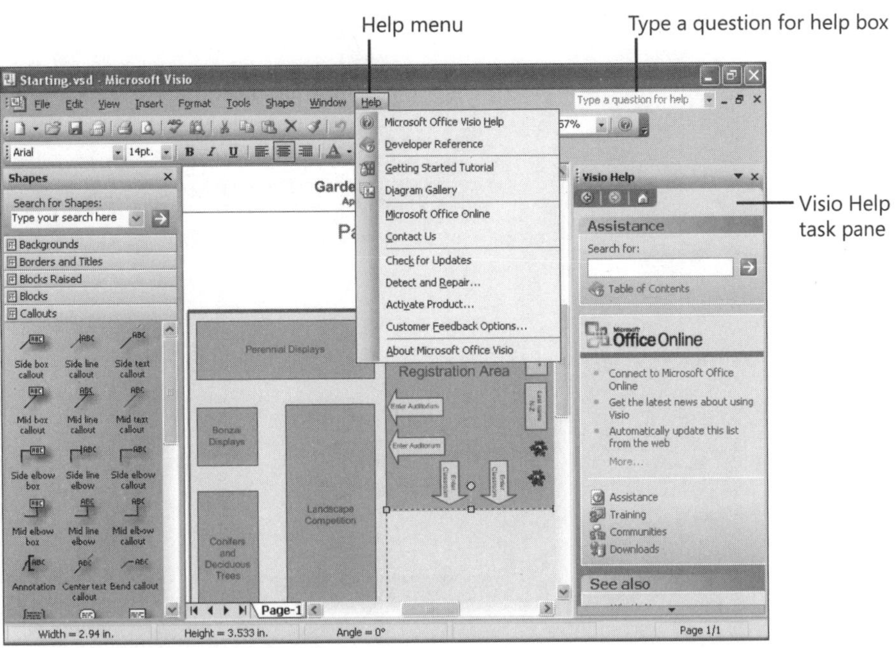

In this exercise, you get help using a particular template and shape, and you search Visio Help using a keyword. You also open the Diagram Gallery to see Visio suggestions for how to use a particular diagram type.

1. Start Visio. In the Choose Drawing Type window, in the **Category** area, click **Charts and Graphs**.
2. In the **Template** area, click **Charts and Graphs**.

   Visio opens a blank drawing page and three stencils.
3. On the **View** menu, click **Task Pane**.
4. Click the down arrow on the **Getting Started** task pane's title bar, and then click **Help**.

The Visio Help task pane appears.

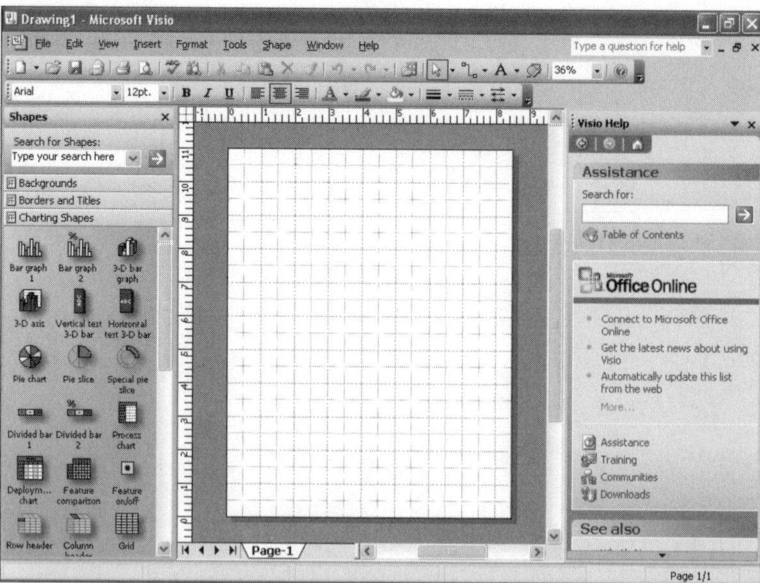

5 In the task pane's **Search for** box, type **Charts and Graphs template**, and then press the Enter key.

Visio displays a list of Help topics for the keyword in the Search Results task pane.

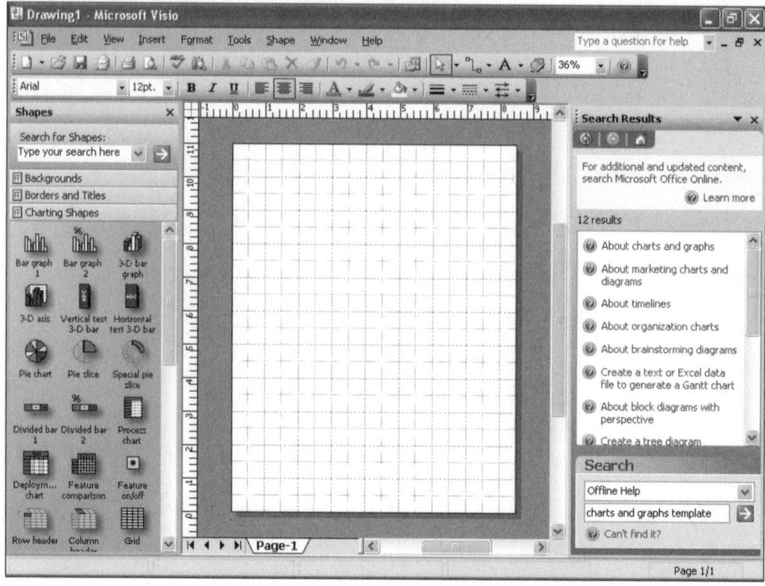

6 In the **Search Results** task pane, click **About charts and graphs**.

The Help window opens to the right of the Visio window and displays the Help topic that you selected.

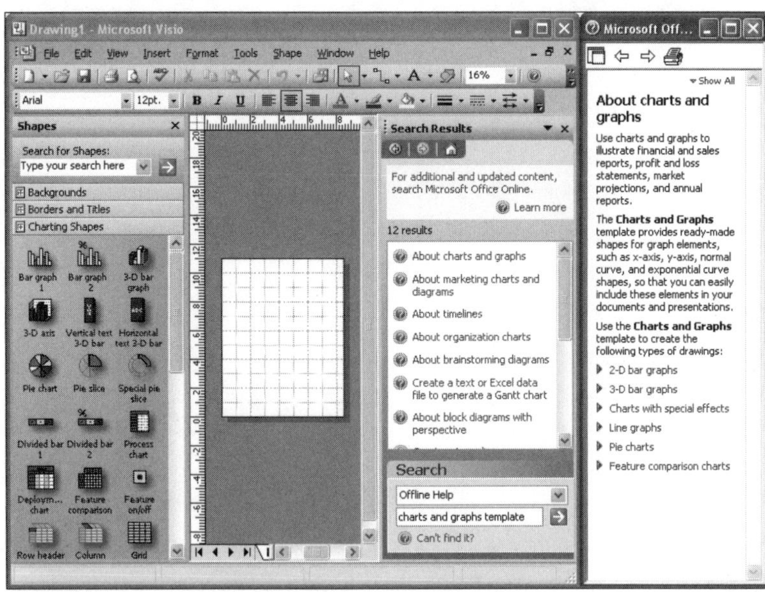

Troubleshooting If you're connected to the Internet while you search Visio Help, the list of Help topics you see in the Search Results task pane might be slightly different than the results shown in this book.

Close

7 In the upper-right corner of the Help window, click the **Close** button to close the window.

The Help window closes and the Visio window is resized.

8 Click the down arrow on the **Search Results** task pane's title bar, and then click **Help** to return to the **Visio Help** task pane.

9 On the Visio menu bar, click in the **Type a question for help** box, type pages, and then press the Enter key.

Visio displays a list of Help topics about pages in the Search Results task pane.

10 In the **Search Results** task pane, click **About dragging shapes onto a drawing page**.

The Help window opens to the right of the Visio window and displays the Help topic that you selected.

11 On the Help window's title bar, click the **Close** button to close the window.

12 On the **Help** menu, click **Diagram Gallery**.

Visio opens the Diagram Gallery window over the Visio window.

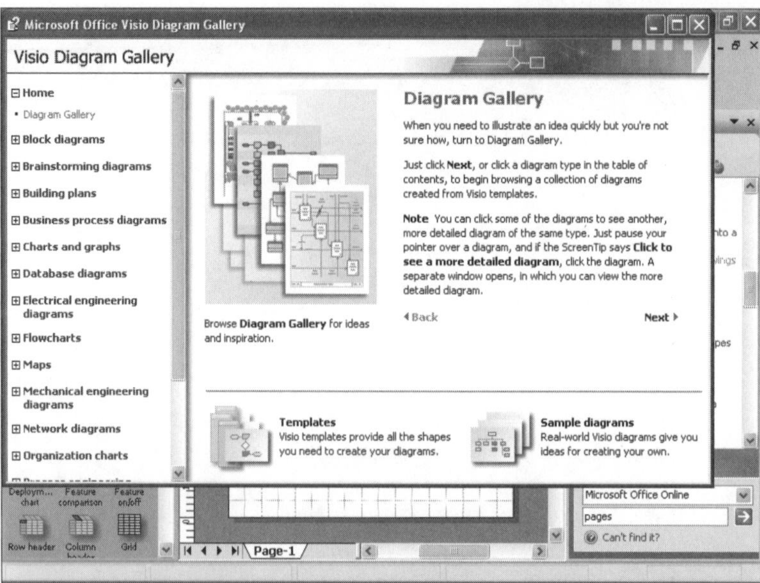

13 In the Diagram Gallery window, in the left pane, click **Charts and graphs.**

14 Under the **Charts and graphs** heading, click **Charts and graphs**.

The Diagram Gallery window displays the selected topic, which shows an example diagram and suggests who might find this type of diagram most useful and how it can be used.

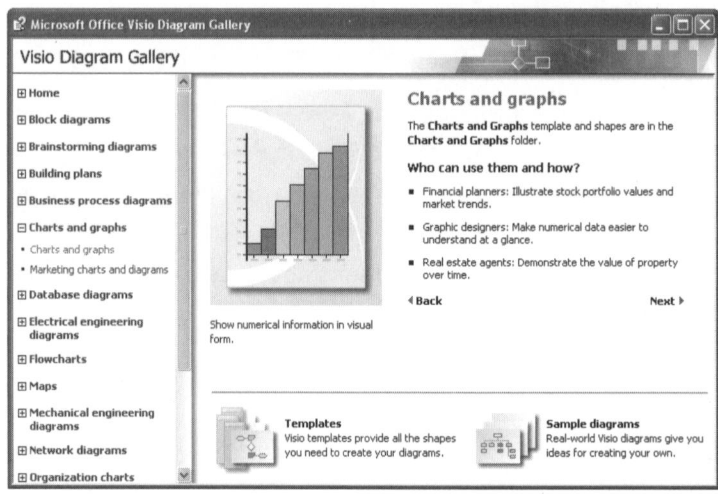

15 On the Diagram Gallery window's title bar, click the **Close** button to close the window.

16 From the **Charting Shapes** stencil, drag the **Bar graph 1** shape onto the drawing page.

17 In the **Custom Properties** dialog box that appears, click **OK**.

18 Right-click the shape on the drawing page, and then click **Help**.

The Help window opens to the right of the Visio window and displays a Help topic that explains how to use the shape.

19 In the Help window's title bar, click the **Close** button to close the window.

20 On the **File** menu, click **Exit**, and in the dialog box that appears, click **No** so that you don't save the diagram.

Visio closes.

Help

Tip When you open a dialog box in Visio, you can get help with each option in the dialog box. To open a dialog box Help topic, click the Help button in the dialog box (usually located in the lower-left corner).

Key Points

- You can create Visio diagrams by using the templates that come with Visio or templates that you can download from the Microsoft Office Online Web site.
- If none of the templates meet your needs, start your diagram by using a template that closely matches the diagram type.
- If you don't know which diagram type to use, browse the Diagram Gallery for inspiration.
- You can customize the Visio drawing environment so you can work efficiently.
- If you don't know which command or tool a toolbar button represents, position the pointer over it to see a ScreenTip.
- You can right-click an item to see its shortcut menu.
- Whenever you're stuck and need help, type your question in the "Type a question for help" box.
- If you need help using a particular template, type the template name in the "Type a question for help" box.
- If you don't know how to use a particular shape, right-click it, and then click Help.

Chapter 2 at a Glance

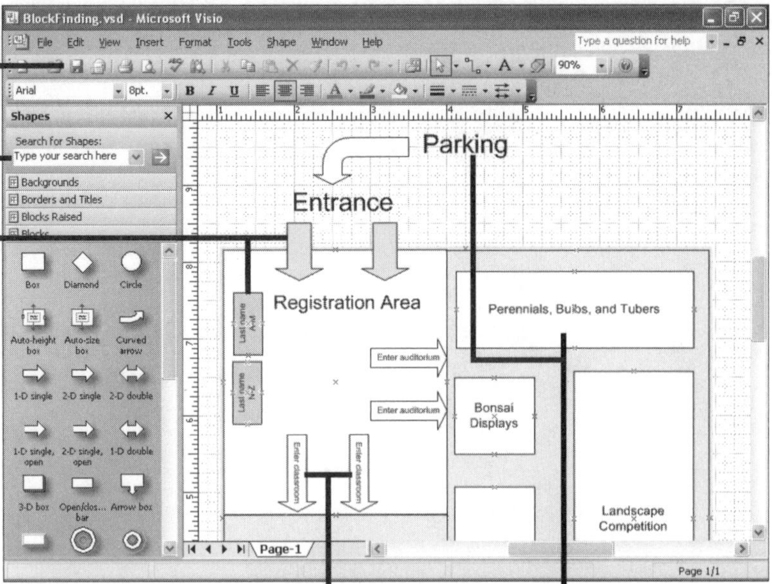

Save diagrams, page 54

Find shapes for diagrams, page 47

Work with 1-D and 2-D shapes, page 28

Move, size, rotate, and copy shapes, page 40

Add text to shapes and the drawing page, page 34

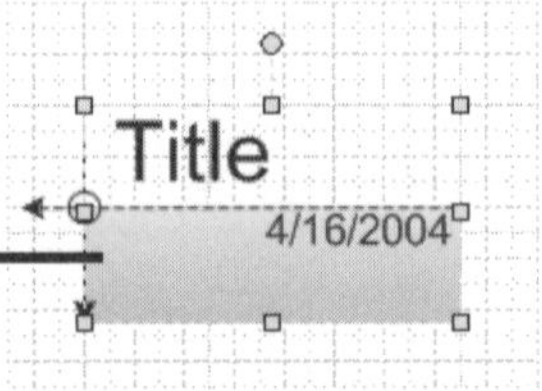

Work with groups, page 46

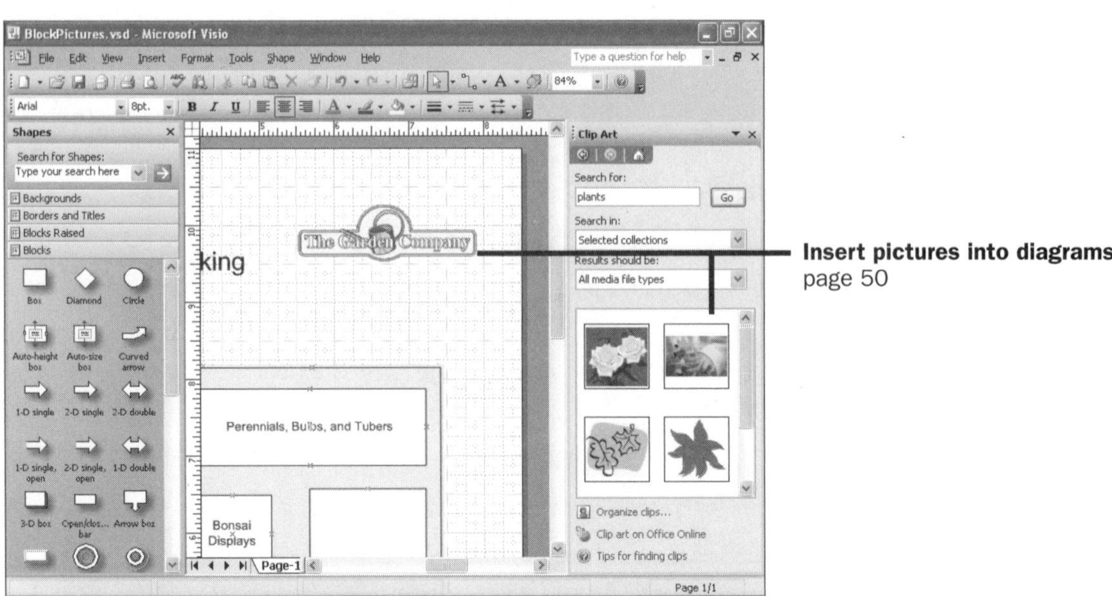

Insert pictures into diagrams, page 50

2 Adding Shapes to Diagrams

In this chapter you will learn to:

- ✔ Work with 1-D and 2-D shapes.
- ✔ Add text to shapes and the drawing page.
- ✔ Move, size, rotate, and copy shapes.
- ✔ Work with groups.
- ✔ Find shapes for diagrams.
- ✔ Insert pictures into diagrams.
- ✔ Save diagrams.

Microsoft Office Visio includes tens of thousands of shapes that you can use to quickly create diagrams. Shapes in Visio can represent both conceptual graphics and real-world objects, such as office furniture and network equipment. Shapes can be as simple as a rectangle that represents a step in a process flowchart, or they can be as complex as a hub in a network diagram. Because shapes can represent real-world objects, you can interact with them in ways that are similar to the ways you interact with the real-world objects. For example, you can use a handle to quickly rotate a chair shape so that it faces a desk. Pie chart shapes have handles that you use to adjust the size of a pie slice. On network hub shapes, you can even drag cables (represented by lines) from the hub to other network equipment shapes. And all Visio shapes include handles that you can drag to resize the shapes. Visio shapes are *smart*; that's what sets them apart from shapes in other programs and clip art.

As you add shapes to your diagrams, you'll need to arrange them on the drawing page. For instance, in a flowchart, you might move one shape at a time, but in an office layout, you might need to move all the shapes at once. You can also add titles to your diagrams or labels to your shapes by simply typing the text you want to add. You can customize the appearance of your diagram by modifying the text and shape *attributes*. If you can't find the shape you need on the stencils associated with the template, you can find shapes on other stencils or on the Web. In addition, you can insert a picture, such as a company logo or a piece of clip art, from another program into your Visio diagram.

In this chapter, you'll work with a block diagram—one of the most commonly used diagram types in Visio—that uses simple box and arrow shapes to represent the layout of a gardening expo hosted by The Garden Company. You'll learn how to work with different types of shapes, add text to shapes, move and size shapes, rotate and copy shapes, and otherwise modify the appearance of shapes. You'll learn how to search for shapes you can use to create diagrams and insert pictures from other programs into your diagrams. Last, you'll save the diagram with file information that can help you identify the file without even opening it.

See Also Do you need only a quick refresher on the topics in this chapter? See the Quick Reference entries on pages xxv–xxvii.

Important Before you can use the practice files in this chapter, you need to install them from the book's companion CD to their default location. See "Using the Book's CD" on page xv for more information.

Working with 1-D and 2-D Shapes

Shapes are the building blocks of all Visio diagrams. To work efficiently with any type of shape in any diagram, you need to understand some basic shape behavior, the differences between the types of Visio shapes, and how to interact with Visio shapes.

One of the fundamentals of interacting with shapes is that you drag shapes–one at a time–from stencils onto the drawing page to add them to a diagram. Another is that before you do something to a shape, such as move it or change its color, you need to *select* it so that Visio knows you want perform an action on that specific shape. Just place the pointer over the shape you want to select, and when a four-headed arrow appears under the pointer, click the shape to select it. You know that a shape is selected when you see *selection handles*. To *deselect* a shape, click the pasteboard or a blank area of the drawing page.

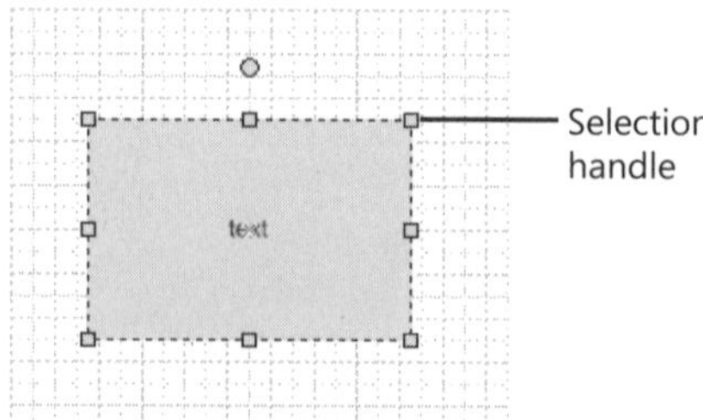

Tip Don't drag shapes back onto stencils to delete them from the drawing page. To delete a shape, select it, and then press the Del key.

All Visio shapes behave like *one-dimensional (1-D)* or *two-dimensional (2-D)* shapes. This difference affects the type of selection handles that appear when you select a shape and the way you work with the shape. 1-D shapes behave like lines and 2-D shapes behave like boxes. This information might not seem consequential now, but as you work with

Visio and eventually create your own shapes, knowing how both types of shapes behave will help you use Visio more skillfully.

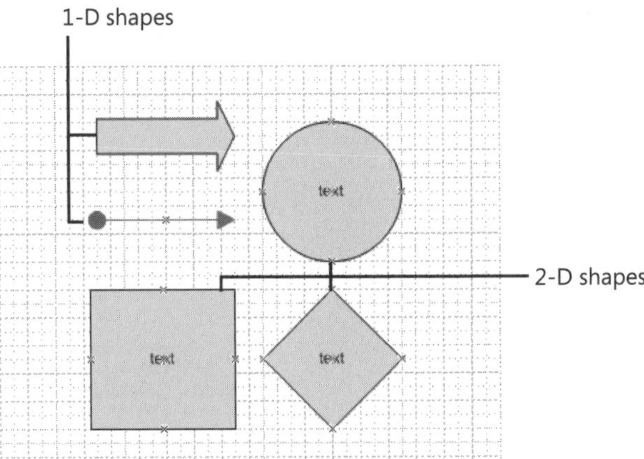

When you select a 1-D shape, two selection handles (called *endpoints*) appear that you can drag to resize the shape. The endpoint at the beginning of a 1-D shape is the *begin point* (represented by a x symbol), and the endpoint at the end of the shape is the *end point* (represented by a + symbol).

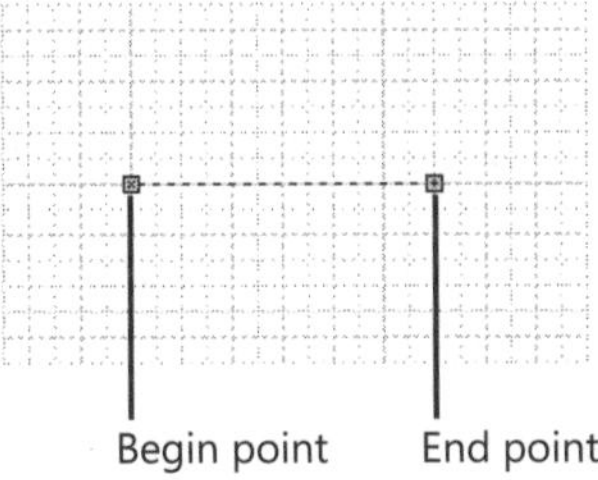

New in Visio 2003

When you select a 2-D shape, a rectangular *selection box* appears around the shape. The selection box has eight selection handles: one handle on each of the four corners and one handle on each side of the selection box. One round *rotation handle* also appears above the selection box. You can drag the rotation handle to rotate a shape or any corner selection handle to resize a shape proportionally.

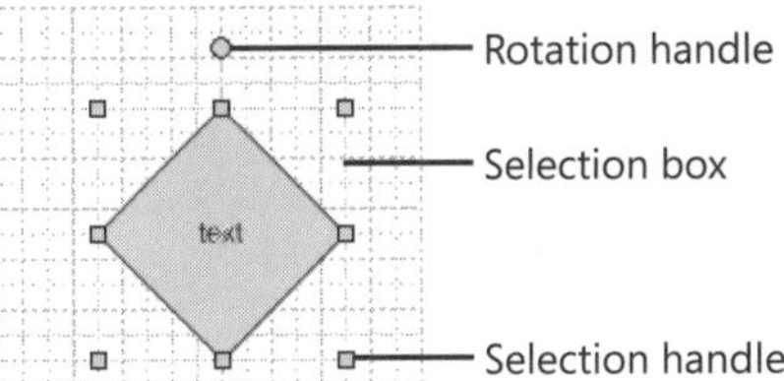

Tip All Visio shapes behave either like 1-D shapes or 2-D shapes. However, some shapes might look 3-D but behave like 2-D shapes, and others might look 2-D but behave like 1-D shapes. You can determine which way a shape will behave by the selection handles that appear when you select it. If, after selecting the shape, you're still confused about a shape's behavior, on the Format menu, click Behavior to see whether the shape will behave like a 1-D or 2-D shape.

In addition to selection handles, some shapes have special handles called *control handles*. When you drag a control handle, it performs an action unique to that shape. For example, the Line-Curve Connector shape has a control handle that adjusts the curvature of the shape's arc, as the ScreenTip explains.

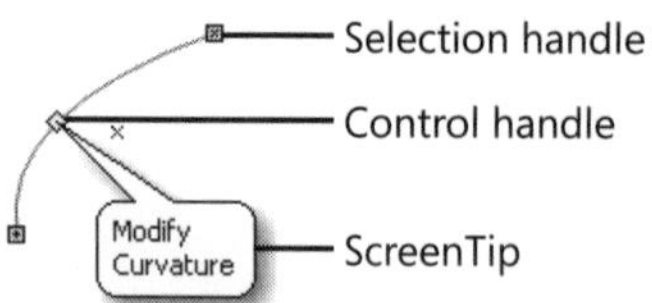

Tip All Visio shape handles—selection, rotation, and control handles—have ScreenTips that explain what you can do with it. If you don't know how to use a particular handle, just pause the pointer over it to display its ScreenTip.

In this short exercise, you practice dragging a few 1-D and 2-D shapes onto the drawing page and selecting them. Then you drag a shape's control handle to change the shape's appearance.

1. Start Visio. In the Choose Drawing Type window, in the **Category** area, click **Block Diagram**.
2. In the **Template** area, click **Block Diagram**.

   Visio opens a blank drawing page and four stencils.
3. On the **View** menu, make sure that both **Rulers** and **Grid** are checked so that the rulers appear in the Visio drawing window and the grid appears on the drawing page.

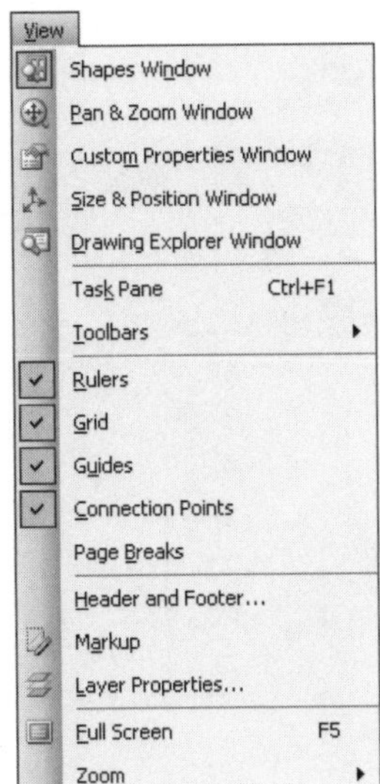

4 In the Shapes window, on the **Blocks** stencil, pause the pointer over the **Box** shape.

A ScreenTip appears that tells you how to use the shape.

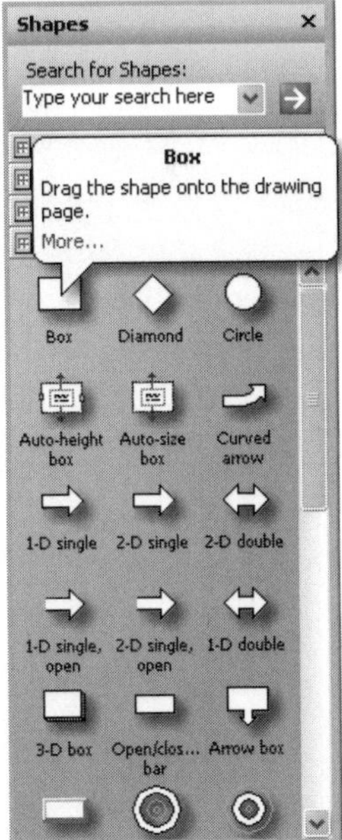

5 Drag the **Box** shape onto the drawing page.

The shape is selected on the drawing page. It's a 2-D shape, so it is surrounded by a selection box with eight selection handles and one round rotation handle.

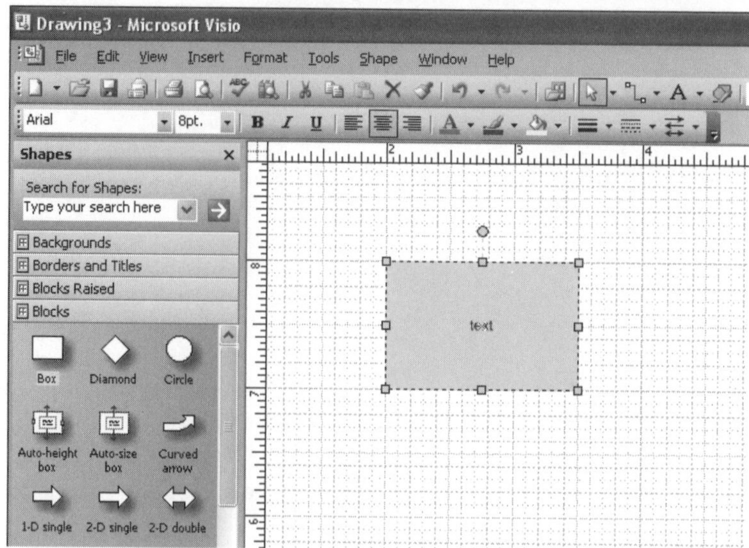

Note As you drag shapes onto the drawing page, notice how they *snap* to the nearest grid line on the page to help you easily position and align them.

6 Click the pasteboard.

The **Box** shape is no longer selected.

Tip You can also press the Esc key to deselect a shape.

7 Position the pointer over the **Box** shape.

four-headed arrow

A four-headed arrow pointer appears, indicating that Visio is ready for you to select the shape.

8 Click the **Box** shape.

The shape is selected again.

9 From the **Blocks** stencil, drag the **1-D Single** shape onto the drawing page.

The shape is selected on the drawing page. This shape is a 1-D shape, so you can see its begin point and end point. The **Box** shape is no longer selected.

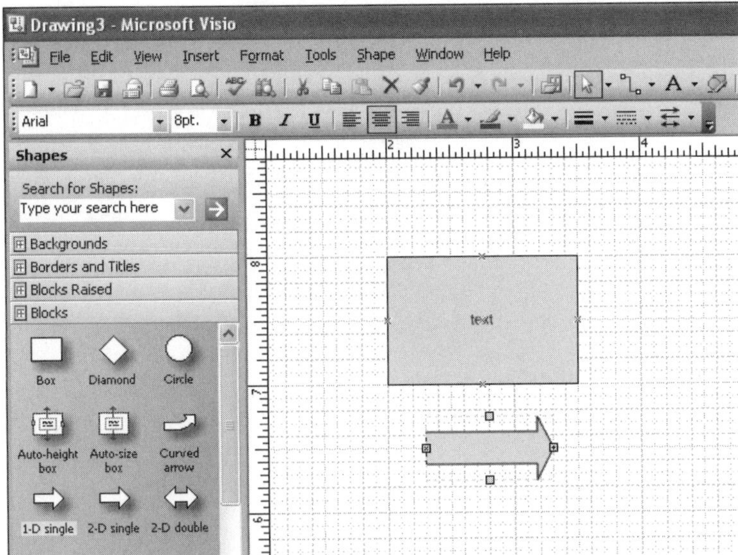

10 From the **Blocks** stencil, drag the **Curved Arrow** shape onto the drawing page.

The shape is selected on the drawing page. It's a 2-D shape, so it is surrounded by a selection box with eight selection handles and one round rotation handle. You can also see two yellow control handles on the shape.

11 Pause the pointer over the control handle on the arrowhead.

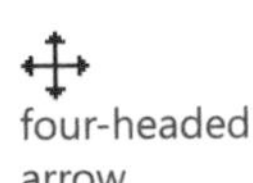
four-headed arrow

A ScreenTip appears that tells you what you can do with the control handle. The pointer changes to a four-headed arrow, indicating that Visio is ready for you to drag the control handle.

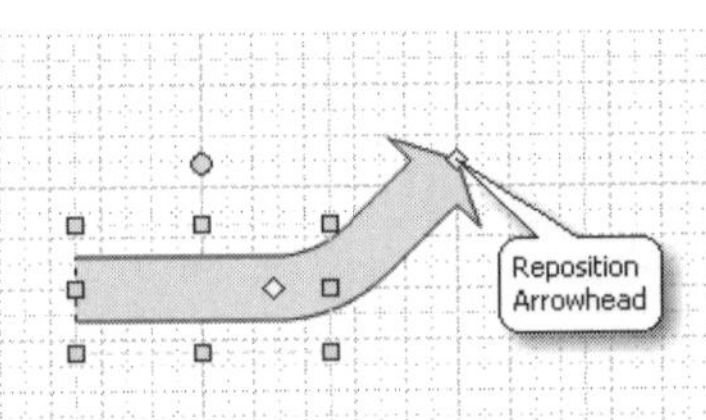

12 Drag the control handle to reposition the arrowhead.

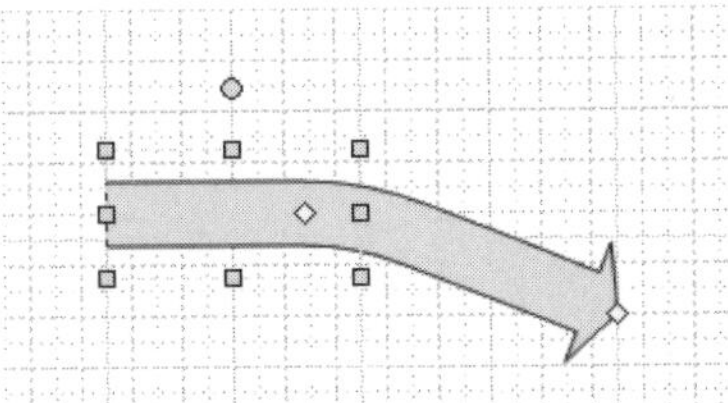

13 On the **File** menu, click **Close**, and then click **No** to close the drawing without saving the changes.

Adding Text to Shapes and the Drawing Page

Most diagrams contain text as well as shapes. By default, most Visio shapes appear either without text or with placeholder text. Adding text or replacing the placeholder text is easy—you simply select the shape and type.

The area in the shape where the text appears is called a *text block*. When you start typing, a blinking cursor appears at the insertion point so that you can keep track of the text placement. The pointer changes to an I-beam when you place it over the text block, indicating that you can click anywhere in the text to insert new text, delete text, or select existing text to replace or format it.

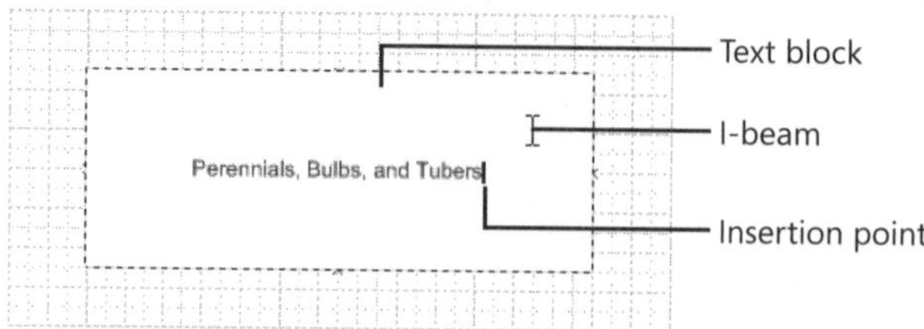

After you add text to a shape, you can format the text using the same methods you would use in any other program in the Microsoft Office System. You can change the font type, size, color, style, and alignment by using the familiar toolbar buttons on the Formatting toolbar. You can also use the Text command on the Format menu. When you want to apply the same text formatting to all the text in a shape, you simply select the shape, and any text changes you make apply to all the text in the shape.

Text Block Tool

Tip You can also move, resize, and rotate a text block independently of its shape by using the Text Block tool. For example, you might want to position the text block for an arrow at the end of the arrow rather than over the center of it. Or you might want the orientation of a text block to be different than its shape orientation. To use the Text Block tool, click the Text Tool down arrow, and then click . Text Block Tool For more information about using the Text Block tool, type "text block tool" in the "Type a question for help" box. Then click the "Rotate, move, and resize a text block" topic.

Text Tool

You can also create a *text-only shape* —text that's not associated with a shape—on the drawing page. For example, you can add a title, footer, or bulleted list to a diagram. Just click the Text Tool button on the Standard toolbar, click the location on the drawing page where you want the text to appear, and then type. After you add a text-only shape to a diagram, you can select, move, rotate, and format it just as you would any other shape.

Note A text-only shape is simply a rectangular shape without a border around it or color inside it.

In this exercise, you work with a diagram that has already been started for you using the Block Diagram template. You drag shapes from a stencil onto the drawing page, add text to shapes, revise the existing text in shapes, add a text-only shape, and then save the diagram.

OPEN the *BlockAddingText* file in the My Documents\Microsoft Press\Visio 2003 SBS\AddingShapes folder.

1. From the **Blocks** stencil, drag the **2-D single** arrow shape onto the drawing page and position it directly below the **Enter auditorium** arrow shape.

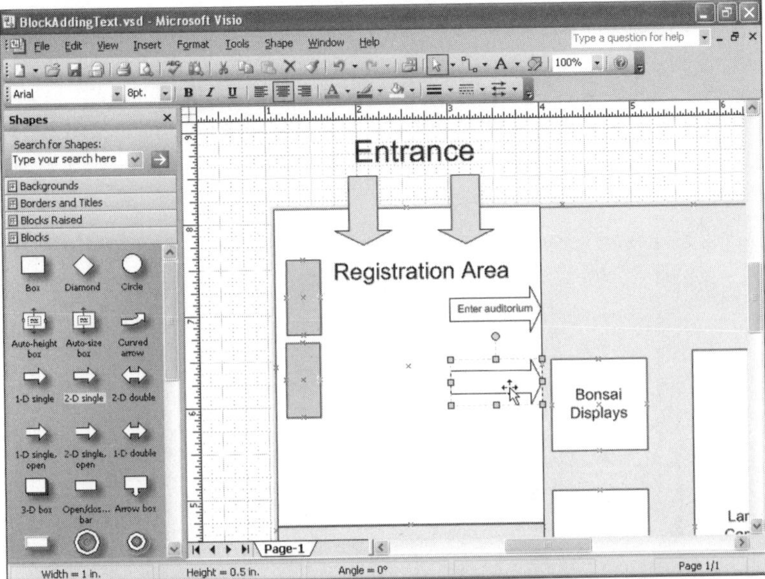

Notice how the shape snaps to the grid, even though the grid is obscured by the white Registration Area shape.

2. With the **2-D single** arrow shape selected, type Enter auditorium.

   As soon as you start typing, the text block opens and a blinking cursor appears in the text block. Visio centers the text in the shape.

   Tip Misspelled words are underlined in red. To correct a misspelled word, right-click the word, and then click the correct spelling on the shortcut menu.

3. Click the pasteboard to close the text block and deselect the shape.

   Tip Another way to deselect the shape is to click a blank area of the drawing page. Alternatively, you can press the Esc key to close the text block, but this action will leave the shape selected.

4 Select the top gold rectangle in the left area of the drawing page. Type Last name, press the Enter key, and then type A-M.

As you type, Visio displays the text block horizontally for ease of reading.

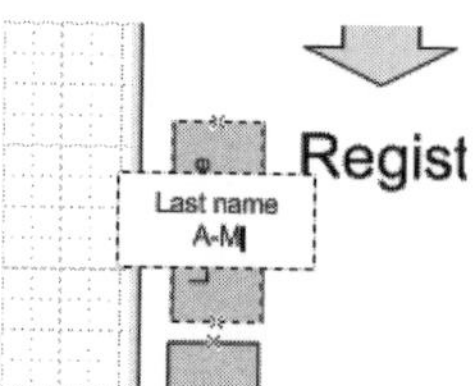

5 Click the pasteboard to close the text block and deselect the shape.

Visio displays the text vertically in the shape.

6 Repeat steps 4 and 5 for the bottom gold rectangle, but type N-Z (instead of A-M).

Visio displays the text vertically in the shape.

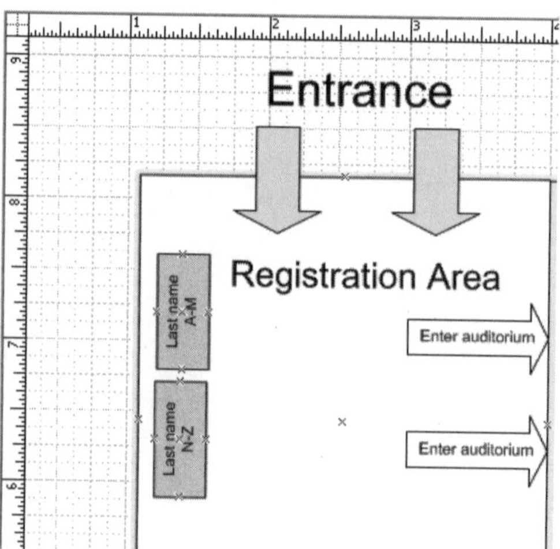

7 From the **Blocks** stencil, drag a **Box** shape onto the drawing page and position it above the **Bonsai Displays** box shape.

8 Align the **Box** shape with the **Bonsai Displays** box shape by snapping the **Box** shape to the grid.

9 With the **Box** shape selected, type Perennials, Bulbs, and Tubers.

Visio adds the text to the shape, centers it, and wraps it to fit inside the shape.

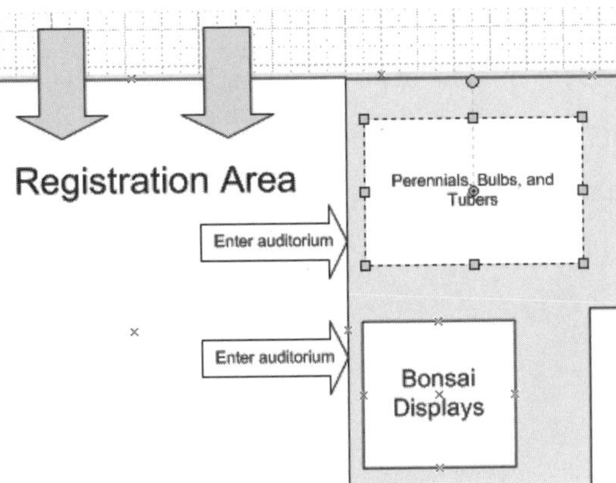

Tip Alternatively, you can open a shape's text block by selecting a shape and pressing the F2 key.

10 Click the pasteboard to close the text block and deselect the shape.

11 From the **Blocks** stencil, drag the **2-D single** shape onto the drawing page and position it below the **Last name N-Z** box.

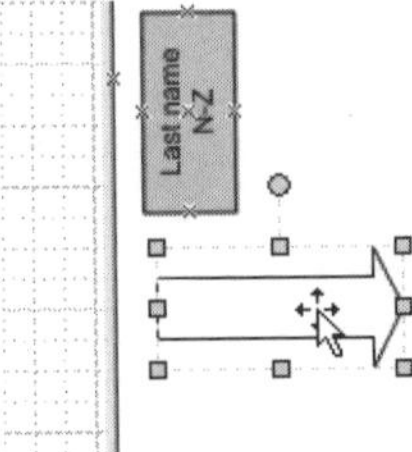

12 With the shape selected, type **Enter classroom**.

Visio adds and centers the text in the shape.

Tip Visio centers the text in most shapes by default. You can change the alignment of the text in a shape by using the alignment buttons on the Formatting toolbar.

13 Click the pasteboard to close the text block and deselect the shape.

14 If you can't see the **Classrooms and Demos** shape on the drawing page, drag the vertical scroll bar (on the right side of the drawing window) down until the shape is visible.

Text Tool

15 On the Standard toolbar, click the **Text Tool** button.

The pointer changes to a text box icon.

16 In the **Classroom and Demos** shape, click to the left of the letter C in Classroom.

The text block opens and a blinking cursor appears at the insertion point.

17 Type **Gardening**, and then press the Space key.

The new text appears in the shape.

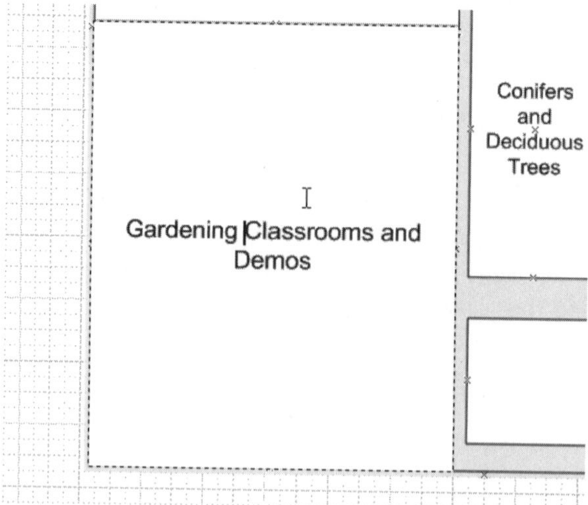

Tip Using the Text Tool button to modify existing text is a good habit to get into. When you just select a shape and type, the new text replaces all the existing text. When you click the Text Tool button before you click the text block, you can select only the text you want to modify.

18 If you can't see the **Perennials, Bulbs, and Tubers** box shape, drag the vertical scroll bar up until the shape is visible.

Pointer Tool

19 On the Standard toolbar, click the **Pointer Tool** button.

20 Click the **Perennials, Bulbs, and Tubers** shape to select it.

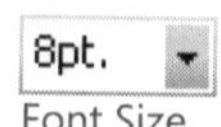

Font Size

21 On the Formatting toolbar, click the **Font Size** down arrow to display a list of font sizes.

22 Click **12 pt.** in the list.

The font size of the text in the selected shape increases to 12 points.

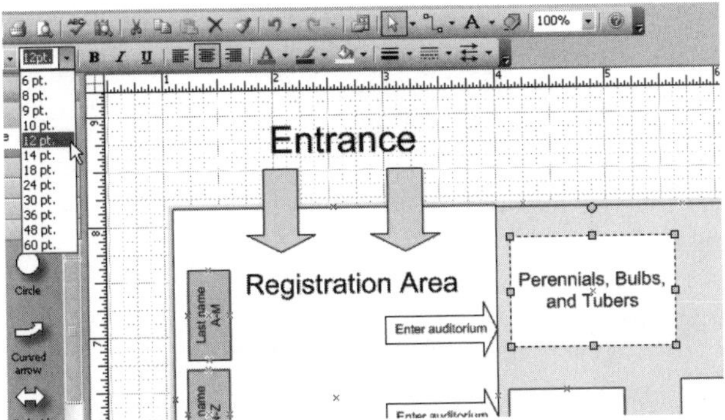

23 If you can't see the top of the drawing page, drag the vertical scroll bar up until it's visible.

24 On the Standard toolbar, click the **Text Tool** button.

25 Approximately one inch above and to the right of the **Entrance** text, click to create a text-only shape.

A text block opens and a blinking cursor appears.

Tip If you click the wrong location, click the pasteboard or press the Esc key, and then try again.

26 In the text block, type Parking.

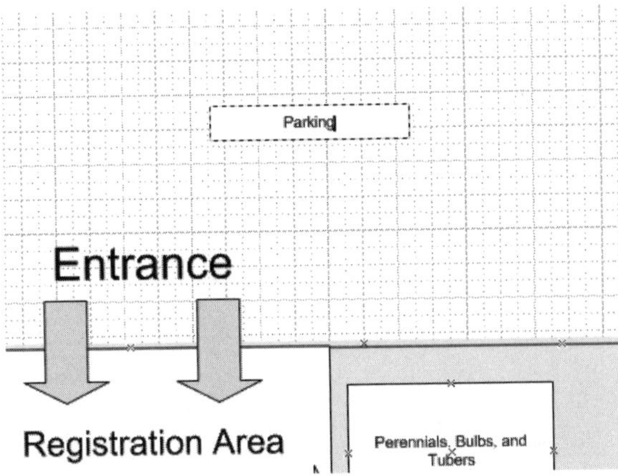

27 Press the Esc key to close the text block.

The text-only shape is selected.

28 On the Formatting toolbar, click the **Font Size** down arrow to display a list of font sizes.

29 Click **24 pt.** in the list.

The font size of the text in the selected shape increases to 24 points.

Save

30 On the Standard toolbar, click the **Save** button to save your changes to the diagram.

CLOSE the BlockAddingText file.

Moving, Sizing, Rotating, and Copying Shapes

As you create your Visio diagrams, you'll need to move shapes around the drawing page, resize shapes, and maybe even rotate and copy them. When you move shapes, you can move one at a time or many shapes at once. Moving one shape is simple–just select the shape and drag it to a new position. Moving multiple shapes at once is as simple as moving one shape. First you select the shapes you want to move, and then you position the pointer over one of the selected shapes. As you drag, all the selected shapes move as one.

One of the most common ways to select multiple shapes is to select one of the shapes and then hold down the Shift key while you select the rest of the shapes. The first shape you select is the *primary shape*. Its selection box turns dark magenta after you click an additional shape while holding down the Shift key. The selection boxes for the other shapes you select, called *secondary shapes*, turn light magenta. Visio also encloses all the selected shapes in a green selection box. Knowing which shape is the primary shape will be useful when you learn about aligning shapes in Chapter 4 and merging shapes in Chapter 10.

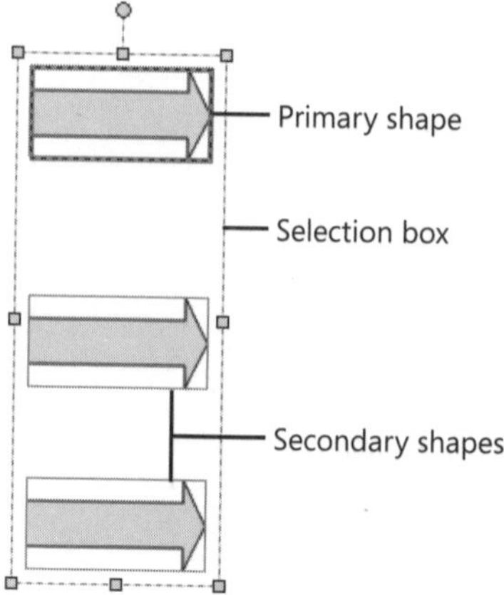

New in Visio 2003

Visio includes several other methods for selecting multiple shapes. If, for example, all the shapes you want to select are in the same area, as they might be in an office layout, you can use the Pointer tool to drag a green *selection net* around the shapes you want to select. After you release the mouse button, everything within the net is selected. You can also use the selection tools on the Pointer Tool menu (on the Standard toolbar) to select multiple shapes without holding down the Shift key. To see the selection tools on the Pointer Tool menu, click the Pointer Tool down arrow.

Tip To view Visio Help topics that tell you how to use the selection tools on the Pointer Tool menu, type the name of the tool in the "Type a question for help" box, and then press the Enter key.

New in Visio 2003

The way you resize a shape depends on whether the shape is 1-D or 2-D. You can drag a 1-D shape's endpoints in any direction to lengthen the shape. When you're working with a 2-D shape, you can change the height or width of the shape by dragging a side, top, or bottom handle. You can also resize the entire shape proportionally by dragging a corner selection handle. To rotate a shape, you can simply drag the shape's rotation handle in the direction you want.

New in Visio 2003

Tip You can resize more than one shape at a time by selecting all the shapes you want to resize and then dragging a selection handle on the green selection box that encloses the selected shapes.

Copying a shape is also a simple procedure. Select a shape, and on the Edit menu, click Copy. Then on the Edit menu, click Paste–just as you would in any program in the Microsoft Office System. With Visio, you can go a step further by copying a shape and positioning it in the same action. To do so, instead of working with commands on menus, hold down the Ctrl key while you drag a shape. This action copies the shape and positions it in the location where you release the mouse button. When you're done creating the copy, make sure you release the mouse button *before* you release the Ctrl key. Otherwise, Visio moves the shape instead of copying it.

In this exercise, you continue working with the block diagram that you updated in the previous exercise. You resize, move, rotate, and copy shapes in the diagram.

OPEN the *BlockMoving* file in the My Documents\Microsoft Press\Visio 2003 SBS\AddingShapes folder.

1. Click the **Perennials, Bulbs, and Tubers** shape to select it.
2. Position the pointer over the middle selection handle on the right side of the shape.

   The pointer turns to a two-headed arrow and displays a ScreenTip.

↔ two-headed arrow

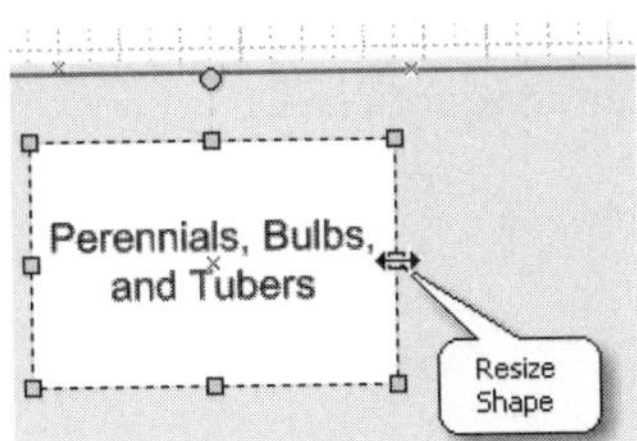

3. Drag the section handle until the right side of the box is aligned with the right side of the **Landscape Competition** shape.
4. To get a closer look, position the pointer over the center of the **Perennials, Bulbs, and Tubers** shape, and hold down Shift+Ctrl while you left-click.

   Visio zooms in, and the **Zoom** box on the Standard toolbar displays the current level of zoom.
5. If you need to adjust the size of the box, drag the selection handle again.
6. Hold down Shift+Ctrl, and then right-click to zoom out.
7. Click the pasteboard to deselect the **Perennials, Bulbs, and Tubers** shape.
8. Position the pointer over the **Enter classroom** shape.

four-headed arrow

   A four-headed arrow pointer appears, indicating that you can select the shape.
9. Click the shape to select it.
10. Position the pointer over the **Enter classroom** shape.

four-headed arrow

   When a four-headed arrow appears, Visio is ready for you to move the shape.
11. Drag the shape to move it down a little.

   Important If you resize a shape accidentally instead of moving it, you can immediately undo your mistake by clicking Undo on the Edit menu; the keyboard shortcut for this command is Ctrl+Z. To avoid making this mistake, don't place the pointer over a selection handle when you want to move a shape. Place the pointer over the middle of the shape, and make sure the pointer changes to a four-headed arrow before you move the shape.
12. Position the pointer over the **Enter auditorium** shape.

   A four-headed arrow pointer appears, so you know can select the shape.
13. Click the top **Enter auditorium** shape to select it.
14. Hold down the Shift key, and then click the bottom **Enter auditorium** shape.

   Visio selects both shapes and encloses the two selected shapes in a green selection box. The selection box for the first shape you select (the primary shape) changes to a dark magenta line. The selection box for the second shape you select (the secondary shape) changes to a light magenta line.

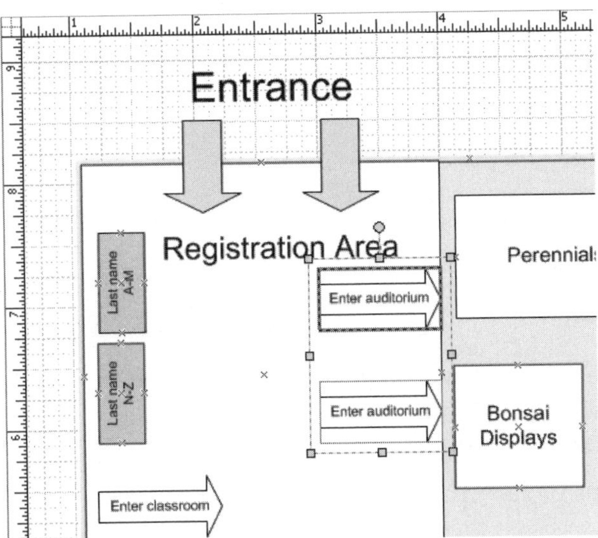

15 Point to the top **Enter auditorium** shape.

When a four-headed arrow appears, you can move the selected shapes.

16 Drag the top shape down approximately one inch.

As you drag, notice that all the selected shapes move at once. Also notice the tick marks that appear on the horizontal ruler to show the shape's position.

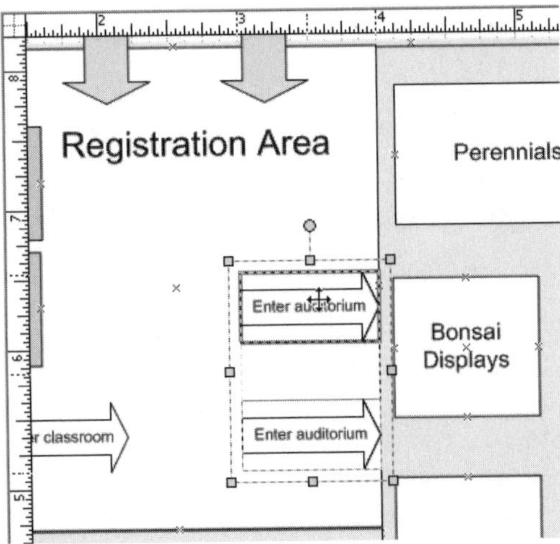

Tip To constrain the direction of shape movement horizontally or vertically, press the Shift key while you drag one or more shapes. To nudge one or more selected shapes just a little, use the arrow keys on your keyboard.

17 Click the pasteboard to deselect both shapes.

18 Select the **Enter classroom** shape, and then position the pointer over the rotation handle on the shape.

circular arrow

The pointer changes to a circular arrow, indicating that Visio is ready to rotate the shape.

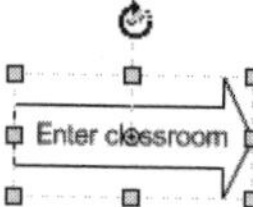

19 Drag the rotation handle to the right until the shape points downward or is rotated clockwise 90 degrees. As you drag the rotation handle, watch the status bar, which shows the angle of rotation for the selected shape.

The shape is rotated clockwise 90 degrees and remains selected.

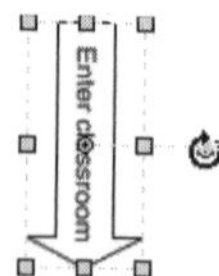

Tip Alternatively, you could right-click the shape, point to Shape on the shortcut menu, and then click Rotate Right.

20 Position the pointer over the selected **Enter classroom** shape, and then hold down the Ctrl key.

plus sign pointer

When a plus sign pointer appears, Visio is ready for you to copy the selected shape.

21 Drag the **Enter classroom** shape to the right to create a copy of the shape, release the mouse button, and then release the Ctrl key.

A copy of the **Enter classroom** shape appears to the right of the original shape.

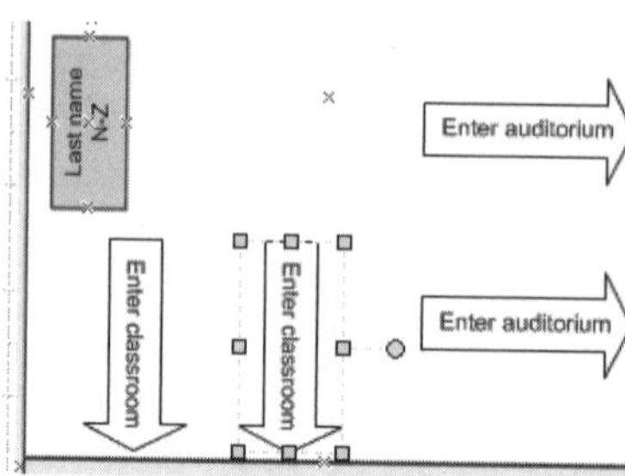

Troubleshooting If you moved the shape instead of copying it, you released the Ctrl key before you released the mouse button. You must release the mouse button first. Press Ctrl+Z to undo your action, and try again.

22 Click the pasteboard to deselect the shape.

23 If you can't see the **Parking** label at the top of the diagram, drag the vertical scroll bar up until it's visible.

24 From the **Blocks** stencil, drag the **Curved Arrow** shape onto the drawing page, and position it to the left of the **Parking** label.

25 On the **Shape** menu, point to **Rotate or Flip**, and then click **Flip Horizontal**.

The shape is flipped horizontally.

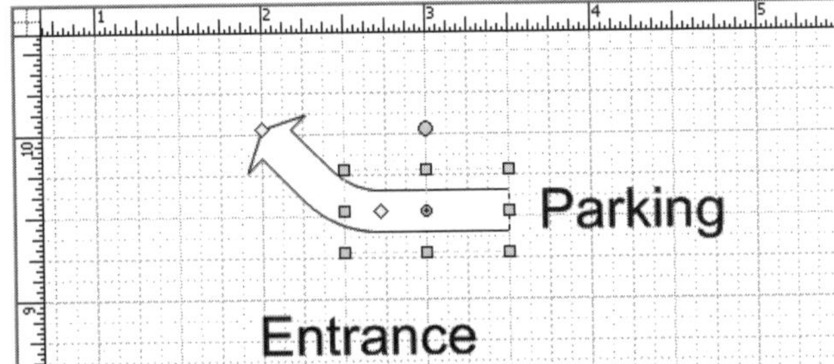

26 Pause the pointer over the yellow control handle at the end of the arrow.

Visio displays a ScreenTip.

27 Drag the control handle down until the shape points toward the **Entrance** label.

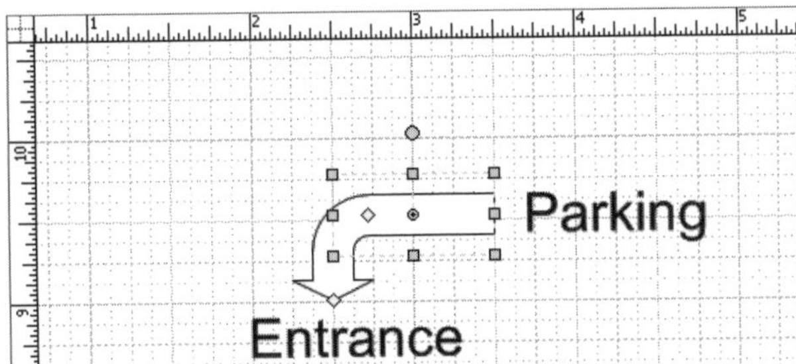

28 If you need to align some of the shapes in your diagram more precisely, select them, and then nudge them using the arrow keys on your keyboard.

Save

29 On the Standard toolbar, click **Save** to save your changes to the diagram.

CLOSE the *BlockMoving* file.

Working with Groups

Up to this point in the book, you've worked with simple individual shapes, such as rectangles, circles, and lines. However, many Visio shapes are made up of several shapes. This type of Visio shape is called a *group*—two or more shapes that function as a unit. For instance, the title block shapes on the Borders and Titles stencil are groups composed of boxes, lines, circles, text, and so on. Instead of dragging each individual piece of a title block onto the drawing page, you can drag the group onto the page. Instead of moving or resizing each piece on the drawing page, you can resize or move the group. You can even rotate a group by using the rotation handle that appears on the group when you select it.

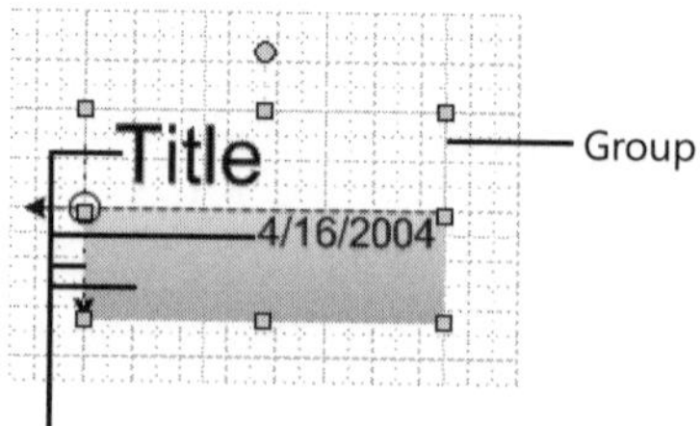

Even though the shapes in a group function as a unit, you can still work with the shapes individually. However, the shapes within groups are often *locked*—protected against particular types of changes—to prevent you from deleting or inadvertently moving them individually when you intended to move the whole group. In other words, you can work with the individual shapes in groups, but your actions are limited depending on the group.

When you *subselect* a shape you want to work with in the group, if that shape is locked, its selection handles are gray instead of green. To subselect a shape within a group, select the group, and then select the individual shape. For example, you can subselect the text in a title block group to replace the placeholder text with your own title and change the text attributes, but you can't delete or move the locked text-only shape.

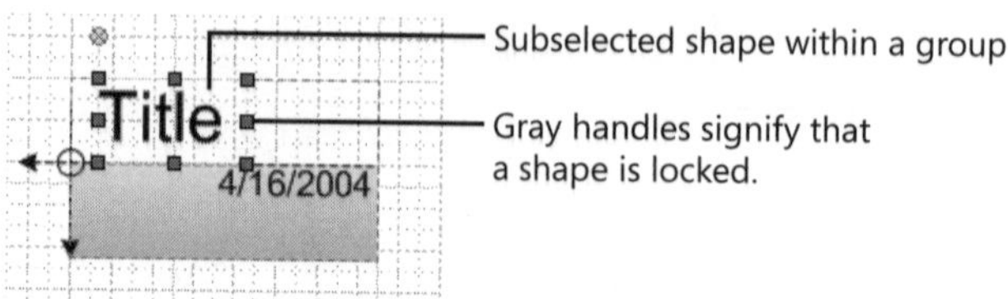

In this short exercise, you practice selecting, moving, and resizing groups. Then you subselect a shape within a group to work with it individually.

1. On the **File** menu, point to **New**, point to **Block Diagram**, and then click **Block Diagram**.

   Visio opens a blank drawing page and four stencils.

2 Click the **Borders and Titles** stencil's title bar to display the shapes on the stencil.

3 From the **Borders and Titles** stencil, drag the **Title block compass** shape onto the drawing page. Notice all the individual shapes that make up the grouped shape.

The shape is selected on the drawing page. Because groups are 2-D shapes, the selection box includes eight selection handles and one round rotation handle.

4 Click the **Title** placeholder text.

Visio subselects the text-only shape within the group.

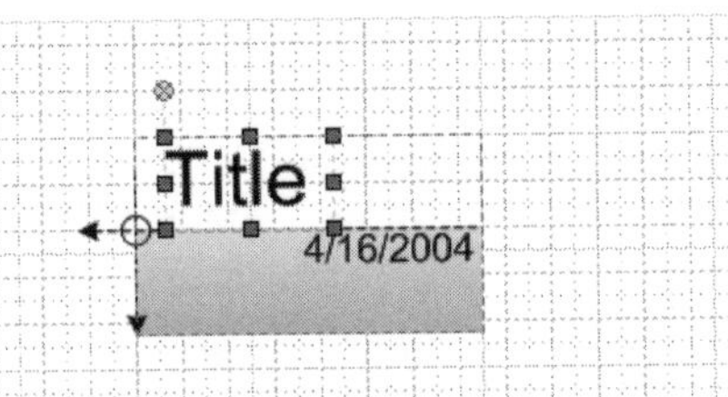

5 Type Garden Expo.

Visio opens the shape's text block, replaces the placeholder text with the new text, and resizes the title block to accommodate the text.

6 Click the blue box below the title to subselect it.

Fill Color

7 On the Formatting toolbar, click the **Fill Color** down arrow, and then click the red color on the palette.

Visio changes the color of the box to red. The rest of the shapes in the group are unaffected.

8 On the **File** menu, click **Close**, and then click **No** to close the drawing without saving the changes.

Finding Shapes for Diagrams

Visio templates open stencils that contain the shapes used most often for a particular diagram type. However, you might want to add shapes to your diagram that aren't on any of the template's stencils. For example, in a brainstorming diagram, you might want to include a text callout shape to highlight a topic, but how do you find the shape you need?

New in Visio 2003

It's easy. In the Shapes window, use the Search for Shapes box to quickly search for shapes on your computer and on the Web. Using this method, it's not necessary to open and browse additional Visio stencils—although you could do that if you wanted to familiarize yourself with shapes on different stencils.

Tip To open a stencil, on the File menu, point to Shapes, point to a category, and then click the name of the stencil you want to open.

To search for shapes quickly by using keywords, type the keyword for the shape you want to find in the Search for Shapes box. For example, to find furniture shapes, you might type **desk** or **chair**. To find callout or annotation shapes, you might type **callout**, **text**, **label**, or **annotation**. Then when you click the arrow next to the Search for Shapes box, Visio searches your computer and the Microsoft Office Online Web site for the shapes that match the keyword.

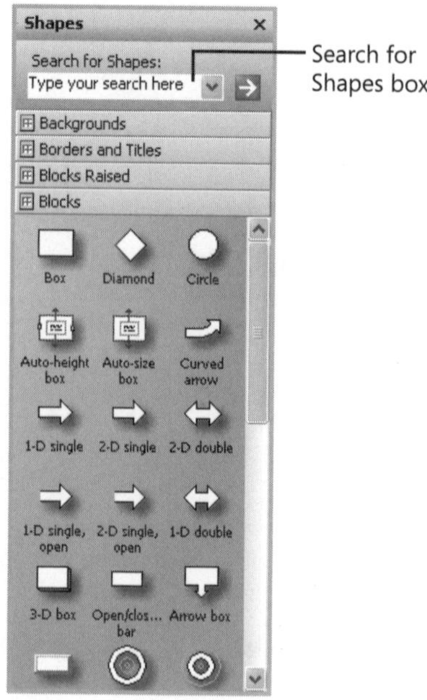

Tip In the Search For Shapes box, you can type more than one keyword and separate them with spaces, commas, or semicolons.

In this exercise, you continue working with the block diagram that you updated in the preceding exercise. You search for shapes that aren't on the stencils opened by the Block Diagram template, and then you drag the shapes you find onto the drawing page.

OPEN the *BlockFinding* file in the My Documents\Microsoft Press\Visio 2003 SBS\AddingShapes folder.

1 In the Shapes window, in the **Search for Shapes** box, type Plants.

2 Click the arrow to the right of the **Search for Shapes** box, or press the Enter key.

Visio searches for shapes with *plants* in the name or keyword stored with the shape.

Tip By default, Visio searches for shapes on your computer and on the Microsoft Office Online Web site. To change the search options, on the Tools menu, click Options, and then click the Shape Search tab.

3 If a dialog box appears telling you that the search results are greater than the specified maximum, click **Yes** to view the results.

4 If you aren't connected to the Internet, a **Shape Search** dialog box might appear telling you that the results are limited to the shapes on your computer. Click **OK**.

Visio completes its search and creates a **Plants** stencil that contains all the shapes it found.

5 From the **Plants** stencil in the Shapes window, drag the **Large plant** shape onto the drawing page directly below the **Last name N-Z** box.

Tip You might need to scroll the Plants stencil to find the Large plant shape.

6 From the **Plants** stencil, drag the **Plant** shape onto the drawing page and position it directly below the **Large plant** shape.

Notice that both of the plant shapes you dragged onto the drawing page are groups because they are composed of two or more shapes that function as a unit.

7 On the **Plants** stencil's title bar, click the stencil icon to the left of the title **Plants**, and then click **Close** on the stencil menu.

The **Plants** stencil closes.

Tip You can save the Plants stencil so that you can use it again to add plants to your diagrams. To do so, click the stencil icon to the left of the stencil's title, click Save, and then in the Save As dialog box, click the Save button. To open the stencil later, on the File menu, point to Shapes, point to My Shapes, and then click Plants.

Save

8 On the Standard toolbar, click the **Save** button to save your changes to the diagram.

CLOSE the BlockFinding file.

Inserting Pictures into Diagrams

Although Visio includes most of the shapes you need for your diagrams, sometimes you need an image that was created in a different program. You can insert a picture–a graphic file–into Visio whether or not the program that created the image is currently installed on your computer.

When you want to add a picture to diagram, you can use the Picture command on the Insert menu or the Clip Art task pane. To display the Clip Art task pane, on the View menu, click Task Pane. Then click the down arrow on the task pane's title bar, and click Clip Art. Adding clip art from the Clip Art task pane to your diagram is as simple as adding a Visio shape from a stencil–you simply drag it onto the drawing page.

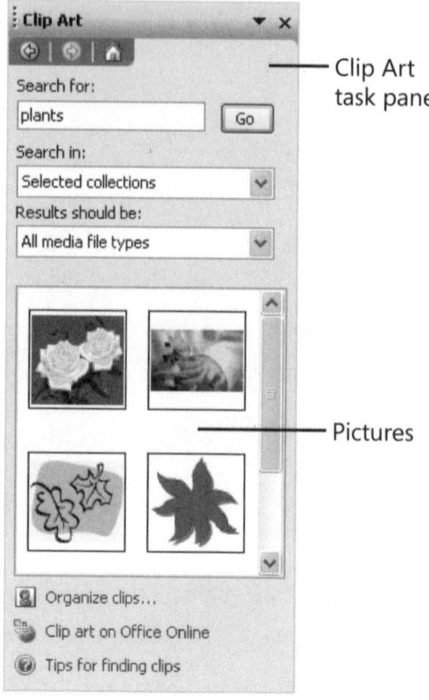

You can insert pictures into Visio diagrams that have been saved in the file formats shown in the following table.

File Format	File Extension
Compressed Enhanced Metafile	.emz
Enhanced Metafile	.emf
Graphics Interchange Format	.gif
Joint Photographic Experts Group File Interchange Format	.jpg
Portable Network Graphics	.png
Scalable Vector Graphics	.svg and .svgz
Tag Image File Format	.tif and .tiff
Windows Bitmap	.bmp and .dib
Windows Metafile	.wmf

After you insert a picture, you can size, position, and *crop* it, which means cut out portions you don't want to appear. You can also format a picture's properties to change its brightness, sharpness, transparency, and other qualities that affect appearance. Visio includes a Picture command on the Format menu that even previews your changes before you apply them.

Tip If you insert a lot of pictures into your diagrams, you can display the Picture toolbar, which includes the Insert Picture button, for quick access to picture formatting commands. Right-click the toolbar area, and then click Picture on the shortcut menu to display the Picture toolbar. This toolbar is usually displayed only when you select a picture on the drawing page. However, if you choose the toolbar from the toolbar shortcut menu, the toolbar will appear at all times; Visio won't hide it when a picture isn't selected.

In this exercise, you insert The Garden Company logo and a piece of clip art into a block diagram, and then you resize the pictures. Then you will you make the logo transparent.

OPEN the *BlockPictures* file in the My Documents\Microsoft Press\Visio 2003 SBS\AddingShapes folder.

1. On the **Insert** menu, point to **Picture**, and then click **From File**.

   Visio opens the My Pictures folder by default.

   Tip Using the Picture command, you can also insert clip art, charts, equations, and photographs from a scanner or digital camera.

2. In the **Look in** box, navigate to the My Documents\Microsoft Press\Visio 2003 SBS\AddingShapes folder.
3. Double-click the **Logo.gif** file.

Visio inserts the logo on the drawing page, selects it, and displays the Picture toolbar.

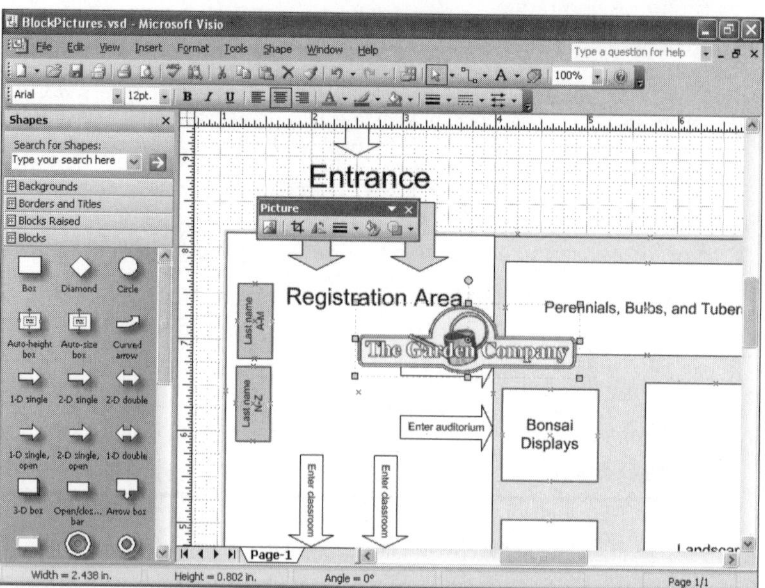

4 Drag the logo to the upper right corner of the drawing page.

5 Drag one of the corner selection handles to make the logo a little smaller.

6 On the Picture toolbar, click the **Transparency** down arrow, and then click **60%**.

Visio makes the logo 60 percent transparent so that the grid shows through.

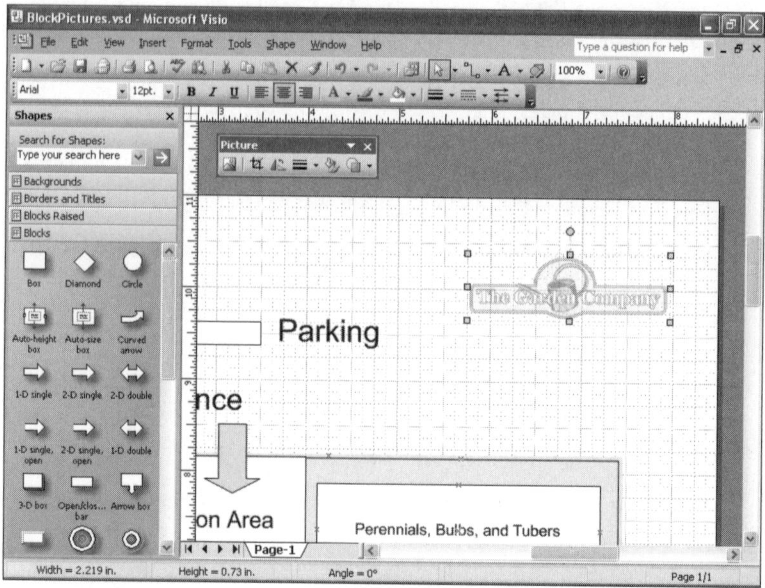

7 On the **View** menu, click **Task Pane**.

Visio displays a task pane to the right of the drawing page.

8 Click the down arrow on the task pane's title bar, and then click **Clip Art**.

Visio displays the **Clip Art** task pane.

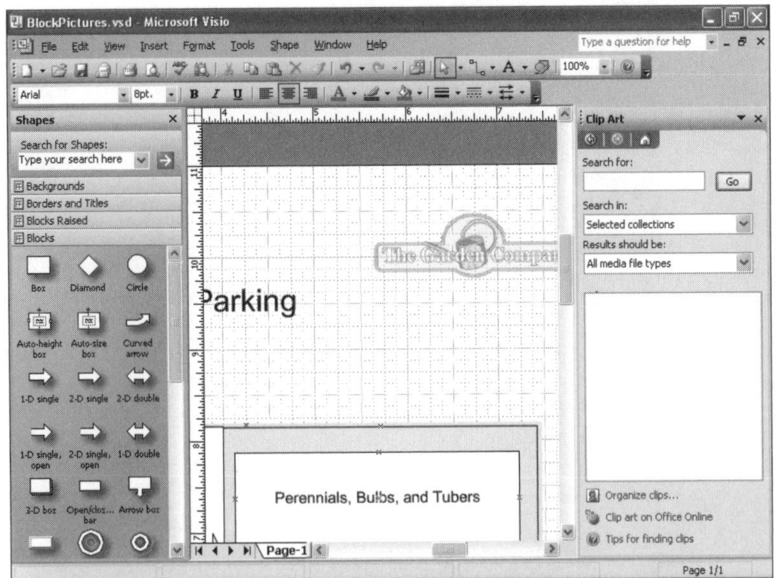

Important If you don't have the Clip Art feature installed on your computer, Visio will prompt you to install it when you try to view the Clip Art task pane. You need to install this feature to complete this exercise.

9 In the **Search for** box, type plant, and, to the right of the **Search for** box, click the **Go** button.

Visio searches your computer for all available clip art that matches the keyword and displays the results in the task pane.

Tip To search for clip art on the Microsoft Office Online Web site, at the bottom of the task pane, click "Clip art on Office Online".

10 Pause the pointer over the **Plant** clip art.

A ScreenTip appears that tells you the dimensions, file size, and file type of the piece of clip art.

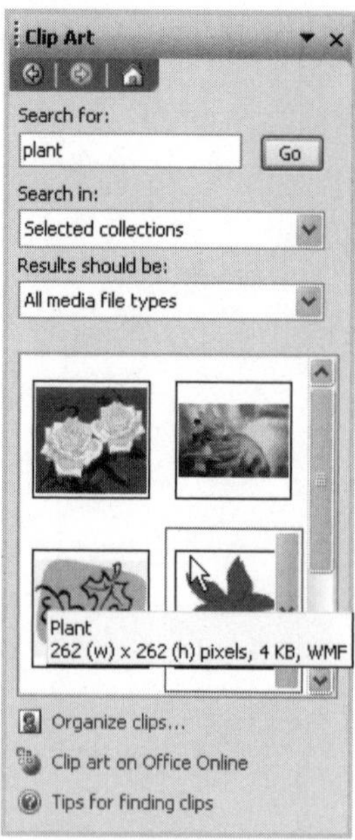

Important The clip art you see on your computer might differ from the images shown in this book, depending on the clip art you have installed.

11 Drag the **Plant** clip art onto the drawing page, and position it in the **Landscape Competition** shape.

12 Drag a corner selection handle on the shape to decrease the size of the shape a little.

13 On the **File** menu, click **Close**, and then click **No** to close the drawing without saving the changes.

Saving Diagrams

Saving a Visio diagram is just as easy as saving a file in any other program in the Microsoft Office System. Just click the Save button on the Standard toolbar or click Save on the File menu. The first time you save a diagram, the Save As dialog box appears so that you can name the file and choose the location where you want to save it. By default, the diagram is saved as a Visio *drawing file* with a .vsd file extension.

In addition, you can record diagram information, such as title, subject, author, manager, and company using the Properties dialog box. This information appears in a ScreenTip when you select the file. This can help identify a file that doesn't have a descriptive file name or that will be distributed to co-workers. For example, typing your name in the

Properties dialog box alerts others who select or open the file that you are the person who created the file.

Important The amount of property information you see and how it's displayed depends on the version of Microsoft Windows you're using and your folder settings.

In this exercise, you create a new drawing that has just a few shapes. Then you type information about the drawing in the Properties dialog box and save the drawing. Last you view the file in the Open dialog box to see its file properties as a ScreenTip.

New

1 On the Standard toolbar, click the **New** down arrow.
2 In the drop-down list, point to **Block Diagram**, and then click **Basic Diagram**.
3 From the **Basic Shapes** stencil, drag several shapes onto the drawing page.
4 On the **File** menu, click **Properties**.

The **Properties** dialog box appears with the **Summary** tab shown. Based on your computer's settings, some properties might appear by default, such as **Language**.

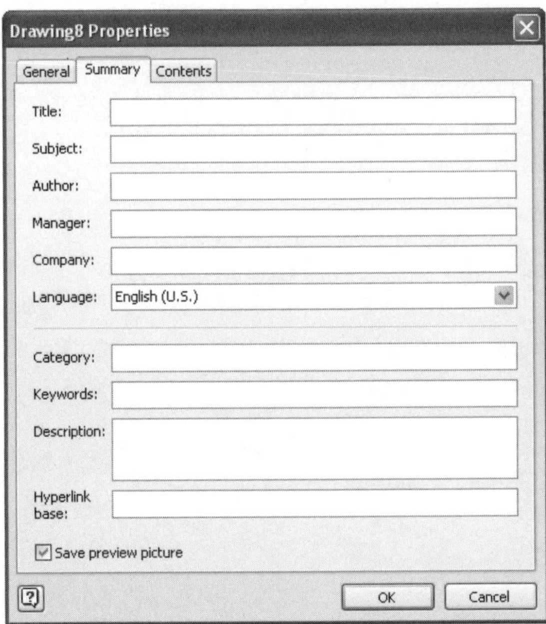

Tip In the Properties dialog box, the "Save preview picture" check box is always selected by default. This option saves a thumbnail preview of your diagram with the Visio drawing file, so when you select the file in a folder, the thumbnail is displayed. If your files don't have descriptive file names, this thumbnail preview will help you identify the file you want to open.

5 In the **Title** box, type Garden Expo Layout.

6 In the **Subject** box, type Garden Expo 2004.

7 In the **Author** box, type Kim Akers.

8 In the **Manager** box, type Olinda Turner.

9 In the **Company** box, type The Garden Company.

10 Click **OK** to close the **Properties** dialog box.

Save

11 On the Standard toolbar, click the **Save** button.

The **Save As** dialog box appears because this is the first time you've saved the drawing.

12 In the **File name** box, type BasicSaving, and then click **Save**.

By default, Visio saves the drawing as a Visio drawing file with a .vsd file extension.

Tip If you want to use a Visio diagram in another program or as an image on the Web, you can save the diagram in the appropriate file format. In the Save As dialog box, in the "Save as type" box, scroll the file list to see the available file formats, such as JPEG File Interchange Format (*.jpg). You can also save a Visio 2003 diagram in the Visio 2002 file format so that people with Visio 2002 can work with the diagram.

13 On the **File** menu, click **Close**.

The **BasicSaving** diagram closes.

14 On the **File** menu, click **Open**.

15 In the **Open** dialog box, pause the pointer over **BasicSaving**.

Visio displays the property information for the file as a ScreenTip. You can also view this information in a folder window or on the desktop.

16 In the **Open** dialog box, click the **Cancel** button.

17 On the **File** menu, click **Exit**.

Key Points

- All Visio shapes behave like 1-D or 2-D shapes. 1-D shapes, such as lines, have endpoints that you can use to shorten or lengthen the shape. 2-D shapes, such as rectangles, circles, diamonds, and triangles, have selection handles that you can use to increase the height or width of shapes.
- You can drag a corner selection handle on a 2-D shape to resize it proportionally. Drag the rotation handle on a 2-D shape to rotate it.
- When the pointer changes to a four-headed arrow pointer, you can move the shape. When the pointer changes to a two-headed arrow pointer, you can resize the shape.
- To copy and position a shape in a single action drag it while holding down the Ctrl key. Be sure to release the mouse button before the Ctrl key; otherwise, you'll move the shape.
- To add text to a shape, select it, and then type your text. To add independent text to a diagram, use the Text tool.
- To work with an individual shape in a group, subselect the shape within the group.
- To find additional shapes for your diagrams type keywords in the Search for Shapes box.
- To insert pictures created in other programs into your diagrams use the Picture command on the Format menu or the Clip Art task pane.
- Save Visio diagrams the same way you save any other Microsoft Office 2003 file. On the File menu, click Save. Or on the Standard toolbar, click the Save button.

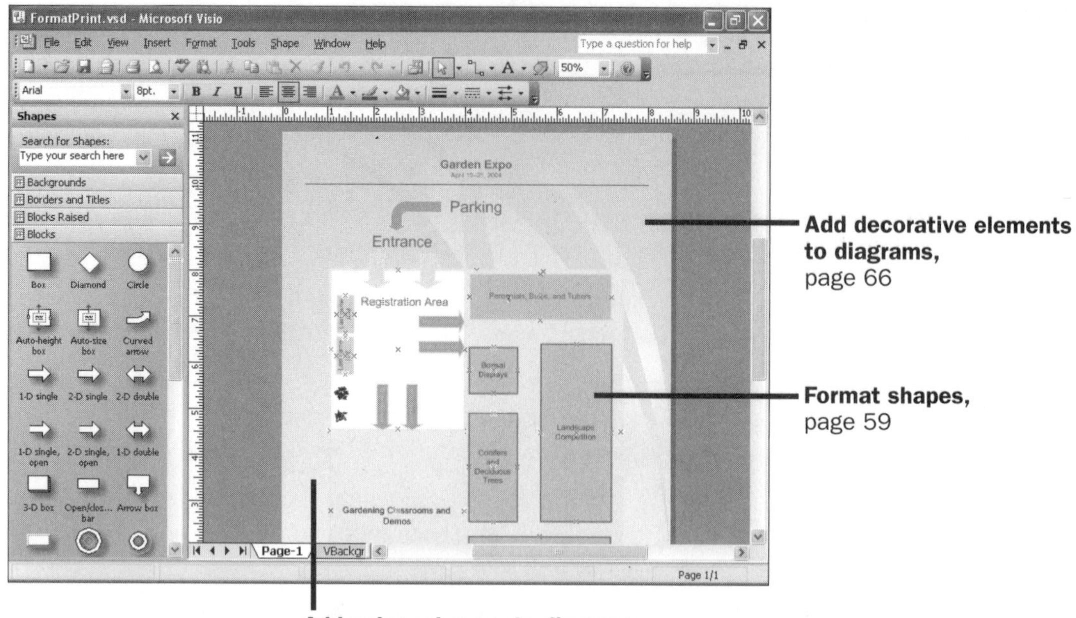

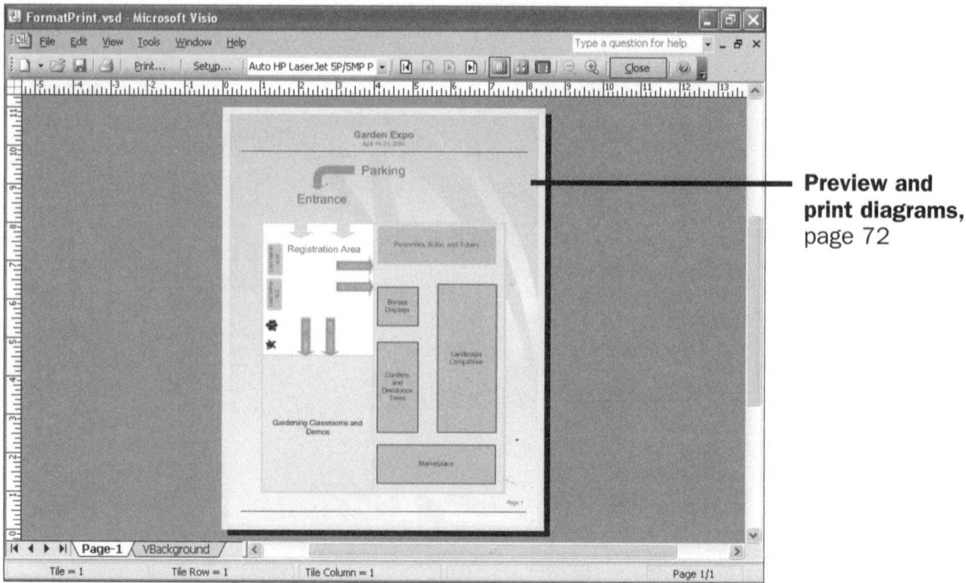

Chapter 3 at a Glance

3 Formatting Shapes and Diagrams

In this chapter you will learn to:

- ✔ Format shapes.
- ✔ Add decorative elements to diagrams.
- ✔ Add color schemes to diagrams.
- ✔ Preview and print diagrams.

You can create effective, professional-looking diagrams simply by dragging Microsoft Office Visio shapes onto the drawing page. However, you might want to personalize or add pizzazz to your diagrams. For example, to ensure that a flowchart captures the attention of your colleagues, you can add colors to the shapes, insert a background image to add interest, and increase the font size of the text to make it easier to see. You can also customize the appearance of the shapes to meet your organization's design specifications. With Visio, formatting shapes and diagrams is easy.

In this chapter you'll learn the quickest methods of formatting shapes and adding finishing touches to diagrams. You'll learn how to add decorative elements, such as ornamental borders and attractive title shapes, to your diagrams. You'll also learn how to format your diagrams with colors that complement a corporate color scheme. When you're done, you'll preview and print your work.

See Also Do you need only a quick refresher on the topics in this chapter? See the Quick Reference entries on pages xxvii–xxix.

Important Before you can use the practice files in this chapter, you need to install them from the book's companion CD to their default location. See "Using the Book's CD" on page xv for more information.

Formatting Shapes

The right *formatting*—a combination of attributes that makes up the appearance of a shape, diagram, or text—can add emphasis and interest to your diagrams and help you communicate more effectively. For example, you can draw attention to important steps in a process by adding high-contrast colors to shapes, or refine the overall look of your diagram by adding something as simple as a shadow to a shape. Every shape in Visio has attributes that you can format:

- The *weight* (thickness), color, pattern, and transparency of the border around a 2-D shape; and the weight, color, pattern, and transparency of a 1-D shape. Use the Line command on the Format menu to change these attributes.
- The color, pattern, and transparency of a 2-D shape's interior, called its *fill*. Use the Fill command on the Format menu to change these attributes.
- The color, pattern, and transparency of a shape's shadow. Use the Fill command on the Format menu to change these attributes.
- The *line ends* on a 1-D shape. Some examples of line ends are arrowheads, diamonds, and circles. Use the Line command on the Format menu to change these attributes.
- The *line caps* (round or square) on a 1-D shape and the corners on a 2-D shape. Use the Line command on the Format menu to change these attributes.
- The text size, style, color, and so on. Use the Text command on the Format menu to change these attributes.

By formatting these shape attributes, you can change the look of a shape or an entire diagram to better convey your message.

Tip A collection of formatting attributes is a called a *style*. A style can include text, line, and fill attributes. Templates include predefined styles that are appropriate for a particular diagram type. To apply a style to your shape, on the Format menu, click Style. Or display the Format Shape toolbar, and specify the styles by using the Line Style, Text Style, and Fill Style buttons. These toolbar boxes list the predefined styles included with the template.

When you drag any shape from a stencil onto the drawing page, it appears with the shape's default formatting. For example, the Box shape on the Blocks stencil has a gray fill color and a solid black border. Text that you type in this shape is black, the font size is 8 points, and the font name is Arial.

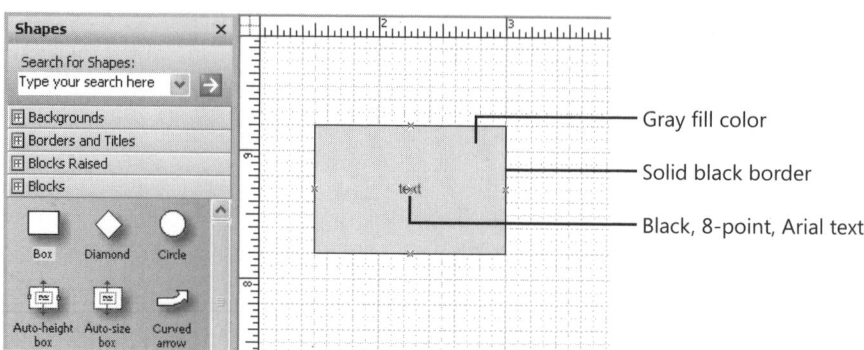

Visio makes it easy to change the default formatting of any shape by using the Text, Line, and Fill commands on the Format menu, or the buttons on the Formatting toolbar. Most of these buttons have drop-down lists with options that you can select. To view the options for a specific button, click the down arrow on the button. For example, to change a shape's fill color, select the shape, click the Fill Color down arrow, and then click the color you want from the palette of colors that appears.

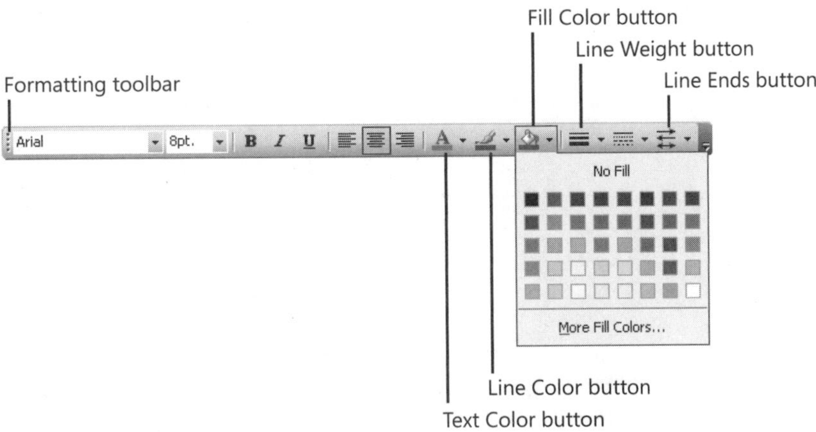

Tip Pause the pointer over any toolbar button to display a ScreenTip that tells you the button's function.

In a diagram that includes many shapes, you can save time by formatting multiple shapes at the same time. Do this by clicking Select All on the Edit menu, and then specifying the attributes you want to apply. Visio applies the changes to all the selected shapes. If you want to apply the same formatting to only some of the shapes in a diagram, hold down the Shift key while selecting the shapes you want to format, and then specify the attributes you want to apply.

Format Painter

If you want to apply the formatting of one shape to other shapes, you can copy the formatting from that shape and apply it to the other ones. The Format Painter tool copies the fill, line, and text attributes of one shape and applies them to another shape. When you click the Format Painter button on the Formatting toolbar, the format of the selected shape is copied. You then click the shape you want to format. If you double-click the Format Painter button, you can format multiple shapes on the drawing page.

In this exercise, you refine an unfinished diagram of the conference hall layout for a gardening expo hosted by The Garden Company. Using the buttons on the Formatting toolbar, you apply a new fill color and line weight to a shape. Then you use the Format Painter tool to copy the formatting from one shape to another. Finally, you change the font size and color of some shapes.

OPEN the *FormatShapes* file in the My Documents\Microsoft Press\Visio 2003 SBS\FormattingShapes folder.

1. Click the **Perennials, Bulbs, and Tubers** shape on the drawing page to select it.

Fill Color

2. On the Formatting toolbar, click the **Fill Color** down arrow.

   A color palette appears.

3. Pause the pointer over a color in the palette to see a ScreenTip that identifies the color.

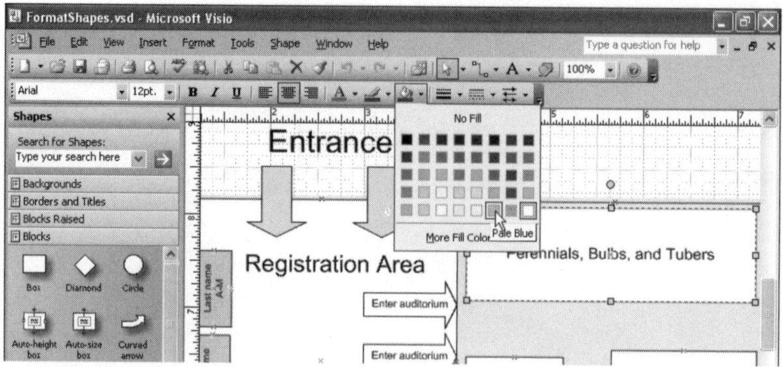

4. Click the pale blue color.

   Visio fills the interior of the shape with the pale blue color. The shape remains selected.

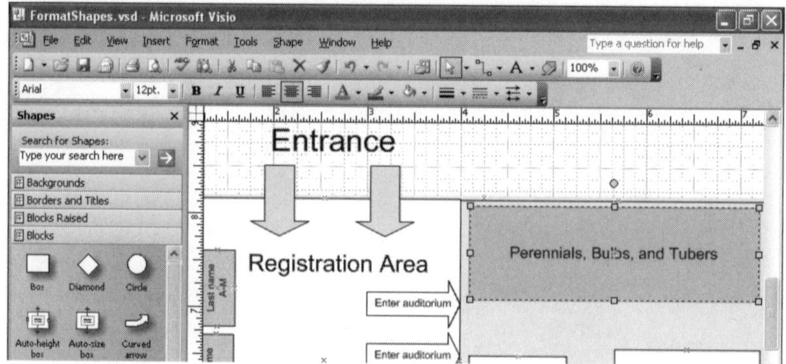

Tip After you choose a color from the color palette, you don't need to view the color palette each time you want to apply that color to a shape. Clicking the Fill Color button will apply the last color you selected from the palate to the shape.

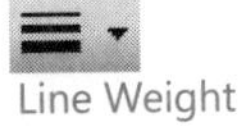
Line Weight

5. On the Formatting toolbar, click the **Line Weight** down arrow to display a list of line weights.
6. Pause the pointer over a weight in the list to see a ScreenTip that describes the weight.
7. Click Line Weight 5.

   Visio applies a thicker border to the shape. The shape remains selected.

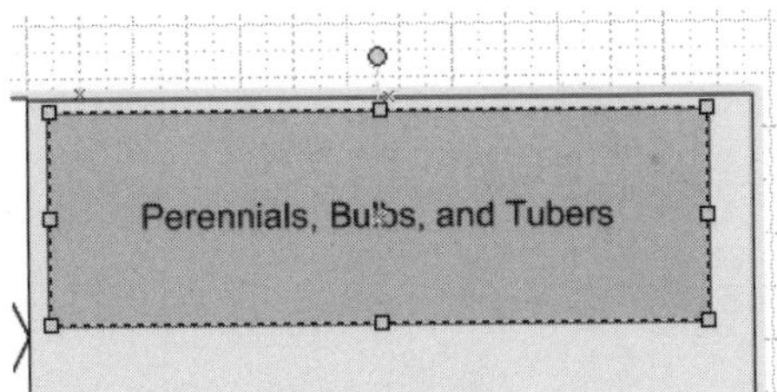

Format Painter

8. On the Formatting toolbar, *double-click* the **Format Painter** button.

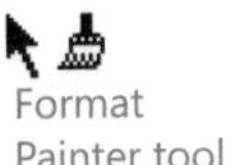
Format Painter tool

   The pointer changes to a black color and a paintbrush appears next to it, indicating that the Format Painter tool is selected and you can now copy the formatting from one shape to another one.

9. One shape at a time, click the **Bonsai Displays** shape, the **Landscape Competition** shape, the **Conifers and Deciduous Trees** shape, and the **Marketplace** shape.

   Visio copies the formatting from the Perennials, Bulbs, and Tubers shape to the selected shapes, changing their fill color to pale blue and line weight to 5.

Troubleshooting If you can copy the formatting from the Perennials, Bulbs, and Tubers shape to only the Bonsai Displays shape, you didn't double-click the Format Painter button. You must double-click the button to copy the formatting to more than one shape. Select the Perennials, Bulbs, and Tubers shape again, double-click the Format Painter button, and then copy the formatting to the rest of the shapes.

10. Press the Esc key to switch back to the Pointer tool.

   The pointer changes back to the Pointer tool icon.

11 Position the pointer above and to the left of the **Last name A-M** shape, and outside the large, green, rectangular shape.

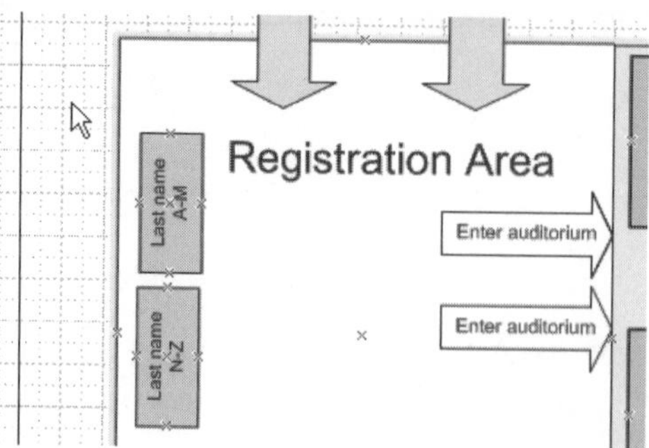

12 Drag a selection box around the **Last name A-M** and **Last name N-Z** shapes.

As you drag, Visio draws the selection box. When you release the mouse button, the two shapes within the box are selected.

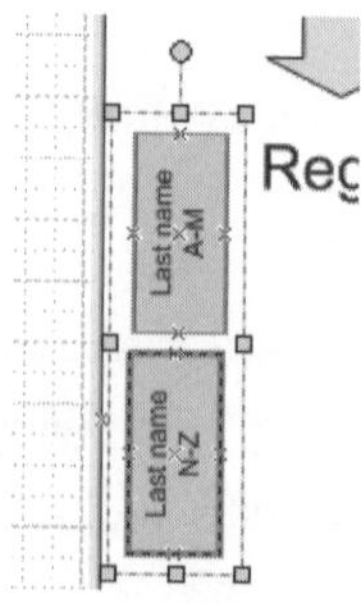

Troubleshooting If you move the large, green, rectangular shape instead of selecting the two shapes, you didn't position the pointer correctly. Press Ctrl+Z to undo your action and try again. Make sure you position the pointer outside the large shape and over a blank area of the drawing page where you can see the grid, and then drag to select the two shapes within the selection box.

8pt.
Font Size

13 On the Formatting toolbar, click the **Font Size** down arrow, and then click **10 pt.** in the list.

Visio increases the text size for both of the selected shapes.

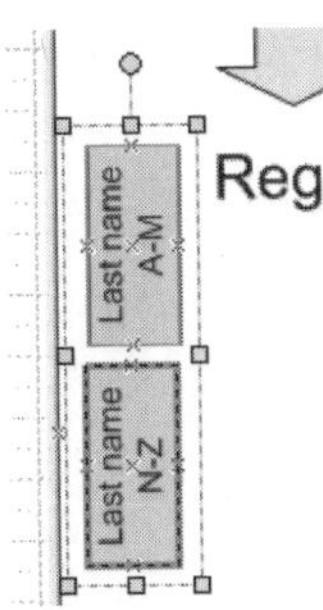

Tip You can also type a number in the Font Size box to change the text size rather than clicking a size in the list.

14 Click the top **Enter auditorium** shape.

15 While holding down the Shift key, click the remaining three arrow shapes in the **Registration Area** shape (the bottom **Enter auditorium** shape and the other two **Enter classroom** shapes).

The first shape you select (the primary shape) has a dark magenta selection box; the other shapes (secondary shapes) have light magenta selection boxes.

Text Color

16 On the Formatting toolbar, click the **Text Color** down arrow to display the color palette.

17 Pause the pointer over a color in the palette to see a ScreenTip that identifies the color.

18 Click the gold color.

Visio changes the text in the four selected arrows to gold.

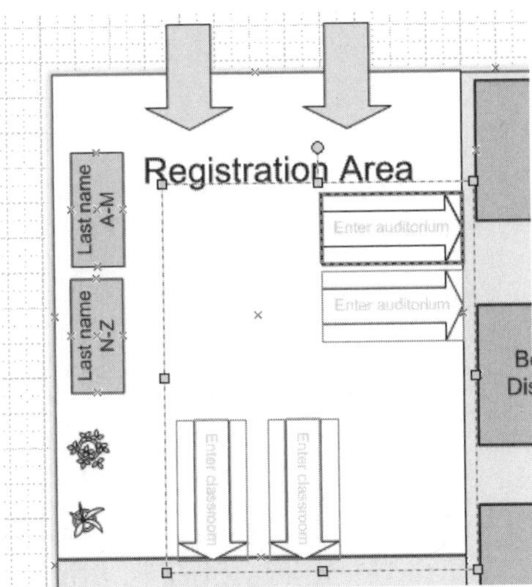

Tip For quick access to all the commands on the Format menu, you can right-click a shape to display its shortcut menu, point to Format, and then click the appropriate command.

19 Click the pasteboard to deselect the shapes.

Save

20 On the Standard toolbar, click **Save** to save your changes to the diagram.

CLOSE the *FormatShapes* file.

Adding Decorative Elements to Diagrams

In addition to formatting shapes, you can format entire diagrams by adding decorative elements, such as borders, title blocks, and backgrounds. A border is a design that appears around all or part of the drawing page. A title block is a formatted title that can include information such as the date created. A background is a pattern that appears behind a diagram, much like wallpaper on the Windows desktop. Borders, title blocks, and backgrounds are all special types of shapes that can add a professional look to your diagram. You'll find many of these shapes on the Backgrounds stencil and the Borders and Titles stencil that opens with many of the business-oriented templates in Visio, including the Block Diagram template. You can add a border, title, or background at any time, but these shapes are usually added as finishing touches just before you print or distribute your diagram.

Visio includes dozens of border, title block, and background shapes. You can add them to a diagram the same way you would add any other shape–by dragging. When you drag a border onto the drawing page, Visio sizes it to fit the drawing page. Most borders include text, such as a title and page number. Visio adds the page number and generic text as a title placeholder, which you can replace with the real title. Some borders and title blocks display the date as well, which, like page numbers, are added by default.

When you add background shapes to your diagrams, Visio sizes them to fit the drawing page. However, they are different from borders in that when you drag a background shape onto the drawing page, Visio first creates a new *background page* named *Vbackground*. The background shape is placed on the new background page so it doesn't get in the way as you move and format the shapes in your diagram. Although it is on a separate page, the background shape on the background page appears on the drawing page and is printed with the diagram.

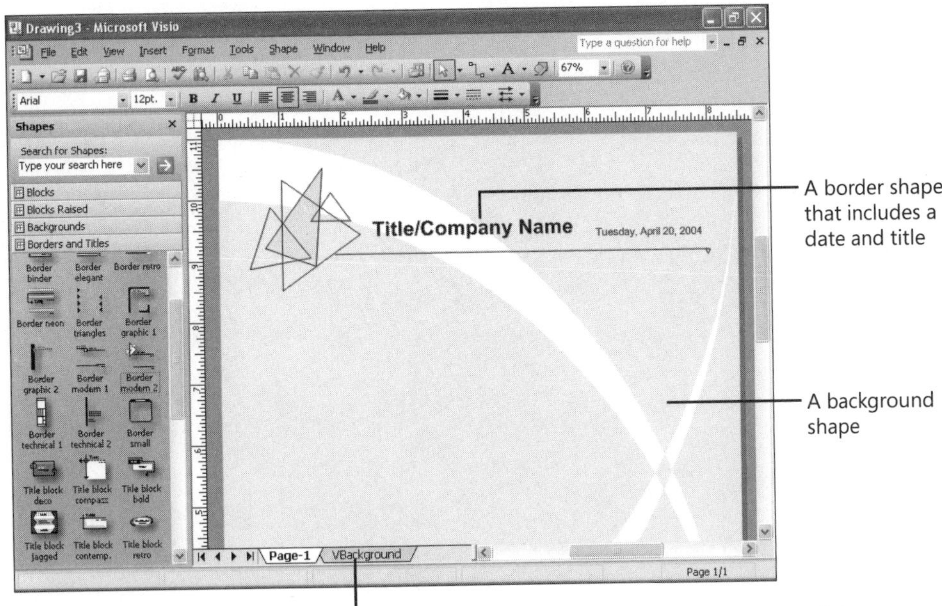

In this exercise, you fine-tune the appearance of the gardening expo layout by adding a border, title block, and background shape to the diagram.

OPEN the *FormatDecorate* file in the My Documents\Microsoft Press\Visio 2003 SBS\Formatting-Shapes folder.

1. Click the **Borders and Titles** stencil to display the shapes on the stencil.
2. From the **Borders and Titles** stencil, drag the **Border Classic** shape onto the drawing page.

   Visio centers and snaps the border shape into place. The shape includes generic title placeholder text, the date at the top of the page, and the page number at the bottom of the page.

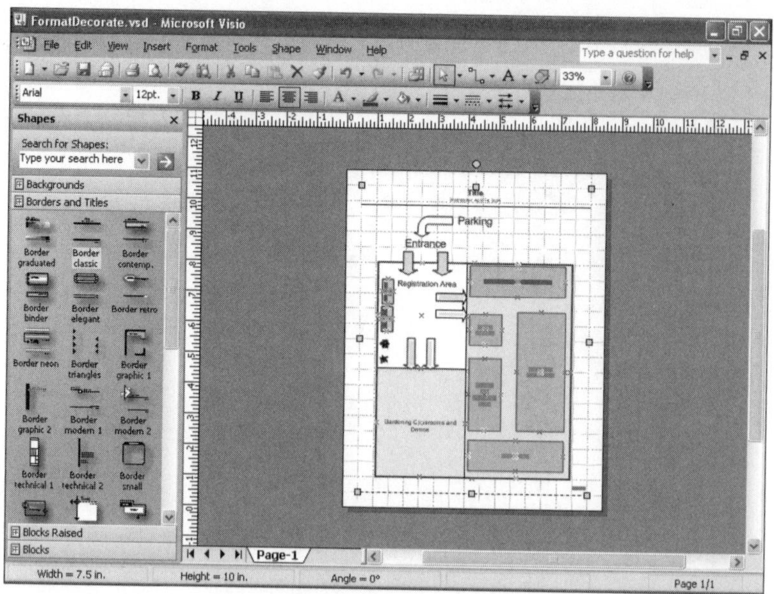

3 Hold down Shift+Ctrl, and then drag a selection box around the generic title placeholder text to zoom in on it.

Visio zooms in on the text.

4 Press the F2 key to open the shape's text block and select the shape's text.

5 Double-click the word **Title** in the text block to select just that word, and then type Garden Expo to replace the placeholder text.

Visio replaces the placeholder text with the new text.

Troubleshooting If you select a title block shape and type, you can inadvertently replace the automatic date text as well as the title. If this happens, immediately press Ctrl+Z, and then try again. Make sure you select only the word *Title*, and then type.

6 Click the date to select it.

7 Type **April 19-21, 2004**.

Visio replaces the old date with the new date.

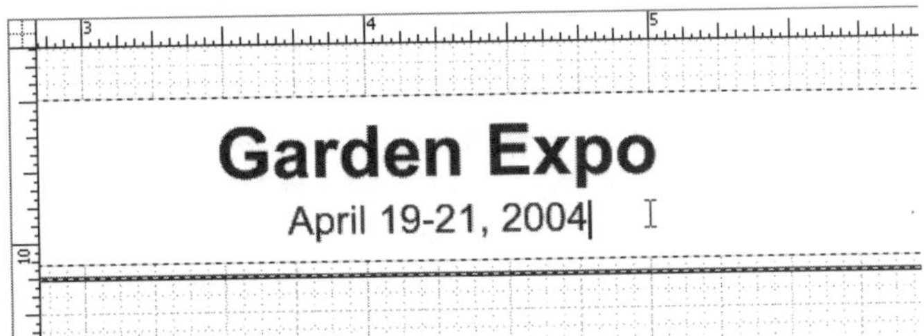

8 Press Ctrl+W to zoom out and view the whole drawing page.

9 Click the **Backgrounds** stencil to display the shapes on the stencil.

10 From the **Backgrounds** stencil, drag the **Background Leaf** shape to the drawing page.

Visio inserts a new page named Vbackground and adds the Background Leaf shape, which appears behind the drawing page, to the background page. Notice the new Vbackground page tab at the bottom of the drawing window.

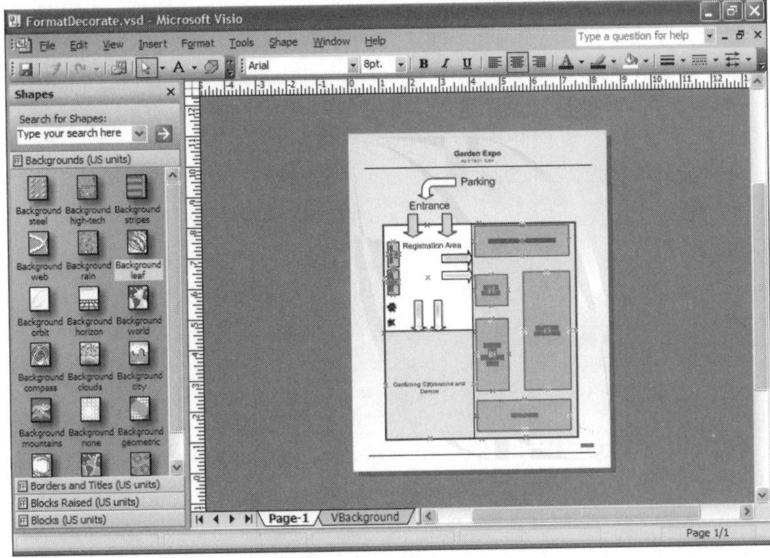

Tip If you add a background shape to your diagram that you don't like, you can immediately undo your action by pressing Ctrl+Z.

Save

11 On the Standard toolbar, click **Save** to save your changes to the diagram.

CLOSE the *FormatDecorate* file.

Using Shapes with Dates

Many of the title block and border shapes display a date when you add them to the drawing page. This special type of text is called a *field*—a type of text that Visio updates with the current date, for example, based on your computer's date and time settings. A date field can display the date in several formats, which are predetermined by the shape you select. However, you can edit date fields to display the date in a different format. For more information about fields, type "text field" in the "Type a question for help" box, and then press the Enter key. In the list of topics, click About text fields. Fields can contain other information, such as page numbers, document information, and custom formulas. To insert a field into a shape, select a shape, and then on the Insert menu, click Field.

Adding Color Schemes to Diagrams

The quickest way to add polish to a diagram is to use a *color scheme*–a set of coordinated colors that Visio applies to all the shapes and text in a diagram. For example, if you're pressed for time, you can right-click the drawing page, and then click Color Schemes on the shortcut menu to change the look of your entire diagram. A color scheme applies colors to the text, line, fill, and shadows of all the shapes in a diagram, including background and border shapes. Color schemes have names that suggest the result; for example, the Forest color scheme applies earth tones, and the Steel color scheme applies shades of gray to the shapes in your diagram. The Color Schemes dialog box stays open after you make a selection so that you can see the effect immediately; if you don't like the result, you can simply choose a different color scheme.

If you have already formatted the shapes in your diagram, you can apply a color scheme without changing the existing colors. The Color Schemes dialog box includes the "Preserve my shape color changes" check box, which preserves the existing formatting in your diagram. If you don't select this check box, the new colors in the color scheme replace your existing formatting.

Troubleshooting Color schemes are designed to work with diagrams based on a business-oriented template, such as block diagrams and flowcharts. If you create a diagram with a template that does not support color schemes, the Color Schemes command does not appear on the shortcut menu when you right-click the drawing page.

In this exercise, you add pizzazz to the layout of a gardening expo hosted by The Garden Company by applying a color scheme.

OPEN the *FormatScheme* file in the My Documents\Microsoft Press\Visio 2003 SBS\FormattingShapes folder.

1 Right-click the drawing page, and then click **Color Schemes** on the shortcut menu to open the **Color Schemes** dialog box.

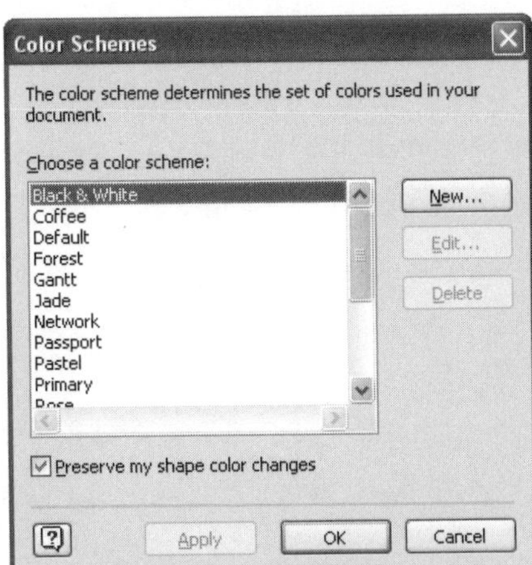

2 In the **Choose a color scheme** list, click **Forest**.

3 Make sure the **Preserve my shape color changes** check box is selected, and then click **Apply**.

Visio applies the color scheme to the diagram, and the Color Schemes dialog box remains open.

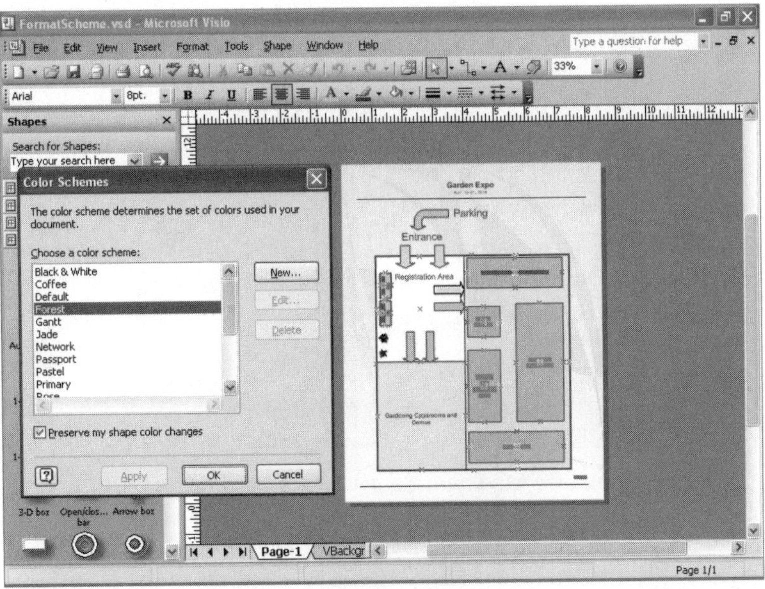

Important Notice that when you apply a color scheme, Visio changes the color of the background as well as the fill and text color of some—but not all—shapes. When the "Preserve my shape color changes" check box is selected, Visio does not apply the color scheme to shapes have been formatted already.

4 In the **Choose a color scheme** list, click **Jade**, and then click **Apply**.

Visio applies the new color scheme to the diagram.

5 Click **OK** to accept the color scheme and close the dialog box.

6 Select the jade-colored arrow labeled **Enter auditorium**.

Selection handles appear around the shape.

Format Painter

7 On the Standard toolbar, click the **Format Painter** button, and then click the white arrow labeled **Enter auditorium**.

Visio applies the color scheme to the shape, overwriting its previous formatting.

Save

8 On the Standard toolbar, click **Save** to save your changes to the diagram.

CLOSE the *FormatScheme* file.

Previewing and Printing Diagrams

Most people share their Visio drawings and diagrams by printing them. Like other programs in the Microsoft Office System, Visio includes a Print Preview command that shows you how your diagram will look when it is printed, as well as a Print Page button on the Standard toolbar that you can click to print one page of your diagram. For more printing options, such as printing all the pages in a diagram or multiple copies of a diagram, you can use the Print command on the File menu.

If your drawing page is larger, smaller, or oriented differently than your printer's paper, you must make adjustments when you print. You can change the size of the drawing page and choose the size of your printer paper in the Page Setup dialog box, which you open by clicking Page Setup on the File menu. The Page Setup dialog box includes a preview area that shows you the effect of various page settings. It includes options on several tabs, but the following two tabs are most important ones to know about when you print:

- The Print Setup tab is where you can specify the size and orientation of the paper in your printer.
- The Page Size tab is where you can change the size and orientation of the drawing page you see on the screen.

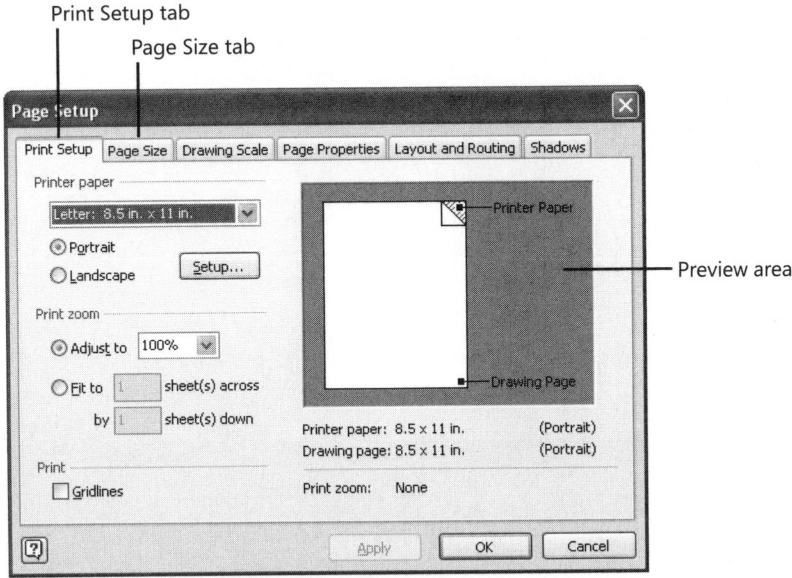

You can also determine where Visio will break a large diagram that spans more than one page by viewing *page breaks*, which are represented by gray lines on the drawing page. To view page breaks, on the View menu, click Page Breaks. If your drawing page fits the size of the paper in your printer, gray lines appear around the drawing page. For the most detailed preview of page breaks and exactly how and where your shapes will be printed, use the Print Preview command. If you have a black and white printer, Visio can preview your diagram in shades of gray so that you can see how it will look when printed.

Fixing Page Orientation Problems

The most common problem people encounter when printing Visio diagrams is a drawing page that is oriented differently than the printer setting. For example, if the drawing page is wider than it is tall (*landscape orientation*), but the printer is set to print in *portrait orientation* (taller than wide), Visio displays a message box that says one or more drawing pages is oriented differently than the printer setting. To correct this problem, click the Page Setup command on the File menu, and then do one of the following:

- Change the drawing page to match the printer's settings. Click the Page Size tab, and then select the Same as printer paper size option.
- Change the printer's settings to match your diagram. Click the Print Setup tab, and then in the Printer paper area, select the option that matches the preview of the drawing page shown in the preview area of the dialog box.

In this exercise, you practice previewing and printing a diagram that shows The Garden Company's gardening expo. You view page breaks first, and then preview the diagram in the Print Preview window. Finally, you compare the printer's paper size setting with the drawing page size in the Page Setup dialog box, and then print the diagram.

Important To complete this exercise, a printer must be connected to your computer.

OPEN the *FormatPrint* file in the My Documents\Microsoft Press\Visio 2003 SBS\FormattingShapes folder.

1. On the **View** menu, click **Page Breaks.**

   Gray lines appear around the drawing page because the diagram fits on a single page.

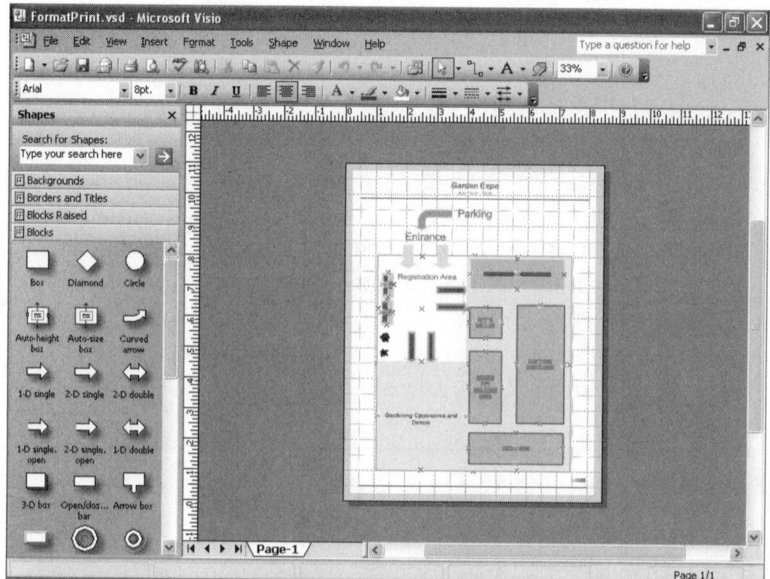

Important If your diagram includes a background page, you might not be able to see the gray lines that represent page breaks.

2. On the **File** menu, click **Print Preview.**

   The Print Preview window opens and displays the Print Preview toolbar.

Important If you have a color printer, your screen will not match the following illustration, which shows the diagram when a black and white printer is selected.

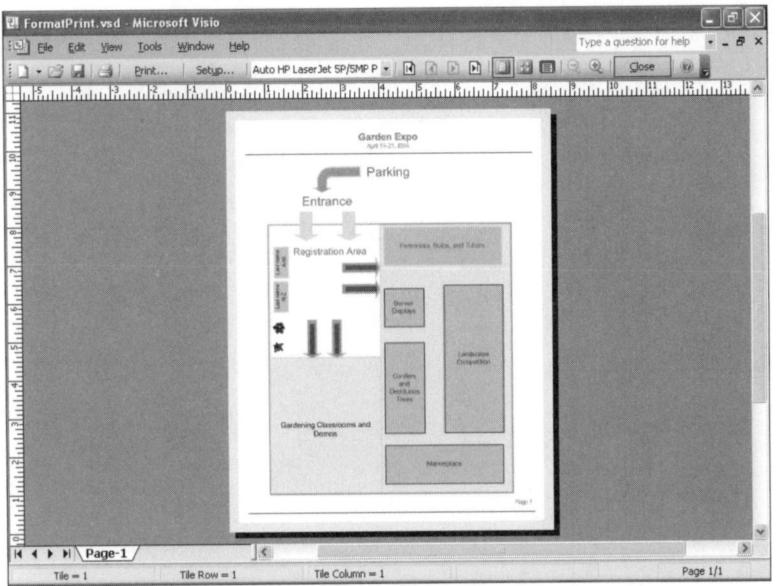

Setup...

3 On the Print Preview toolbar, click **Setup**.

The Page Setup dialog box appears with the Print Setup tab displayed.

4 In the **Printer paper** area, make sure **Letter** is selected in the text box and that the **Portrait option** is selected.

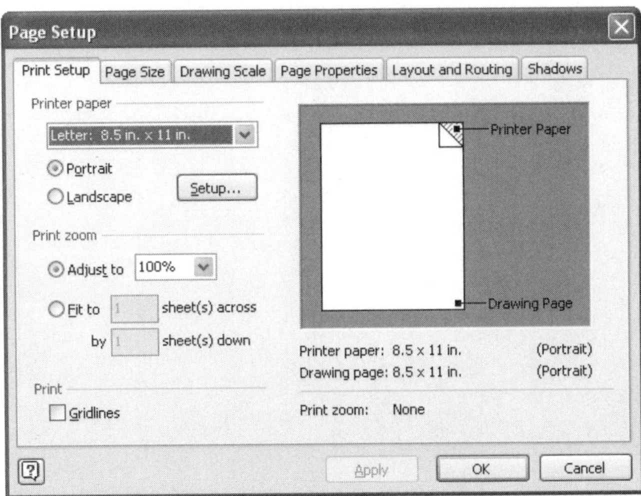

Tip Use the preview area in the Page Setup dialog box to verify that the printer paper setting and drawing page match in size and orientation. The printer's current size and orientation settings are listed below the preview picture in the dialog box.

5 Click the **Page Size** tab to display the settings for the drawing page.

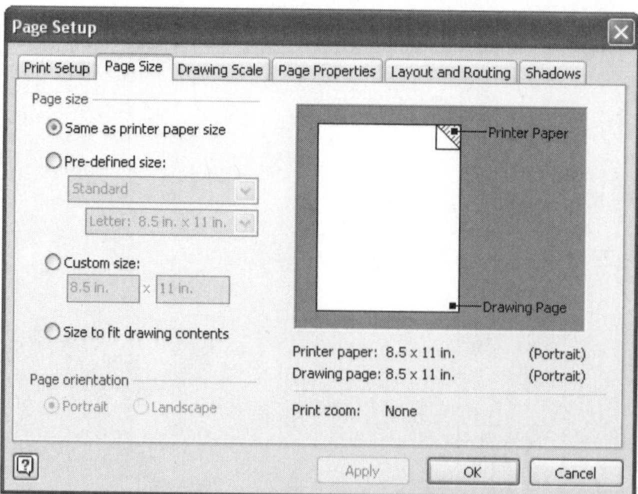

6 In the **Page size** area, make sure **Same as printer paper size** option is selected, and then click **OK** to close the dialog box.

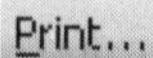

7 On the Print Preview toolbar, click **Print** to open the **Print** dialog box. Notice that **All** is selected in the **Print range** area and **Number of copies** is set to **1**.

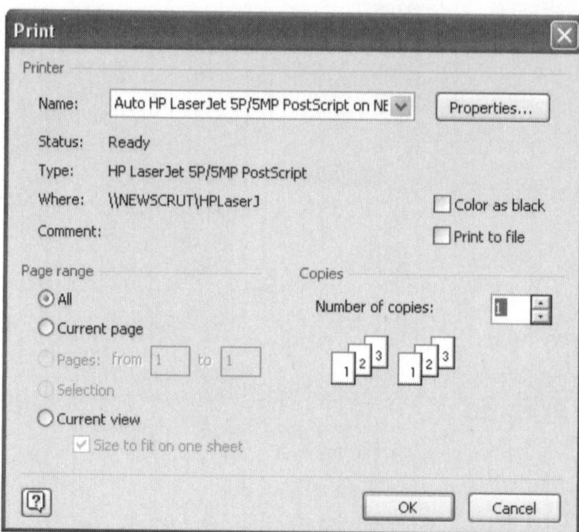

Troubleshooting Make sure you click the button labeled Print. If you click the Print Page button instead, Visio does not display the Print dialog box and instead prints the current page.

8 Click **OK** to print your diagram.

Troubleshooting To troubleshoot any problems you might encounter when printing, refer to Visio Help. In the "Type a question for help" box, type "troubleshoot printing," and then press the Enter key. In the list of results, click Troubleshoot printing to view that topic.

9 On the Print Preview toolbar, click **Close**.

The Print Preview window closes and the drawing page is displayed.

Print Page

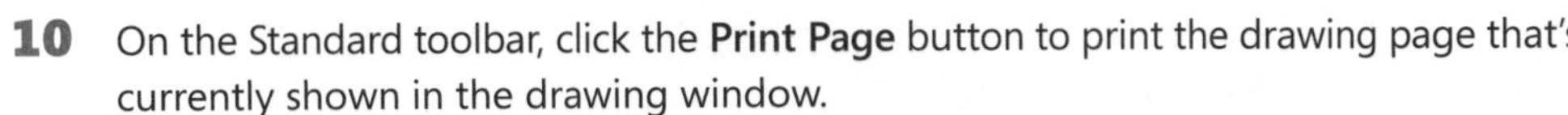

10 On the Standard toolbar, click the **Print Page** button to print the drawing page that's currently shown in the drawing window.

Save

11 On the Standard toolbar, click **Save** to save your changes to the diagram.

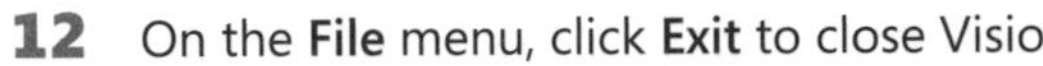

12 On the **File** menu, click **Exit** to close Visio.

Key Points

- To format shapes, use the commands on the Format menu or the buttons on the Formatting toolbar.
- To quickly copy all the formatting from one shape to another shape, use the Format Painter tool. Double-click the tool to copy the formatting from one shape to multiple shapes.
- To add borders, backgrounds, or titles to your diagrams, drag a shape from the Borders and Titles stencil or the Backgrounds stencil onto the drawing page.
- To apply a color scheme to your diagram, right-click the drawing page, and then click Color Schemes. If Color Schemes doesn't appear on the shortcut menu, the template that you used to start your diagram doesn't support color schemes.
- To check or change any page settings, on the File menu, click Page Setup. When you print your diagrams, make sure the size and orientation of the drawing page matches the printer settings.
- To preview your diagram, on the File menu, click Print Preview.
- To print the drawing page that's currently shown in the drawing window, click the Print Page button on the Standard toolbar.

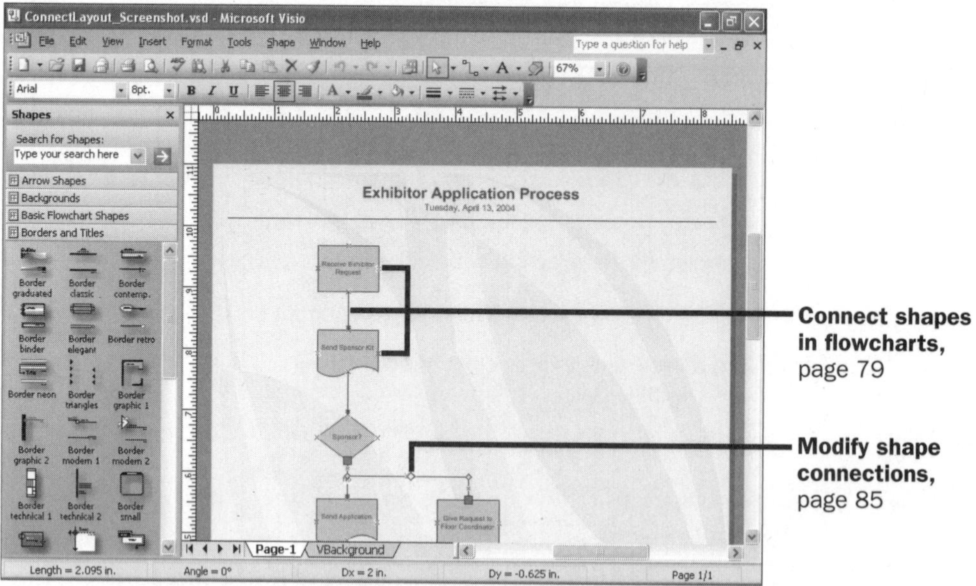

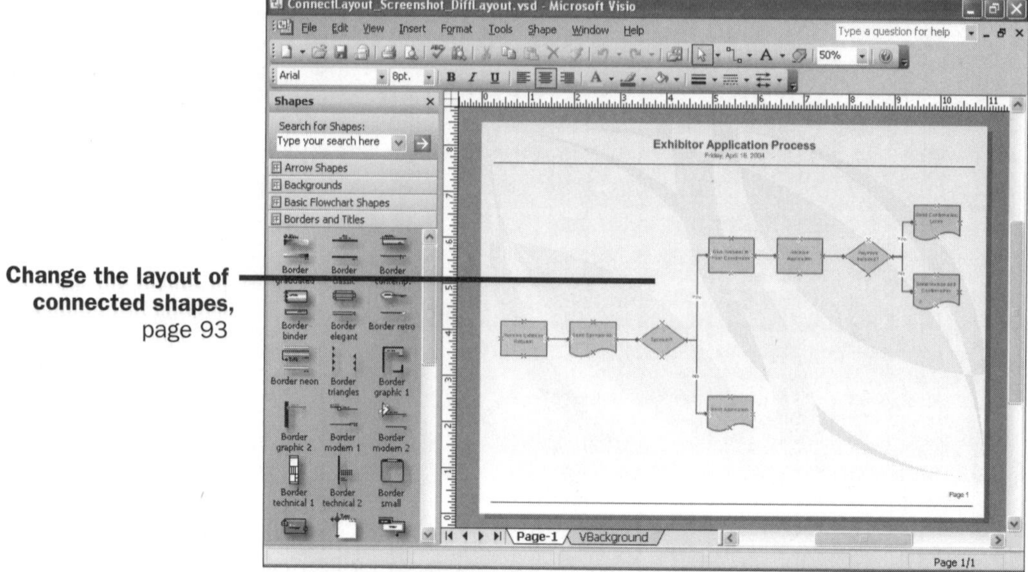

Chapter 4 at a Glance

4 Connecting Shapes

In this chapter you will learn to:

- ✔ Connect shapes in flowcharts.
- ✔ Modify shape connections.
- ✔ Change the layout of connected shapes.

Many types of Microsoft Office Visio diagrams depict related ideas, relationships, or sequences by showing shapes that are connected with lines. For example, a flowchart shows each of the steps in a process as a series of shapes connected by lines. Organization charts show employee relationships as a hierarchy of shapes connected by lines. Network diagrams use lines to show equipment connected to hubs. Visio makes it easy to connect the shapes in these diagrams by using *connectors*—1-D shapes (usually lines or arrows) that connect 2-D shapes, such as the process shapes in a flowchart. If you rearrange the connected 2-D shapes, the connectors stay attached to the shapes and are rerouted for you, so you don't waste time redrawing lines. In some diagrams, such as flowcharts, you can even drag a 2-D shape between two connected shapes, and Visio reroutes the connector and connects all three shapes.

This chapter shows you how to connect shapes and work with connectors in a flowchart. However, the techniques that you use to connect flowchart shapes apply to other types of diagrams as well. As you modify shape connections and arrange connected shapes, you can take advantage of several layout tools that help you evenly distribute, align, and position shapes. You can even change the orientation of all the connected shapes in a diagram; for example, you can change the layout in a flowchart from top to bottom and from left to right.

See Also Do you need only a quick refresher on the topics in this chapter? See the Quick Reference entries on pages xxix–xxxi.

Important Before you can use the practice files in this chapter, you need to install them from the book's companion CD to their default location. See "Using the Book's CD" on page xv for more information.

Connecting Shapes in Flowcharts

Flowcharts are the ideal diagrams for visually representing business processes. For example, if you need to show the flow of a custom-order process through various departments within your organization, you can use a flowchart. Visio includes several different flowchart templates; however, the most common type of flowchart uses simple shapes to represent the basic elements in a business process, as shown in the following table.

Shape Name	Shape	What It Represents
Process		Steps in a business process
Decision		Decisions in a business process
Document		Steps that result in or require documentation
Data		Steps that require data

You add connectors between these flowchart shapes to show relationships between them and the sequence of steps in a process. Flowchart connectors are usually lines with arrowheads that can include text to clarify the process being depicted. When you draw a connector (or when Visio draws it for you), the endpoints of the connector *glue* to the shapes–that is, Visio creates a bond that won't break unless you move a connector endpoint or delete the connector. When you select a connector that is glued to a shape, the connector's endpoints turn red, indicating that the connector will be rerouted when you move the connected shapes.

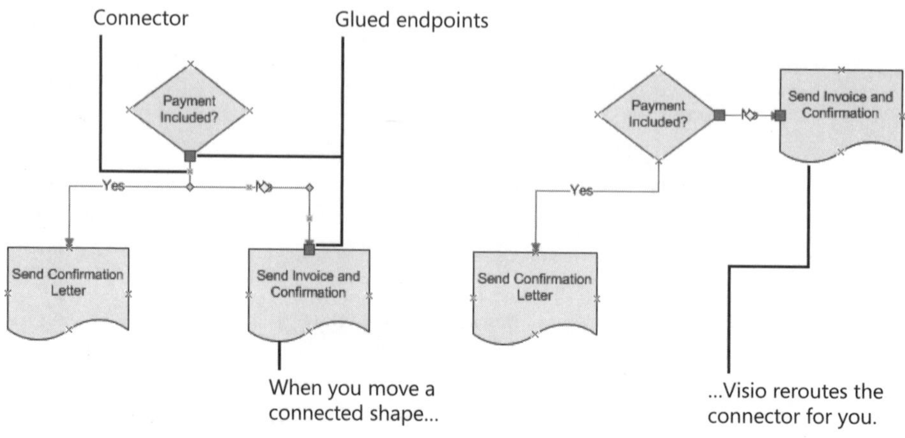

Connector Tool

There are several methods of connecting shapes. For flowchart shapes, it's best to use the Connector tool, which you access by clicking the Connector Tool button on the Standard toolbar. You can connect shapes with the Connector tool in two ways:

- You can add shapes to the drawing page first, and then use the Connector tool to draw connectors between shapes.
- You can use the Connector tool to drag shapes from a stencil onto the drawing page so that each shape you drag is connected to the selected shape on the page. Visio draws the connectors for you.

Important To connect shapes as you drag them onto the drawing page, make sure you select the Connector tool *before* you drag the shapes onto the drawing page.

As you drag a flowchart shape onto the drawing page, a *dynamic grid* appears as a dotted line through the shape to show you how to align it with respect to the shapes already on the page.

In this exercise, you start a new diagram based on the Basic Flowchart template. You drag several shapes onto the drawing page using the Connector tool so that Visio draws the connector and connects the shapes for you. You add text to the connectors to indicate a *yes* or *no* decision. Then you draw your own connector between two shapes using the Connector tool.

1. Start Visio. In the Choose Drawing Type window, in the **Category** area, click **Flowchart**. In the **Template** area, click **Basic Flowchart**.

   The Basic Flowchart template opens a blank drawing page and the Basic Flowchart Shapes, Backgrounds, Arrow Shapes, and Borders and Titles stencils.

Connector Tool

2. On the Standard toolbar, click the **Connector Tool** button.

   The pointer displays a connector icon.

3. From the **Basic Flowchart Shapes** stencil, drag a **Process** shape onto the drawing page and position it near the top of the page.
4. From the **Basic Flowchart Shapes** stencil, drag a **Decision** shape onto the drawing page and position it below the **Process** shape.

Visio draws a connector between the shapes. The connector has an arrowhead at its end point, which is the default connector style for the Basic Flowchart template.

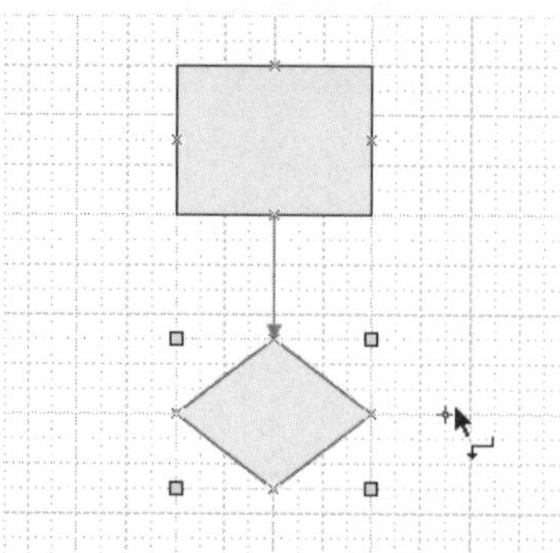

5 From the **Basic Flowchart Shapes** stencil, drag a **Document** shape onto the drawing page and position it to the right of the diamond-shaped **Decision** shape.

Visio draws a connector between the Decision and Document shapes.

Tip You can use the dynamic grid to align the Document and Decision shapes.

6 Click the **Decision** shape to select it.

7 From the **Basic Flowchart Shapes** stencil, drag another **Process** shape onto the drawing page and position it below the **Decision** shape.

Visio draws a connector between the Decision and Process shapes.

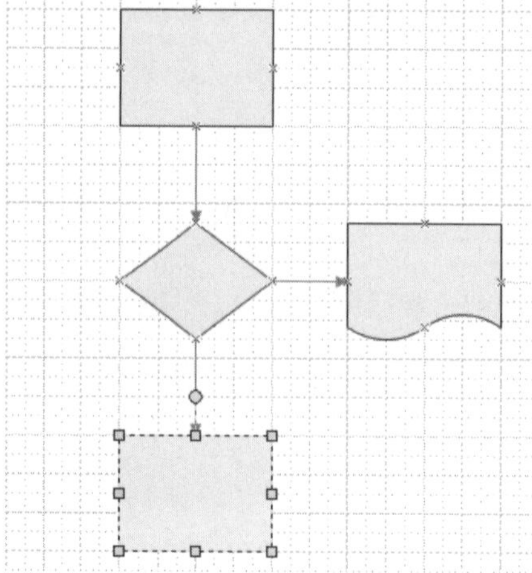

Tip Visio can number the shapes in your flowchart for you. To specify the numbering settings, on the Tools menu, point to Add-Ons, point to Visio Extras, and then click Number Shapes.

Pointer Tool

8 On the Standard toolbar, click the **Pointer Tool** button.

9 Click the top **Process** shape to select it.

10 Hold down Shift+Ctrl and left-click the top **Process** shape to zoom in on it.

11 With the top **Process** shape selected, type Contact workshop presenters.

The text is added to the shape.

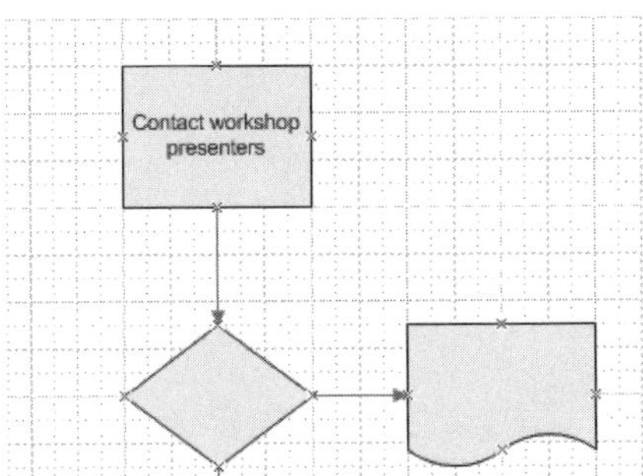

12 Select the **Decision** shape, and type Presenter available?

13 Select the **Document** shape, and type Send presenter kit and contract.

14 Select the bottom **Process** shape, and type Contact exhibitors.

15 Click the connector between the **Decision** shape and the **Document** shape to select it.

The connector's endpoints turn red, indicating that the connector is glued to the shapes and will be rerouted when you move the connected shapes.

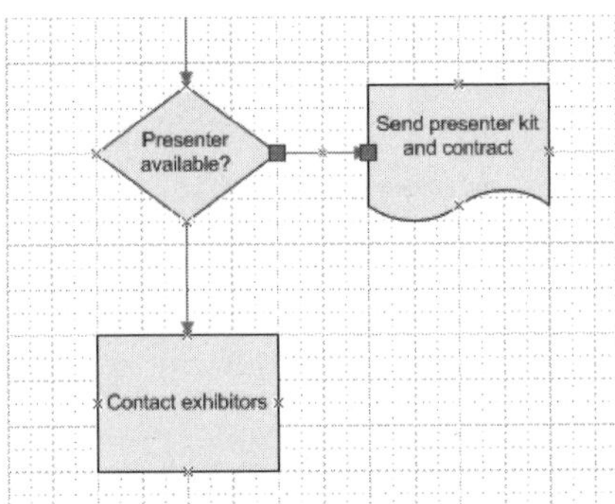

16 With the connector selected, type Yes.

The text is added to the connector.

17 Select the connector between the **Decision** shape and the bottom **Process** shape, and then type No.

The text is added to the connector.

18 Click the pasteboard to deselect the shape.

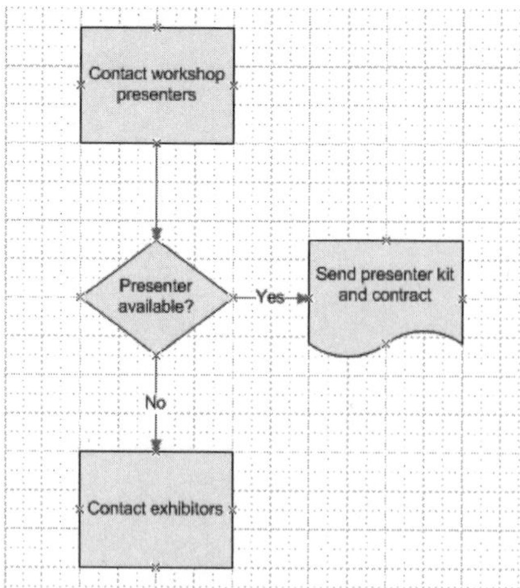

19 From the **Basic Flowchart Shapes** stencil, drag a **Decision** shape onto the drawing page and position it below the **Send presenter kit and contract** shape.

20 On the Standard toolbar, click the **Connector Tool** button.

The pointer displays a connector icon.

21 Position the pointer over the **Contact exhibitors** shape.

A red border appears around the shape.

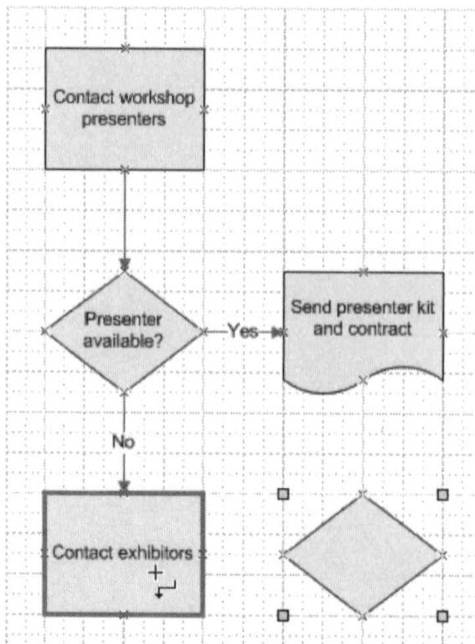

22 Drag to the **Decision** shape on the right until a red border appears around the **Decision** shape.

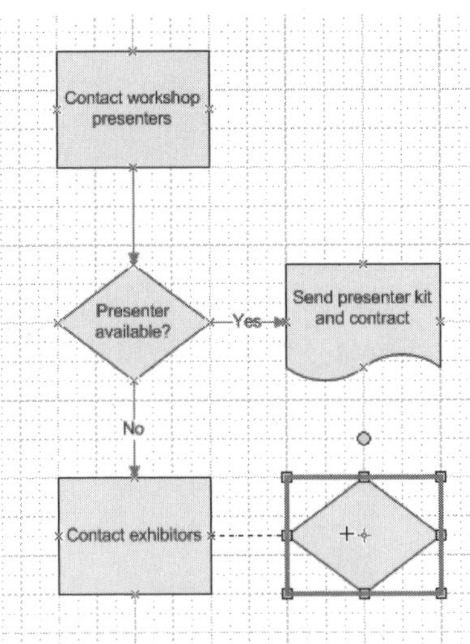

23 Release the mouse button.

Visio draws a connector between the two shapes.

24 With the connector selected, type Yes.

25 On the Standard toolbar, click the **Pointer Tool** button.

26 Select the **Decision** shape, and then type Exhibitor available?.

27 Click the pasteboard to deselect the shape.

28 On the **File** menu, click **Save As** to open the **Save As** dialog box.

29 In the **File name** box, type ConnectFlowchart, and then click the **Save** button to save the flowchart.

CLOSE the *ConnectFlowchart* file.

Modifying Shape Connections

New in Visio 2003

Not only does Visio make it easy to create connections in diagrams, it also makes it easy to modify those connections. Perhaps you need to add a missing step to a flowchart or adjust a series of steps to make a process more efficient. Maybe you need some of the connectors in a flowchart to be rerouted in a specific way. With Visio, you can insert shapes between shapes that are already connected and move shapes around while the connections stay intact, which makes modifying a flowchart painless.

The method you use to connect shapes in a flowchart determines how the connectors are rerouted and how much control you have over where connectors are attached to shapes. In the previous exercise, you connected shapes with a *shape-to-shape connection*; that is, you connected shapes without specifying a point of connection. When you move shapes connected by a shape-to-shape connection, the connector reroutes and connects the shapes between the two closest points on the shapes. When you insert a shape between two shapes that are connected by a shape-to-shape connection, Visio connects all three shapes. For most types of flowcharts, shape-to-shape connections are sufficient because you don't usually need to control the exact point of connection on each shape. When you select the connector between two shapes with a shape-to-shape connection, the glued connector endpoints are large, light red, and have no begin point or end point symbols.

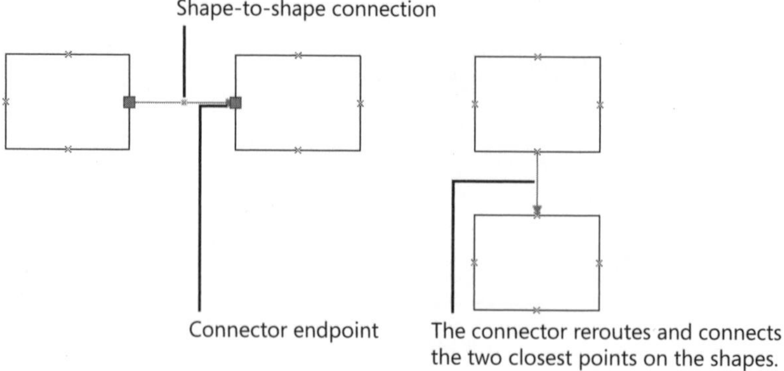

When you use the Connector tool to drag shapes onto the drawing page and connect them, Visio creates shape-to-shape connections by default. To draw a shape-to-shape connection yourself, you place the Connector tool over one of the shapes until you see a red border around the shape. Then you drag to the other shape, and when you see a red border around it, release the mouse button.

There might be times when you're working within design constraints that, for example, require all Yes connectors to flow from the right side of the shapes and all No connectors to flow downward in a flowchart. When you need total control over your shape connections, you can connect shapes with a *point-to-point connection*, which connects specific points on the shapes. When you move shapes connected by a point-to-point connection, the connector stays connected to those specific points, regardless of where you move the shapes. When you add a shape between two shapes already connected by a point-to-point connection, Visio connects all three shapes at specific connection points. When you select the connector between shapes connected by a point-to-point connection, the glued endpoints on the connector are small, dark red, and include begin and end point symbols.

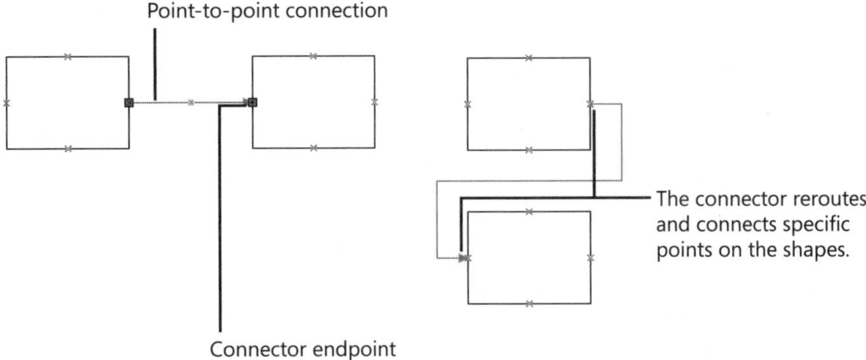

To create a point-to-point connection, instead of positioning the Connector tool over the shape, you position it over a *connection point*—a specific point, represented by a blue x symbol.

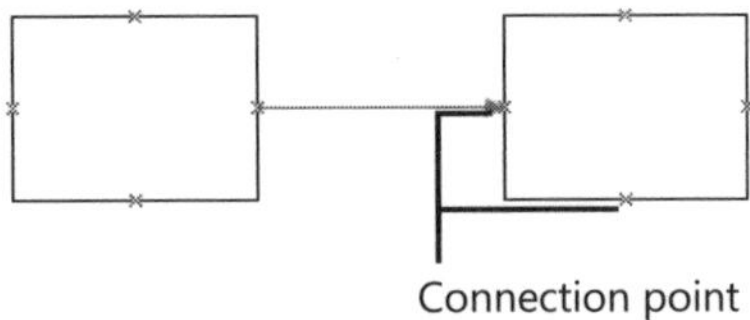

When you place the Connector tool over a connection point on a shape, a small red box appears. Then you drag the connector to the small red box around the connection point on the shape to which you are connecting.

Tip You can use both shape-to-shape connections and point-to-point connections in a flowchart. You can also create your own connection points. For information about creating connection points and the different types of connection points, type "connection points" in the "Type a question for help" box. Then read the "About connection points" and "Work with connection points" Help topics.

In this exercise, you move a flowchart shape to a new position and see how the connector moves with the shape. You also insert a flowchart shape between two shapes that are already connected. Then you move two shapes that are connected by a shape-to-shape connection and create a point-to-point connection between them using the Connector tool. Finally, you modify a connector segment and attach a connector endpoint to a different shape.

OPEN the *ConnectModify* file in the My Documents\Microsoft Press\Visio 2003 SBS\ConnectingShapes folder.

1. Drag the **Contact workshop presenters** shape up approximately one inch.

   The connector is resized but stays connected to the shape.

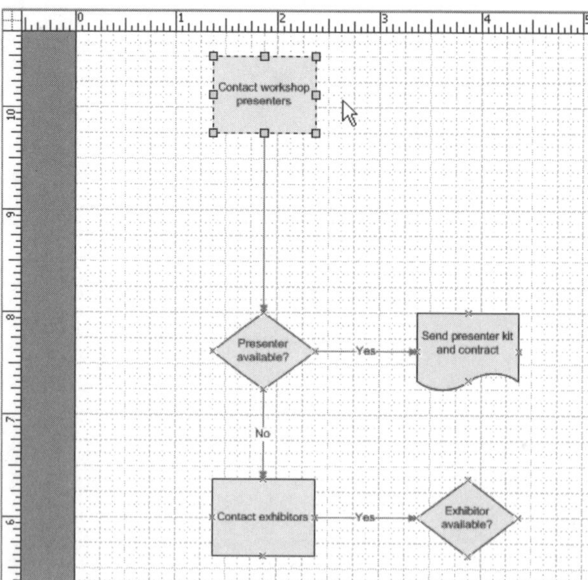

2. From the **Basic Flowchart Shapes** stencil, drag a **Process** shape onto the drawing page and position it on the connector between the **Contact workshop presenters** shape and the **Presenter available?** shape.

scissors icon

   As you hold the Process shape over the connector, the pointer changes to a scissors icon, indicating that you can cut, or split, the existing connection and reconnect all three shapes in the series.

3. Release the mouse button.

   Visio connects all three shapes in the series.

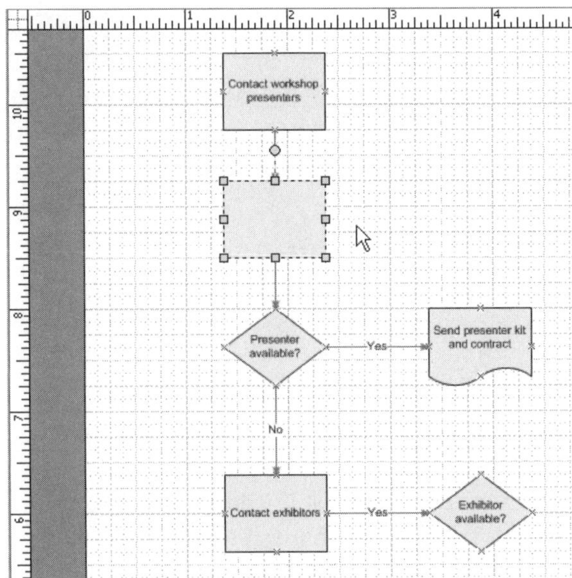

Important Not all templates and connectors support connector-splitting behavior. To determine whether a template and connector support this behavior, drag a shape onto a connector between two shapes. If the connector is rerouted around the shape rather than attaching to it, the template, connector, or both don't support this behavior. To determine whether a particular connector supports splitting behavior, right-click the connector, point to Format on the shortcut menu, and then click Behavior to see the Connector splitting settings.

4 With the **Process** shape selected, type **Send follow-up e-mail.**

Visio zooms in so that you can easily read the text as you type.

5 Click the pasteboard to deselect the shape and zoom out again.

6 Select the connector between the **Contact exhibitors** shape and the **Exhibitor available?** shape.

The endpoints on the connector are large and light red, indicating that the shapes are connected with a shape-to-shape connection.

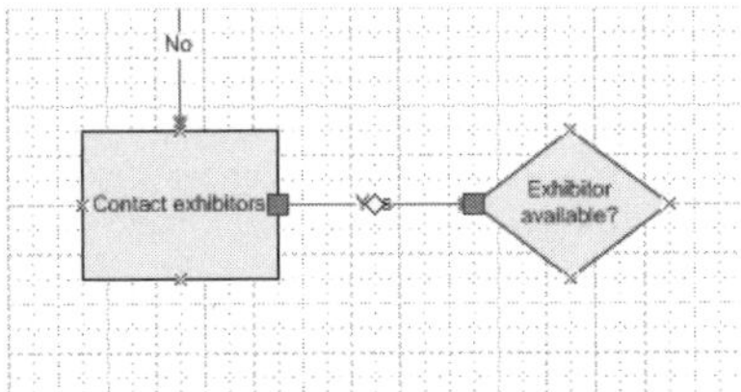

7 Drag the **Exhibitor available?** shape below the **Contact exhibitors** shape, and use the dynamic grid to align the two shapes.

The connector is rerouted and connects the shapes between the two closest points.

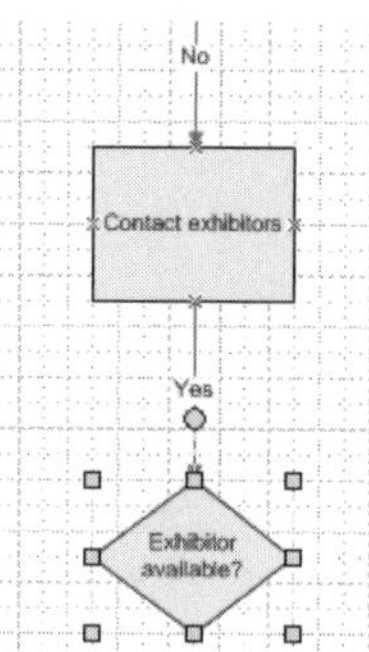

8 Select the rest of the connectors in the flowchart—one by one—and notice that all the shapes in the flowchart are connected with shape-to-shape connections.

9 From the **Basic Flowchart Shapes** stencil, drag a **Document** shape onto the drawing page. Use the dynamic grid to position it to the right of the **Exhibitor available?** shape and align it with the **Send presenter kit and contract** shape.

10 Click the pasteboard to deselect the shape.

Connector Tool

11 On the Standard toolbar, click the **Connector Tool** button.

12 Position the pointer over the right connection point on the **Exhibitor available?** shape.

A small, dark-red box encloses the connection point, indicating that you can draw a connector starting from that connection point.

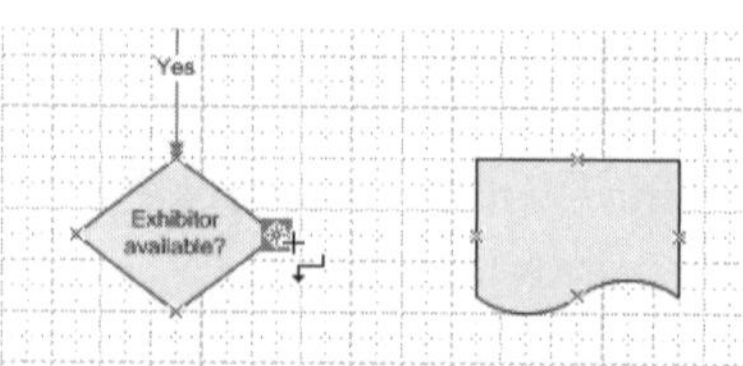

13 Drag to the left connection point on the **Document** shape.

A red box encloses the connection point on the Document shape.

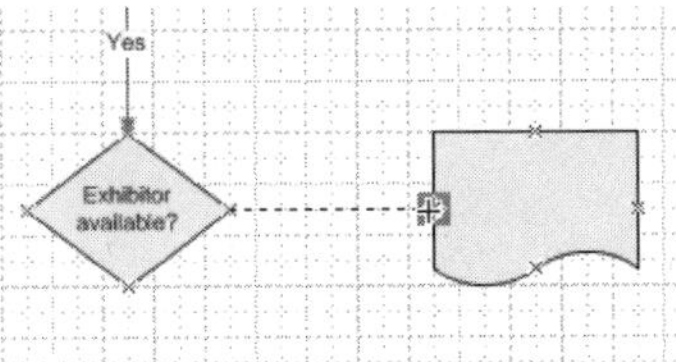

14 Release the mouse button.

Visio draws the connector and connects the two shapes using a point-to-point connection. Notice the small, dark-red endpoints on the connector, which indicate a point-to-point connection.

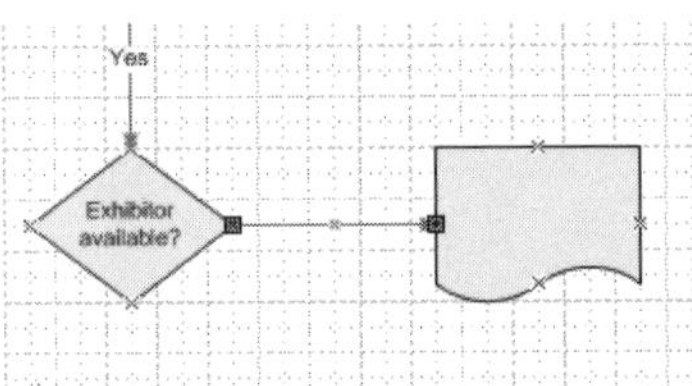

15 With the connector selected, type Yes.

Visio zooms in so that you can see the text as you type.

Pointer Tool

16 On the Standard toolbar, click the **Pointer Tool** button.

17 Select the **Document** shape, and type Send informational kit.

18 Click the pasteboard to deselect the shape.

19 Drag the **Send informational kit** shape below the **Exhibitor available?** shape.

Visio reroutes the connector, but the shapes remain connected at the same connection points.

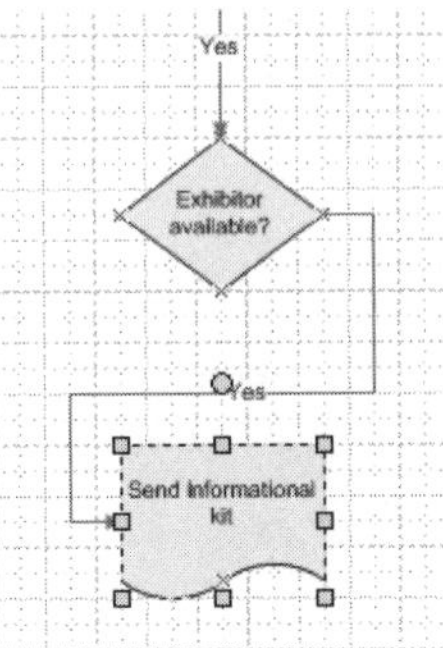

20 Select the connector between the **Send informational kit** shape and the **Exhibitor available?** shape.

21 Position the pointer over a midpoint on the right side of connector.

A ScreenTip appears.

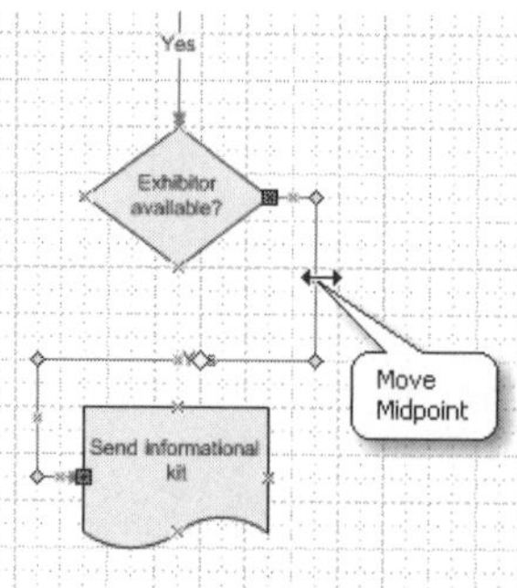

22 Drag the midpoint a little to the right to move that segment of the connector.

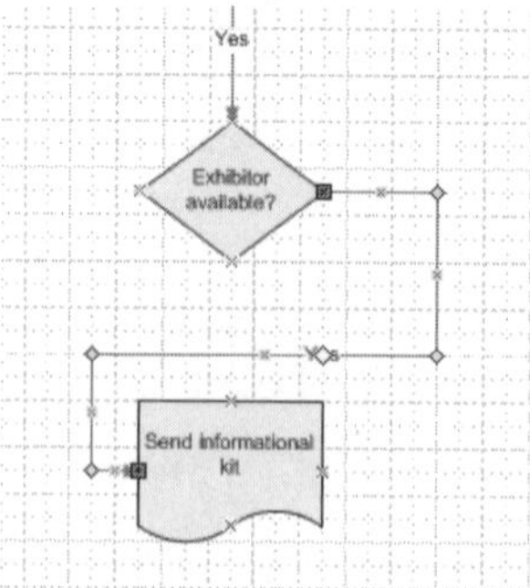

Tip Connectors have a shortcut menu just as other shapes do. You can use the commands on a connector's shortcut menu to access commands that are unique to connectors, such as the Right-Angle Connector, Straight Connector, and Curved Connector commands. Right-click a connector to display its shortcut menu.

23 Move the **Send informational kit** shape up, and position it to the right of the **Send presenter kit and contract** shape.

The connector stays attached to both connection points on the shapes.

24 Select the connector between the **Send informational kit** shape and the **Exhibitor available?** shape.

25 Place the pointer over the red connector endpoint on the **Exhibitor available?** shape.

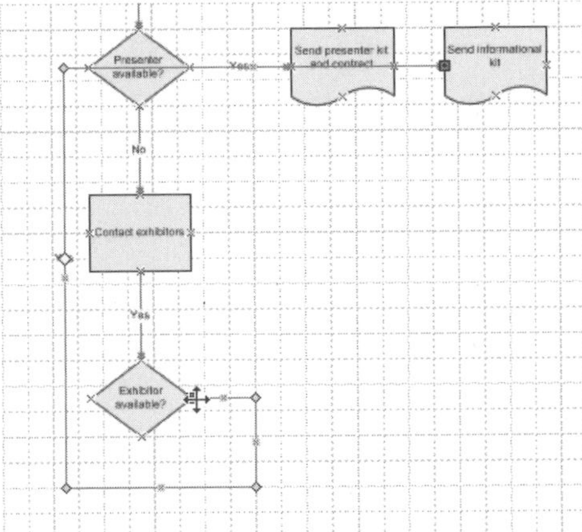

26 Drag the endpoint to the right connection point on the **Send presenter kit and contract** shape.

Visio glues the endpoint to the connection point on the Send presenter kit and contract shape and creates a new point-to-point connection.

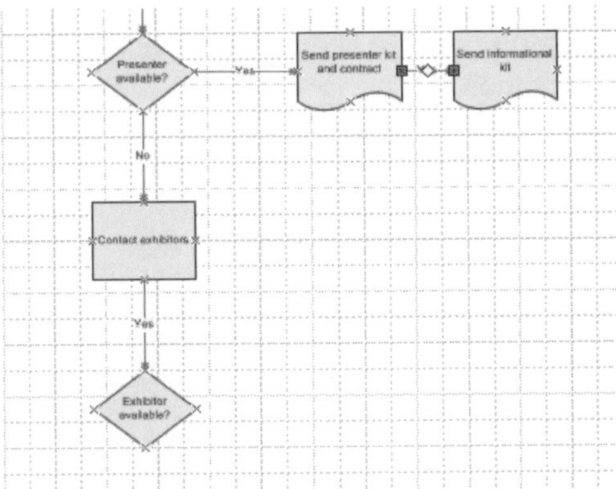

Save

27 On the Standard toolbar, click **Save** to save your changes to the diagram.

CLOSE the *ConnectModify* file.

Changing the Layout of Connected Shapes

Although flowchart layouts often flow from top to bottom, you can connect shapes from left to right, right to left, or even in a circular fashion. You can change the direction of the connected shapes in a diagram by using the Lay Out Shapes command on the

Shape menu. As long as you've created shape-to-shape connections throughout a diagram, you can change the entire layout and reroute connectors.

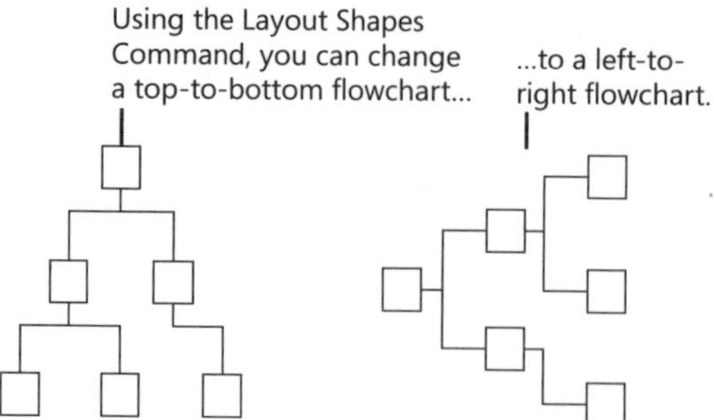

In addition, if you need to update a large flowchart to include a new process, you can use the Lay Out Shapes command to realign the diagram. For example, you can add a new shape to an existing flowchart. After you connect the new shape, you can use the Lay Out Shapes command to adjust the layout and realign all the shapes.

Troubleshooting When you change the layout of a diagram, you might find that it no longer fits on the drawing page. In this case, you can change the page size or orientation by clicking Page Setup on the File menu. Then click the Page Setup tab, and select a different page size or orientation.

You can also adjust the spacing between three or more shapes at a time by using the Distribute Shapes command on the Shape menu. When you distribute shapes vertically, the spacing is defined by the top and bottom shapes in the selection. When you distribute shapes horizontally, the spacing is defined by the leftmost and rightmost shapes in the selection.

Tip When you distribute shapes, the order in which you select the shapes is not important.

You can use the Align Shapes command on the Shape menu to align two or more shapes. When you align shapes, the order in which you select the shapes *is* important. The secondary shapes you select align with the first selected shape (the primary shape). The primary shape is indicated by its dark-magenta selection box.

In this exercise, you use the Lay Out Shapes command to change a top-to-bottom flowchart to a left-to-right flowchart. You distribute several shapes so that they are evenly spaced, and then you align some shapes.

OPEN the *ConnectLayout* file in the My Documents\Microsoft Press\Visio 2003 SBS\ConnectingShapes folder.

1 On the **Shape** menu, click **Lay Out Shapes** to open the **Lay Out Shapes** dialog box.

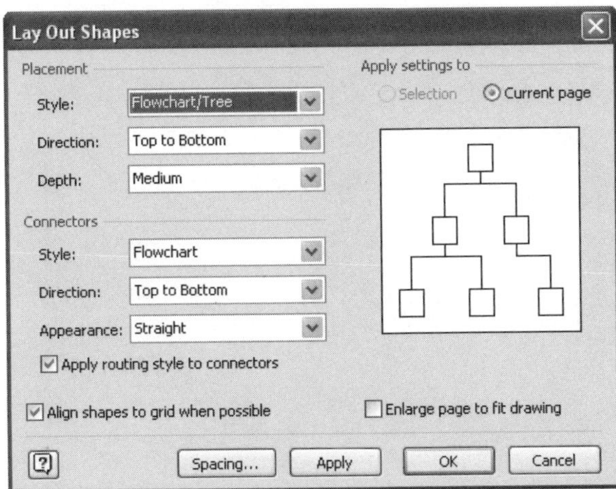

Tip You can also change the layout of selected shapes in a diagram. To do this, first select the shapes whose layout you want to change, and then on the Shape menu, click Lay Out Shapes.

2 In the **Placement** area, click the down arrow in the **Direction** box, and then click **Left to Right.**

A preview of the new layout appears in the preview area.

3 Click **OK**.

Visio changes the flowchart layout to left to right, but some shapes extend beyond the drawing page onto the pasteboard.

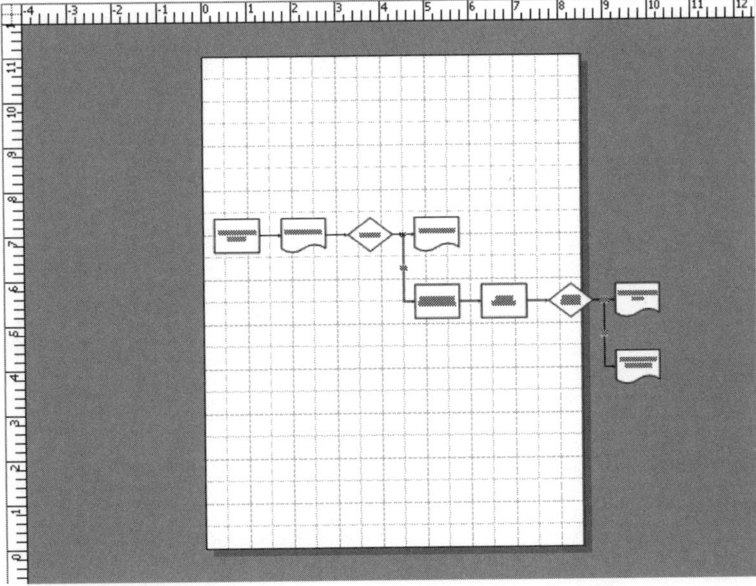

4 On the **File** menu, click **Page Setup** to open the **Page Setup** dialog box.

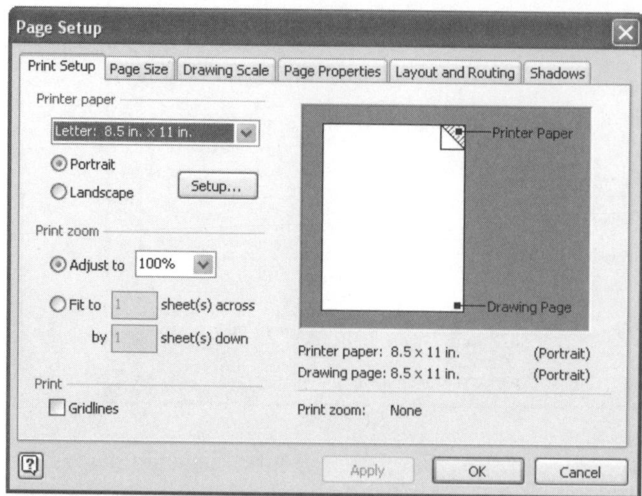

5 Click the **Page Size** tab, and then in the **Page size** area, click **Pre-defined size**.

6 In the **Page orientation** area, click **Landscape**.

A preview of the new page orientation appears in the preview area.

7 Click **OK**.

The drawing page is now set to a landscape orientation (wider than it is tall); however, the flowchart is slightly off center.

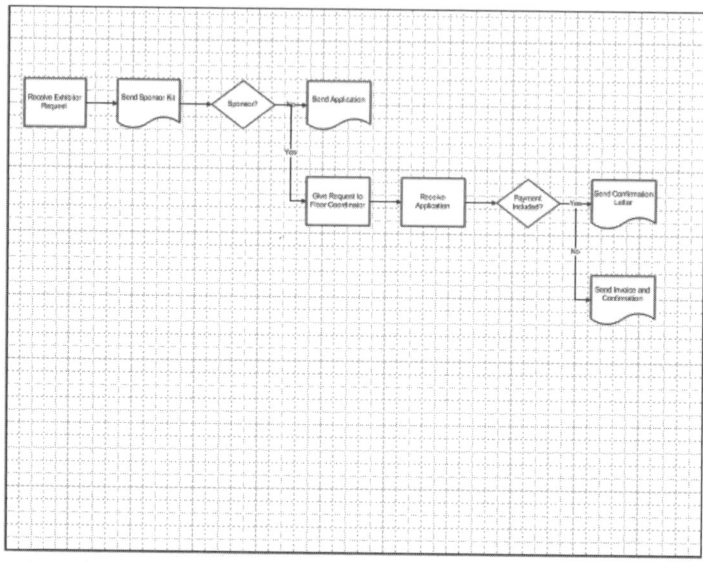

8 On the **Shape** menu, click **Center Drawing**.

Visio centers the flowchart on the drawing page.

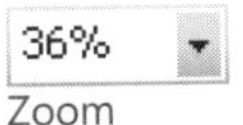

Zoom

9 On the Standard toolbar, click the **Zoom** down arrow, and then click **100%**.

Visio zooms in to the center of the drawing page.

10 If you can't see the shapes on the right side of the flowchart, drag the horizontal scroll bar until you can see the **Payment Included?** shape, the **Send Confirmation Letter** shape, and the **Send Invoice and Confirmation** shape.

11 Select the **Payment Included?** shape, hold down the Shift key, and select the **Send Confirmation Letter** shape and the **Send Invoice and Confirmation** shape.

Visio selects all three shapes.

12 On the **Shape** menu, click **Distribute Shapes** to open the **Distribute Shapes** dialog box.

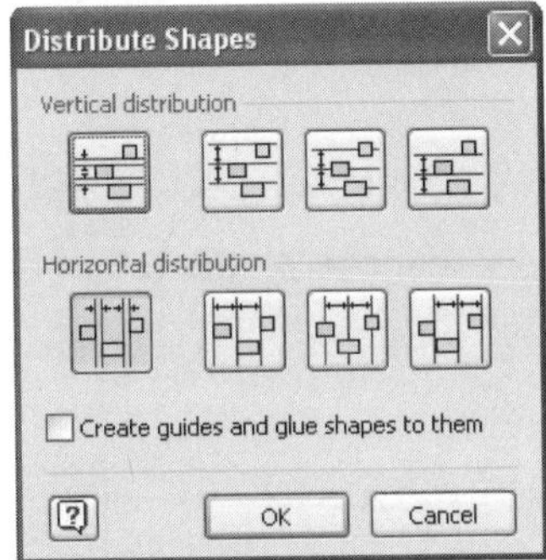

13 In the **Vertical distribution** area, click the leftmost button, and then click **OK**.

Visio positions the shapes so the spacing between them is even.

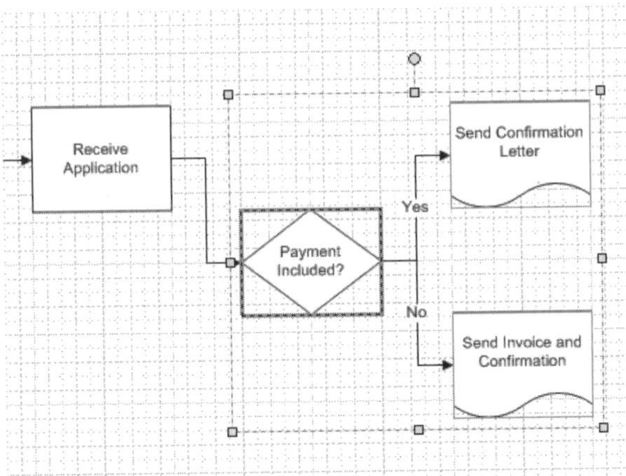

14 Select the **Payment Included?** shape, hold down the Shift key, and select the **Receive Application** shape and the **Give Request to Floor Coordinator** shape.

Visio selects all three shapes. The first shape you selected, Payment Included?, is the primary shape.

15 On the **Shape** menu, click **Align Shapes** to open the **Align Shapes** dialog box.

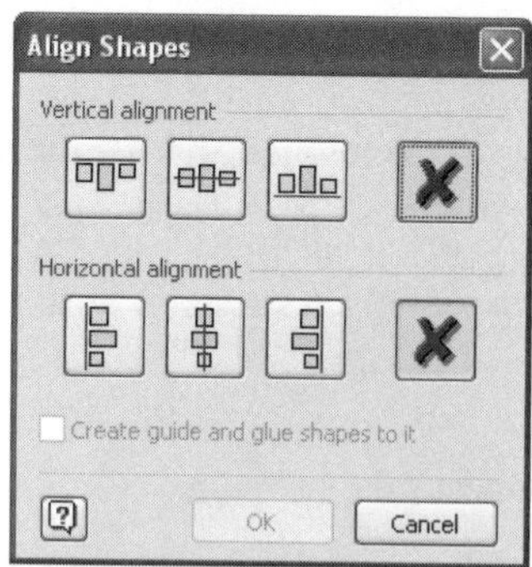

16 In the **Vertical alignment** area, click the leftmost button, and then click **OK**.

Visio aligns the top of the secondary shapes with the top of the primary shape.

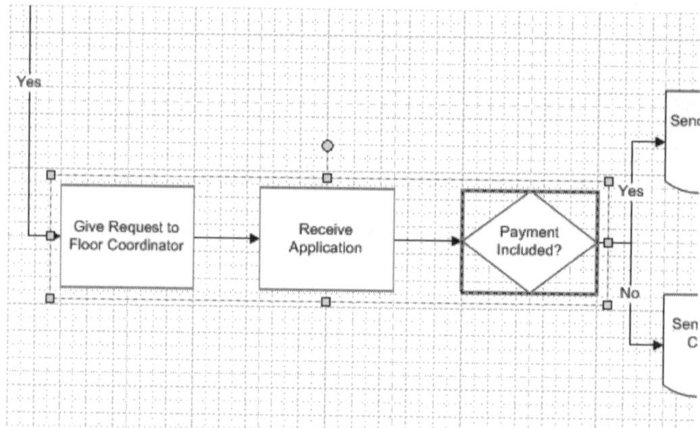

Tip For quick access to the Distribute Shapes and Align Shapes commands, use the Distribute Shapes and Align Shapes buttons on the Action toolbar. To display this toolbar, right-click the toolbar area, and then click Action on the shortcut menu.

Save

17 On the Standard toolbar, click **Save** to save your changes to the diagram.

CLOSE the *ConnectLayout* file.

Key Points

- Diagrams, such as flowcharts, organization charts, and network diagrams, include connectors that represent process sequences, employee relationships and hierarchies, and physical relationships among pieces of equipment.
- You use the Connector tool to create connections in flowcharts. Connectors are 1-D shapes that connect 2-D shapes. In flowcharts, connectors are usually lines or arrows.
- Connectors can be glued to the shapes that they connect. You can break the bond by moving a connector endpoint or deleting the connector. Connectors that are glued to shapes are represented with a red endpoint.
- You can create two types of connections in Visio diagrams: shape-to-shape connections and point-to-point connections. Shape-to-shape connections connect shapes at the two closest points. Point-to-point connections connect shapes at specific connection points. When you move a shape connected by a point-to-point connection, the connector stays attached to the connection point.
- You can add text to a connector the same way you would any other shape—by selecting the connector and typing. Each connector also has a shortcut menu; right-click the connector to display it.
- You can reroute connectors by dragging an endpoint to a new shape or connection point, or by dragging a midpoint on a connector segment. Delete a connector by selecting it and pressing the Del key.
- You can change the layout of all the shapes in your flowchart by clicking Lay Out Shapes on the Shape menu.
- You can distribute three or more shapes evenly by using the Distribute Shapes command on the Shape menu.
- You can align two or more shapes by using the Align Shapes command on the Shape menu. Visio aligns the secondary shapes with the primary shape.

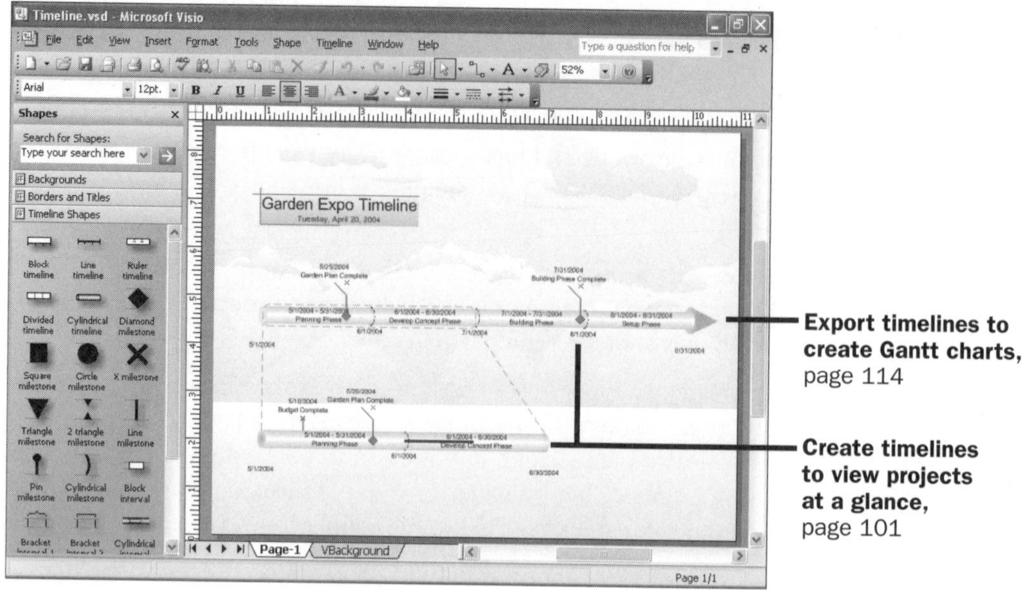

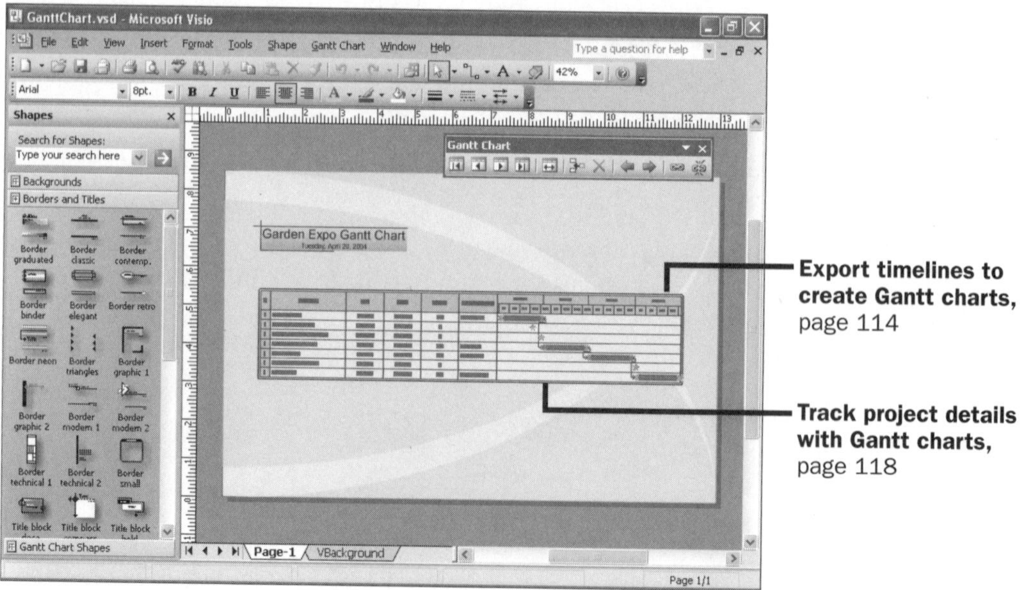

Chapter 5 at a Glance

5 Creating Project Schedules

In this chapter you will learn to:

- ✔ Create timelines to view projects at a glance.
- ✔ Export timelines to create Gantt charts.
- ✔ Track project details with Gantt charts.

Effective project schedules are vital to a successful project. Project schedules help you track project dates, milestones, phases, and tasks. Although there are many ways to create project schedules, the finished product should make it easy to see the progress of the project from the big picture down to the details.

In Microsoft Office Visio, you can use *timelines* to visualize your overall project plan and present this information to executives and others who need to grasp it quickly. For project managers or team members who need more detail, you can create *Gantt charts* that display project specifics in a visual form that's easy to comprehend. Timelines and Gantt charts can help you keep your project on track, and they ultimately contribute to the success of your project.

In this chapter, you'll learn how to use Visio timelines and Gantt charts to track projects and display progress visually. You'll learn how to create a timeline to view the project schedule at a glance, export the timeline data to create a Gantt chart, and track project details with the Gantt chart.

See Also Do you need only a quick refresher on the topics in this chapter? See the Quick Reference entries on pages xxxi–xxxii.

Important Before you can use the practice files in this chapter, you need to install them from the book's companion CD to their default location. See "Using the Book's CD" on page xv for more information.

Creating Timelines to View Projects at a Glance

When you're planning a project, timelines help you visualize the big picture and identify the project's scope. They come in handy when you want to present high-level project information to those who need to view this information at a glance. You can begin creating your timelines during brainstorming sessions and modify them as your project plans develop.

A timeline is a graphic that represents a specific period of time and the events that occur during that period. Timelines are particularly good at showing an overview of a project—project status, history of events, and what's to come. They also usually include milestones and interval markers.

New in Visio 2003

Your project-schedule diagrams can include one or more timelines on a drawing page, and the timelines can be synchronized. For example, you can use an *expanded timeline* to represent a segment of the primary timeline, and then work with the expanded timeline individually to show more detail. You can add milestones or intervals to the expanded timeline just as you would to the primary timeline. The items you add to the expanded timeline don't appear on the primary timeline. However, any shape you add to the primary timeline also appears on the expanded timeline and is synchronized with the shape on the primary timeline. Think of the primary timeline as the complete high-level view of events, and the expanded timeline as a more detailed glimpse into a particular portion of that time period. You can use this synchronized timeline method to display various levels of information for one project—all on one page—in easy-to-understand form.

Milestones represent significant events or dates in a schedule, such as the date the building phase of a project is complete. They can highlight dates when you want to evaluate the progress of your project and make necessary decisions or adjustments. *Interval markers* specify a length of time. Use them to represent the beginning and end of a process or phase. For example, you could use an interval marker to represent the time period of a building phase in a project. You can even show the percentage of the interval that's complete as a line on the interval marker.

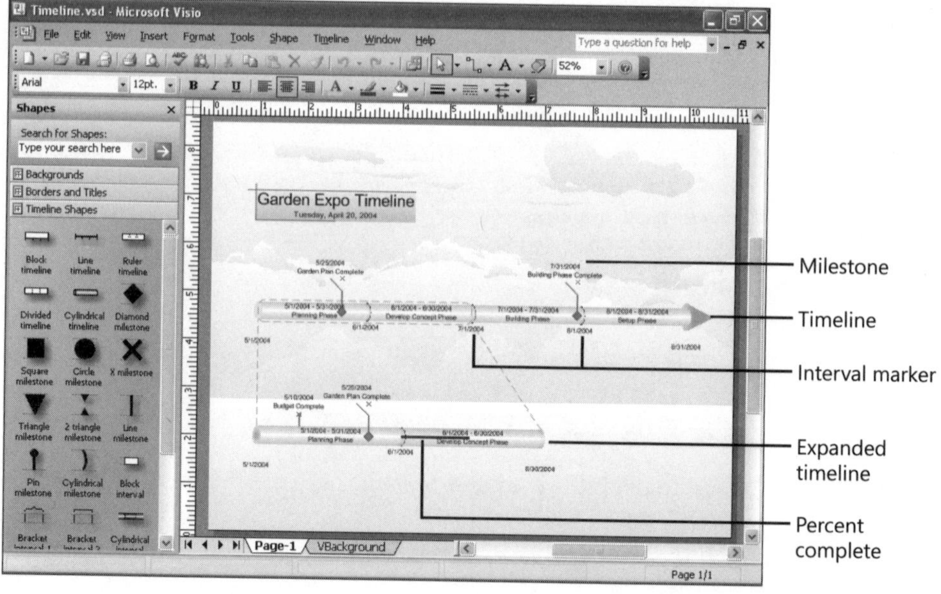

New in Visio 2003

Create timelines with the Timeline template by adding shapes that represent milestones and interval markers to a timeline. After you add shapes to the timeline, you can reposition the shapes by dragging them. Visio updates a shape's date according to its position on the timeline. You can also right-click a shape and reconfigure it by clicking the appropriate command on the shape's shortcut menu. Visio repositions the shape on the timeline according to the shape's date.

In this exercise, you create a primary timeline and an expanded timeline. You add interval markers and milestones to both timelines, and then add a title and background to the diagram.

1. Start Visio. In the Choose Drawing Type window, in the **Category** area, click **Project Schedule**.
2. In the **Template** area, click **Timeline**.

   Visio opens the Timeline template, which opens a blank drawing page and the Timeline Shapes, Borders and Titles, and Backgrounds stencils. This template also inserts a Timeline menu on the Visio menu bar.

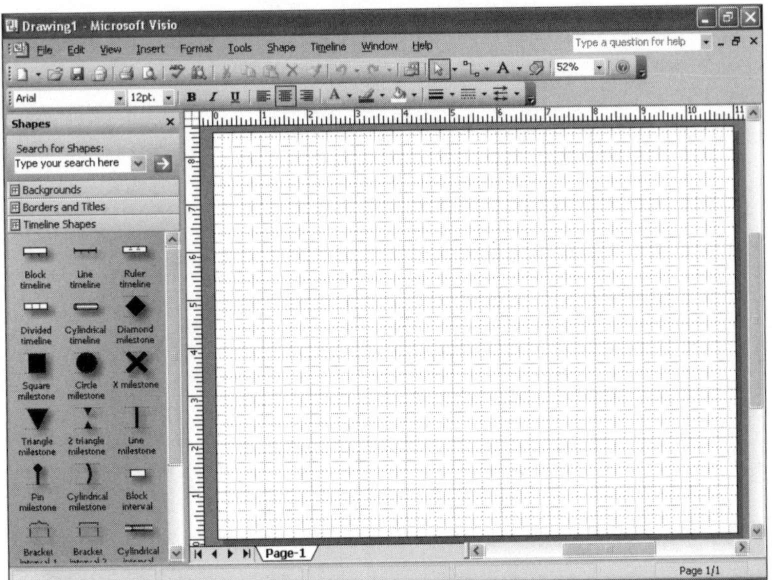

Tip If you already have project data in a Microsoft Office Project, Microsoft Office Excel, or text file format, you can import it into Visio by using the Import Timeline Wizard. After you open the Timeline template, drag a timeline onto the drawing page and configure it. Then on the Timeline menu, click Import Timeline Data. Follow the steps in the wizard to import the project data.

3 From the **Timeline Shapes** stencil, drag a **Cylindrical timeline** shape onto the drawing page.

The Configure Timeline dialog box appears.

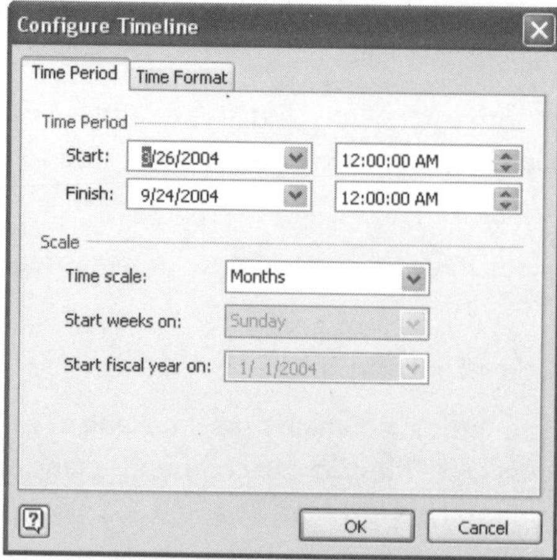

4 In the **Start** box, click the down arrow to display a monthly calendar. In the calendar, click the left or right arrow to display the month of May, and then select the start date for the timeline by clicking **1**.

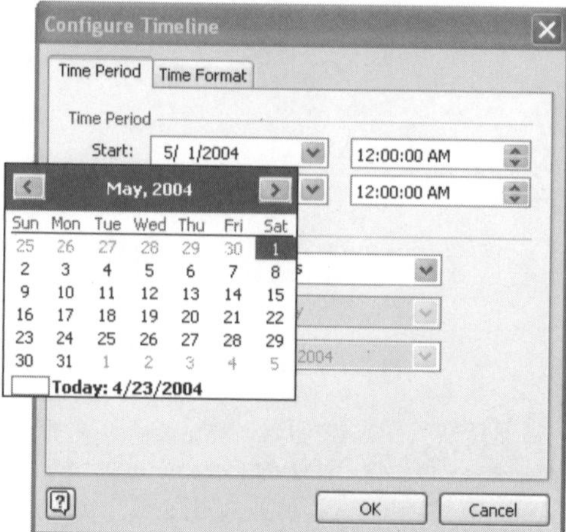

5 In the **Finish** box, click the down arrow to display a monthly calendar. In the calendar, click the left or right arrow to display the month of August, select the finish date for the timeline by clicking **31**, and then click **OK**.

Visio positions the timeline on the drawing page and adds dates to it.

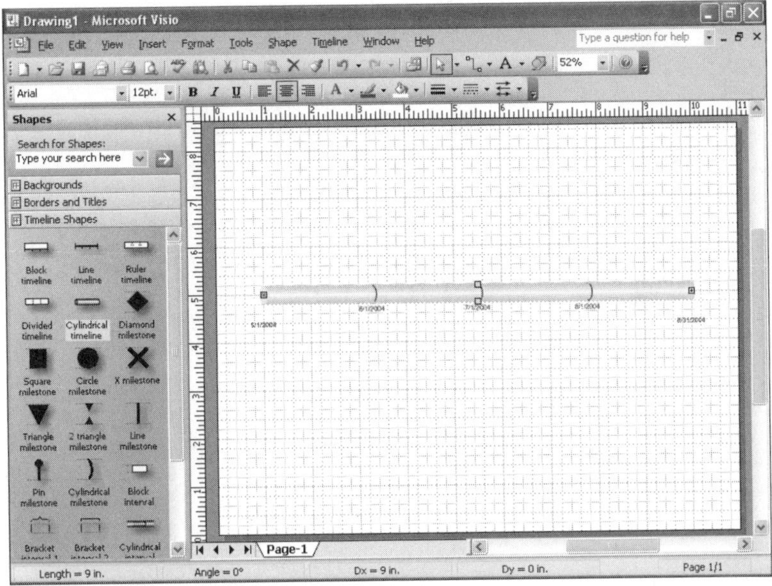

Tip To reconfigure the timeline, right-click it, and then click Configure Timeline on the shortcut menu. Notice the shortcut menu also includes commands for changing the timeline type and date and time formats.

6 To add an arrowhead to the right end of the timeline, right-click the timeline, and then click **Show Finish Arrowhead**.

Visio adds an arrowhead to the right end of the timeline.

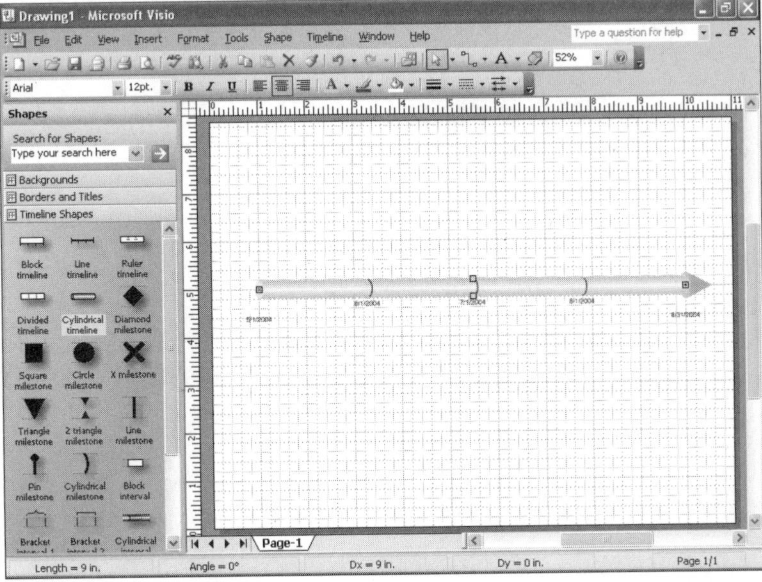

Tip To change the orientation of a timeline, select the timeline, and then on the Shape menu, point to Rotate or Flip, and click the appropriate command.

7 From the **Timeline Shapes** stencil, drag a **Cylindrical interval** shape onto the left area of the timeline.

The Configure Interval dialog box appears.

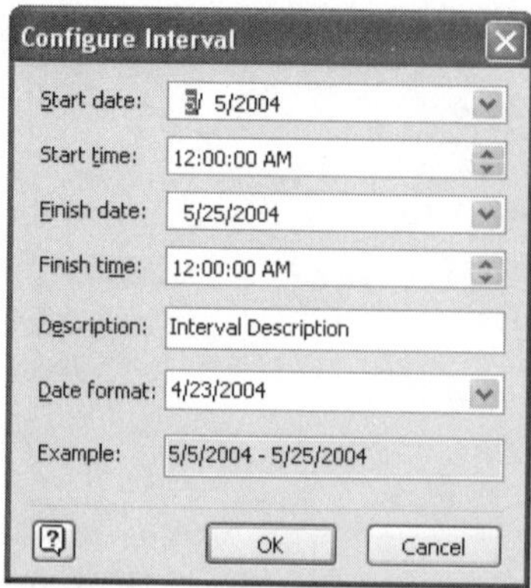

8 In the **Start date** box, click the down arrow to display a monthly calendar. In the calendar, click the left or right arrow to display the month of May, and select the start date for the interval by clicking **1**.

9 In the **Finish date** box, click the down arrow to display a monthly calendar. In the calendar, click the left or right arrow to display the month of May, and select the finish date for the interval by clicking **31**.

10 In the **Description** box, select the placeholder text, and replace it by typing Planning Phase.

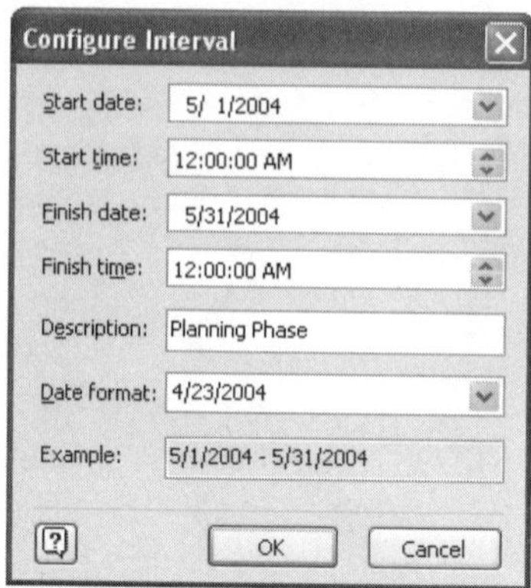

11 Click **OK**.

Visio positions the interval shape in the correct position on the timeline.

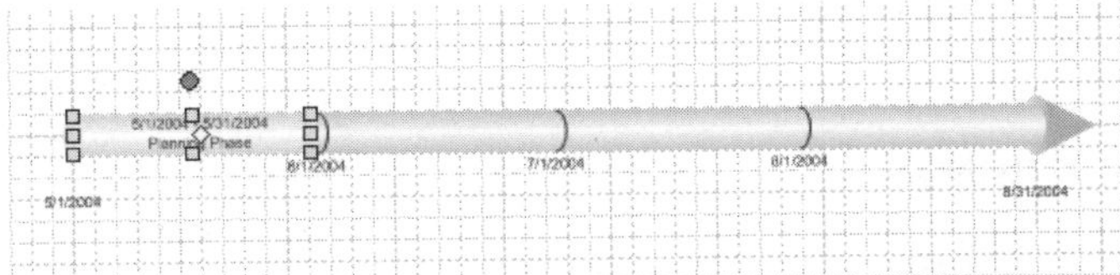

Tip To reconfigure the interval, right-click it, and click Configure Interval on the shortcut menu. To quickly modify the interval description, select the shape, press the F2 key to open the shape's text block, and type a new description. Notice the shortcut menu also includes commands for changing the interval type and showing the percentage of the interval that's complete.

12 From the **Timeline Shapes** stencil, drag three more **Cylindrical interval** shapes onto the timeline and configure them with the information shown in the following table.

Start Date	Finish Date	Label
6/1	6/30	Develop Concept Phase
7/1	7/31	Building Phase
8/1	8/31	Setup Phase

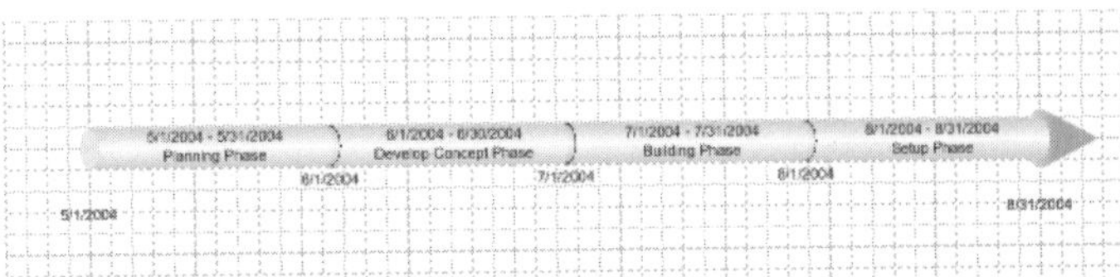

13 From the **Timeline Shapes** stencil, drag a **Diamond milestone** shape anywhere on the timeline.

The Configure Milestone dialog box appears.

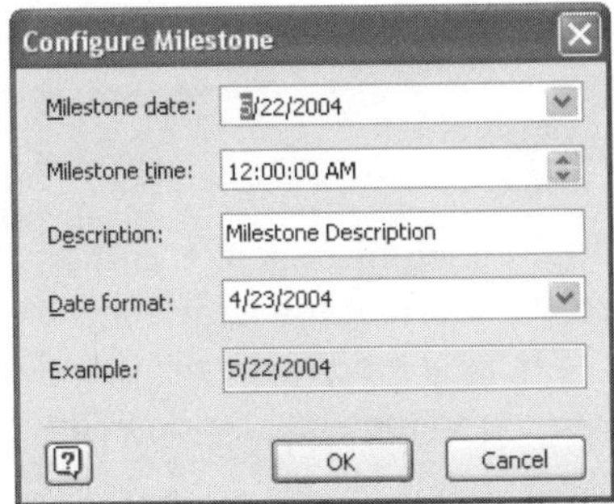

14 In the **Milestone date** box, click the down arrow to display a monthly calendar. In the calendar, click the left or right arrow to display the month of July, and select the milestone date by clicking **31**.

15 In the **Description** box, select the placeholder text, and replace it by typing **Building Phase Complete**.

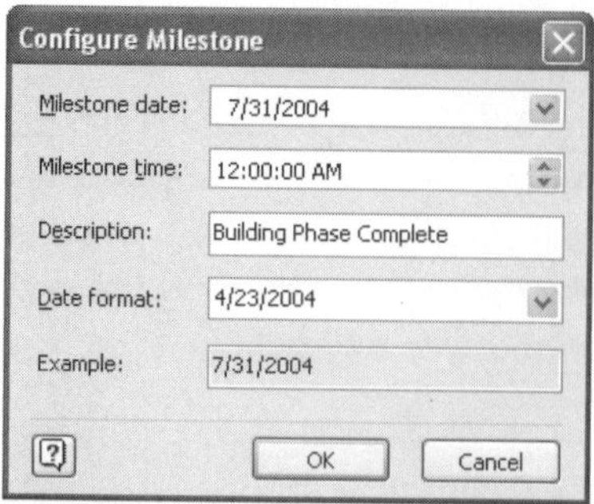

16 Click **OK**.

Visio positions the milestone shape on the timeline.

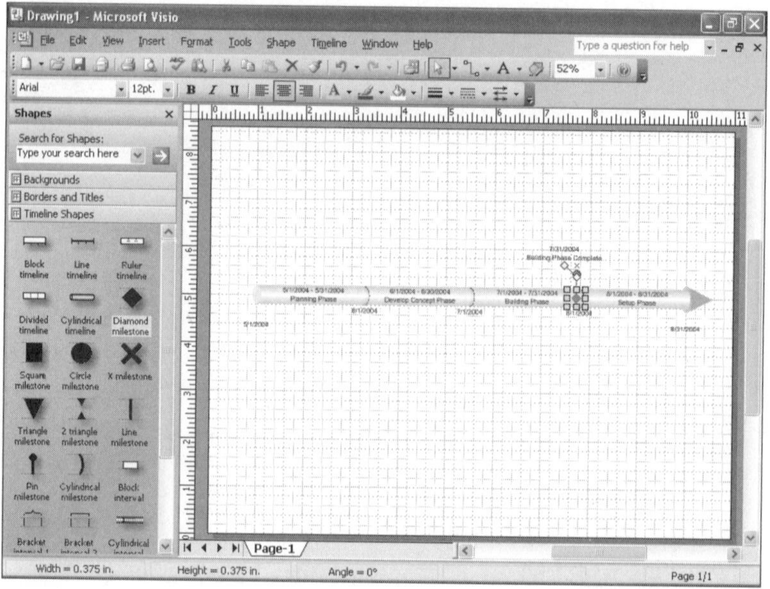

Tip To reconfigure the milestone, right-click it, and click Configure Milestone on the shortcut menu. Notice the shortcut menu also includes commands for changing the milestone type. To quickly modify the milestone description, select the shape, press the F2 key to open the shape's text block, and type a new description.

17 From the **Timeline Shapes** stencil, drag an **Expanded timeline** shape onto the drawing page and position it below and left-aligned with the primary timeline.

The Configure Timeline dialog box appears.

18 In the **Start** box, click the down arrow to display a monthly calendar. In the calendar, click the left or right arrow to display the month of May, and select the start date for the timeline by clicking **1**.

19 In the **Finish** box, click the down arrow to display a monthly calendar. In the calendar, click the left or right arrow to display the month of June, and select the start date for the timeline by clicking **30**.

20 Click **OK**.

Visio adds an expanded timeline for May and June to the drawing page. On the expanded timeline, Visio adds intervals that are synchronized with the intervals on the primary timeline. Gray dashed lines associate the two timelines and indicate the section of the primary timeline that the expanded timeline represents.

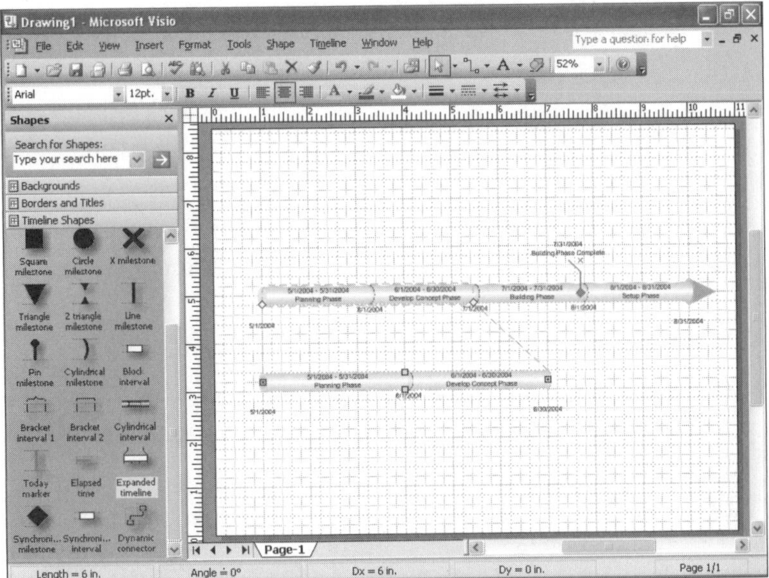

21 From the **Timeline Shapes** stencil, drag a **Pin milestone** shape onto the expanded timeline.

The Configure Milestone dialog box appears.

22 In the **Milestone date** box, click the down arrow to display a monthly calendar. In the calendar, click the left or right arrow to display the month of May, and select the milestone date by clicking **10**.

23 In the **Description** box, select the placeholder text, and replace it by typing **Budget Complete**.

24 Click **OK**.

Visio positions the milestone shape on the expanded timeline. Notice that the milestone doesn't appear on the primary timeline.

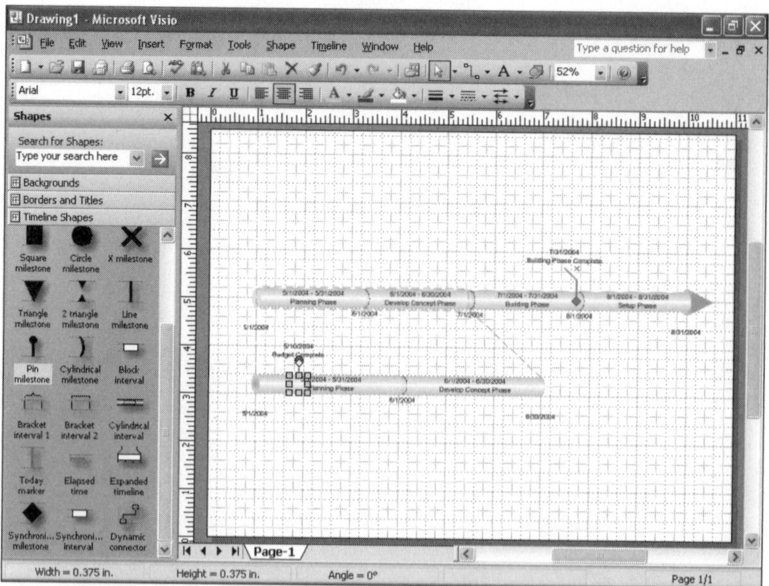

25 From the **Timeline Shapes** stencil, drag a **Diamond milestone** shape onto the primary timeline.

The Configure Milestone dialog box appears.

26 In the **Milestone date** box, click the down arrow to display a monthly calendar. In the calendar, click the left or right arrow to display the month of May, and select the milestone date by clicking **20**.

27 In the **Description** box, select the placeholder text, and replace it by typing **Garden Plan Complete**.

28 Click **OK**.

Visio positions the milestone shape on the primary timeline. Notice that the milestone also appears on the expanded timeline.

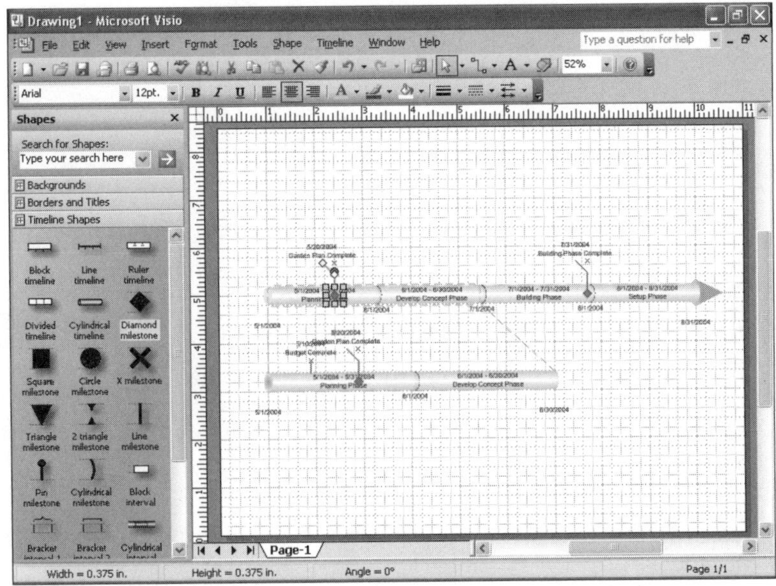

29 Right-click the **Garden Plan Complete** milestone on the primary timeline, and click **Configure Milestone** on the shortcut menu.

30 In the **Milestone date** box, click the down arrow to display a monthly calendar. In the calendar, select the milestone date by clicking **25**, and then click **OK**.

Visio repositions the milestone shape on both timelines.

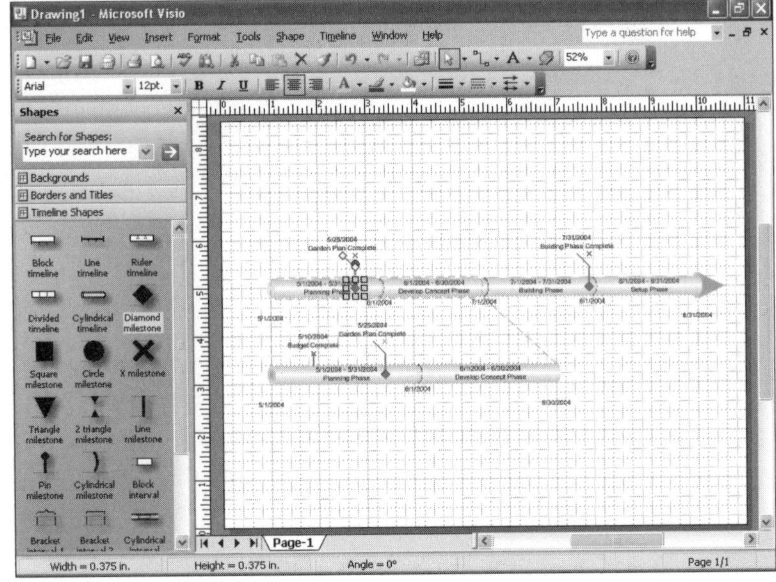

31 Right-click the **Develop Concept Phase** interval marker on the expanded timeline, and click **Set Percent Complete** on the shortcut menu.

32 In the **Percent Complete** box, type 50, and then click **OK**.

33 Right-click the **Develop Concept Phase** interval marker on the expanded timeline, and click **Show Percent Complete** on the shortcut menu.

Visio shows the percent complete with a line on the interval marker. Notice the line appears on the expanded timeline, but not on the primary timeline.

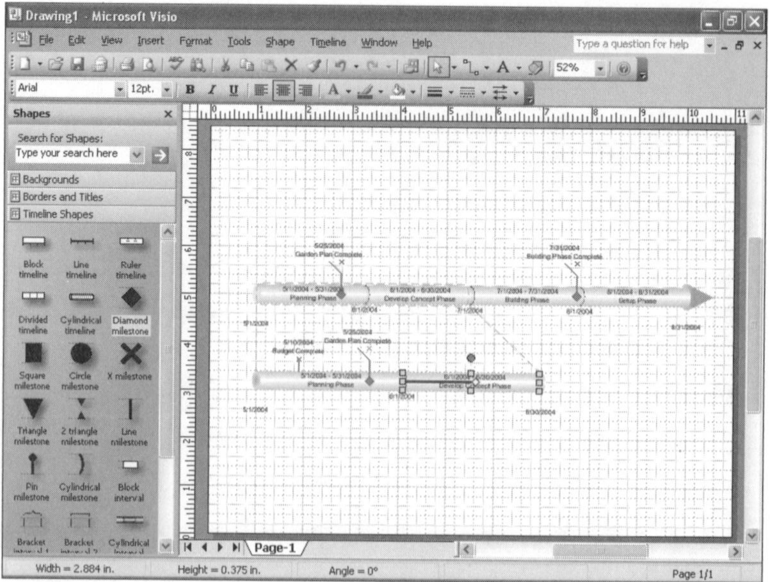

34 To add a background to the diagram, click the **Backgrounds** stencil, and drag the **Background mountains** shape onto the drawing page.

Visio adds a mountain background to the diagram.

35 To add a title to the diagram, click the **Borders and Titles** stencil, drag the **Title block contemp.** shape onto the drawing page, and position it in the upper-left corner of the page.

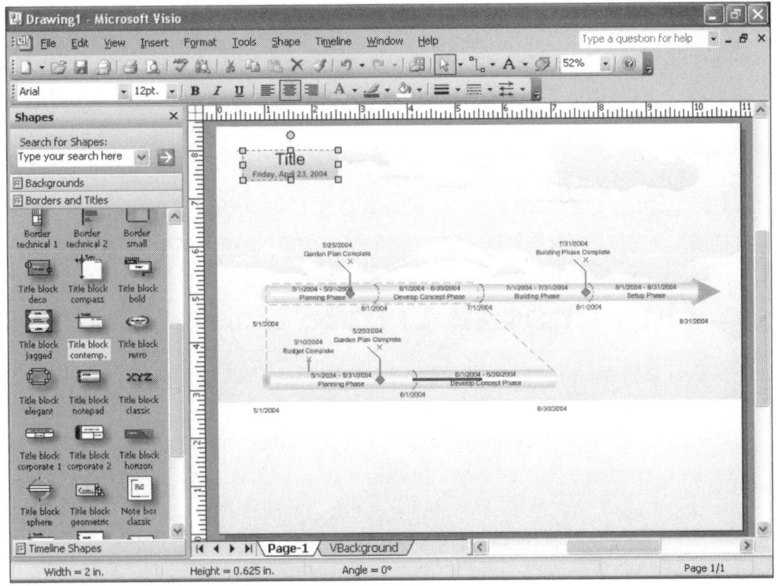

36 With the **Title block contemp.** shape selected, press the F2 key.

37 Highlight the word **Title**, and type **Garden Expo Timeline**.

The shape expands to fit your title.

38 Click the pasteboard to close the text block and deselect the title shape.

39 Click the title shape, and drag it to align it with the left edge of the timeline.

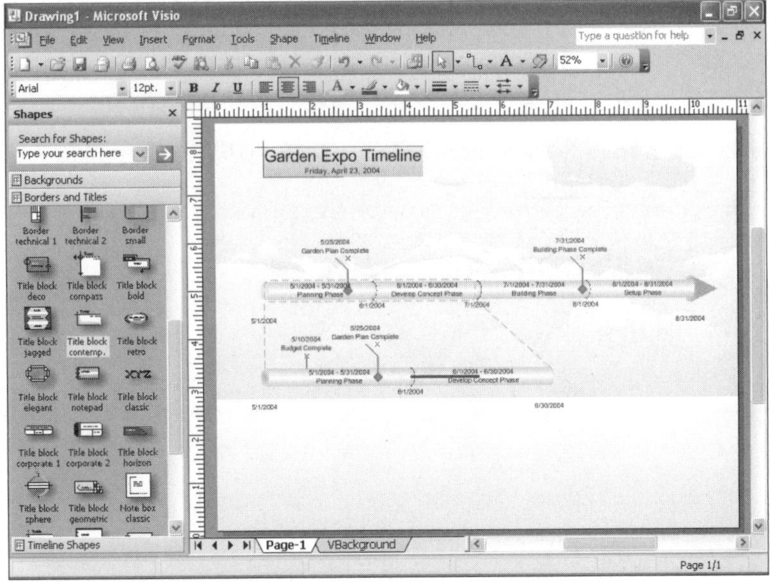

40 On the **File** menu, click **Save As** to open the **Save As** dialog box.

41 In the **File name** box, type Timeline, and then click the **Save** button to save the diagram.

CLOSE the *Timeline* file.

Tip For more information about creating timelines, type Timeline in the "Type a question for help" box in the upper-right corner of the Visio window.

Exporting Timelines to Create Gantt Charts

When you use Visio diagrams to schedule your projects, you usually start by visualizing the big picture with timelines, and then you create Gantt charts to display project details. Instead of creating a Gantt chart from scratch, you can export your timeline data to the Microsoft Office Project file format with the Export Timeline Data command. You can use this data to create a Visio Gantt chart by using the Import Project Data Wizard, which is available on the Gantt Chart menu in a diagram started using the Gantt Chart template.

Tip As you revise your Gantt charts, you'll no doubt make changes to the overall schedule as well. Just as you can export timeline data to create Gantt charts, you can also export Gantt chart data to create new timelines by using the Export Project Data Wizard, which you can start by clicking the Export command on the Gantt Chart menu.

In this exercise, you open an existing timeline, and use the Export Timeline Data command to export the timeline data. Then you use the Import Project Data Wizard to create a Gantt chart from that data.

Important To complete this exercise, you need Microsoft Office Project (version 2000 or later) installed on your computer. If you don't have Project installed, the Export Timeline Data command doesn't appear on the Timeline menu.

OPEN the *Timeline* file in the My Documents\Microsoft Press\Visio 2003 SBS\CreatingSchedules folder.

1 Select the primary timeline on the drawing page.

Troubleshooting You must select a timeline on the drawing page before you can export timeline data. To quickly select a timeline, click either edge of the timeline.

2 On the **Timeline** menu, click **Export Timeline Data**.

3 A message appears that asks you if you'd like to export all markers on the timeline's expanded child timelines. Click **No**.

The Export Timeline Data dialog box appears.

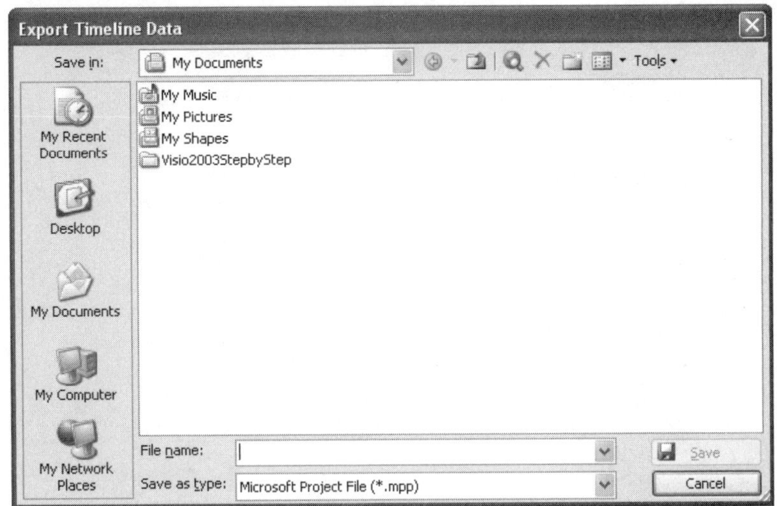

4 In the **File name** box, type TimelineData, and then click **Save**.

Visio saves the timeline data in Microsoft Project File (*.mpp) file format and in the My Documents folder by default.

Tip You can open the exported timeline data in Project to plan your projects in more detail and incorporate them into other enterprise schedules.

5 When you see a message stating that the project has been successfully exported, click **OK**.

6 On the **File** menu, point to **New**, point to **Project Schedule**, and then click **Gantt Chart**.

Visio opens the Gantt Chart template and three stencils, and the Gantt Chart Options dialog box appears. When you open the Gantt Chart template, a Gantt Chart menu and toolbar also appear.

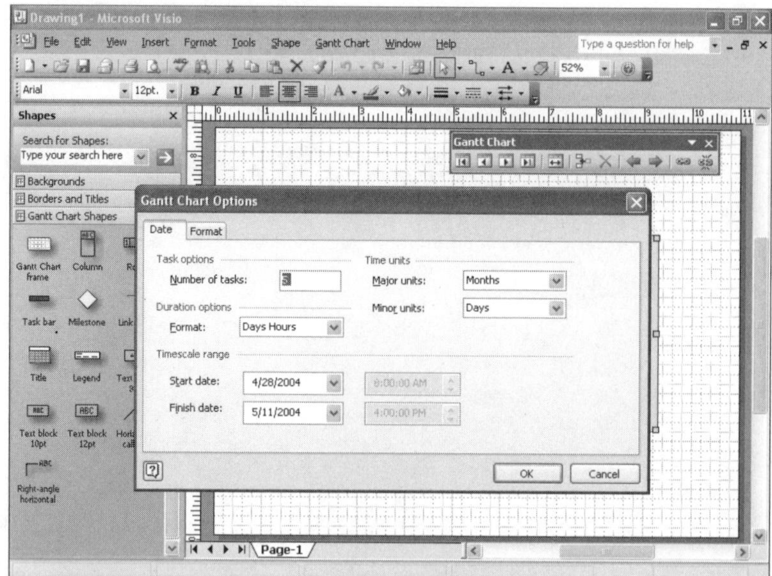

7 In the **Gantt Chart Options** dialog box, click **Cancel**.

Visio deletes the Gantt chart frame from the drawing page and closes the Gantt Chart Options dialog box.

8 On the **Gantt Chart** menu, click **Import**.

The first page of the Import Project Data Wizard appears.

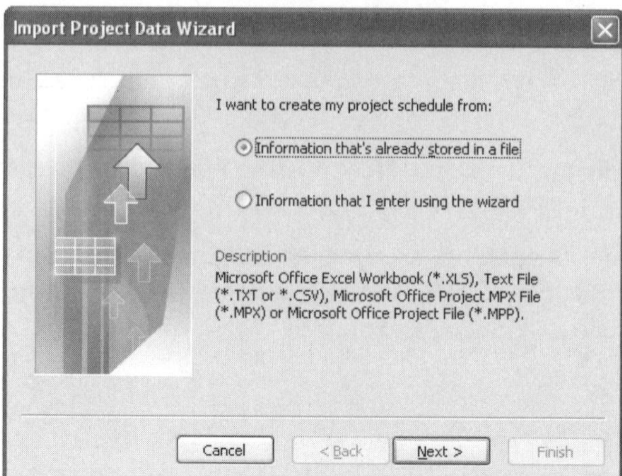

9 On the first page of the **Import Project Data Wizard**, select the **Information that's already stored in a file** option, and then click **Next**.

10 On the second page of the **Import Project Data Wizard**, click **Microsoft Office Project File**, and then click **Next**.

11 On the third page of the **Import Project Data Wizard**, click **Browse**, navigate to the My Documents folder, double-click **TimelineData**, and then click **Next**.

12 On the fourth page of the **Import Project Data Wizard**, click **Next**.

The wizard populates the pages with information used most often in Gantt charts, so you don't need to make any changes and can accept the default information.

13 On the fifth page of the **Import Project Data Wizard**, click **Next**.

By default, Visio includes all tasks from the data in the Gantt chart.

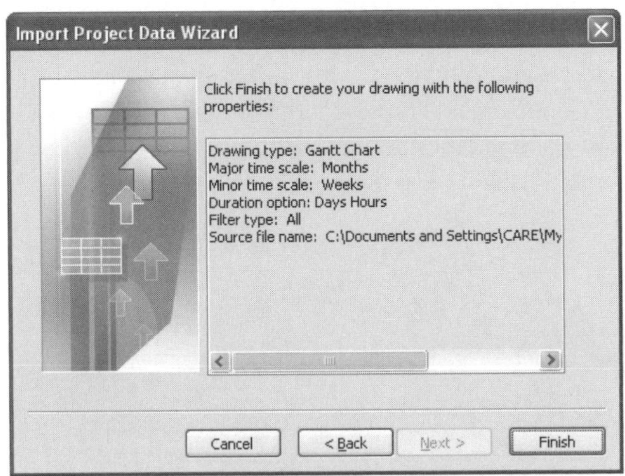

14 On the last page of the **Import Project Data Wizard**, click **Finish**.

Visio creates the Gantt chart from the timeline data.

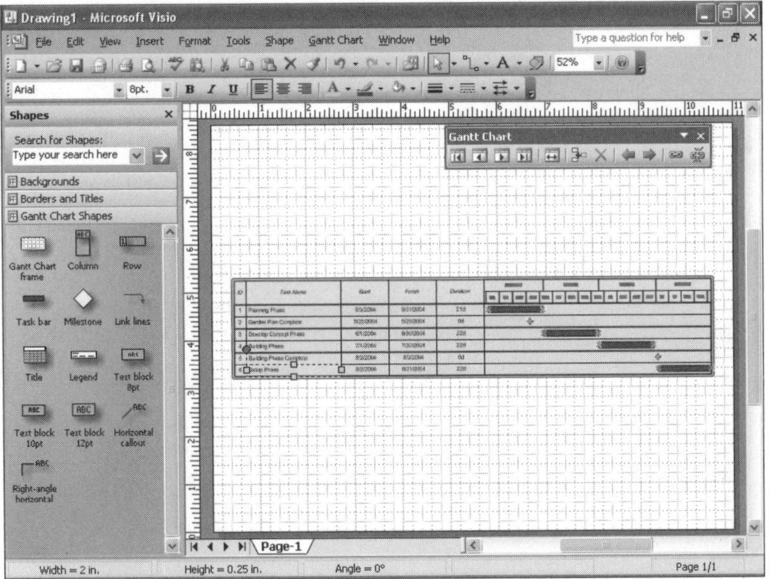

15 On the **File** menu, click **Save As** to open the **Save As** dialog box.

16 In the **File name** box, type **NewGantt**, and then click the **Save** button to save the drawing.

CLOSE the *NewGantt* file.

Tracking Project Details with Gantt Charts

Just as you use Visio timelines to view your project at a glance, you use Gantt charts to manage the project details. With Gantt charts, you can track the details of each project task, create task dependencies, see how changes to one task affect another, and quickly identify task owners and status. A Gantt chart includes a list of project tasks and details about the tasks, *Gantt bars* that represent the duration of each task, and a timescale. With Gantt charts, you can track the specifics that project managers and project members need to complete their tasks and keep the project on schedule.

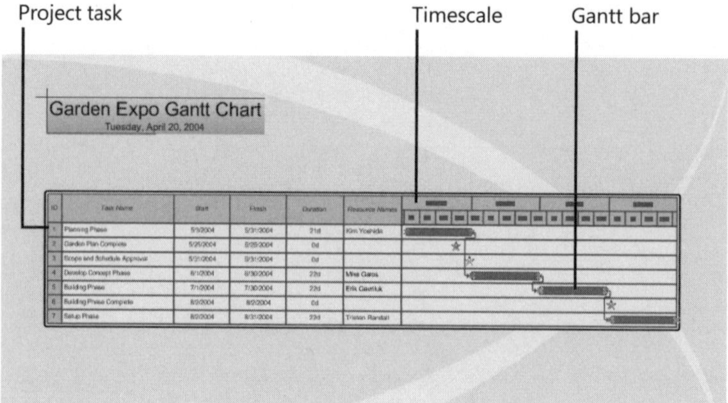

You can create Gantt charts from existing timeline data by using the Import Project Data Wizard or from scratch by using the Gantt Chart template. To create a Gantt chart from scratch, on the File menu, point to New, point to Project Schedule, and then click Gantt Chart. Then use the Gantt Chart Options dialog box to configure and format your Gantt chart.

After you create a Gantt chart from existing data or from scratch, you add rows and columns to the chart. Each row represents a task, and each Gantt bar in a row represents the duration of the task. Each column represents project data you want to track, such as start date, end date, percentage complete, resource name, and task notes.

You can also show that one task can't start until another ends by creating task dependencies. To create task dependencies, you select the Gantt bar for the task that starts first, select the bar for the next task, and then link the bars. Visio draws arrows between the linked tasks.

In this exercise, you open the Gantt chart you created in the previous exercise and track task details by creating task dependencies, inserting columns, and creating new tasks. For visual appeal, you also add a title and background to the diagram.

OPEN the *NewGantt* file in the My Documents\Microsoft Press\Visio 2003 SBS\CreatingSchedules folder.

1. Select the first blue Gantt bar in the chart.

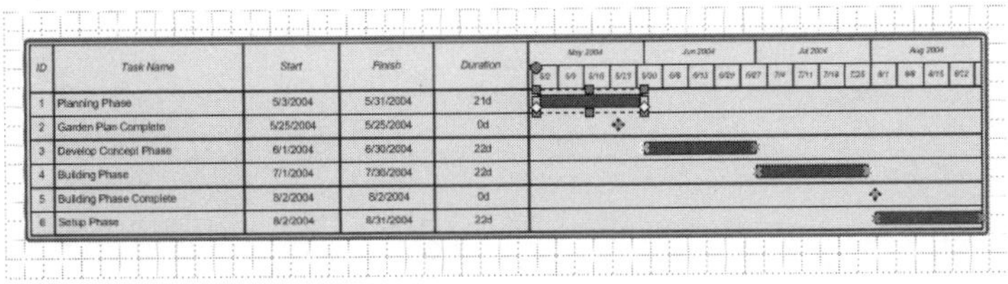

2. Hold down the Shift key while you select the three other Gantt bars, from top to bottom.

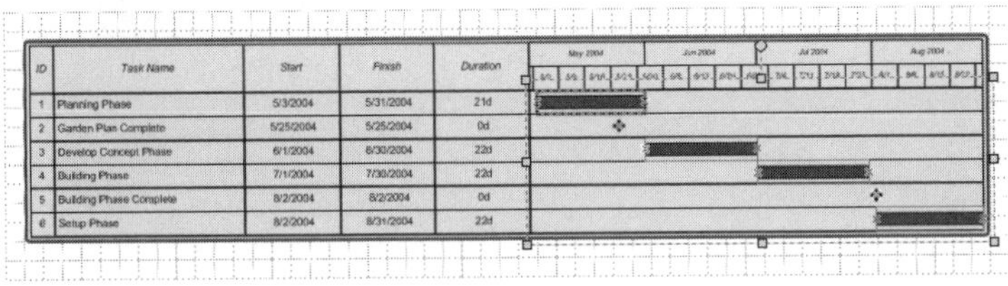

   Important The order in which you select and link the tasks is important. Select the Gantt bar for the task that starts first, the bar for the task that can't start until the other ends, and so on. The bar you select first (the primary shape) is enclosed by a dark magenta selection box. The selection boxes for the other bars (secondary shapes) are light magenta, and the selection box for all the shapes is green.

3. To create task dependencies, on the **Gantt Chart** menu, click **Link Tasks**.

   Visio links the selected tasks with lines.

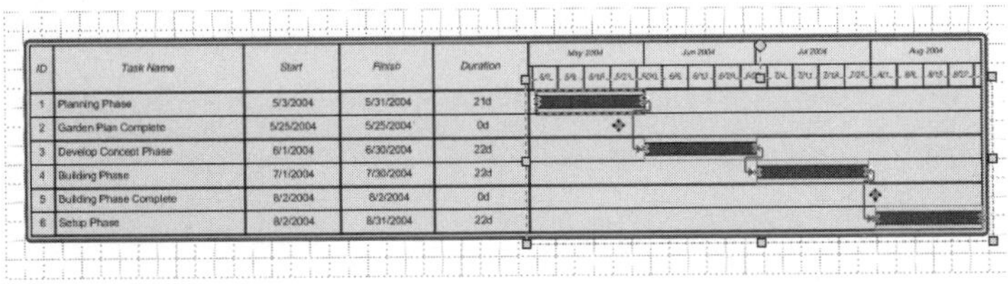

   Tip Alternatively, you could right-click one of the selected tasks, and click Link Tasks on the shortcut menu. To unlink tasks, select the tasks you want to unlink, right-click one of the selected tasks, and then click Unlink Tasks on the shortcut menu.

4 Press the Esc key to deselect everything.

5 To track more task details, right-click the **Duration** column, and then click **Insert Column**.

The Insert Column dialog box appears.

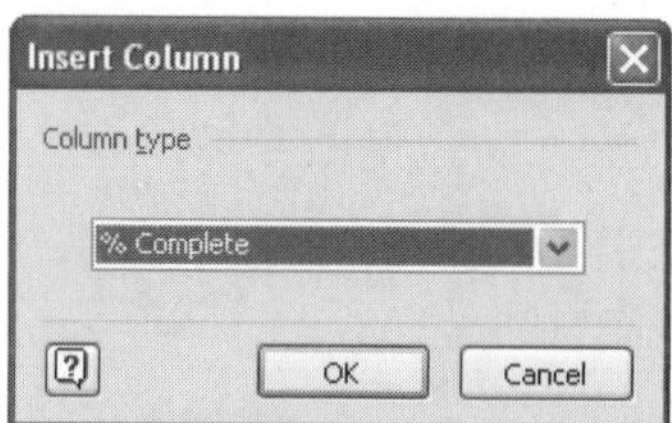

6 To add column with which you can track each task owner, click the down arrow, click **Resource Names** in the list, and then click **OK**.

Visio inserts the Resource Names column after the Duration column.

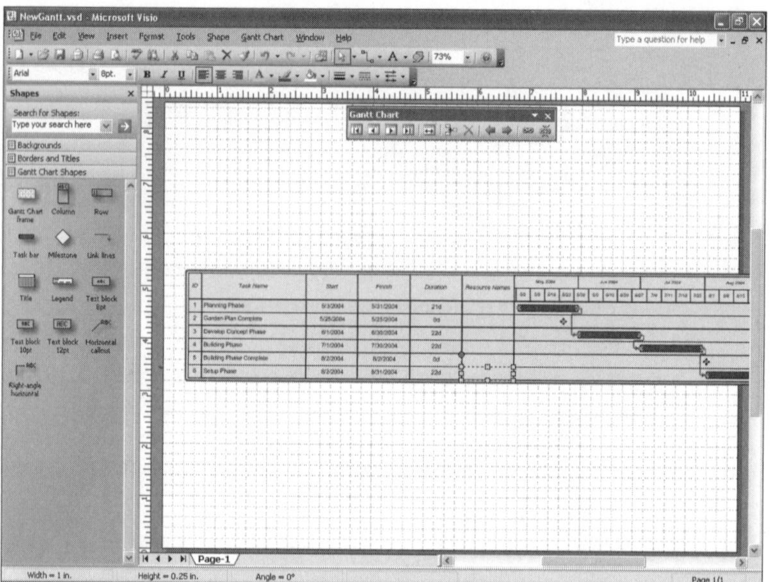

7 On the **Shape** menu, click **Center Drawing**.

Visio centers the Gantt chart on the drawing page.

8 Select the first cell in the **Resource Names** column, and type Kim Akers.

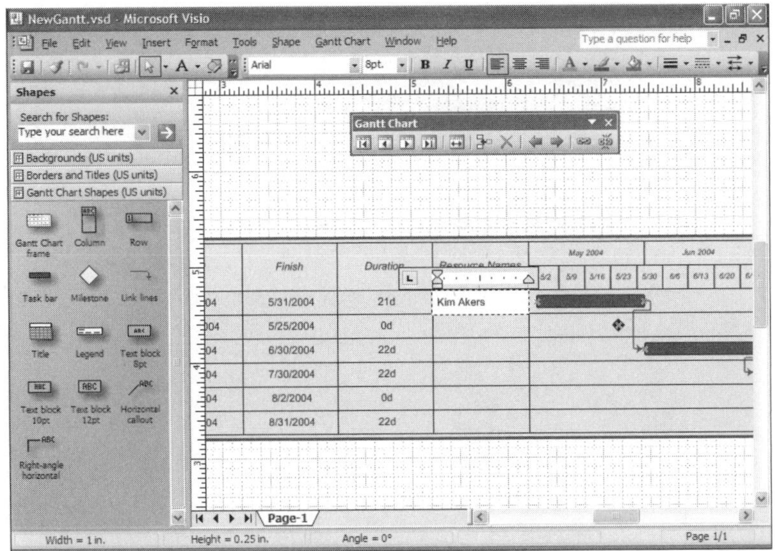

9 Skip the second cell, select the third cell in the **Resource Names** column, and type Mike Gahrns.

10 Select the fourth cell in the **Resource Names** column, and type Eric Gruber.

11 Skip the fifth cell, select the last cell in the **Resource Names** column, and type Linda Randall.

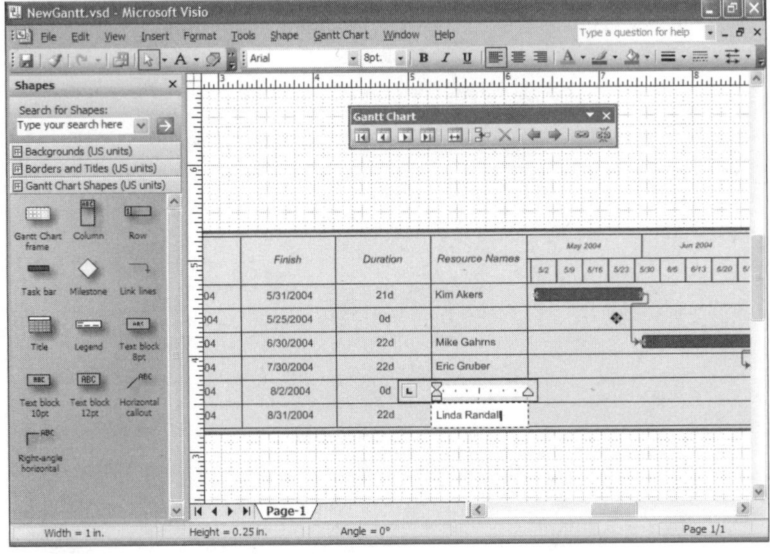

12 To add one more milestone to the Gantt chart, in the **ID** column, right-click 3 (the third row), and then click **New Task** on the shortcut menu.

Visio inserts a row before the Develop Concept Phase task row and selects the Task Name cell in the new row.

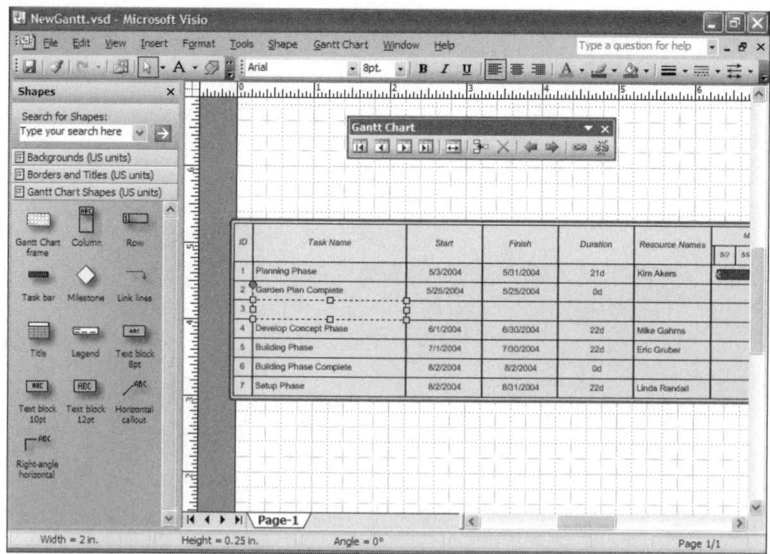

Tip You can add more tasks to the end of your Gantt chart by selecting the Gantt chart frame and dragging it down. You can delete tasks at the end of the chart by dragging the Gantt chart frame back up.

13 With the **Task Name** cell for the new milestone selected, type Scope and Schedule Approval.

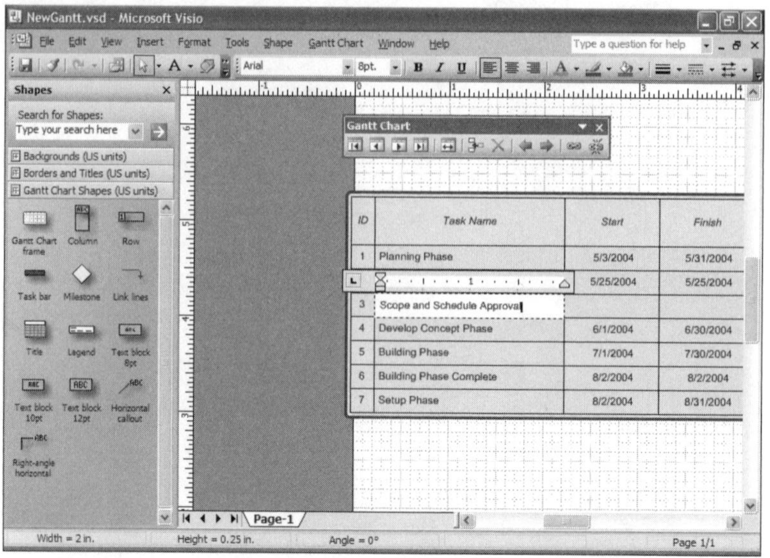

14 Select the **Start** cell for the new milestone.

Visio inserts default task information for you.

15 Type 5/31, and click the drawing page outside the Gantt chart.

Visio changes the finish date to match the start date of the milestone.

16 To make this task a milestone, select the **Duration** cell for the task, type 0 because milestones don't have duration, and then click the drawing page outside the Gantt chart.

Visio changes the Gantt bar to a diamond.

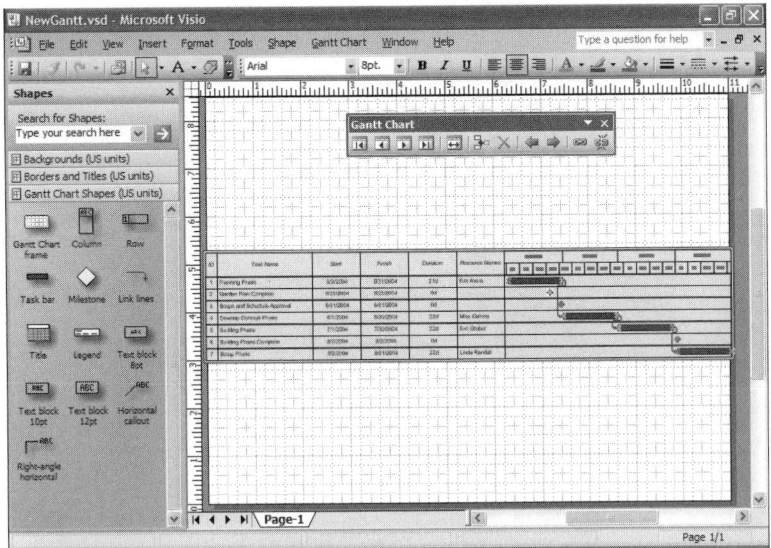

17 To change the milestone shape to a star for all the milestones in the Gantt chart, on the **Gantt Chart** menu, click **Options**.

The Gantt Chart Options dialog box appears.

18 Click the **Format** tab, and in the **Shape** drop-down list, click **Star**.

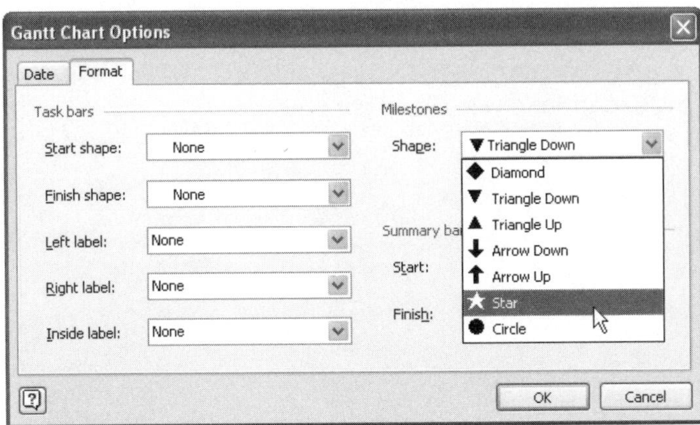

19 Click **OK**.

Visio changes the milestone shapes in the Gantt chart from diamonds to stars.

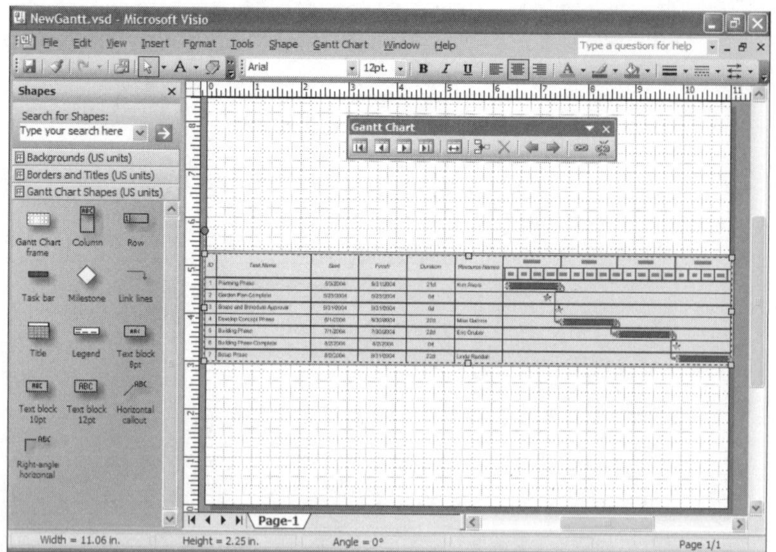

20 To change the drawing page size so the Gantt chart fits on the page, on the **File** menu, click **Page Setup**.

The Page Setup dialog box appears.

21 Click the **Page Size** tab, and in the **Page size** area, select the **Custom size** option. In the **Custom size** area, type 13 in the first box.

22 Click **OK**.

Visio widens the drawing page.

23 On the **Shape** menu, click **Center Drawing**.

Visio centers the Gantt chart on the drawing page.

24 To add a background to the diagram, click the **Backgrounds** stencil, and drag the **Background web** shape onto the drawing page.

Visio creates a background for the diagram.

25 To add a title to the diagram, click the **Borders and Titles** stencil, drag the **Title block contemp.** shape onto the drawing page, and position it in the upper-left corner of the page.

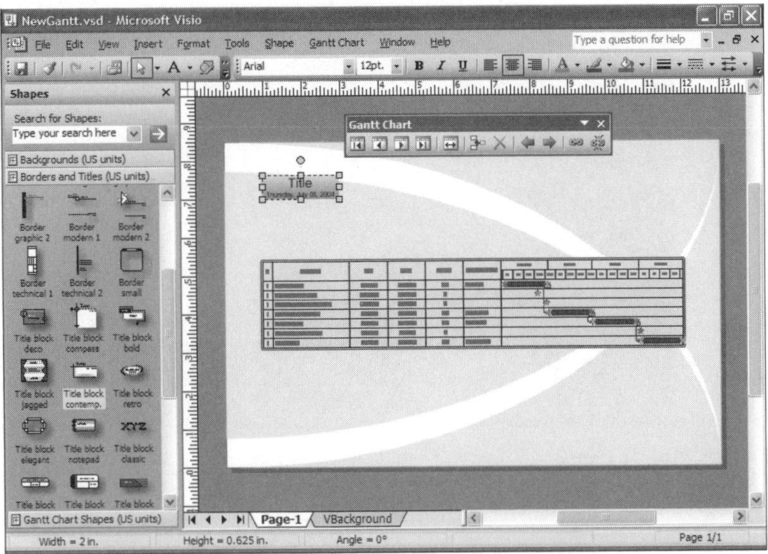

26 With the **Title block contemp.** shape selected, press the F2 key.

27 Highlight the word **Title**, and type a new title, Garden Expo Gantt Chart.

The shape expands to fit your title.

28 Click the pasteboard to close the text block and deselect the title shape.

29 Click the title shape, and drag it to align it with the left edge of the Gantt chart.

30 To add a color scheme to your timeline, right-click the drawing page, and click **Color Schemes**.

The Color Schemes dialog box appears.

31 In the **Choose a color scheme** list, click **Coffee**, and then click **OK**.

Visio changes the color scheme of the diagram.

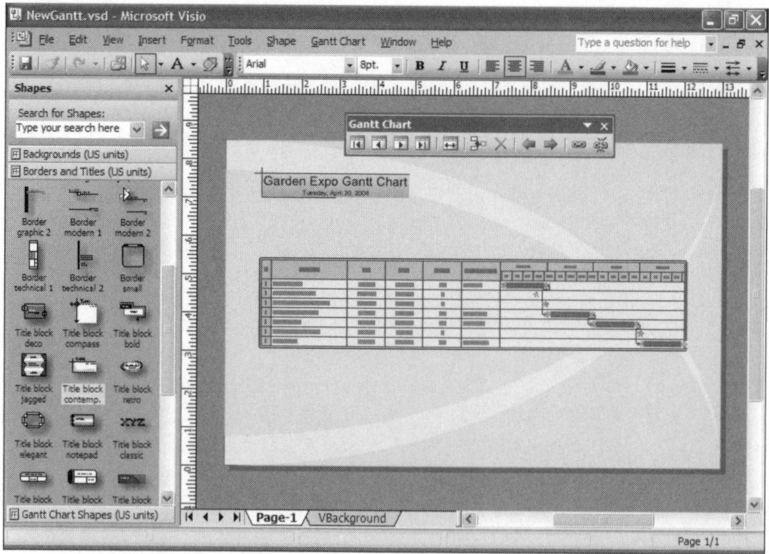

32 On the **File** menu, click **Save As** to open the **Save As** dialog box.

33 In the **File name** box, type **GanttChart**, and click the **Save** button to save the diagram.

CLOSE the *GanttChart* file.

Tip For more information on creating Gantt charts, type "Gantt chart" in the "Type a question for help" box in the upper-right corner of the Visio window.

Key Points

- A timeline is a graphic that represents a specific period of time and the events that occur during that time. Timelines are particularly good at showing an overview of a project–project status, a history of events, and what's to come. Use the Timeline template in the Project Schedule category to create timelines.
- Use expanded timelines to show a segment of the primary timeline in more detail.
- With Gantt charts, you can track the details of each project task, create task dependencies, see how changes to one task affect another, and quickly identify task owners and status. Use the Gantt Chart template in the Project Schedule category to create timelines.
- You can create timelines from scratch or from existing data. To import data to create timelines, open the Timeline template, and on the Timeline menu, click Import Timeline Data. To export data from a timeline, on the Timeline menu, click Export Timeline Data.
- You can create Gantt charts from scratch or from existing data. To import data to create Gantt charts, open the Gantt chart template, and on the Gantt Chart menu, click Import. To export data from a Gantt chart, on the Gantt Chart menu, click Export.
- When you export data from Visio timelines and Gantt charts, Visio saves the data in Microsoft Office Project file format so you can work with the data in Project.
- Right-click the shapes in timelines and Gantt charts to see their formatting options.

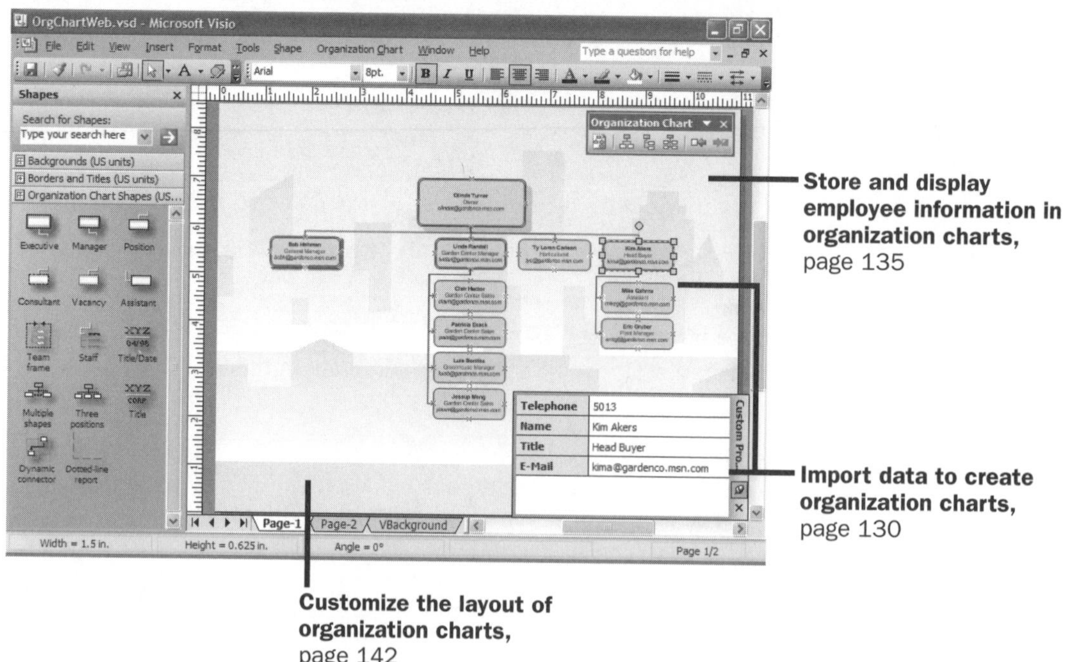

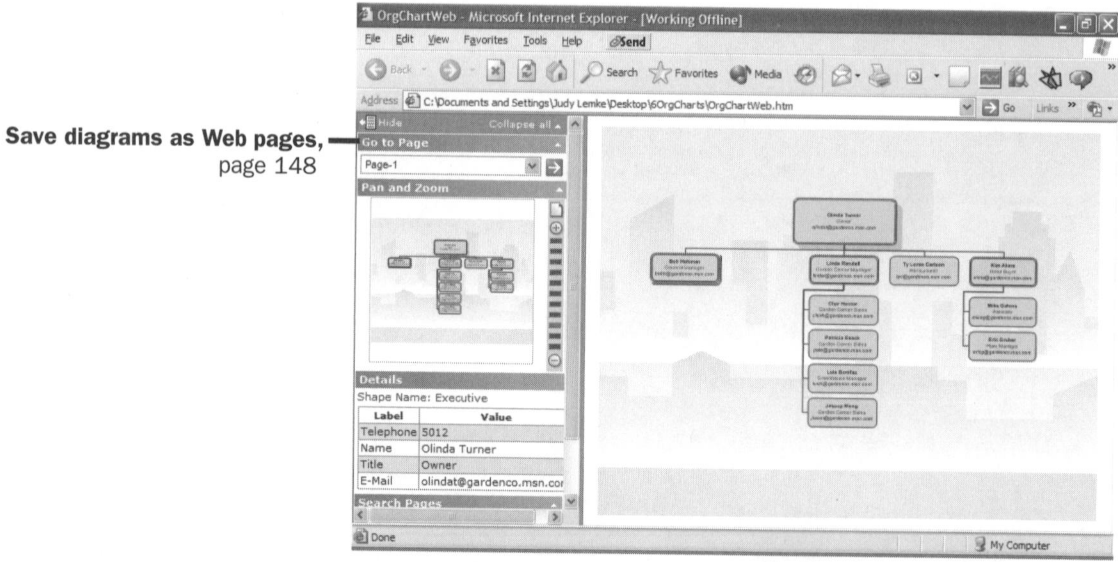

Chapter 6 at a Glance

6 Creating Organization Charts

In this chapter you will learn to:

- ✔ Import data to create organization charts.
- ✔ Store and display employee information in organization charts.
- ✔ Customize the layout of organization charts.
- ✔ Save diagrams as Web pages.

New in Visio 2003

Organization charts are used to visually document the groups within an organization—such as departments and teams—and their reporting relationships. Using the Organization Chart template in Microsoft Office Visio, you can easily create organization charts by dragging shapes, which represent people within an organization, onto the drawing page. By taking advantage of the intelligent behavior of these shapes, you can show employee relationships within an organization. For example, when you drag shapes on top of other shapes, Visio positions and connects the shapes for you, creating the reporting hierarchy as you add shapes to the drawing page. Shapes in organization charts can also store information about the people and relationships within the organization, and you can show as much or little of that information as you choose. You can also rearrange the shapes in a chart and create synchronized copies of departments without redrawing the hierarchy from scratch.

With the Organization Chart Wizard template, you have even more options. The template includes a step-by-step approach to building organization charts from information stored in data files or information that you enter in the wizard. If you already have organization data stored in a file and you don't want to create a chart from scratch, or if you prefer entering data into a wizard rather than dragging shapes onto a drawing page, this template is for you. You can also share an organization chart—or any type of Visio diagram—by saving it as a Web page and publishing it to a Web site, such as a corporate intranet site. Colleagues or team members in any location can easily view the chart with a Web browser at any time of day or night, making global collaboration easier.

In this chapter, you import human resources data from a Microsoft Office Excel spreadsheet to create an organization chart for The Garden Company. You view the additional data stored with each shape, modify the data, display some of the data in the chart, and then format the text in all the shapes. You change the layout of the organization chart, insert a hyperlink, and add color and a background to enhance the appearance of the chart. Finally, you save the chart as a Web page and view it in a Web browser.

See Also Do you need only a quick refresher on the topics in this chapter? See the Quick Reference entries on pages xxxii–xxxiv.

Important Before you can use the practice files in this chapter, you need to install them from the book's companion CD to their default location. See "Using the Book's CD" on page xv for more information.

Importing Data to Create Organization Charts

Today, many organizations maintain human resources information in electronic form. With the Organization Chart Wizard template, you can create an organization chart by importing employee information already stored in corporate data sources such as databases and data files. If the organizational structure changes, you can simply update the chart rather than having to re-create it–a huge timesaver, especially for large organizations. You can import organization data from Microsoft Office Excel spreadsheets (.xls), text files (.txt), Microsoft Office Exchange Server directories, Microsoft Office Access databases (.mdb), or any ODBC-compliant (Open Data Base Connectivity) database application.

Important For the Organization Chart Wizard template to work, the source data must be properly formatted and include, at minimum, data identifying unique employee names and the managers to whom they report. In an Excel spreadsheet, columns of information represent data fields that can be imported to create an organization chart. For example, a human resources spreadsheet might include columns listing each person's name, manager, department, title, e-mail address, phone number, and office number.

New in Visio 2003

With the Organization Chart Wizard template, you first specify the data source you want to use to import the data, and then you determine which columns contain the information for the organization chart. In a typical chart, Visio uses an Employee Name field and a Reports to field (the manager's name) to specify the reporting structure. That means that every employee name in the data source must be associated with the name of the manager to whom the employee reports (except the person at the very top of the organization). For example, if Luis Bonifaz (employee) reports to Bob Hohman (manager), the data source must include both of those pieces of information so that Visio can structure the organization chart correctly.

Next, you select the data fields you want to appear in the organization chart and identify the additional fields you want to import as custom properties. *Custom properties* are categories of information that are stored with each shape and that correspond to data. For example, a Manager shape might include a Telephone custom property, and the telephone number would be the custom property data. Custom property data might not be displayed in the chart, but it is additional information about each employee. For example, custom properties for a shape might include Name, Manager, Department, Title, E-mail Address, Phone Number, and Office Number. However, your organization chart might display only each employee's name and title. The additional custom property data can be viewed through the Custom Properties window in Visio, but it doesn't appear in the organization chart.

Tip Depending on the size and number of shapes in your organization charts, you might need to periodically zoom in to the drawing page to see the shapes and text more clearly.

In this exercise, you import data from an Excel spreadsheet to generate an organization chart for The Garden Company. In addition to importing the Name and Reports to fields, you import data identifying the title, telephone number, and e-mail address for each employee.

Tip For help creating organization charts, type "organization chart" in the "Type a question for help" box on the right side of the menu bar.

USE the *TGC Employees.xls* file located in the My Documents\Microsoft Press\Visio 2003 SBS \CreatingCharts folder.

1. Start Visio. In the Choose Drawing Type window, in the **Category** area, click **Organization Chart**. In the **Template** area, click **Organization Chart Wizard**.

   The Organization Chart Wizard template opens a drawing page, three stencils, and the first page of the Organization Chart Wizard.

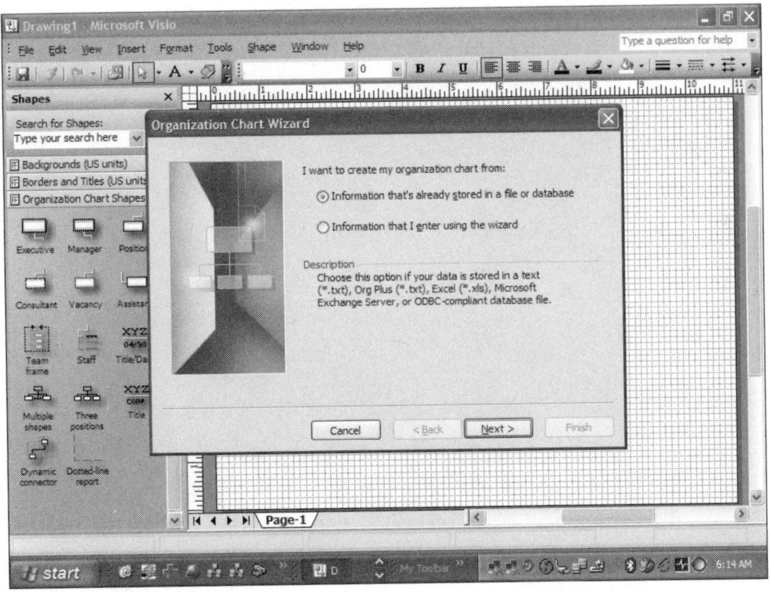

2. On the first page of the **Organization Chart Wizard**, make sure the **Information that's already stored in a file or database** option is selected, and then click **Next**.

   The next page of the wizard appears, prompting you to identify the type of data source from which you are importing.

3. Make sure the **A text, Org Plus (*.txt) or Excel file** option is selected, and then click **Next**.

   The next page of the wizard appears, prompting you to locate the file that contains the organization information.

4. Click **Browse**, navigate to the My Documents\Microsoft Press\Visio 2003 SBS \CreatingCharts folder, and then double-click **TGC Employees.xls**.

   The wizard displays the file and its path.

5. Click **Next**.

   The next page of the wizard appears, prompting you to choose the columns in the spreadsheet that contain the information that defines your organization.

6. In the **Name** box, make sure **Name** is displayed, and in the **Reports to** box, make sure **Manager** is displayed. Click **Next**.

   The next page of the wizard appears, prompting you to choose the fields you want to display in your organization chart.

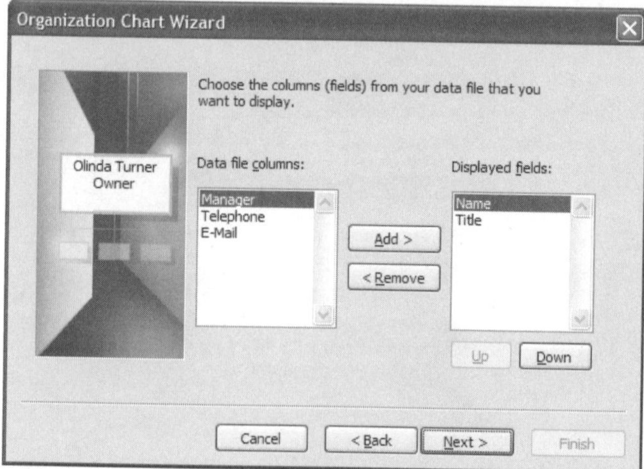

7. Make sure the **Displayed fields** list displays **Name** and **Title**. Click **Next**.

   The next page of the wizard appears, prompting you to choose additional columns (or fields) to import into your organization chart as custom properties.

8. In the **Data file columns** box, click **Telephone**, and then click the **Add** button to move **Telephone** to the **Custom Property fields** box.

Telephone is listed in the Custom Property fields box.

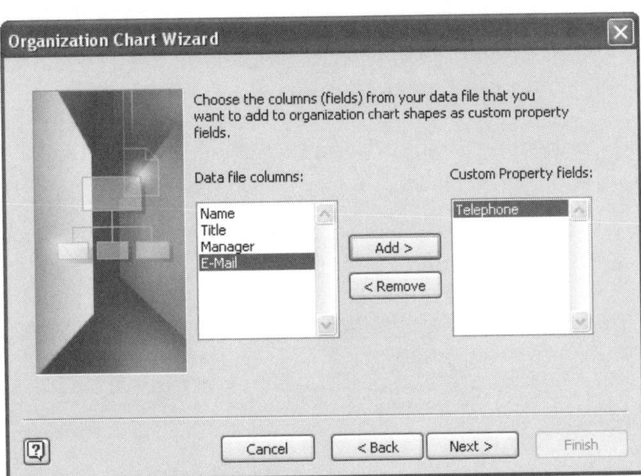

9 Repeat the previous step to add **E-Mail** to the **Custom Property fields** box. Click **Next**.

The next page of the wizard appears, asking you whether you want Visio to break your organization chart across pages.

10 Make sure the **I want the wizard to automatically break my organization chart across pages** option is selected, and then click **Finish**.

The wizard imports the data according to the specifications you entered, and Visio creates the organization chart on the drawing page. The Organization Chart Wizard template also opens an Organization Chart menu and toolbar.

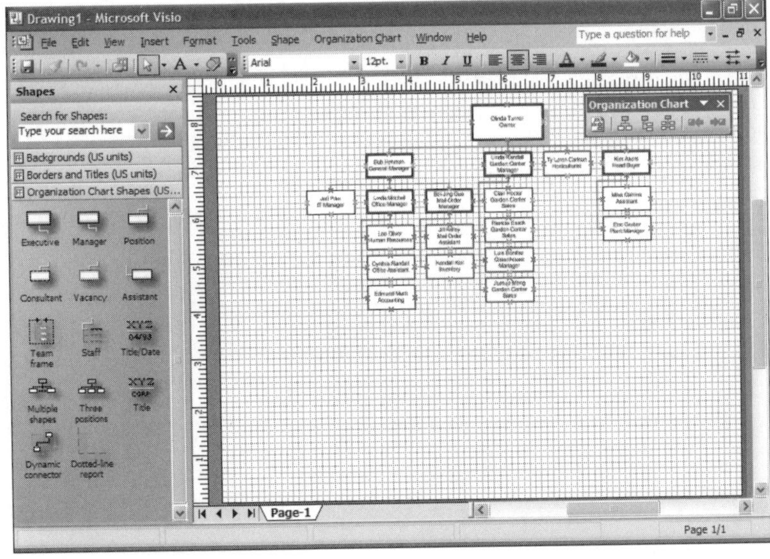

11 From the **Organization Chart Shapes** stencil, drag a **Consultant** shape onto the **Jeff Pike** shape.

Tip At this point in the exercise, you might need to periodically zoom in to the drawing page to see the shapes and text more clearly.

12 In the **Connecting Shapes** dialog box, select the **Don't show this message again** option, and then click **OK**.

Visio positions the Consultant shape below the Jeff Pike shape and draws a connector between the two shapes.

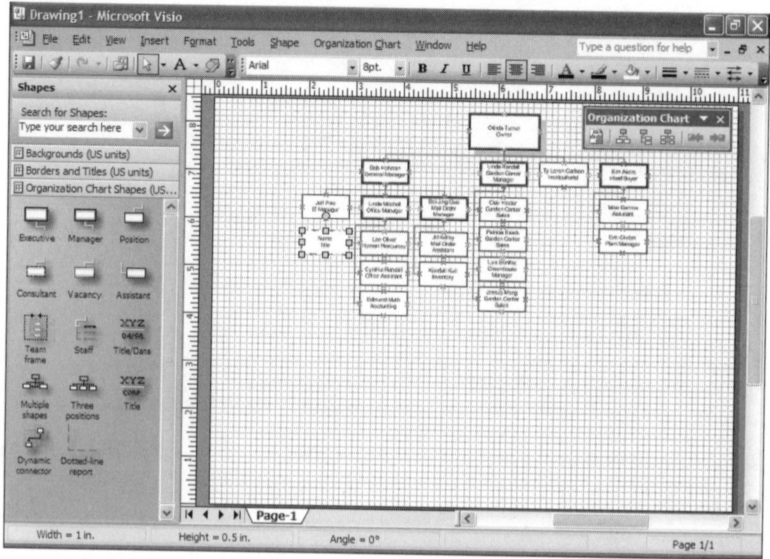

Tip To create your own organization charts from scratch or revise existing ones, simply drag shapes on top of each other as you did in the previous step. Visio positions and connects the shapes to create the organization hierarchy for you.

13 With the shape selected, press F2 to open the shape's text block.

14 Type **Jay Hamlin**, press Enter, and then type **Network Consultant**.

Visio displays the employee's name and title in the shape.

Tip You can also add up to 50 employee shapes to your organization chart at once by using the Multiple shapes shape on the Organization Chart Shapes stencil. Just drag it on top of the shape that represents the manager to whom all the employees report, and then in the dialog box, select the number of and type of shapes you want to add.

15 Click the pasteboard to close the text block and deselect the shape.

Notice that this shape has a dashed-line border, which indicates that the shape represents a consultant.

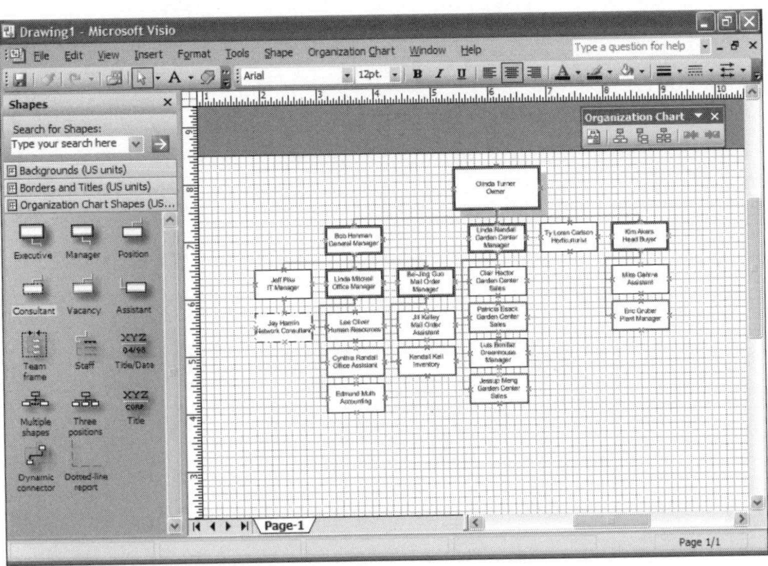

16 On the **File** menu, click **Close**, and then click **No** when Visio asks you if you want to save the changes to the drawing.

Visio and the drawing close.

Storing and Displaying Employee Information in Organization Charts

You can store custom property data with shapes in any Visio diagram. In organization charts, you can use custom property data for reports, reference, or as shape text in charts to store more descriptive detail about an employee. The default custom properties for organization chart shapes are Department, Telephone, Name, Title, and E-mail. By default, the Name and Title properties are shown in the shapes in a chart.

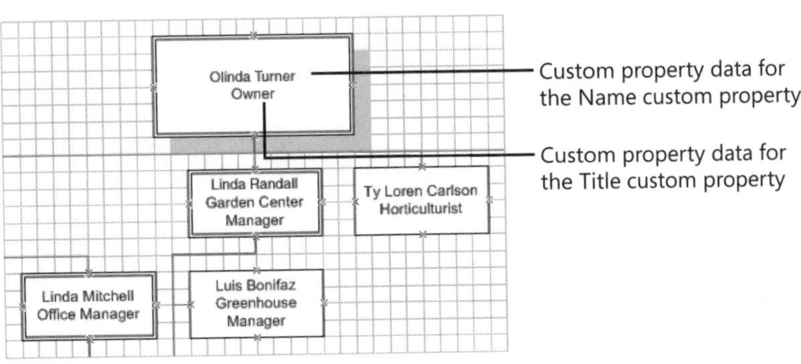

Custom property data for the Name custom property

Custom property data for the Title custom property

The other default custom properties are stored with the shapes but not shown in the chart. You can display them by clicking the Options command on the Organization Chart menu and then clicking the Fields tab in the Options dialog box. In Visio, you can view the hidden custom property data by using the Custom Properties window, or by right-clicking a shape and clicking Properties on the shape's shortcut menu.

You can also change custom property data in the Custom Properties window by selecting the data you want to change and typing new data. You can format the text in all the shapes at once by clicking the Options command on the Organization Chart menu and then clicking the Text tab in the Options dialog box. You can also format individual shapes by selecting the shape text and formatting it as you would any other text.

In this exercise, you open an organization chart. You view the custom properties of a couple of shapes and change the data for one of them. You display e-mail address data in all the shapes, widen the shapes to accommodate the new information, and then format the text that appears in all the shapes.

OPEN the *OrgChart* file in the My Documents\Microsoft Press\Visio 2003 SBS\CreatingCharts folder.

1 On the **View** menu, click **Custom Properties Window**.

The Custom Properties window appears with no data displayed because a shape isn't selected.

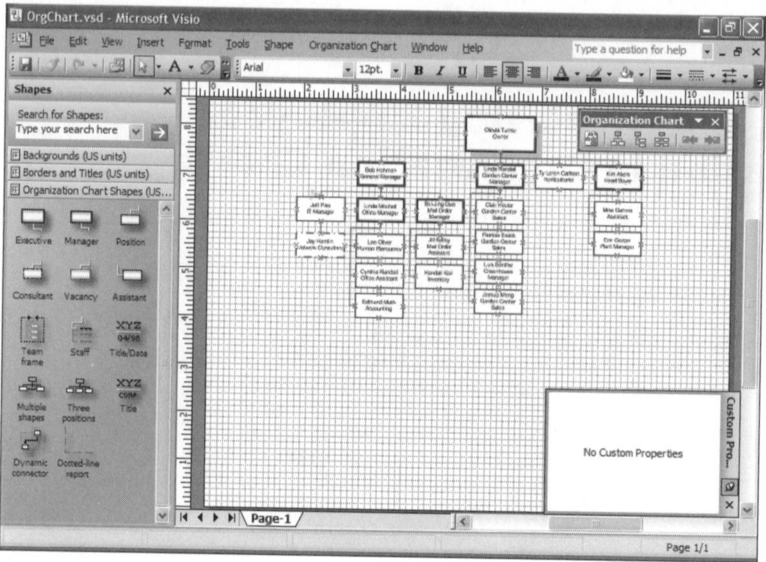

Custom Properties Window

Tip You can also open the Custom Properties window by clicking the Custom Properties Window button on the View toolbar. To display the View toolbar, right-click the toolbar area, and click View on the shortcut menu.

2 Click the **Olinda Turner** shape.

The Custom Properties window displays the telephone, name, title, and e-mail custom property data for Olinda Turner.

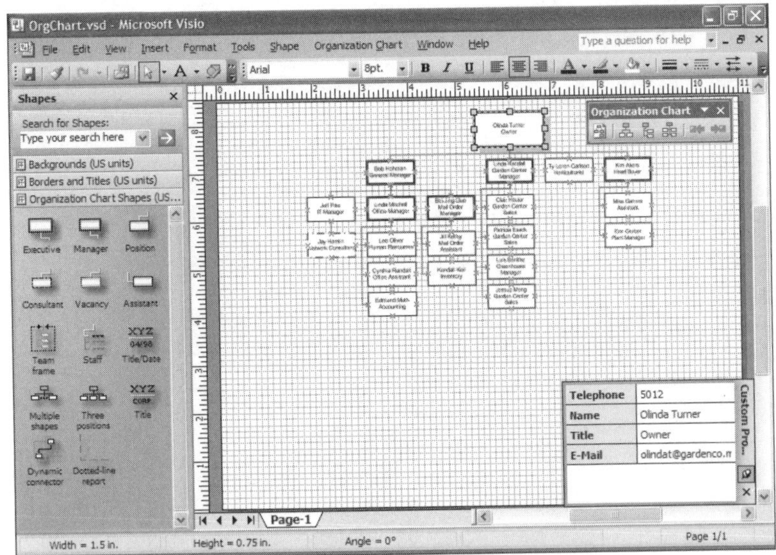

Troubleshooting Zoom in to the drawing page to see the shapes and text more clearly. You can also move the Organization Chart toolbar if it obstructs your view of a shape. To move the toolbar, position the pointer over the toolbar's title, and then drag it to a different location.

3 Position the pointer over the left side of the Custom Properties window, and then drag to the left to widen the window so you can see all of the data in the window.

When the pointer changes to a two-headed arrow, drag to resize the window.

4 Click the **Ty Loren Carlson** shape.

The Custom Properties window displays the telephone, name, title, and e-mail custom property data for Ty Loren Carlson.

5 In the Custom Properties window, click the **Telephone** box, type **5025**, and press the Enter key.

The Telephone box displays the new number.

Tip You can also view, change, and create new custom properties in the Custom Properties dialog box. To view this dialog box, right-click a shape, and then click Properties on the shortcut menu. To create new custom properties, in the Custom Properties dialog box, click the Define button.

6 Click the **Jay Hamlin** shape.

The Custom Properties window displays the name and title custom property data for Jay Hamlin.

7 In the Custom Properties window, click the **Telephone** box, type 6025, and press the Enter key.

The Telephone box displays the number.

8 In the Custom Properties window, click the **E-Mail** box. Then type c_jayh@gardenco.msn.com, and press the Enter key.

The E-Mail box displays the e-mail address.

9 On the **Organization Chart** menu, click **Options** to open the **Options** dialog box.

10 In the **Options** dialog box, click the **Fields** tab.

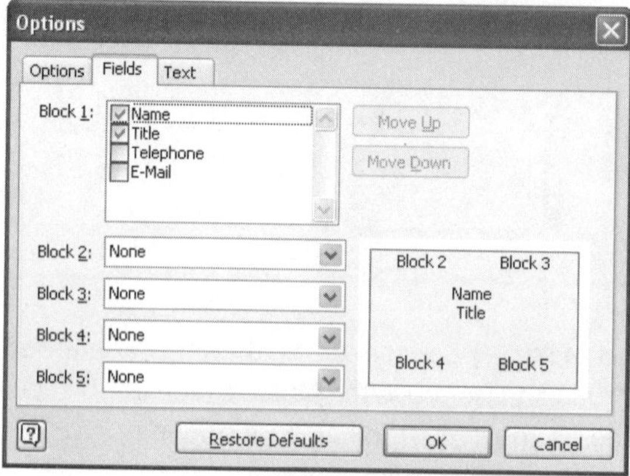

11 In the **Block 1** area, select **E-Mail** to add a checkmark next to it.

Notice that the preview area on the right side of the dialog box shows you where the e-mail custom property data will appear in the shape.

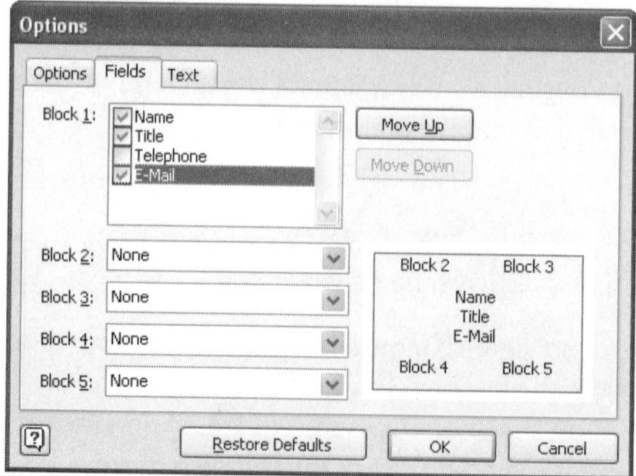

Tip To add information to the other text blocks in the shapes in an organization chart, click the down arrow next to the block you want to use, and then click the custom property you want to display.

12 Click **OK**.

13 When a message box appears asking if you want the shape's height adjusted to accommodate the additional information and your drawing automatically arranged, click **Yes**.

The shapes on the chart are enlarged to display the name, title, and e-mail for each position; however, the information still looks a bit cramped in the shapes.

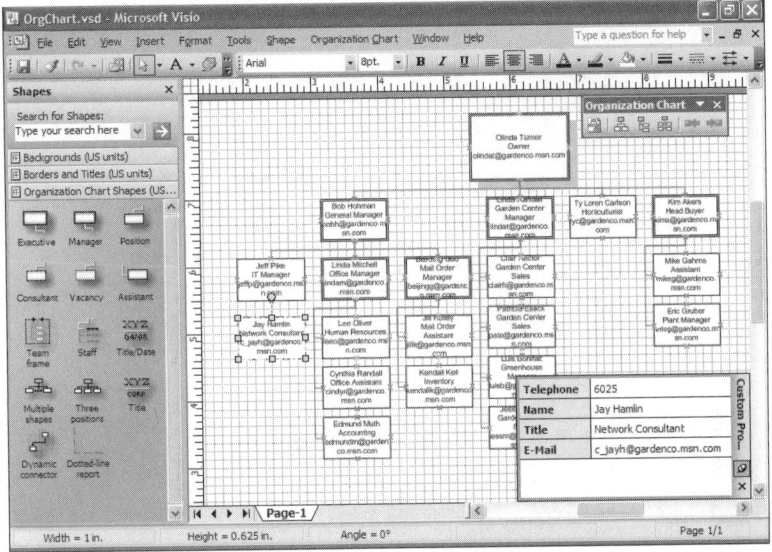

14 On the **Organization Chart** menu, click **Options** to open the **Options** dialog box.

15 On the **Options** tab, in the **Shape display** area, highlight the text in the **Width** box, and then type 1.5.

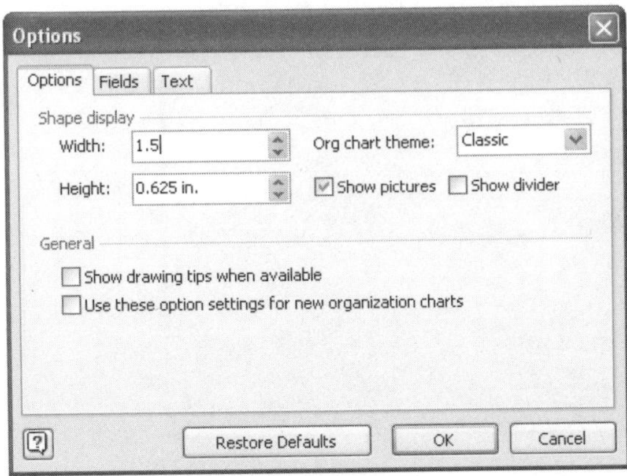

16 Click **OK**.

17 When a message box appears asking if you want your drawing automatically arranged, click **Yes**.

Visio widens the shapes in the chart to 1.5 inches and rearranges them on the drawing page.

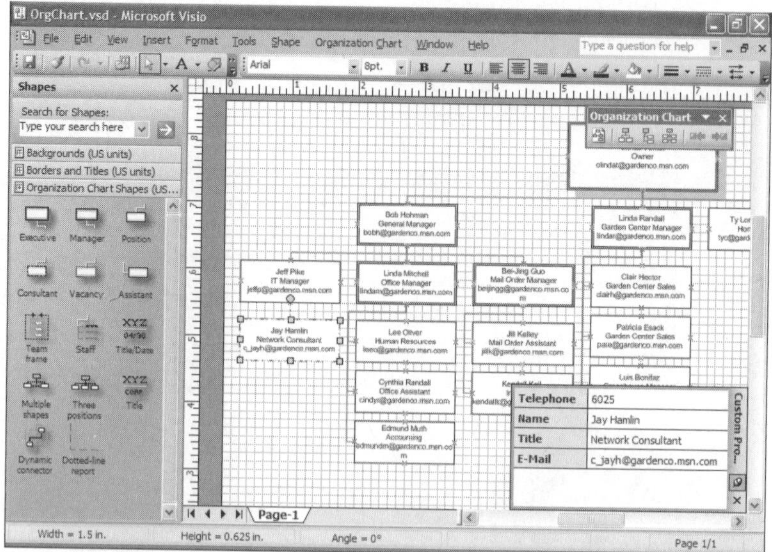

18 On the **Organization Chart** menu, click **Options** to open the **Options** dialog box.

19 Click the **Text** tab.

20 Make sure **Name** is displayed in the **Fields** box, and in the **Style** area, select the **Bold** check box to add that formatting to the names in the organization chart shapes.

21 In the **Fields** box, click **E-Mail**, and in the **Style** area, select the **Italic** check box to italicize the e-mail addresses in the organization chart shapes.

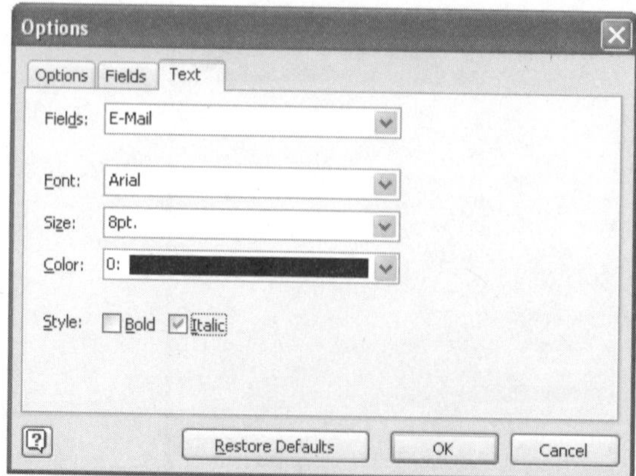

22 Click **OK**.

Visio formats the names and e-mail addresses in the shapes.

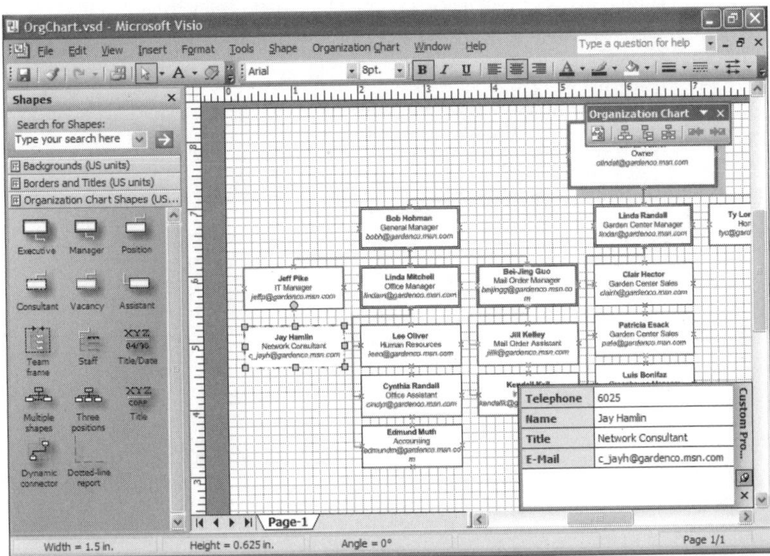

Tip To insert a picture into a shape, right-click the shape, and then click Insert Picture on the shortcut menu.

23 Select the **Olinda Turner** shape.

24 Right-click the shape, and then click **Show Divider Line** on the shortcut menu.

Visio inserts a divider line under the owner's name.

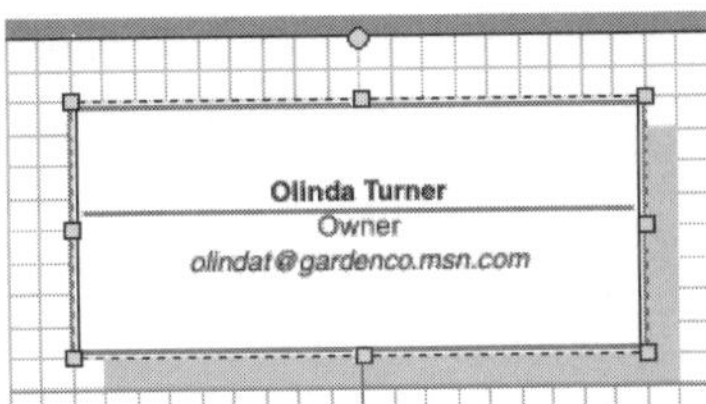

25 Right-click the shape, and then click **Hide Divider Line** on the shortcut menu to hide the line.

Close

26 For an unobstructed view of the organization chart, click the **Close** button on the Custom Property window to close the window.

27 On the **File** menu, click **Close**, and then **No** so Visio doesn't save the chart.

Visio and the chart close.

Customizing the Layout of Organization Charts

New in Visio 2003

Visio includes a number of tools that you can use to rearrange the shapes in your organization chart, so you can modify the way the chart looks without wasting valuable time reconnecting the shapes in the reporting structure. You can change the location of individual shapes or the layout of all the shapes in a department by using the buttons on the Organization Chart toolbar. You can also change individual reporting relationships.

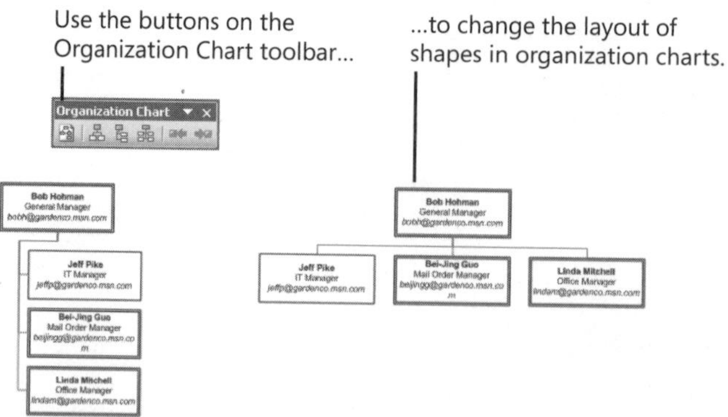

Charts that represent large or complex organizations can be arranged on several pages so you don't need to cram the entire chart onto one drawing page. You can quickly build a multiple-page organization chart by creating synchronized copies of departments on pages in the drawing file. For example, on the first page of a chart, select a manager shape with subordinate employees that make up a department or team, and then create a synchronized copy of it. Visio cuts the subordinates from the first page, creates a new page, and then places the manager and the subordinates on the new page. A shape representing the manager remains on the first page, indicating that a synchronized copy is on another page in the drawing file. Any changes you make to the text or custom properties for any synchronized shape applies to all synchronized copies of it on other pages. If the manager changes her name and you update her name on the first page of the chart; that change ripples throughout all the synchronized copies of the shape on other pages. Synchronized copies save time, help you manage large organization charts, and make it easier to maintain accurate and consistent organization charts.

You can customize your organization charts further by adding hyperlinks to easily navigate between synchronized copies and pages of a complex organization chart. You could, for example, link the drawing page for a customer service department to the department Web site on the corporate intranet, making it easy to access more information about the group. To insert a hyperlink for a shape, select it, and then click Hyperlinks on the Insert menu. To insert a hyperlink for a drawing page, make sure nothing on the page is selected, and then click Hyperlinks on the Insert menu. Finally, you can add more visual appeal to your organization charts by adding a background, changing the color scheme and the theme for the chart. Use the Options command on the Organization Chart menu to change the organization chart theme for an organization chart from classic (shapes with square corners) to contemporary (shapes with round corners).

In this exercise you change the layout of some of the shapes in the organization chart. You create a synchronized copy of one department on a new page, and then insert a hyperlink linking the manager shape on the first page to its copy on the second page. Finally, you add a background to the chart, and change the color scheme and design theme of the chart.

OPEN the *OrgChartLayout* file in the My Documents\Microsoft Press\Visio 2003 SBS\CreatingCharts folder.

1 Select the **Bob Hohman** shape.

Vertical Layout

2 On the Organization Chart toolbar, click the **Vertical Layout** button.

Align Left

3 On the Vertical Layout submenu, click the **Align Left** button.

The subordinates in Bob Hohman's department are left aligned under the Bob Hohman shape. Some shapes appear below the bottom of the drawing page.

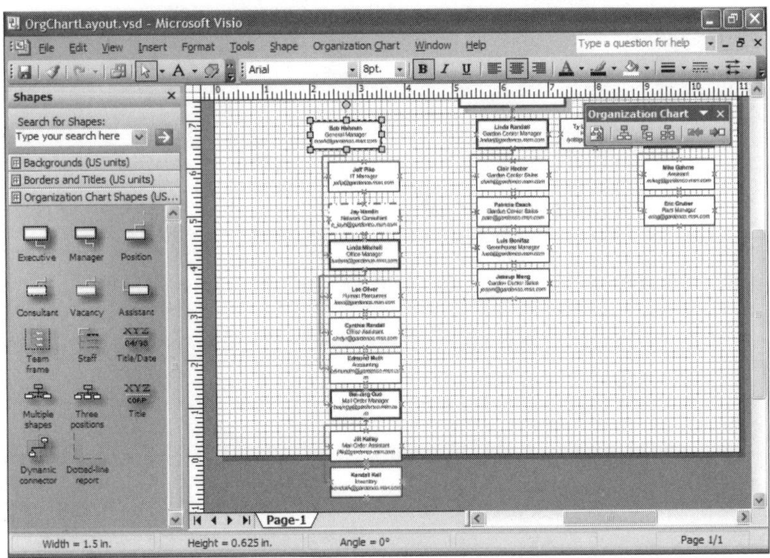

Tip Another way to change the layout of all or part of an organization chart is to select the shape at the highest level of the staffing group you want to change, and then on the Organization Chart menu, click Arrange Subordinates. Click the layout style you want, and then click OK. You can also right-click the shape, and then click Arrange Subordinates on the shortcut menu.

4 With the **Bob Hohman** shape selected, on the **Organization Chart** menu, point to **Synchronize**, and then click **Create Synchronized Copy**.

The Create Synchronized Copy dialog box appears, asking whether you want the synchronized copy placed on a new page.

5 In the **Create Synchronized Copy** dialog box, make sure the **New page** option is selected. Select the **Hide subordinates on original page** check box, and then click **OK**.

Visio inserts a second page in the chart and places Bob Hohman's department on it.

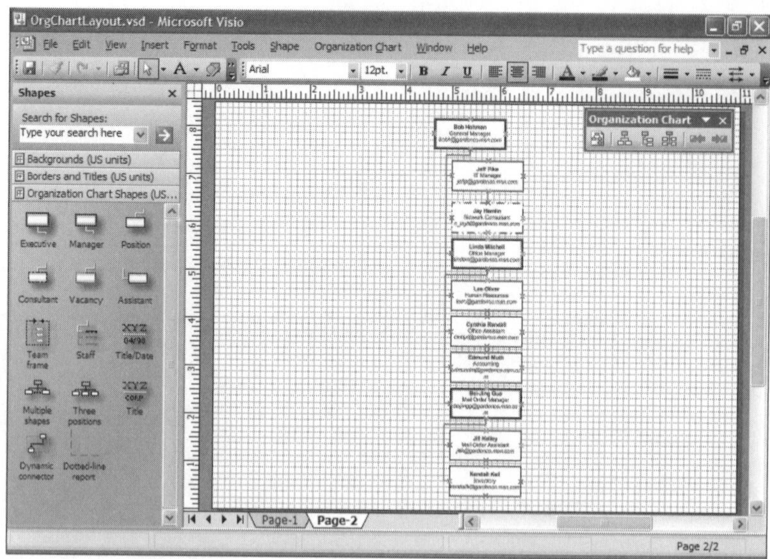

6 Select the **Bob Hohman** shape.

Horizontal Layout

7 On the Organization Chart toolbar, click the **Horizontal Layout** button.

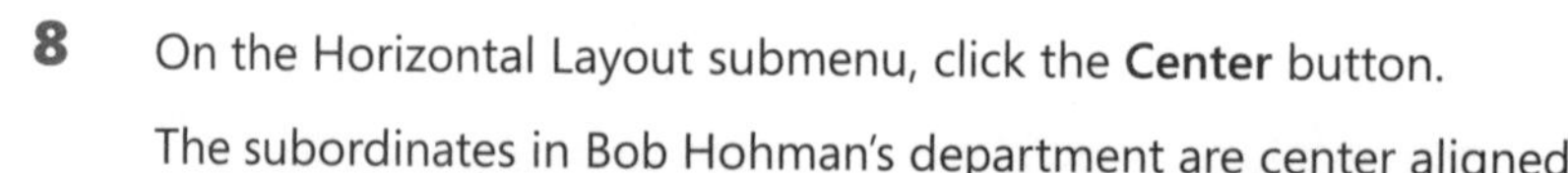

Center

8 On the Horizontal Layout submenu, click the **Center** button.

The subordinates in Bob Hohman's department are center aligned.

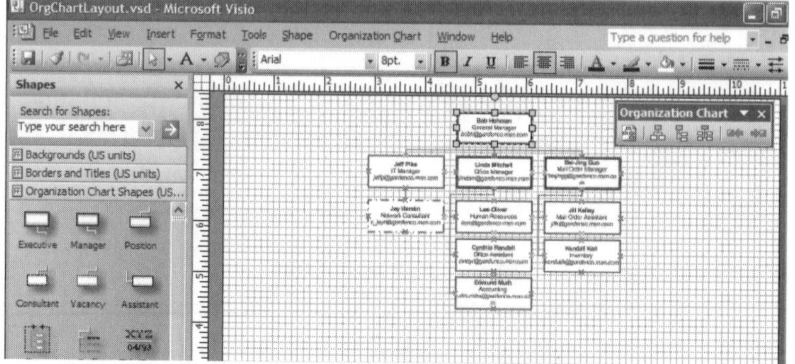

9 On the **Shape** menu, click **Center Drawing**.

Visio centers the shapes on the drawing page.

10 On the **View** menu, click **Custom Properties Window**.

The Custom Properties window opens and displays the custom property data for Bob Hohman.

11 Click the **Telephone** box, type **5041**, and then press Enter to change the telephone number.

Visio changes the telephone number for Bob Hohman.

12 Click the **Page-1** tab to go to the first page of the chart.

13 Select the **Bob Hohman** shape to view the custom properties for the shape.

Visio displays the updated phone number for Bob Hohman, and his subordinates are hidden from view on this page of the chart. Custom property data for the Bob Hohman shape is synchronized on both pages.

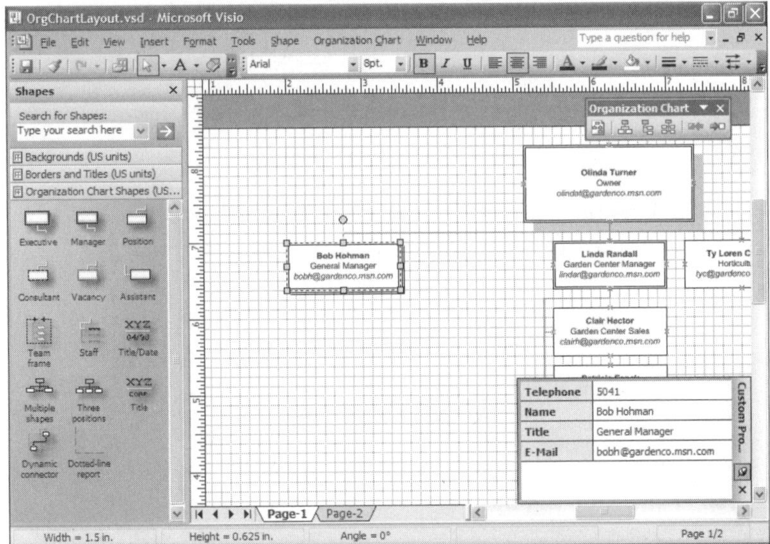

Important Changes to shape text and custom properties apply to all synchronized copies of the shape. However, changes such as adding, deleting, or moving a shape apply only to the page on which you are working; these changes aren't synchronized. If you want to show a manager's subordinates on page where they're hidden, right-click the manager shape, and then click Show Subordinates.

14 With the **Bob Hohman** shape selected, on the **Insert** menu, click **Hyperlinks** to open the **Hyperlinks** dialog box.

15 Click the **Browse** button next to the blank **Sub-address** box.

The Hyperlink dialog box appears.

16 In the **Hyperlink** dialog box, click the **Page** down arrow, and then click **Page-2**. Click **OK**.

The Hyperlink dialog box closes, and the Hyperlinks dialog box shows Page-2 in the Sub-address box.

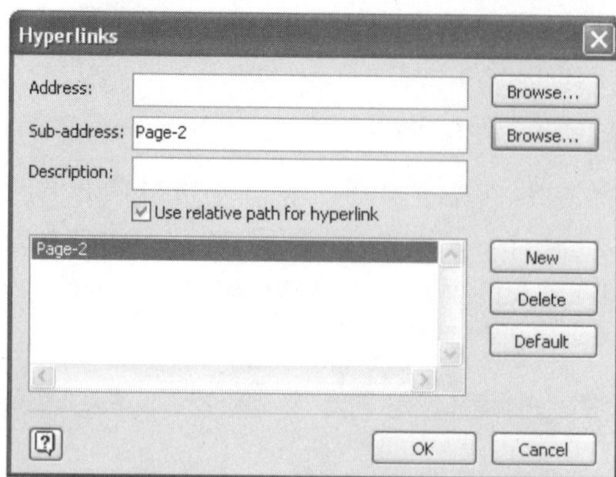

17 Click **OK** to close the **Hyperlinks** dialog box.

18 Pause the pointer over the **Bob Hohman** shape.

hyperlink pointer

A hyperlink pointer indicates that a hyperlink is associated with the shape. A ScreenTip identifies the name of the link as Page-2.

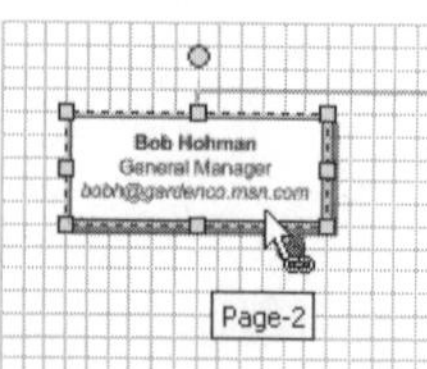

19 Right-click the **Bob Hohman** shape, and then click **Page-2** on the shortcut menu.

Visio displays Page-2 of the chart.

20 Click the **Cynthia Randall** shape to select it.

Move Up

21 On the Organization Chart toolbar, click the **Move Up** button.

Visio moves the Cynthia Randall shape above the Lee Oliver shape.

Tip You can also compare different versions of organization charts. Use the Compare Organization Data command on the Organization Chart menu to generate a report that lists the differences between current and previous versions of a chart.

22 Click the **Close** button on the Custom Property window to close the window.

23 On the **Organization Chart** menu, click **Options** to open the **Options** dialog box.

24 In the **Org chart theme** box, click the down arrow, select **Contemporary**, and then click **OK**.

Visio changes the design theme for all the drawing pages in the chart.

25 Right-click the drawing page, and then click **Color Schemes** on the shortcut menu.

The Color Schemes dialog box appears.

26 In the **Color Schemes** dialog box, click **Coffee**, and then click **OK**.

Visio changes the color scheme for all the drawing pages in the chart.

27 Click the **Backgrounds** stencil, and then drag the **Background city** shape onto the drawing page.

Visio adds the background shape to the drawing page.

28 Click the **Page-1** tab to go to the first page of the chart.

Notice that the first page of the chart doesn't include a background.

29 On the **File** menu, click **Page Setup**, and then click the **Page Properties** tab.

30 In the **Background** box, click the down arrow, and then select **VBackground**.

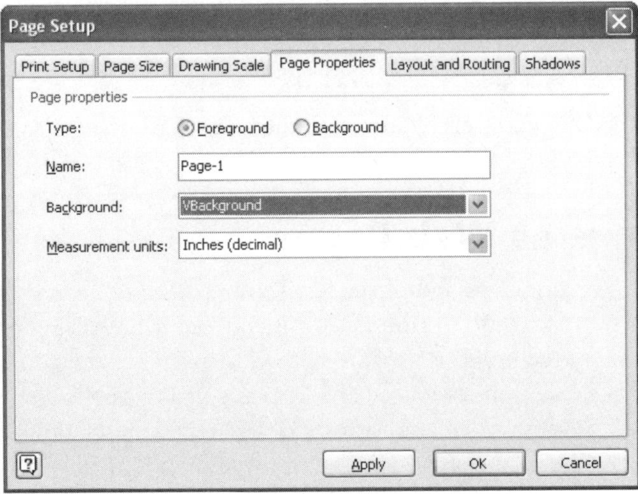

31 Click **OK**.

Visio adds the background to the first page and applies the color scheme to it.

32 On the **Edit** menu, click **Select All** to select all the shapes on the drawing page.

33 Drag one of the shapes to move all the shapes at once and center them on the drawing page.

34 Right-click the drawing page, and then click **Color Schemes** on the shortcut menu.

The Color Schemes dialog box appears.

35 In the **Color Schemes** dialog box, click **Forest**, and then click **OK**.

Visio changes the color scheme for the shapes in the chart.

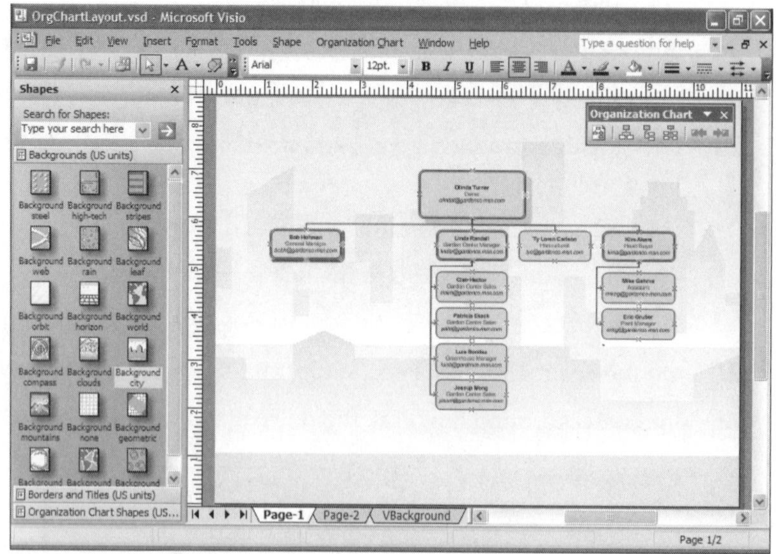

36 On the **File** menu, click **Close**, and then click **No** so you don't save the changes to the chart.

Saving Diagrams as Web Pages

By saving Visio drawings and diagrams as Web pages, you can share information with colleagues over a corporate intranet or with anyone who has a Web browser over the Internet. Many organizations use this method to make information available to employees across the organization—even if they don't have Visio. Web-based organization charts can help employees understand team and departmental relationships and can visually explain organizational changes. Each employee shape can also store custom property data so that these charts can be a source of up-to-date employee information, such as employee office location, telephone number, e-mail address, and so on.

Using Visio, publishing your diagrams to the Web or an intranet site is as easy as saving a file. Visio adds the HTML codes necessary to display the diagram in a Web browser, so all you have to do is make sure your diagram looks the way you want it to. To save a Visio diagram as a Web page, just click Save as Web Page on the File menu as you would for any other Office 2003 file. Navigation elements included in your diagrams, such as hyperlinks and page tabs, are retained in the Web page and any supporting images are saved in a folder that corresponds to the Web page.

In this exercise, you save an organization chart as a Web page. Then you view the Web page in your default Web browser, view custom property date in the Details pane, and navigate between pages using a hyperlink and the Go to Page pane.

Important You need a Web browser, such as Microsoft Internet Explorer, to complete this exercise.

OPEN the *OrgChartWeb* file in the My Documents\Microsoft Press\Visio 2003 SBS\CreatingCharts folder.

1 On the **File** menu, click **Save as Web Page**.

The Save As dialog box appears with OrgChartWeb.htm displayed in the File name box.

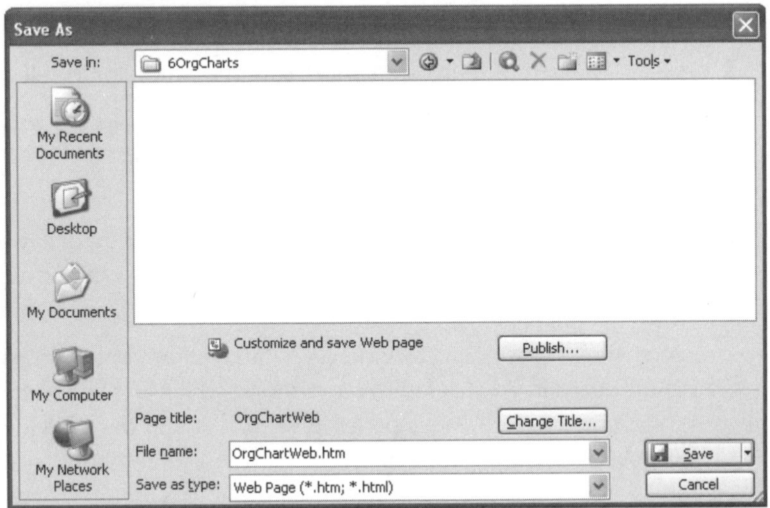

Tip The file name is displayed in the browser's title bar when you view the Web page. To change the title displayed on the title bar, click the Change Title button in the Save As dialog box.

2 In the **Save As** dialog box, click **Publish** to open the **Save As Web Page** dialog box.

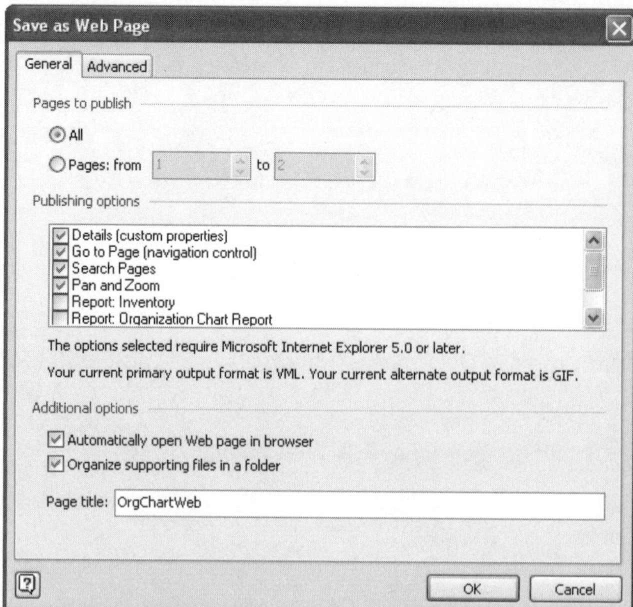

3 In the **Pages to Publish** area, make sure the **All** option is selected.

4 In the **Publishing options** area, make sure the **Details (custom properties)**, **Go to Page (navigation control)**, **Search Pages**, and **Pan and Zoom** check boxes are selected.

5 In the **Additional options** area, make sure the **Automatically open web page in browser** and **Organize supporting files in a folder** check boxes are selected, and then click **OK**.

A progress bar appears as Visio saves the diagram as a Web page. The organization chart opens in your default Web browser, which also shows the blank Go To Page, Details, and Search Pages panes in the left side of the browser window. Visio saves the Web page and supporting files for it in a folder that corresponds to the Web page file.

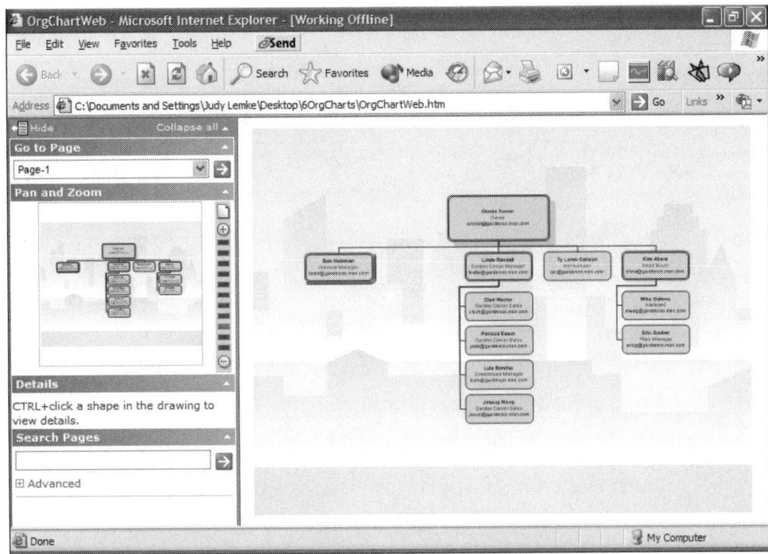

6 Hold down the Ctrl key as you click the **Olinda Turner** shape to view its custom property data in the **Details** pane to the left of the drawing page.

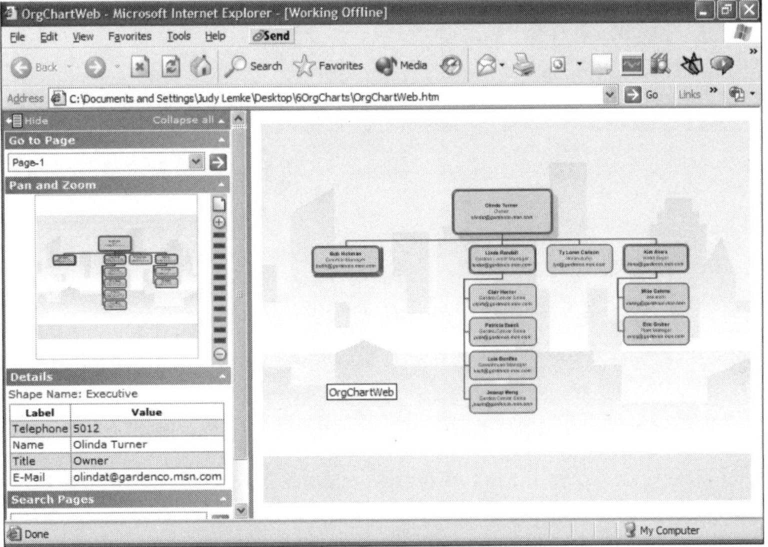

7 Pause the pointer over the **Bob Hohman** shape.

The pointer changes to a hand to indicate that the shape includes a hyperlink. A ScreenTip also appears.

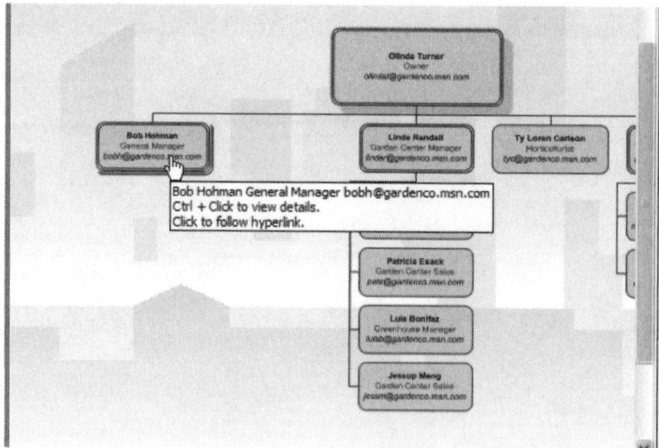

8 Click the **Bob Hohman** shape.

Visio displays Page-2, which contains the shapes that represent the employees in Bob Hohman's department. Notice that Page-2 appears in the Go to Page pane to the left of the organization chart.

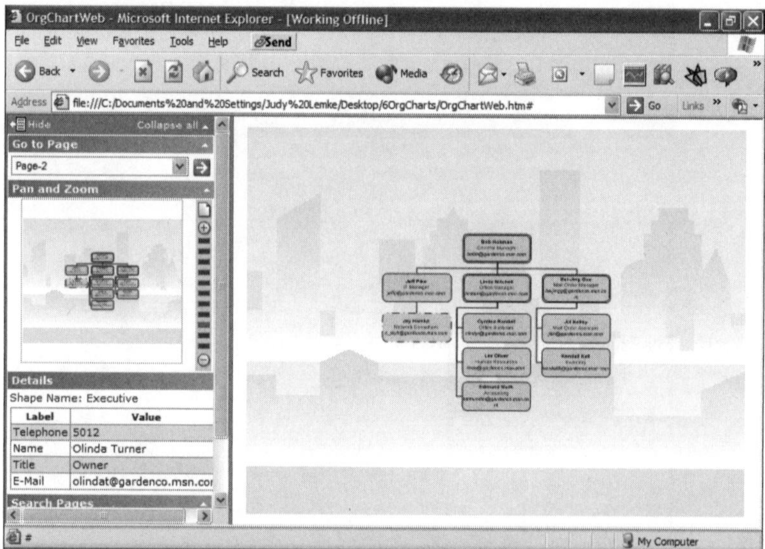

9 In the **Go to Page** pane, click the down arrow, click **Page-1**, and then click the green arrow to return to the first page.

10 In the Web browser, on the **File** menu, click **Close**.

The Web page closes, and your original Visio diagram appears.

11 On the **File** menu, click **Close**, and then click **No** so you don't save the changes to the chart.

Key Points

- You can create organization charts from scratch by starting with the Organization Chart template and dragging shapes on top of one another to create reporting relationships.
- You can create organization charts from information stored in data files or information you enter in a wizard by using the Organization Chart Wizard template.
- You can use the Custom Properties window to view custom property data, such as e-mail address and telephone number, not shown in organization chart shapes.
- You can use the Options command on the Organization Chart menu to display custom property data as text and format the text in all the shapes in a chart at once.
- You can use the Organization Chart menu and toolbar to rearrange shapes in an organization chart.
- You can create synchronized copies of departments or teams in large organizations to build multiple-page organization charts that show an overview of the organization on the first page and department details on the rest of the pages in the drawing file.
- You can save any Visio diagram as a Web page by clicking Save as Web Page on the File menu.

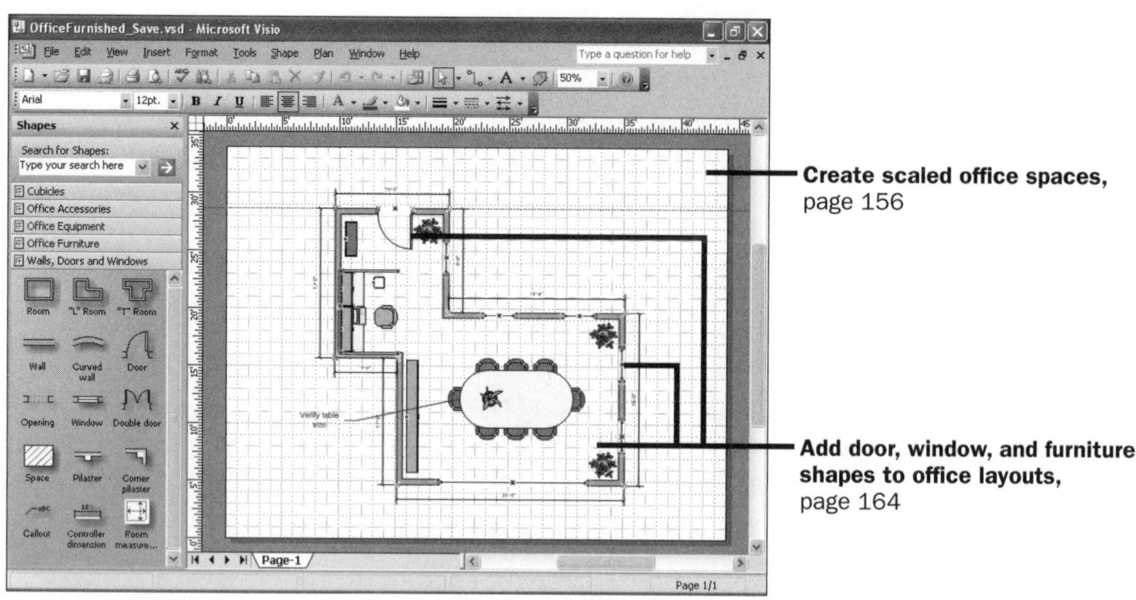

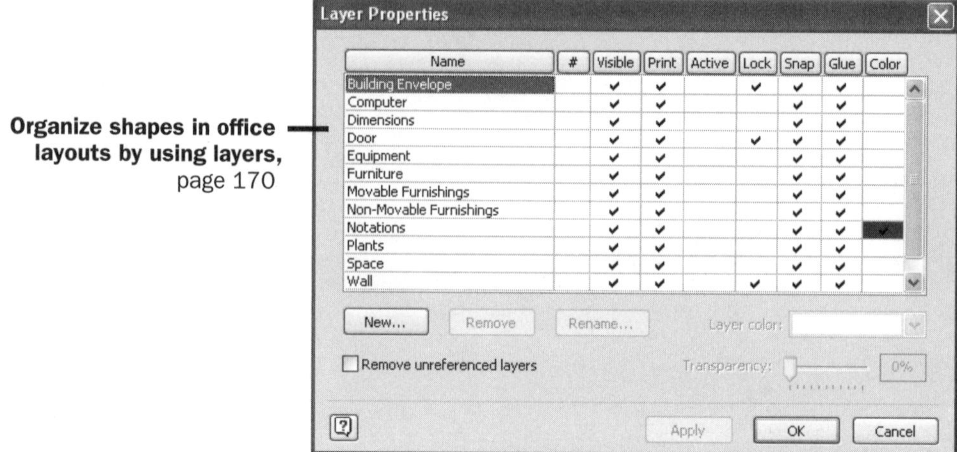

Chapter 7 at a Glance

7 Laying Out Office Spaces

In this chapter you will learn to:

- ✔ Create scaled office spaces.
- ✔ Add door, window, and furniture shapes to office layouts.
- ✔ Organize shapes in office layouts by using layers.

Think of something big–a house, an office building, or your backyard. Using Microsoft Office Visio, you can diagram a large object on a small drawing page by using a *drawing scale*, which represents the relationship between the object's size in the real world and its size on the page. Like a map that depicts a 10-mile stretch of highway with a 1-inch line, a scaled diagram represents physical space and objects at a ratio or a fraction of their real size. A drawing scale isn't only for large objects–you can draw very small objects, such as watch mechanisms or printed circuits, at a larger scale as well. When you start a Microsoft Office Visio diagram with a scaled template, Visio sets up the drawing scale that's appropriate for the drawing type, and the shapes on the stencils included with the template conform to the scale automatically when you drag them onto the drawing page.

Important This chapter demonstrates creating a scaled office layout. However, you can use the methods in this chapter to create any kind of scaled building plan—no matter how big or small it is. Visio Professional 2003 includes scaled templates that you can use to create everything from warehouses or industrial plants to plans for a home.

In this chapter, you create the layout for an office and conference space for The Garden Company. You work with the Office Layout template to first create the walls, and then you add door, window, and furniture shapes to the diagram. Last, you organize the shapes in the office layout on layers, which is an efficient method for managing and differentiating categories of shapes.

See Also Do you need only a quick refresher on the topics in this chapter? See the Quick Reference entries on pages xxxv–xxxvi.

Important Before you can use the practice files in this chapter, you need to install them from the book's companion CD to their default location. See "Using the Book's CD" on page xv for more information.

Creating Scaled Office Spaces

New in Visio 2003

The Office Layout template makes it easy to create scaled office space diagrams with architectural details, such as pilasters (rectangular wall projections like columns) and door swing (the space needed to open or close a door). Because Visio creates diagrams with architectural and engineering precision, your scaled diagrams are as accurate as your measurements.

All Visio templates have a default drawing scale, but for most business diagrams, such as flowcharts or organization charts, that scale is 1:1—that is, no scale. In the Office Layout template, the default drawing scale is ½ inch to 1 foot, which means that a shape that is ½ inch wide on the drawing page represents an object that is 1 foot wide in the real world. Visio sets up the drawing page using the template's scale and *units of measure*, which are typically inches (although Visio includes metric templates as well). If you prefer to measure shapes in yards or meters or some other measurement unit, you can click the Page Setup command on the File menu, which is also how you change the drawing scale for a diagram. In addition, the Office Layout template adds the custom Plan menu, which includes commands specifically for working with floor plans.

When you start a diagram with a scaled template, the units of measure for the drawing scale appear on the rulers. Part of what you have to do when working in any scaled diagram is grow accustomed to measuring distance in real-world units. For example, if your drawing scale is ½ inch to 1 foot on letter-sized paper (11 by 8½ inches), the rulers show that the page represents a space that is 22 feet long and 17 feet wide.

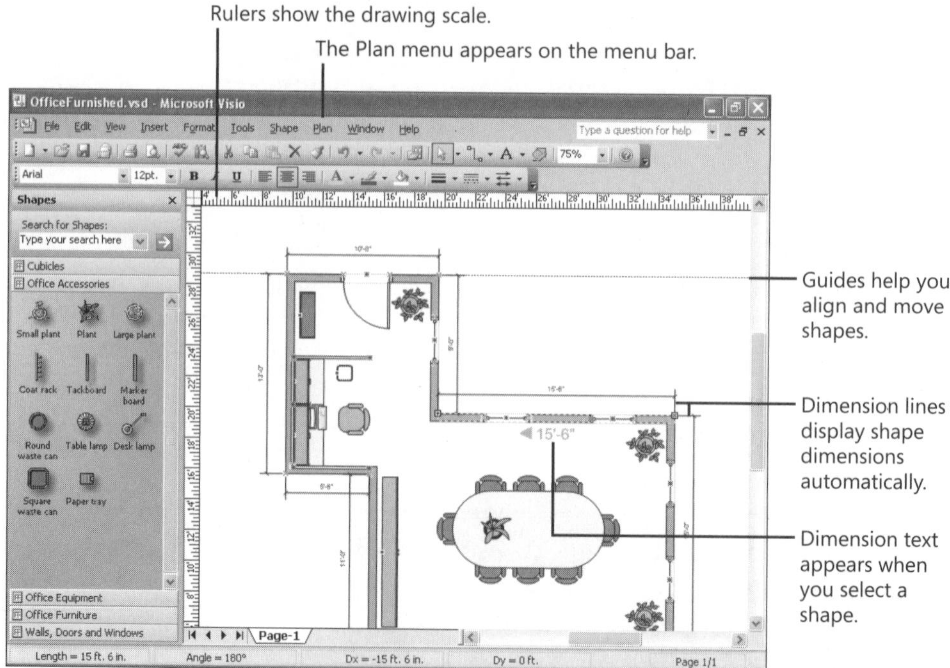

You start an office layout by adding shapes that represent the structure of the office space. One way to do this is to drag wall shapes onto the drawing page and rotate them into position. Where two walls meet, Visio joins their corners for a smooth look. All the other structural shapes, such as doors and windows, are designed to snap to the wall shapes in an office layout. Alternatively, you can use the Space shape, which represents a 10-foot by 10-foot area, to create the office structure. For this technique, you first create a patchwork of space shapes, and then you unite them into a single area by using the Union command, which merges the shapes to create a new shape–that is, one that represents the entire office space. Last, you convert the new shape (the office space) into walls. This sounds time consuming, but most people find it faster and easier than dragging a lot of individual wall shapes–one at a time–onto the drawing page.

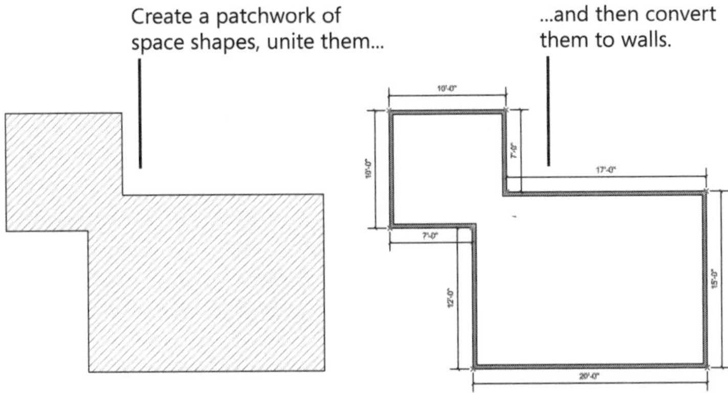

When you need to measure areas precisely, Visio offers several helpful shortcuts. Some shapes display their own dimensions–for example, the Space shape displays 100 sq. ft. The status bar below the drawing page reflects the real-world units of measure, so you can see at a glance how large shapes are in the real world. *Guides*–visual reference lines–help you align shapes to an exact point as well. Shapes connect to guides to ensure perfect alignment, and you can even drag a guide to move all the shapes connected to it. As you move or resize walls, the shape's dimensions and its dimension text and lines are updated automatically. To show the dimension text for a shape, select the shape. To add a dimension line to a shape, use the Controller dimension shape on the Walls, Doors, and Windows stencil.

In this exercise, you start a new office layout with the Office Layout template and use the Page Setup command to change the drawing scale. You use Space shapes to build a scaled office space, unite the shapes to create a new space shape, and then convert the space shape to walls. Then you resize some of the shapes, add dimension lines to them, and connect them to guides that help you position them.

Tip If you have Visio Professional 2003, you can insert AutoCAD drawings into your Visio architectural diagrams or start a diagram with a building shell already created in a CAD (computer-aided design) program. For more information about inserting and using AutoCAD drawings, type AutoCAD in the "Type a question for help" box.

1 Start Visio. In the Choose Drawing Type window, in the **Category** area, click **Building Plan**. In the **Template** area, click **Office Layout**.

   The template opens a blank, scaled drawing page and the Walls, Doors, and Windows stencil, Office Furniture stencil, Office Equipment stencil, Office Accessories stencil, and Cubicles stencil. The Plan menu is added to the menu bar. The rulers reflect the default architectural drawing scale (½″= 1′0″) for the Office Layout template.

2 On the **File** menu, click **Page Setup** to open the **Page Setup** dialog box.

3 Click the **Drawing Scale** tab.

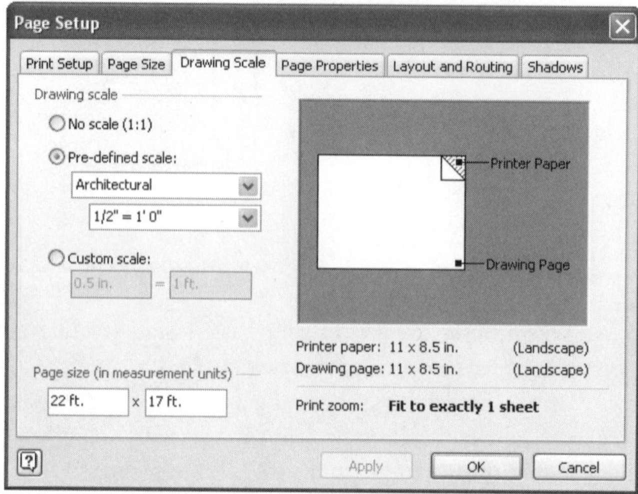

4 In the **Pre-defined scale** area, click the down arrow on the second box, scroll up, and then click **¼″ = 1′0″**.

   Visio changes the drawing scale for the diagram and recalculates the dimensions displayed in the Page size (in measurement units) boxes at the bottom of the dialog box.

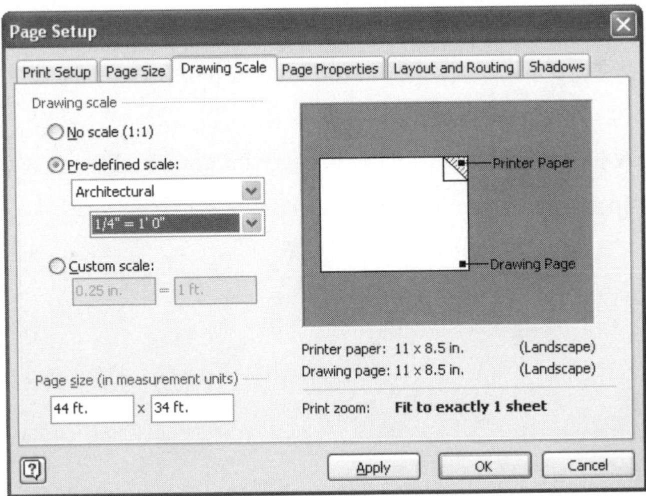

5 Click **OK**.

The rulers display the new drawing scale and show that the drawing page represents an area 44 feet wide by 34 feet tall.

6 From the **Walls, Doors, and Windows** stencil, drag a **Space** shape onto the drawing page and position it so that its top edge is at the 24-foot mark shown on the vertical ruler and its left edge is at the 10-foot mark shown on the horizontal ruler.

The Space shape includes dimension text that is automatically updated when you resize the shape.

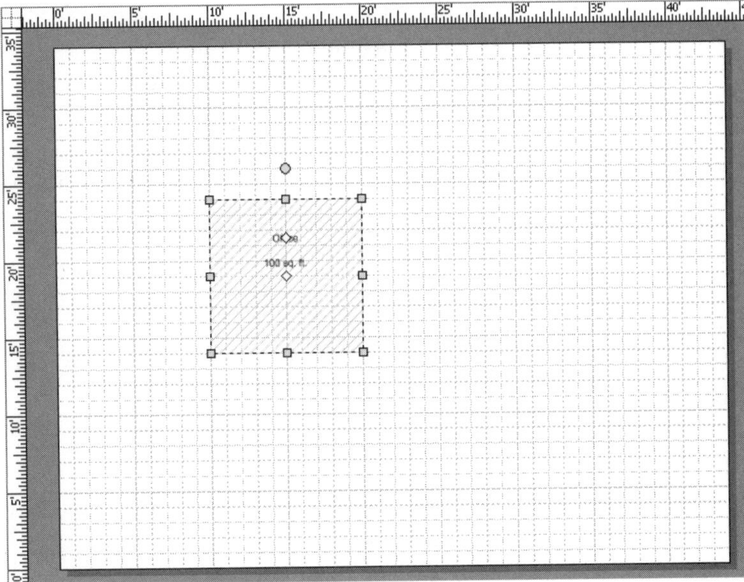

Tip As you drag a shape, Visio displays dotted lines on the rulers and measurements in the status bar that show you the shape's exact position on the drawing page.

7 Drag a second **Space** shape onto the drawing page and position it so that its upper-left corner overlaps the lower-right corner of the first **Space** shape.

The Space shape remains selected.

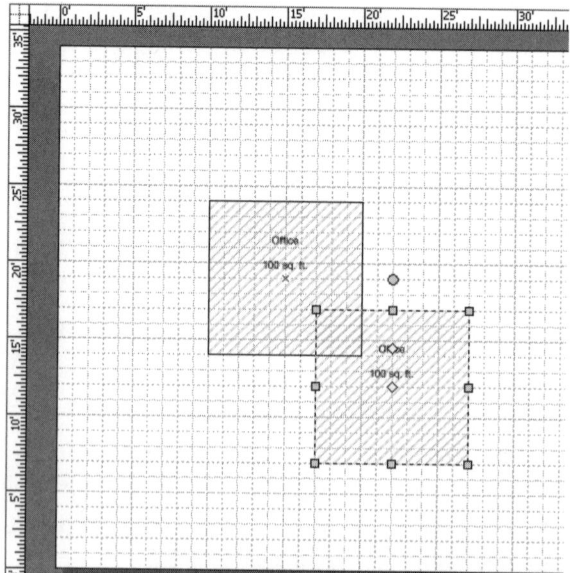

8 On the selected **Space** shape, drag the right-middle selection handle to the right to increase the width of the shape to 20 feet. Use the **Width** field in the status bar at the bottom of the drawing page window to determine the shape's width.

Visio updates the measurement displayed on the shape to 200 sq. ft.

9 On the same shape, drag the lower-middle selection handle down to increase the height of the shape to 15 feet. Use the **Height** field in the status bar at the bottom of the drawing page window to determine the shape's height.

Visio updates the measurement displayed on the shape to 300 sq. ft.

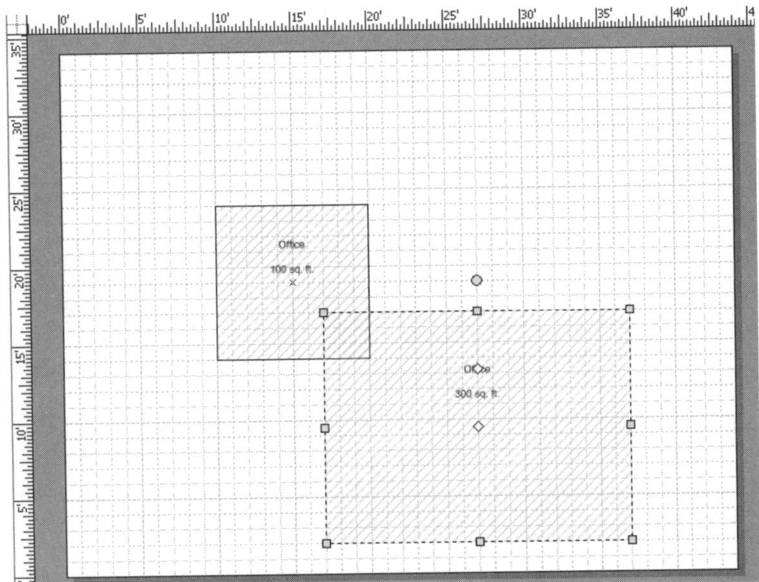

10 Hold down the Shift key while you select the other **Space** shape so that both shapes are selected.

11 On the **Shape** menu, click **Operations**, and then click **Union**.

Visio unites the two shapes into one shape.

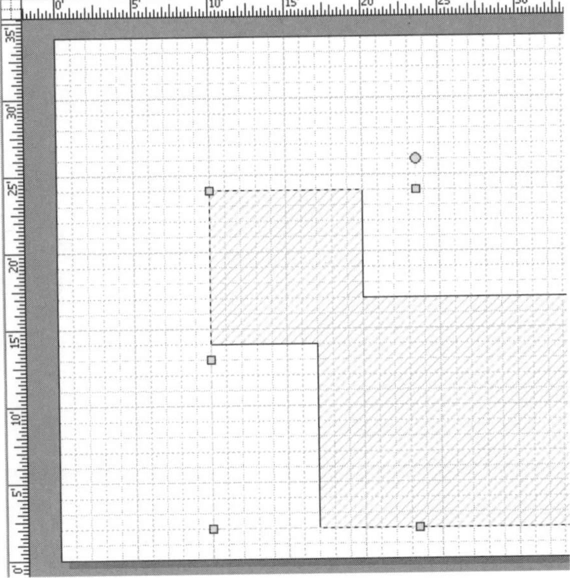

12 With the shape selected, on the **Plan** menu, click **Convert to Walls**.

The Convert to Walls dialog box appears.

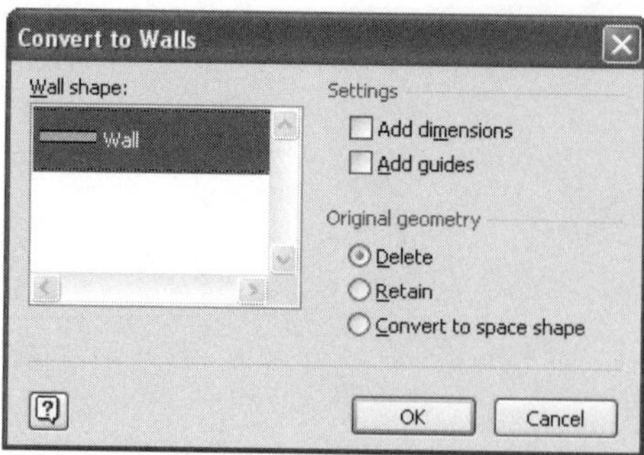

Tip Another way to create walls is to use the Line or Rectangle tool to draw a rough approximation of the walls, and then use the Convert To Walls command.

13 In the **Settings** area, select the **Add dimensions** check box, and then click **OK**.

Visio displays a status bar as it converts the perimeter of the shape to wall shapes and adds dimension lines to each wall.

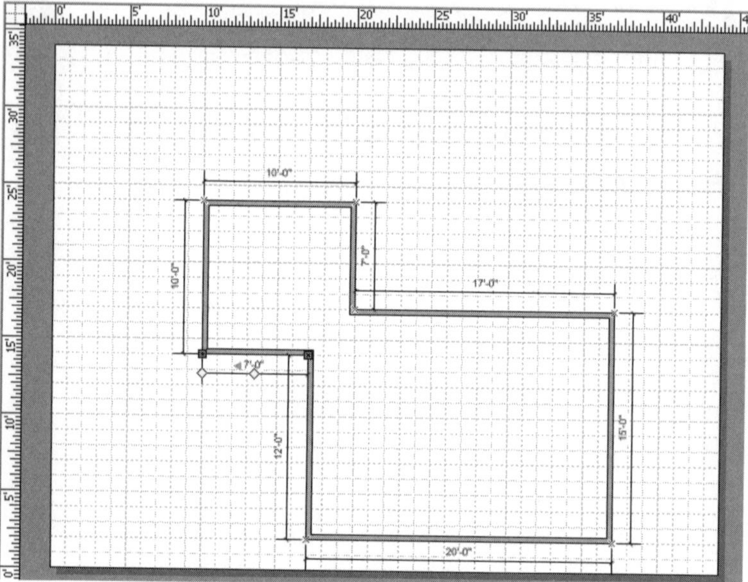

14 Select the top 10-foot wall.

Visio displays the dimension text (10´-0″) for the wall.

15 Right-click the same 10-foot wall, and then click **Add a Guide** on the shortcut menu.

Visio adds a guide to the wall shape's top edge and connects the other two adjoining walls to the guide so that you can move them together. The guide is selected and appears green.

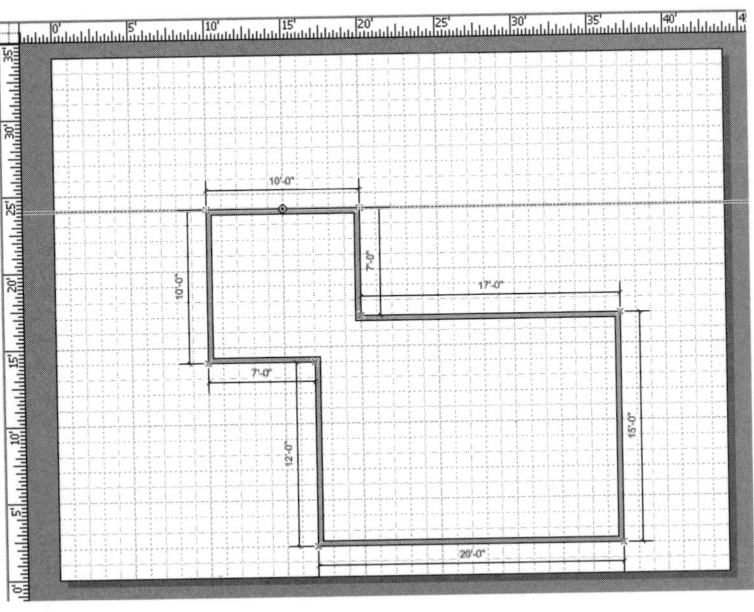

two-headed arrow

16 Pause the pointer over the guide, and when a two-headed arrow appears, drag the guide up 3 feet to the 27-foot mark on the vertical ruler.

Visio moves the guide and all three walls that are connected to it to the new position and updates the dimension lines.

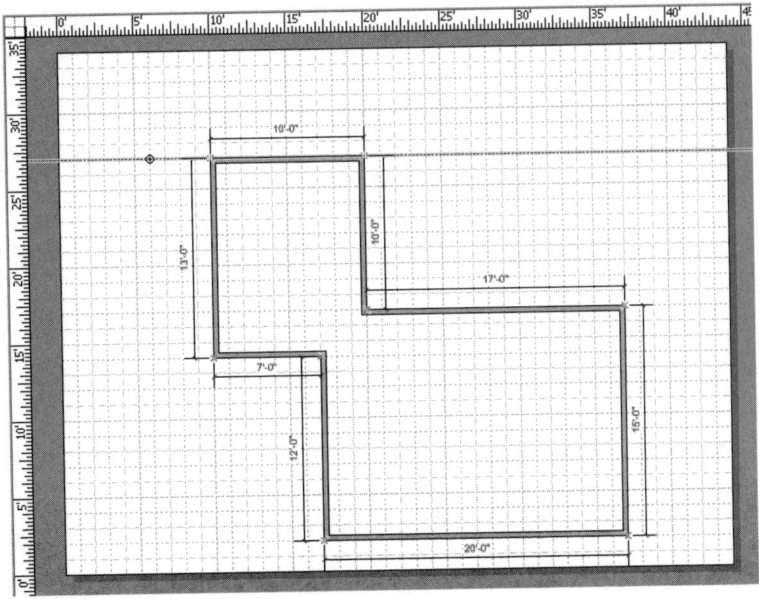

17 Press the Esc key to deselect of the guide.

The deselected guide appears blue.

Tip To select a guide, click it just as you would any shape. To add a guide to the drawing page, position the pointer over the horizontal ruler for a horizontal guide or the vertical ruler for a vertical guide, and then drag. As you drag, the guide appears on the drawing page. To delete a guide from the drawing page, select it, and then press the Del key.

Save

18 On the Standard toolbar, click the **Save** button to open the **Save As** dialog box.

19 In the **File name** box, type NewOffice, and then click **Save** to save the diagram.

CLOSE the *NewOffice* file.

Tip Although office layouts are a common type of scaled diagram, you can define a scale for any drawing type in Visio. For example, you can create maps, parts diagrams, and physical network diagrams to scale by using the Page Setup command on the File menu to define a drawing scale.

Adding Door, Window, and Furniture Shapes to Office Layouts

One of the many advantages of creating a scaled diagram with a scaled template is that the template includes shapes that are designed to work in the default drawing scale. The Office Layout template includes many specialized shapes that are designed to work in an architectural drawing scale and that have unique smart behavior. Wall shapes join together to form smooth corners. Door and window shapes snap into place on top of walls, rotating if necessary to match the wall's orientation. Dimension shapes display the dimensions of the shape they're connected to, and they stay connected to the shape when you move it.

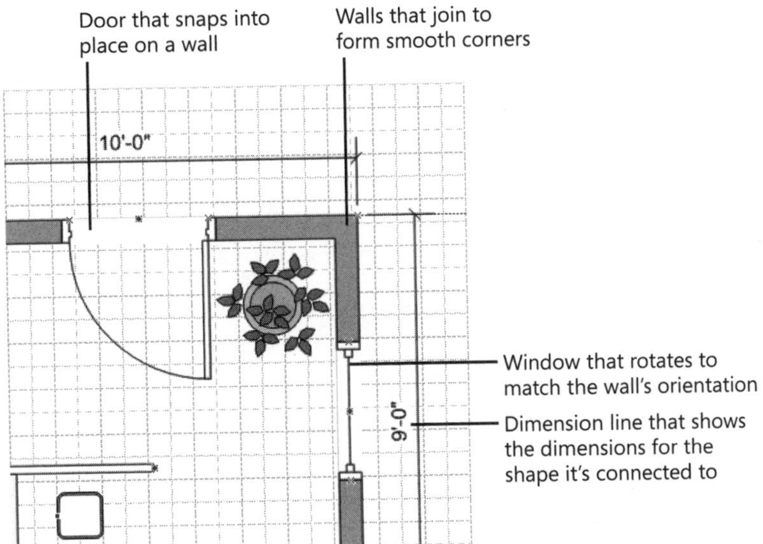

Office Layout shapes are designed only in standard architectural sizes. Because of this, some shapes are locked to prevent you from manually resizing them with the pointer. To change their size, you must modify the property that controls the shape's dimensions. For example, a Door shape has a Door Width property that you can set to 24, 28, 30, 36, 48, 60, or 72 inches–standard door widths. Visio resizes the shape based on your selection. You can change a shape's properties by using the Properties command on shape's shortcut menu, which contains other specialized commands for modifying the shape. For example, you can't rotate or flip a door to change its orientation. Instead, you must use the Reverse In/Out Opening command or Reverse Left/Right Opening command on the shape's shortcut menu so that Visio rotates or flips the shape for you.

Tip Right-click an office layout shape to see its shortcut menu of commands that you can use to modify the shape.

In this exercise, you add door, window, and furniture shapes to an office layout. You use shortcut menu commands to modify the door and window shapes. Last, you add furniture to the office and conference space.

OPEN the *OfficeWalls* file in the My Documents\Microsoft Press\Visio 2003 SBS\LayingOutSpaces folder.

1 From the **Walls, Doors, and Windows** stencil, drag the **Door** shape onto the drawing page and position it in the middle of the top 10-foot wall.

Visio connects the door to the wall. Red selection handles indicate that the shapes are connected, and gray handles indicate that the door is locked to prevent manual resizing. The door shape's dimension text appears while the shape is selected.

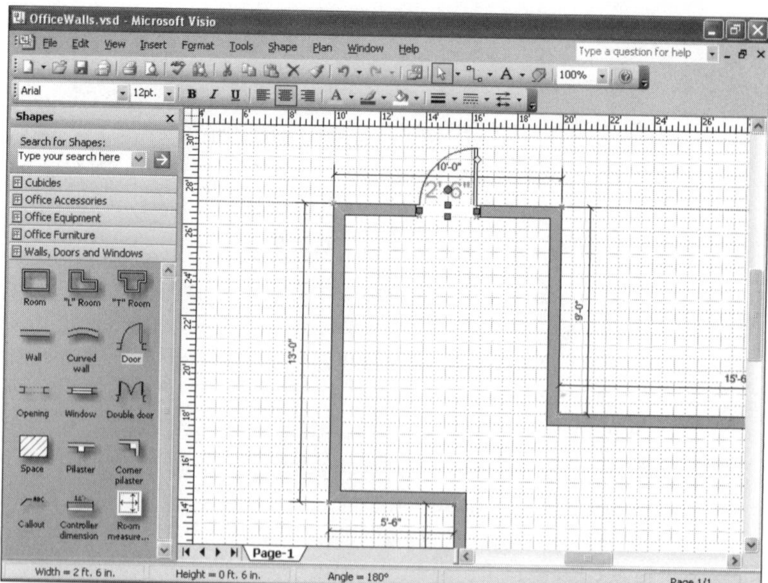

2 Right-click the door to display its shortcut menu, and then click **Properties**.

The Custom Properties dialog box appears and lists properties for the door.

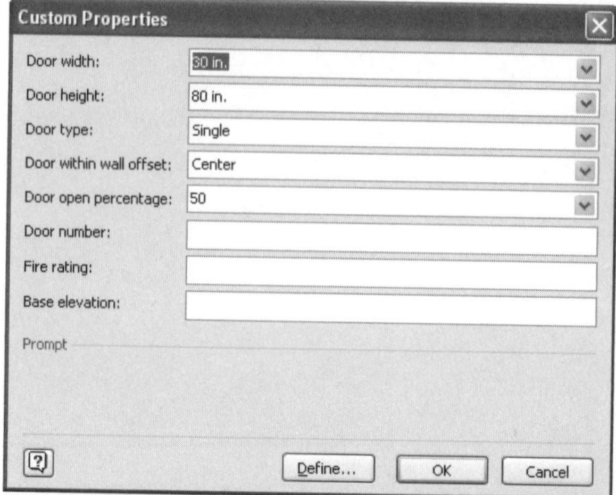

Troubleshooting If you have trouble displaying the shape's shortcut menu, make sure you are right-clicking the shape and not the grid on the drawing page behind the shape. To ensure that you right-click the shape, position the pointer over the shape text, one of the shape's lines, or the white box that appears in the middle of the shape when it's selected, and then right-click.

3 In the **Door width** box, click the down arrow to display a list of dimensions, and then click **36 in**. Click **OK**.

Visio widens the door and updates its dimensions to 3′-0″.

4 Right-click the door to display its shortcut menu again, and then click **Reverse In/Out Opening**.

Visio flips the door opening so that it swings down into the office.

5 From the **Walls, Doors, and Windows** stencil, drag a **Window** shape onto the vertical wall to the right of the door.

Visio flips the window to match the wall's orientation and connects the window to the wall shape, displaying red and gray selection handles. The window shape's dimension text appears while the shape is selected.

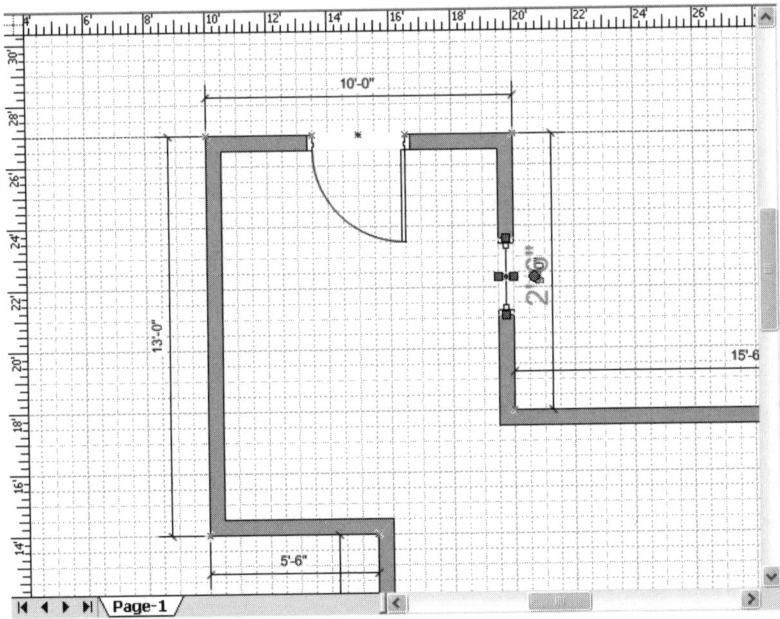

6 Drag the window's bottom selection handle until the shape is 3 feet wide. Use the **Width** field in the status bar at the bottom of the drawing page window to determine the shape's width.

Visio widens the window and updates its dimensions to 3′-0″.

7 From the **Walls, Doors, and Windows** stencil, drag a **Window** shape onto the left side of the 15-foot, 6-inch wall.

Visio connects the window to the wall shape, displaying red and gray selection handles. The window shape's dimension text appears while the shape is selected.

8 Drag the right selection handle on the window you just added to the wall to increase the width of the window to 3 feet. Use the **Width** field in the status bar at the bottom of the drawing page to determine the shape's width.

Visio widens the window and updates its dimensions to 3′-0″.

Tip You can set the display options for one or all the walls, doors, and windows in an office layout at once. For example, you can show or hide all the door frames and swings, window sills and sashes, and wall reference lines in a diagram. To set the display options for all the shapes in a diagram at once, on the Plan menu, click Set Display Options. To set the display options for a single shape, right-click the shape you want to change, and then click Set Display Options on the shortcut menu.

9 Hold down the Ctrl key while you drag the window to the right to duplicate the shape and position the copy on the wall to right of the original.

Visio connects the duplicate window to the wall.

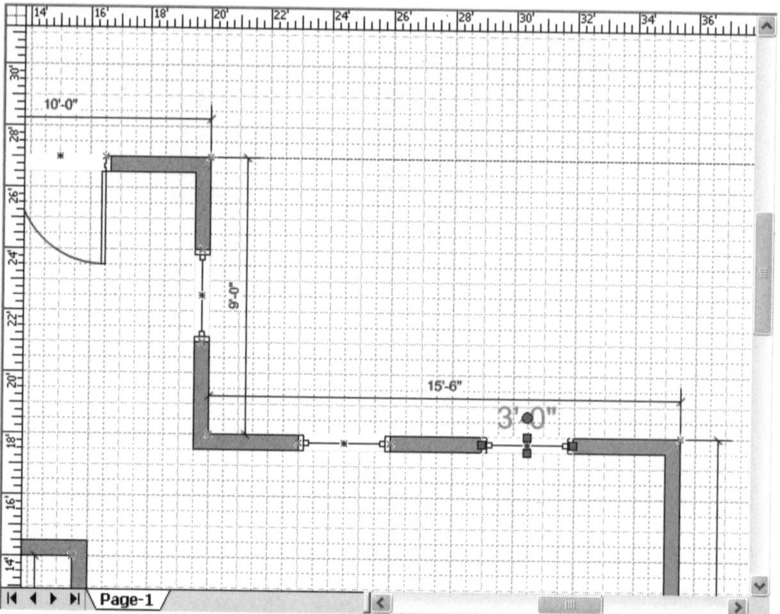

Troubleshooting If you move the window instead of copying it, press Ctrl+Z to undo your action, and then try again. Make sure you release the mouse button before you release the Ctrl key so Visio copies the window instead of moving it.

10 Click the **Cubicles** stencil. From the **Cubicles** stencil, drag the **Straight workstation** shape into the corner of the office opposite the door.

Visio adds the shape to the drawing page.

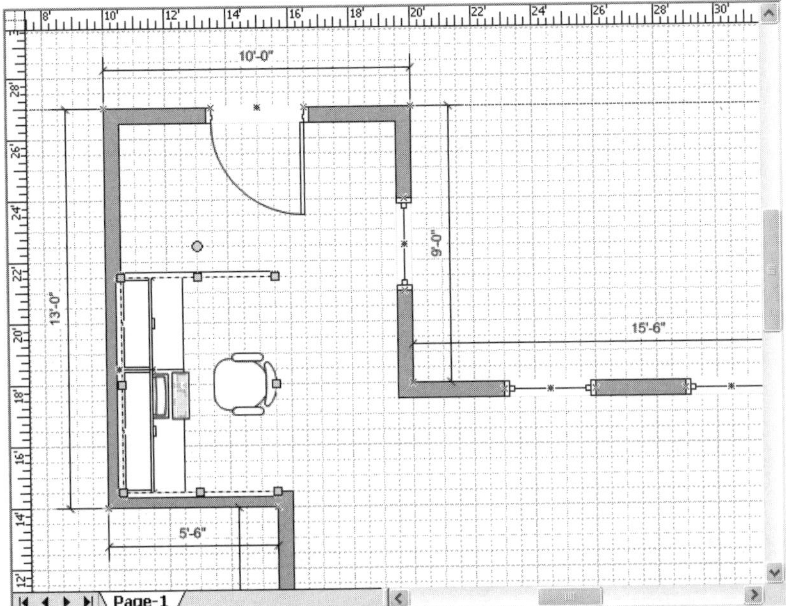

11 Click the **Office Furniture** stencil (at the bottom of the Shapes window). From the **Office Furniture** stencil, drag the **Multi-chair racetrack** shape into the empty room.

Visio adds the shape to the drawing page. The shape is selected.

12 With the shape selected, on the **Shape** menu, point to **Rotate or Flip**, and then click **Rotate Left**.

The shape rotates 90 degrees to the left.

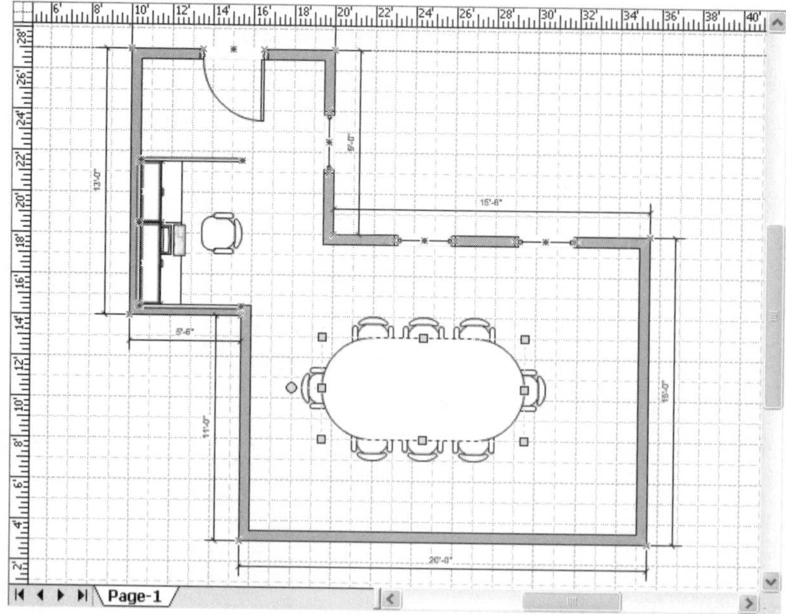

13 On the **File** menu, click **Close**, and then click **No** to close the drawing without saving the changes.

Organizing Shapes in Office Layouts by Using Layers

For some drawing types in Visio, shapes are preassigned to *layers*—categories that help you organize and manage related shapes. Visio can show, hide, lock, print, snap, glue, and color and change the transparency of shapes based on their layer assignment. Layers give you a great deal of flexibility over what you want to display and how you want categories of shapes to behave or look. For example, a space plan with everything but the electrical equipment and structural shapes, such as walls, doors, and windows, hidden would be very helpful in determining the best cable routes for the office. You can accomplish this by hiding anything that's not on the electrical or structural layers, or setting particular layers as non-printing layers. It's also common to lock the structural shapes, such as walls, doors, and windows, in a layout after they're in place so that you don't inadvertently move them while adding furniture to the office layout. You can temporarily hide all the annotation shapes, such as callouts and dimension lines, to make it easier to see and move furniture shapes. Layers open up all these options to you.

Layers are also used when more than one person revises or reviews a diagram. For example, in an office layout, the building shell can be locked and then handed off to an electrician, who adds wiring on one layer, and then to a plumber, who adds pipes on another layer. That way, each person can add to the diagram without disturbing another person's work. A shape can be assigned to a single layer, to several layers, or to no layer at all. For example, if you use the drawing tools to create a shape, that shape is not assigned to a layer. You can, however, choose to assign the shape to an existing layer or create a new layer. Fortunately, the shapes included with the Office Layout template are already assigned to predefined layers that are built into the template and added to your diagram—a feature that can save you a lot of time if you're work extensively with layers.

Tip To quickly see which layers a shape is assigned to, display the Format Shape toolbar, and then view the Layer list. To display the Format Shape toolbar, right-click the toolbar area, and then click Format Shape on the shortcut menu.

Visio includes two commands for working with layers. The Layer command on the Format menu displays a shape's layer assignments and allows you to create and remove layers. The Layer Properties command on the View menu opens the Layer Properties dialog box, which you use to control the appearance and behavior of the shapes assigned to layers.

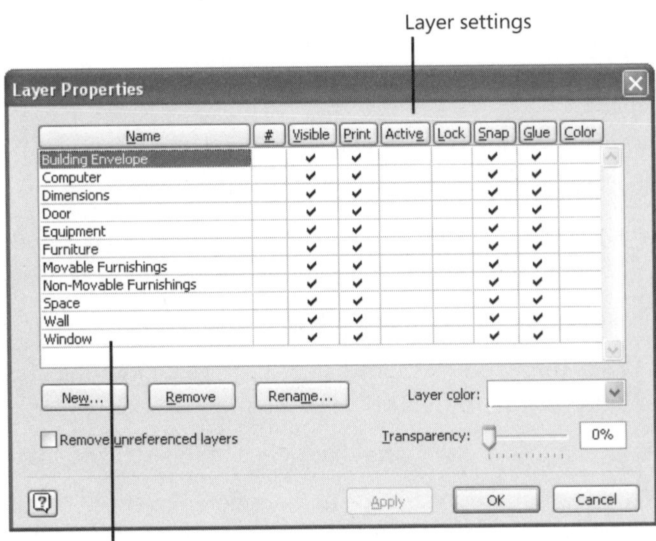

Pre-defined layers in a typical office layout

Important This exercise demonstrates working with layers in an office layout. However, you can use the methods in this exercise to work with layers in any Visio diagram.

In this exercise, you determine which layers some shapes are assigned to, and then you change the layer properties for some layers. You add a callout to the diagram and color code it by using layer properties. Last, you create a new layer, assign shapes to it, and then change its properties.

OPEN the *OfficeFurnished* file in the My Documents\Microsoft Press\Visio 2003 SBS\LayingOutSpaces folder.

1 Select the conference table, and then on the **Format** menu, click **Layer**.

The Layer dialog box appears and shows the layers to which the shape is assigned. In this case, the conference table (the Multi-chair racetrack shape) is assigned to the Furniture layer and Moveable Furnishings layer.

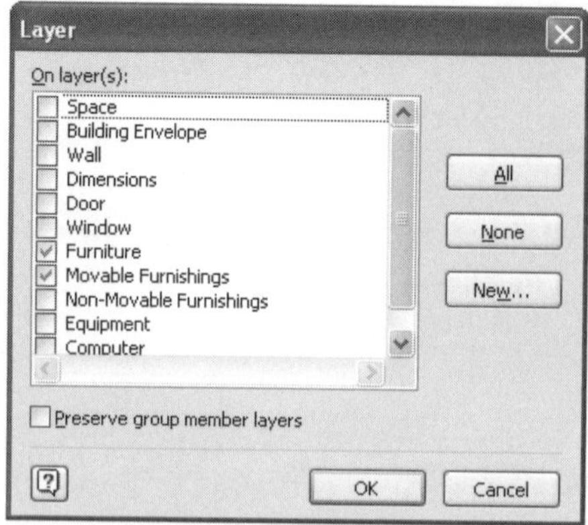

2 Click **Cancel** to close the **Layer** dialog box.

3 Select a wall shape, and then on the **Format** menu, click **Layer**.

The Layer dialog box appears with the Building Envelope layer and the Wall layer selected, indicating that the wall shape is assigned to those two layers.

4 Click **Cancel** to close the **Layer** dialog box.

5 From the **Walls, Doors, and Windows** stencil, drag a **Callout** shape onto the drawing page, and position it to the left of the lower-leftmost wall.

Visio adds a callout to the diagram that points to the left. The shape is selected.

6 Drag the endpoint of the callout line and position it over the middle of the conference table.

As you drag the endpoint to the middle of the table, Visio highlights the table with a red border to indicate that you're creating a shape-to-shape connection. The callout text flips to the other side of the callout line, and the callout connects to the table so that when you move the table, the callout moves with it. The Callout shape remains selected.

7 With the **Callout** shape selected, type **Verify table size**.

Visio adds the text to the callout and resizes the text block so that the text fits within it.

8 Press the Esc key to close the text block.

The Callout shape remains selected.

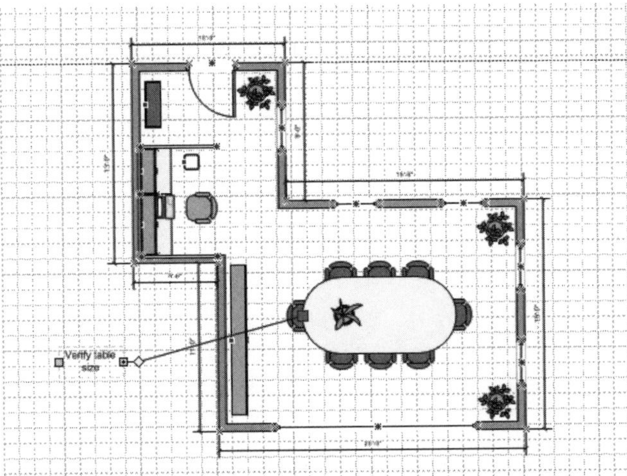

9 On the **View** menu, click **Layer Properties** to open the **Layer Properties** dialog box.

10 In the **Building Envelope** row, click the **Lock** column.

A check mark appears in the Lock column in the Building Envelope row, indicating that all shapes on the Building Envelope layer are locked—in other words, you can't select them.

11 Click the **Lock** column for the **Door**, **Wall**, and **Window** rows—one row at a time.

Visio locks the shapes assigned to the Door, Wall, and Window layers and a check mark appears in the specified rows.

12 In the **Notations** row, click the **Visible** column to deselect it.

There is no check mark in the Visible column, indicating that all shapes on the Notations layer are hidden.

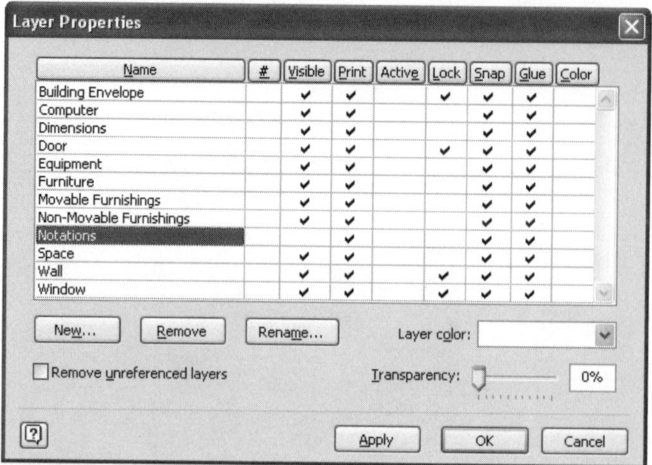

13 Click **OK**.

Visio updates the layers in the office layout with the new layer properties. The Callout shape is no longer visible.

14 Select a door shape.

Nothing happens—the shape is locked, so you can't select it. The walls and windows are also locked.

15 On the **View** menu, click **Layer Properties** to display the **Layer Properties** dialog box again.

16 In the **Notations** row, click the **Visible** column to select it.

A check mark appears in the Visible column in the Notations row, indicating that all shapes on the Notations layer are visible.

17 In the **Notations** row, click the **Color** column.

A check mark appears in the Color column in the Notations row, indicating that all shapes on the Notations layer are color-coded gray (the color that appears by default in the column and in the Layer Color box).

18 In the **Layer Color** box, click the down arrow, scroll up, and then click color **04:** (blue).

In the Notations row, the column is shaded blue to signify that the shapes on the Notations layer are color-coded blue.

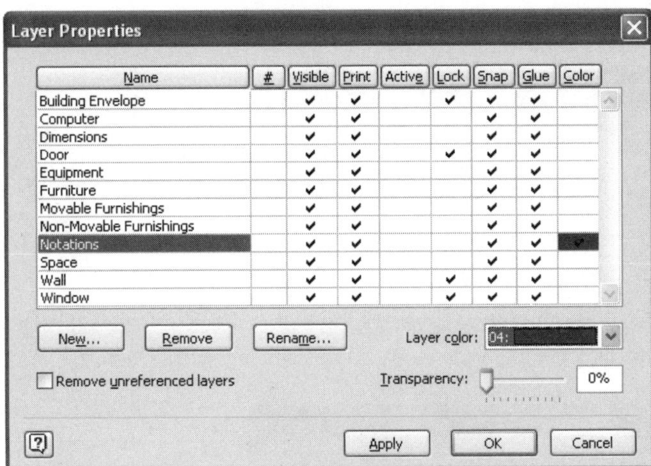

19 Click **OK**.

Visio changes the color of the Callout shape, which is on the Notations layer, to blue.

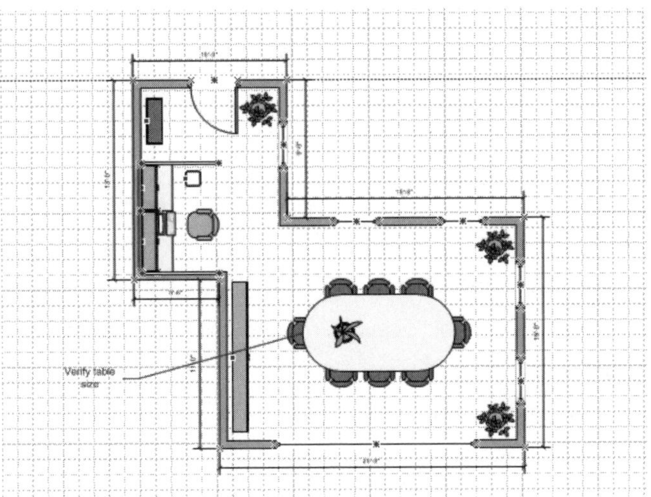

20 Select a plant.

21 Hold down the Shift key while you select the rest of the plants in the office layout.

All four plants in the diagram are selected.

22 On the **Format** menu, click **Layer** to open the **Layer** dialog box.

23 In the **Layer** dialog box, click **New**.

The New Layer dialog box appears.

24 In the **New Layer** dialog box, type Plants.

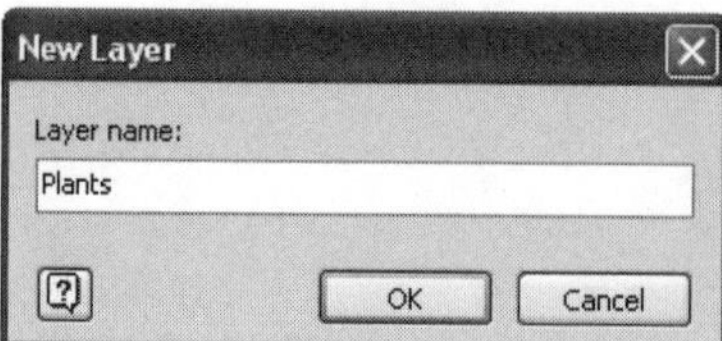

25 Click **OK**.

Visio closes the New Layer dialog box, adds the Plants layer to the layer list in the Layer dialog box, and selects the Plants layer to assign the selected plant shapes to it.

26 Click **OK**.

Visio closes the Layer dialog box and assigns the plant shapes to the Plants layer.

27 On the **View** menu, click **Layer Properties** to display the **Layer Properties** dialog box again.

28 In the **Plants** row, click the **Visible** column to deselect it. Click **OK**.

The plants in the office layout aren't visible.

29 Repeat steps 27 and 28, but *select* the **Visible** option to display the plants again.

Save

30 On the Standard toolbar, click the **Save** button to save the changes to the diagram.

CLOSE the *OfficeFurnished* file.

Troubleshooting Many of the shapes included with the Office Layout template are groups, such as the plant shapes on the Office Accessories stencil and the conference table shapes on the Office Furniture stencil. To add color to the individual shapes in the group, subselect the individual shapes, and choose a formatting option. For example, you can subselect a chair in the Multi-chair racetrack shape, and then click the Fill Color button on the Formatting toolbar to apply a color to that chair.

Key Points

- You can create a scaled diagram with a scaled template so that the drawing scale is already defined and the stencils that the template opens contain shapes appropriate for the drawing scale.
- You can change the drawing scale for a diagram by clicking Page Setup on the File menu, and then clicking the Drawing Scale tab.
- You can create walls by positioning Space shapes on the drawing page, uniting them by using the Union command, and then converting them to walls by using the Convert to Walls command on the Plan menu.
- You can easily add doors and windows to walls by dragging them on top of the walls. Visio orients the doors and windows for you.
- You can change the size of doors and windows by either dragging a shape's end-point or right-clicking the shape, clicking Properties on the shortcut menu, and specifying the shape's width.
- You can set the display options for all the spaces, walls, doors, and windows in an office layout at once by clicking Set Display Options on the Plan menu. You can set the display options for a single shape by right-clicking it and then clicking Set Display Options on the shortcut menu.
- You can see a shape's dimensions by selecting it. To add a dimension line to shape, use the Controller dimension shape on the Walls, Doors, and Windows stencil.
- You can create a new layer and assign a shape to it at the same time by selecting one or more shapes on the drawing page and then clicking Layer on the Format menu.
- You can change the properties for all the shapes assigned to a layer by clicking Layer Properties on the View menu.

Connect shapes in network diagrams,
page 179

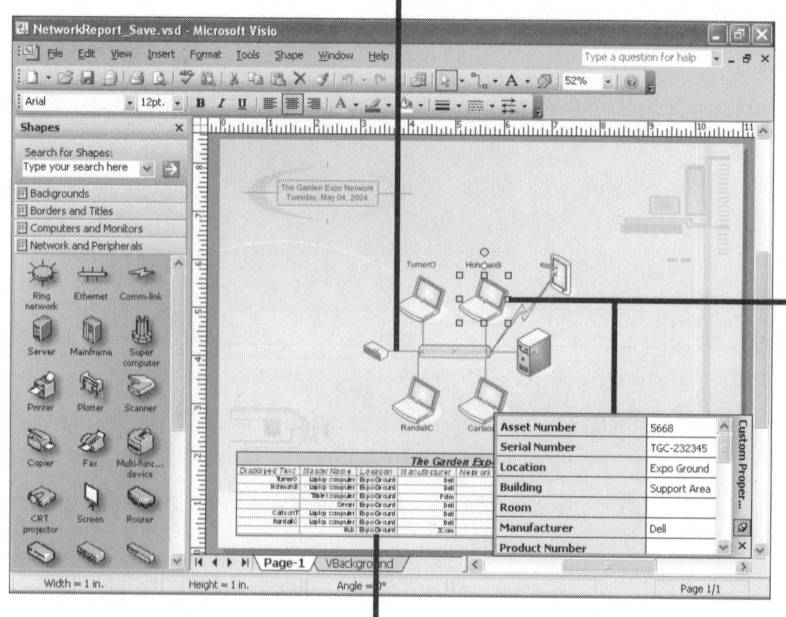

Store information with network shapes,
page 186

Create network reports,
page 190

Chapter 8 at a Glance

8 Creating Network Diagrams

In this chapter you will learn to:

- ✔ Connect shapes in network diagrams.
- ✔ Store information with network shapes.
- ✔ Create network reports.

Organizations of any size can use network diagrams to plan, document, and troubleshoot network infrastructures. Using the Basic Network Diagram template in Microsoft Office Visio, you can diagram a wide variety of computer and network equipment and their physical and logical relationships. You can also store data, such as serial number, location, manufacturer, network name, product description, and so on, with the equipment shapes in a network diagram. You can then use that data to create your own network reports that you can store in spreadsheets or display in your network diagrams.

In this chapter, you create a diagram of the proposed network infrastructure for the Garden Expo hosted by The Garden Company. You add information to the network equipment shapes in the diagram, and then use that information to create a hardware report for the network.

See Also Do you need only a quick refresher on the topics in this chapter? See the Quick Reference entries on pages xxxvi–xxxvii.

Important Before you can use the practice files in this chapter, you need to install them from the book's companion CD to their default location. See "Using the Book's CD" on page xv for more information.

Connecting Shapes in Network Diagrams

New in Visio 2003

You can quickly and easily create a network diagram that includes information such the type of equipment, how it is connected to the network, and the most effective configuration, by using the Basic Network Diagram template. You simply drag shapes onto the drawing page and experiment with their arrangement until you achieve the result you want.

The first step in creating a network diagram is to determine which type of *network ring* or *backbone*—the part of the network that handles the major data traffic—you want to use. Then you drag the backbone shape onto the drawing page, followed by each hardware shape in the network. After you position the network equipment shapes around the backbone, you drag control handles from the backbone shape to connect the hardware shapes to the backbone. Finally, you add text to the shapes as you would any other Visio shape. It really is that easy.

In this exercise, you diagram The Garden Company's local area network (LAN) for the Garden Expo. You drag an Ethernet shape (the backbone of the network) onto the drawing page, connect laptop computers and other components directly to the backbone, and then add descriptive text to some of the network equipment shapes. Finally, you add a background, title, and color scheme to the diagram.

Tip If you need help creating network diagrams, type **network diagram** in the Type a question for help box.

1. Start Visio. In the Choose Drawing Type window, in the **Category** area, click **Network**. In the **Template** area, click **Basic Network Diagram**.

   The template opens a blank drawing page and the Network and Peripherals stencil, Computers and Monitors stencil, Borders and Titles stencil, Backgrounds stencil.

2. From the **Network and Peripherals** stencil, drag an **Ethernet** shape to the center of the drawing page.
3. Click the **Computers and Monitors** stencil.
4. From the **Computers and Monitors** stencil, drag a **Laptop computer** shape onto the drawing page, and position it above the **Ethernet** shape.
5. From the **Computers and Monitors** stencil, drag another **Laptop computer** shape onto the drawing page, and position it above the **Ethernet** shape and to the right of the other **Laptop computer** shape.
6. Repeat the steps 4 and 5, this time positioning the two **Laptop computer** shapes below the **Ethernet** shape.

7 Select the **Ethernet** shape.

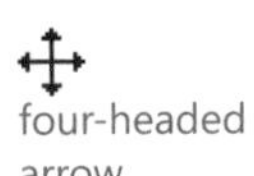
four-headed arrow

8 Position the pointer over the yellow, upper-left control handle on the **Ethernet** shape, and then when the pointer changes to a four-headed arrow, drag the control handle to the connection point in the middle of the upper-left **Laptop computer** shape.

Visio connects the two shapes. The connector remains selected and the endpoint is red, indicating that it is glued to the Laptop computer shape.

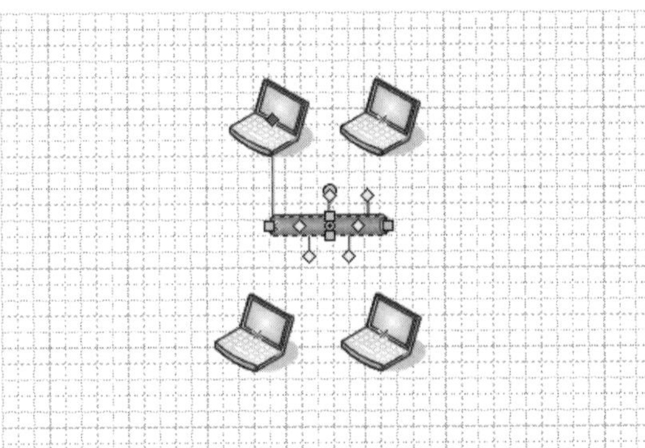

9 Repeat step 8 to create connections to the **Ethernet** shape for each of the remaining **Laptop computer** shapes. Each time, drag a different control handle to a **Laptop computer** shape.

All four laptop computers are connected to the Ethernet shape.

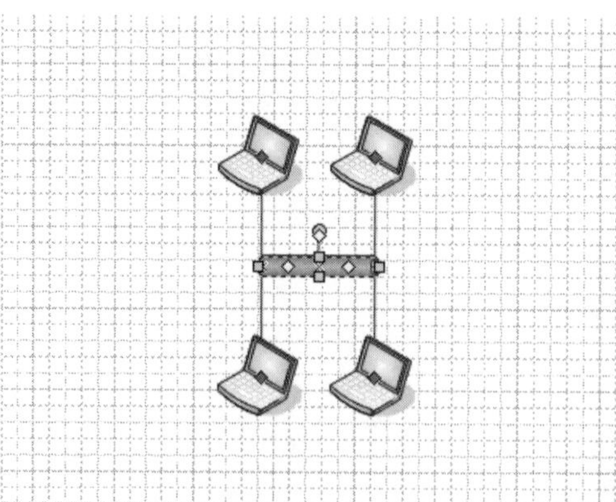

10 Click the **Network and Peripherals** stencil.

11 From the **Network and Peripherals** stencil, drag a **Server** shape onto the drawing page, and position it to the right of the **Ethernet** shape.

12 From the **Network and Peripherals** stencil, drag a **Hub** shape onto the drawing page, and position it to the left of the **Ethernet** shape.

13 Select the **Ethernet** shape.

14 Position the pointer over one of the control handles (represented by a yellow diamond) on the **Ethernet** shape, and when the pointer changes to a four-headed arrow, drag the control handle to the connection point in the middle of the **Server** shape.

Visio connects the two shapes. The connector remains selected and the endpoint is red, indicating that it is glued to the Server shape.

15 Position the pointer over one of the control handles (represented by a yellow diamond) on the **Ethernet** shape, and when the pointer changes to a four-headed arrow, drag the control handle to the connection point in the middle of the **Hub** shape.

Visio connects the two shapes. The connector remains selected and the endpoint is red, indicating that it is glued to the Hub shape.

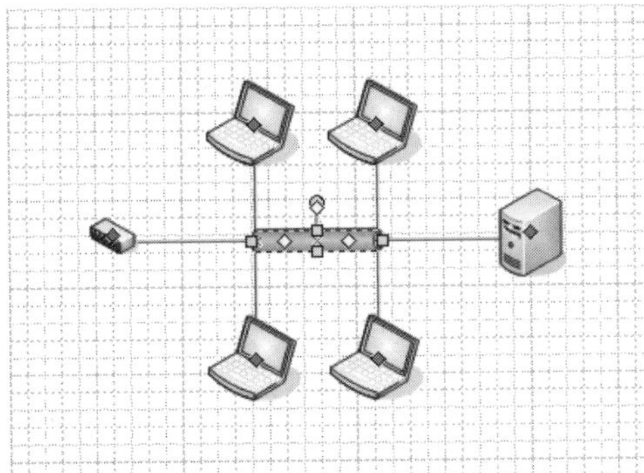

16 Click the **Computers and Monitors** stencil.

17 From the **Computers and Monitors** stencil, drag a **Tablet computer** shape onto the drawing page, and position it above and to the right of the **Ethernet** shape.

18 Click the **Network and Peripherals** stencil.

19 To indicate the transmission of data from the **Tablet computer** shape to the network, drag a **Comm-link** shape onto the drawing page, and position it anywhere in the top half of the diagram.

20 Drag the **Comm-link** shape's right endpoint to the middle connection point on the **Tablet computer** shape.

Visio connects the two shapes. The connector remains selected and the endpoint is red, indicating that it is glued to the Tablet computer shape.

21 Drag the **Comm-link** shape's left endpoint to the right connection point on the **Ethernet** shape.

Visio connects the two shapes. The connector remains selected and the endpoint is red, indicating that it is glued to the Ethernet shape.

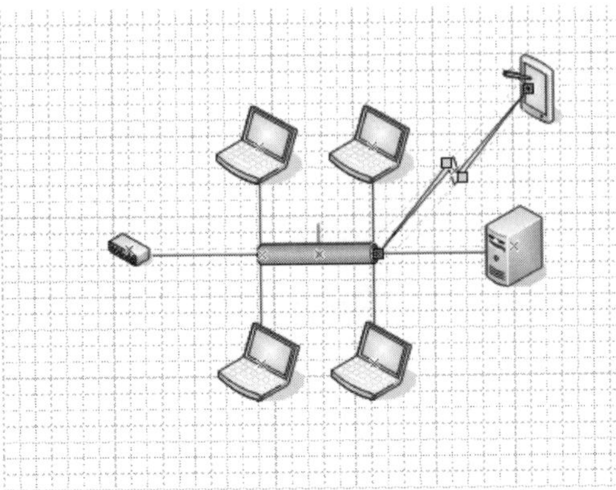

22 Double-click the upper-left **Laptop computer** shape to open the shape's text block.

23 Type TurnerO, and then press the Esc key to close the shape's text block.

The shape remains selected and a new control handle appears on top of the shape text.

24 Drag the new control handle above the **TurnerO** shape to position the text above the shape.

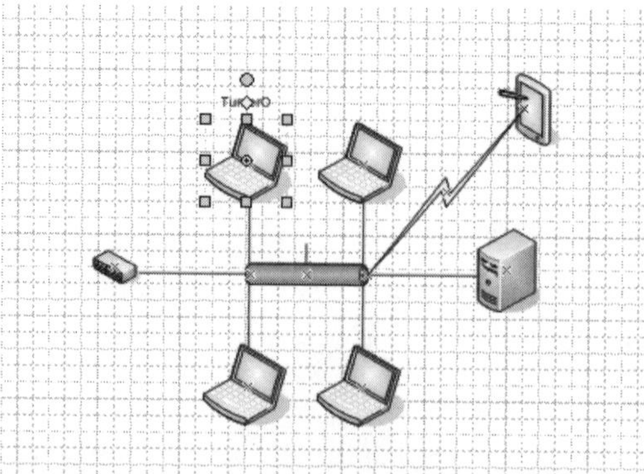

25 Double-click the lower-left **Laptop computer** shape to open the shape's text block, type RandallC, and then press the Esc key to close the shape's text block.

26 Double-click the lower-right **Laptop computer** shape to open the shape's text block, type CarlsonT, and then press the Esc key to close the shape's text block.

27 Double-click the upper-right **Laptop computer** shape to open the shape's text block, type HohmanB, and then press the Esc key to close the shape's text block.

The shape remains selected and a new control handle appears on top of the shape text.

28 Drag the new control handle above the **HohmanB** shape to position the text above the shape.

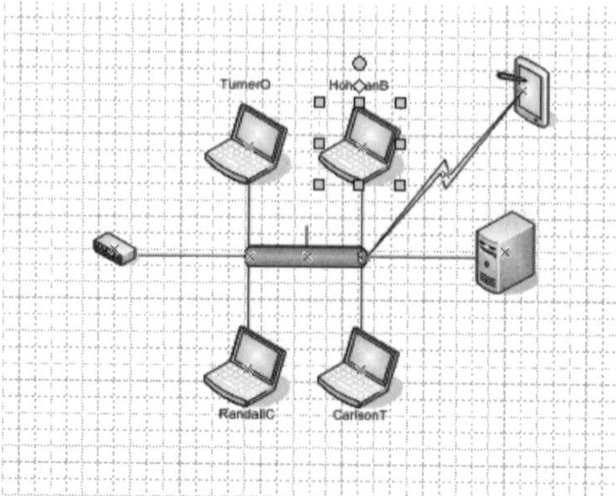

29. Click the **Backgrounds** stencil.
30. From the **Backgrounds** stencil, drag the **Background high-tech** shape onto the drawing page.

    Visio adds a VBackground page to the drawing file and places the background shape on it.
31. Click the **Borders and Titles** stencil.
32. From the **Borders and Titles** stencil, drag the **Title block sphere** shape onto the drawing page, and position it in the upper-left corner of the drawing page.
33. With the shape selected, press F2 to open the shape's text block.
34. Highlight the placeholder text, Company Name/Title, and then type The Garden Expo Network to replace it.

    The shape's width increases to fit the new text.
35. Click the pasteboard to deselect the shape.
36. Right-click the drawing page, and then click **Color Schemes** on the shortcut menu to open the **Color Schemes** dialog box.
37. In the **Color Schemes** dialog box, click **Jade**, and then click **OK**.

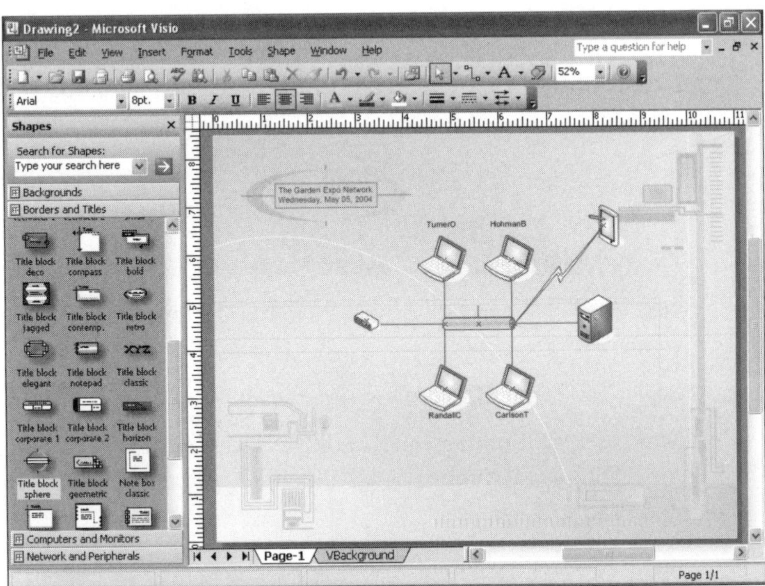

38. On the **File** menu, click **Save**.
39. In the **Save As** dialog box, in the **File name** box, type Network.
40. In the **Save As** dialog box, click the **Save** button to save the diagram.

CLOSE the *Network* file.

Storing Information with Network Shapes

Network equipment shapes have default custom properties, which you can use to store data with the shapes. These properties include manufacturer, product number, part number, product description, and serial number. You can also define new custom properties for a specific shape or for all the instances of a shape in a diagram.

To view custom property information for a shape, on the View menu, click Custom Properties Window, and then select the shape. The shape's custom properties and corresponding data appears in the Custom Properties window. Alternatively, you can right-click a shape, and then click Properties on the shortcut menu. You can define a new custom property for all the instances of a shape in a diagram by using the Document Stencil, which includes all the shapes in your diagram. If you edit a shape on the Document Stencil, the changes ripple throughout all the instances of the shape in the diagram.

Tip You can also create custom property *sets* for shapes in a diagram. A custom property set is a set of related custom properties. To create a custom property set for a shape, right-click the Custom Properties window, and then click Custom Property Sets on the shortcut menu. In the Custom Property Sets window, define the set. For more information about defining and working with custom property sets, type custom property set in the "Type a question for help" box.

In this exercise, you view the custom properties assigned to several of the network equipment shapes in your network diagram. You also create a new custom property for all the Laptop computer shapes in the diagram to identify which employee uses each computer.

OPEN the *NetworkStore* file in the My Documents\Microsoft Press\Visio 2003 SBS\CreatingNetworks folder.

1 On the **View** menu, click **Custom Properties Window**.

   No custom property data appears in the Custom Properties window because a shape isn't selected.

2 Select the **TurnerO** shape.

   The Custom Properties window displays a list of the custom properties for the shape, including Asset Number, Serial Number, Location, Building, Room, Manufacturer, and Product Number.

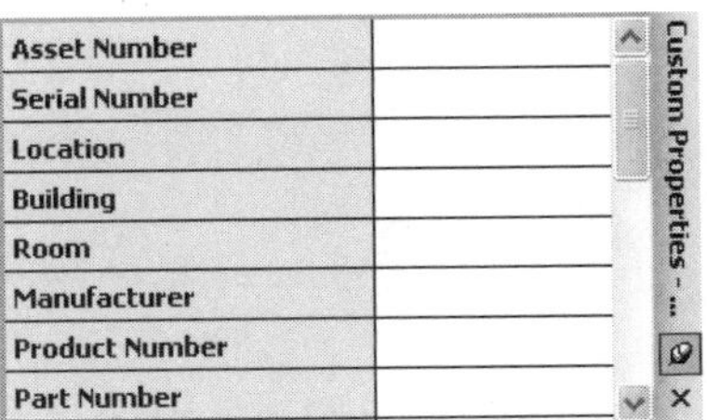

Shapes

3 On the Standard toolbar, click the **Shapes** button, and then click **Show Document Stencil**.

The Document Stencil appears in the Shapes window and displays each shape in your diagram.

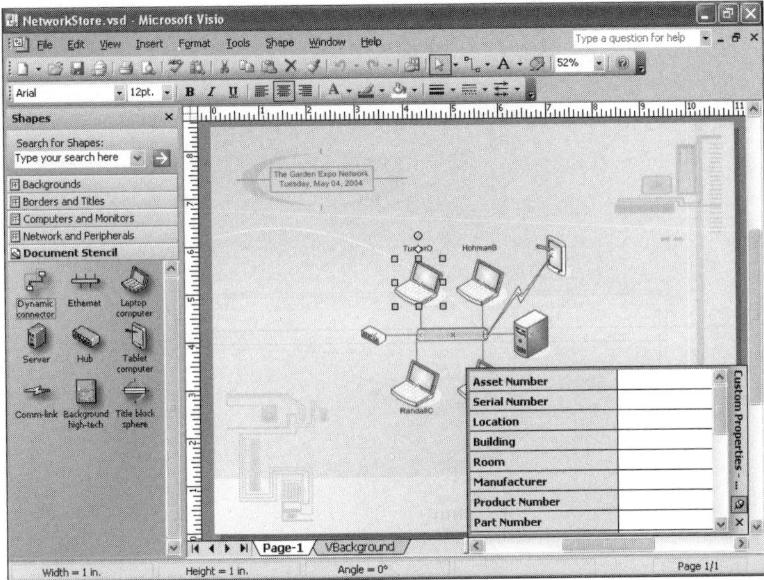

4 In **Document Stencil**, right-click the **Laptop computer** shape, point to **Edit Master**, and then click **Edit Master Shape**.

The Laptop computer shape appears in a drawing window that covers your entire diagram. No custom property data appears in the Custom Properties window because the shape isn't selected.

5 Select the **Laptop computer** shape.

The custom properties for the shape appear in the Custom Properties window.

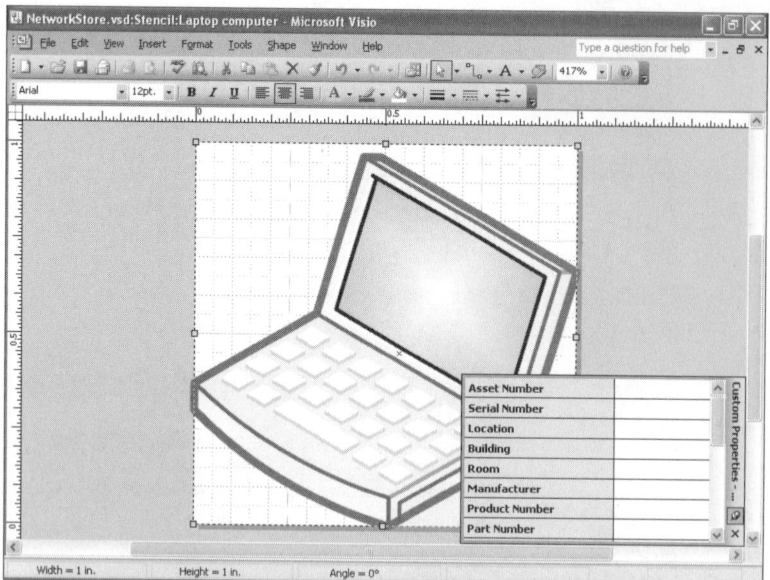

6 Right-click in the Custom Properties window, and then click **Define Properties** on the shortcut menu.

The Define Custom Properties dialog box appears.

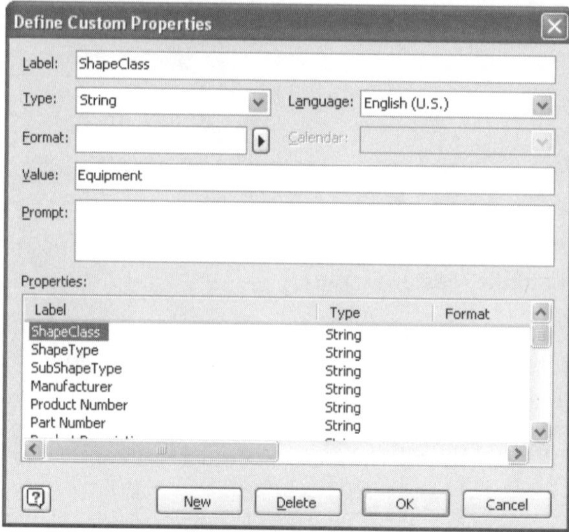

7 In the **Define Custom Properties** dialog box, click **New**.

A property called Property25 is added and highlighted in the Properties box at the bottom of the dialog box.

8 In the **Label** box, type **User Name**, and then click in the **Prompt** box.

9 In the **Prompt** box, type **Enter the name of the employee who uses this device** to create a ScreenTip for the new custom property. Click **OK**.

The Define Custom Properties dialog box closes.

10 Scroll to the end of the list in the Custom Properties window to see the new **User Name** custom property at the end of the list.

Custom Properties - ...	
MAC Address	
Community String	
Network Description	
Hard Drive Capacity	
CPU	
Memory	
Operating System	
User Name	

Close Window

11 Click the **Close Window** button to the right of the **Type a question for help** box in the upper-right corner of the drawing window.

12 When a message appears asking if you want to update the **Laptop computer** shape and all of its instances on the drawing page, click **Yes**.

The drawing window closes and Visio adds the new custom property to all the Laptop computer shapes in the diagram and on the Document Stencil.

13 Right-click the **Document Stencil** title bar, and then click **Close**.

The Document Stencil closes.

14 Click the **HohmanB** shape, and then scroll to the bottom of the list in the Custom Properties window.

The User Name box has been added to the HohmanB shape. Now you can document the individuals that use each laptop computer in the organization.

Tip You can quickly create a custom property for a single instance of a shape. Rather than editing the shape in the Document Stencil, select the shape on the drawing page. Right-click the Custom Property window, and then click Define Properties on the shortcut menu. In the Define Custom Properties dialog box, click New, and then enter the information for the new property.

15 Position the pointer over the **User Name** box to see the ScreenTip that appears for the custom property.

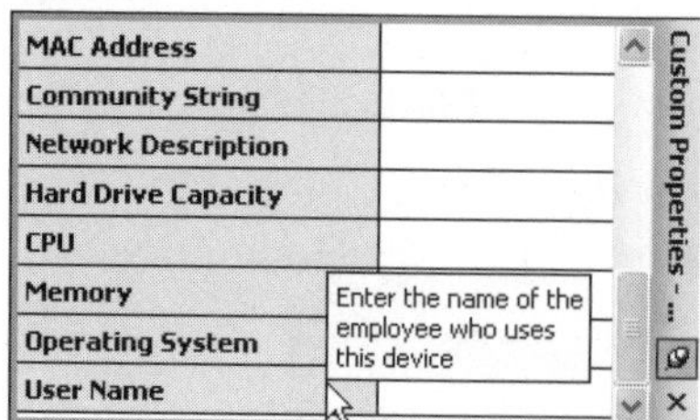

16 In the Custom Properties window, click the **User Name** box, type **Bob Hohman**, and then click the pasteboard to deselect the property.

17 On the **File** menu, click **Close**, and then click **No** when Visio asks you if you want to save the changes to the drawing.

Visio and the drawing close.

Creating Network Reports

You can create a report on the equipment in your network diagrams by using the custom property data stored in the diagram. Visio includes several standard report types, such as the Inventory and Network Device report. You can also define your own report by creating a *report definition*—a set of criteria that specifies which shapes and custom properties are included in the report, as well as the format to use. You create report definitions or modify existing ones by using the Report Definition Wizard, which guides you through the process of specifying the criteria for your report. You run the report by clicking the Reports command on the Tools menu. You can save the results in a spreadsheet, an XML file, or a Web page, or you can display the report as a Visio shape—a specialized shape that displays the report data directly on the drawing page in your network diagram.

In this exercise, you create a new report definition, specifying which shapes and custom properties to include in it, and then you display the report as a Visio shape in the network diagram.

OPEN the *NetworkReport* file in the My Documents\Microsoft Press\Visio 2003 SBS\CreatingNetworks folder.

1 Click one of the network equipment shapes in the diagram, then hold down the Shift key, and click all the other network equipment shapes except the **Ethernet** shape.

2 On the **Tools** menu, click **Reports** to open the **Reports** dialog box.

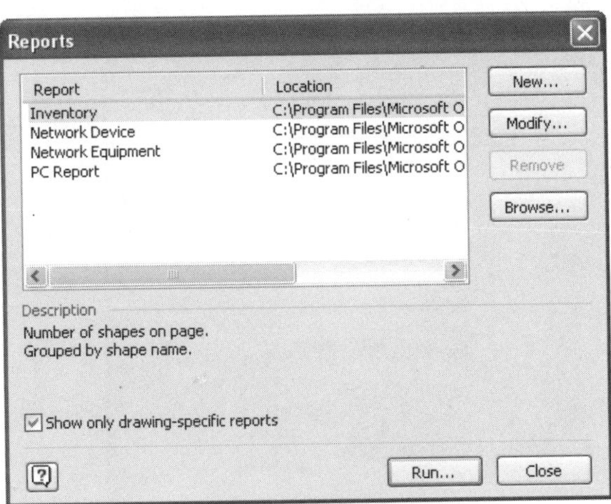

3 In the **Reports** dialog box, click **New**.

The first page of the Report Definition Wizard appears.

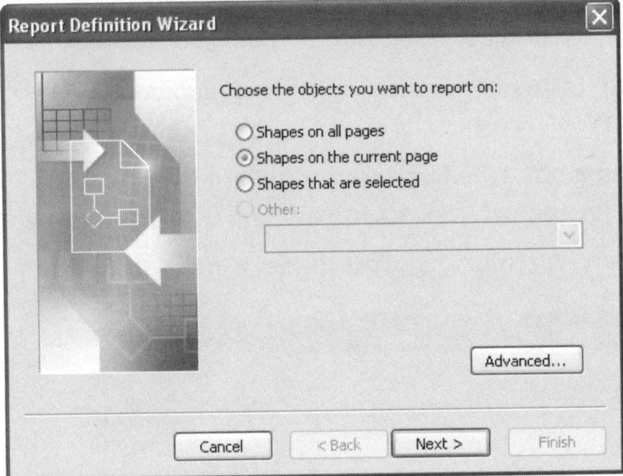

4 On the first page of the **Report Definition Wizard**, select **Shapes that are selected**, and then click **Next**.

The second page of the wizard appears, asking you to select the properties you want to include as columns in your report.

5 Select the **<Displayed Text>**, **<Master Name>**, **Location**, **Manufacturer**, **Network Name**, **Product Description**, **Serial Number**, and **User Name** check boxes.

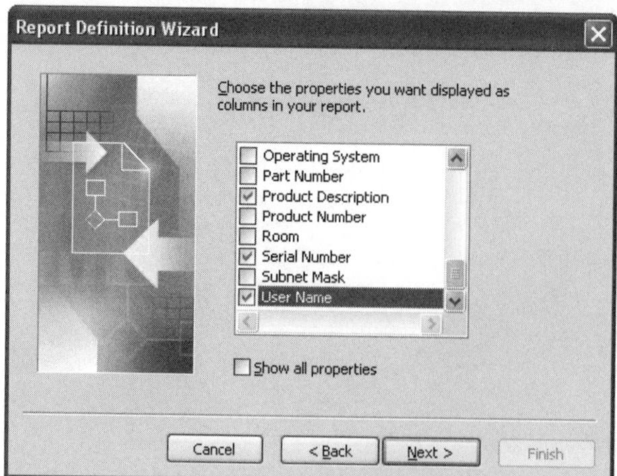

6 Click **Next**.

The third page of the wizard appears, asking you to title the report.

7 In the **Report Title** box, type **The Garden Expo Network**, and then click **Next**.

The fourth page of the wizard appears, asking you to name the custom report definition you're creating.

8 In the **Name** box, type **Network Equipment Report**. In the **Description** box, type **Includes all network equipment and is sorted by shape name.**

9 On the same wizard page, select the **Save in this drawing** option.

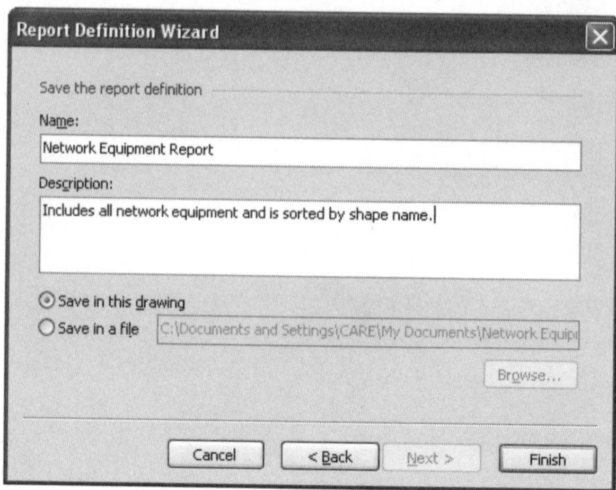

10 Click **Finish**.

The Reports dialog box reappears, listing the Network Equipment Report in the Report column.

11 In the **Reports** dialog box, make sure **Network Equipment Report** is highlighted.

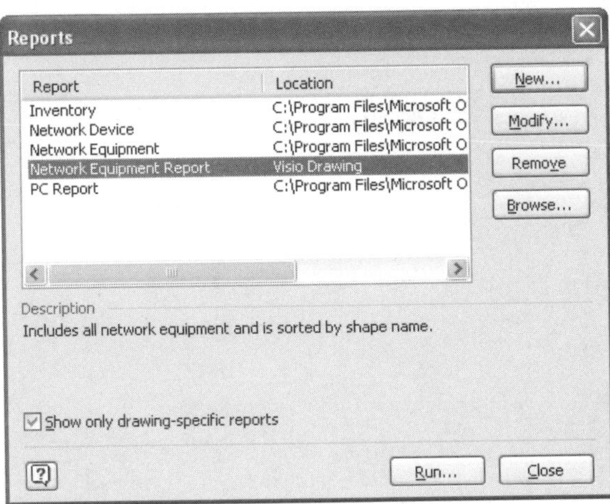

12 Click **Run**.

The Run Report dialog box appears.

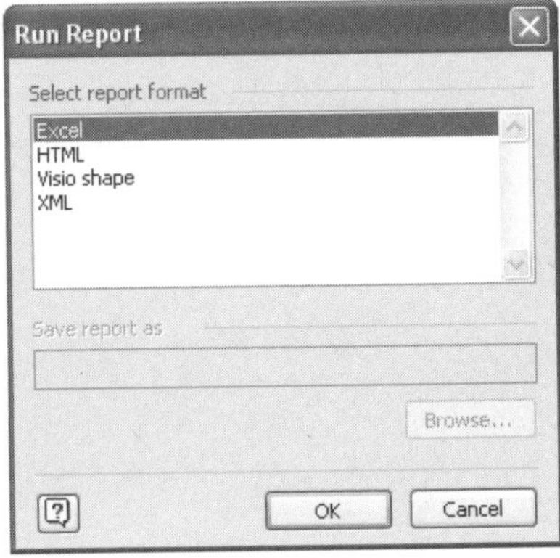

Tip To run an existing report, on the Tools menu, click Reports. Click the report you want, and then click Run. In the Run Report dialog box, select the format for the report, and click OK.

13 In the **Run Report** dialog box, in the **Select report format** box, click **Visio shape**, and then click **OK**.

Visio generates the report and places it at the bottom of the drawing page in a Visio shape that looks like a table.

14 Drag the shape to the bottom of the drawing page.

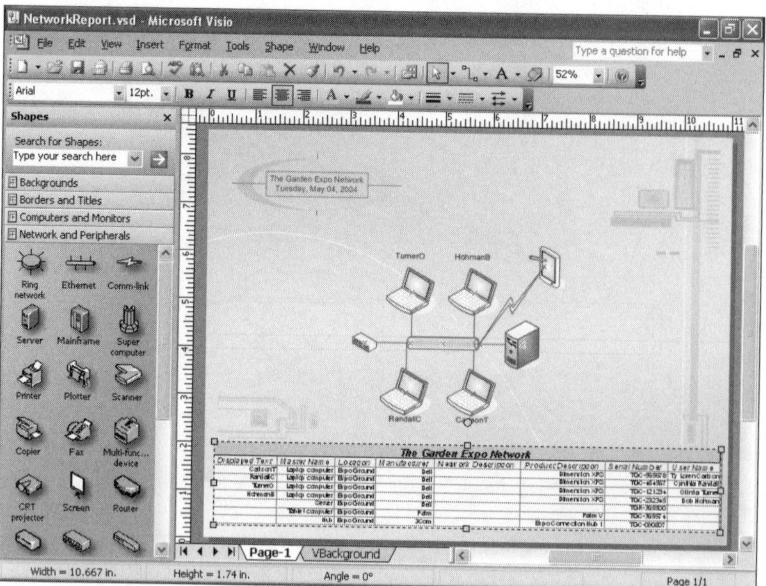

15 On the **File** menu, click **Close**, and then click **No** so you don't save the changes to the diagram.

Key Points

- You can connect network equipment shapes to backbone shapes, such as Ethernet or Ring network shapes, in network diagrams by dragging control handles from the backbone shape to the middle of the network equipment shape.
- You can store network equipment information with shapes by using custom properties. To view a shape's custom property data, select the shape, and then on the View menu, click Custom Properties Window. You can also right-click a shape, and then click Properties on the shortcut menu.
- You can define a new custom property for all the instances of a shape in your diagram. Open the Document Stencil, and then on that stencil, double-click the shape to which you want to add the custom property. Select the shape in the drawing window, and then add the custom property.
- You can define a new custom property for a single shape. Select the shape, right-click the Custom Properties window, and then click Define Properties on the shortcut menu.
- You can run a predefined network report or create your own network report definition. On the Tools menu, click Reports. To create your own report definition, click New in the Reports dialog box.

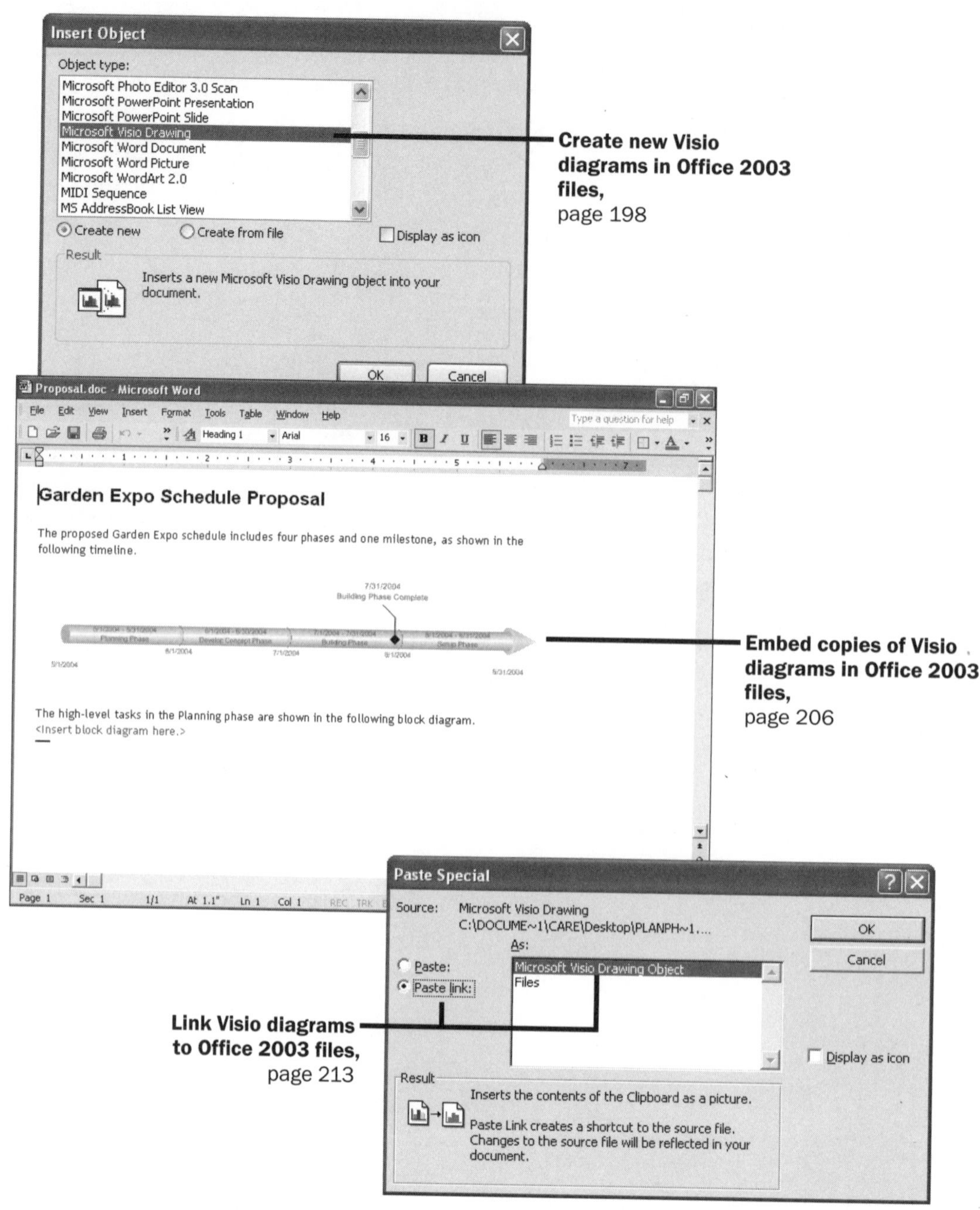

Chapter 9 at a Glance

9 Using Visio Diagrams with the Microsoft Office System

In this chapter you will learn to:

- ✔ **Create new Visio diagrams in Office 2003 files.**
- ✔ **Embed copies of Visio diagrams in Office 2003 files.**
- ✔ **Link Visio diagrams to Office 2003 files.**

Microsoft Office Visio diagrams can support, strengthen, and clarify the information in Microsoft Office 2003 files, such as Microsoft Office Word documents, Microsoft Office PowerPoint presentations, and Microsoft Office Excel spreadsheets. For example, you can incorporate Visio diagrams to enhance the text in Word documents, illustrate the points on PowerPoint slides, support the calculations in Excel spreadsheets, and so forth. The results clearly have more impact than words or numbers alone.

You can use any of the following methods to incorporate Visio diagrams into Office 2003 files:

- Create a new Visio diagram directly in an Office 2003 file. For example, you might want to create a diagram to illustrate a point on a PowerPoint slide. The diagram you create becomes part of the PowerPoint file. Use this method when you don't need to save the diagram as a separate Visio drawing file.
- *Embed* a copy of a Visio diagram in an Office 2003 file. For example, you might want to copy part of a Visio diagram and paste it into a Word document. The copy you embed becomes part of the Word file. Use this method when you don't want any changes you make to the copy of the diagram to appear in the original Visio drawing file, and vice versa.
- *Link* a Visio diagram to an Office 2003 file. For example, you might want to link an entire diagram to a Word document and keep the linked copy up-to-date. Any changes you make to the original Visio drawing file are reflected in the Word file. The diagram you link to the Office 2003 file doesn't become part of the file, so the Office 2003 file size stays at a minimum. Use this method when you want to synchronize the original diagram and the copy in the Office 2003 file.

You can modify the Visio diagrams you incorporate into Office 2003 files by double-clicking the diagram in the file. Visio opens inside the file and replaces many of the program's menus and toolbars with Visio menus and toolbars so that you use Visio shapes, menus, and drawing tools to modify the diagram. When you're finished, you click anywhere outside the diagram to return to the Office 2003 program.

Important This chapter demonstrates incorporating Visio diagrams into Word documents, so Word must be installed on your computer to complete the exercises in this chapter. You can use the general methods outlined in this chapter to incorporate Visio diagrams into any program or Office 2003 file that supports *object linking and embedding*; however, this chapter's instructions are specific to Word.

In this chapter, you'll learn how to create a new Visio diagram within a Word document, embed a copy of a Visio diagram in a Word document, and link a Visio diagram to a Word document. You'll also learn how to modify Visio diagrams in a Word document.

See Also Do you need only a quick refresher on the topics in this chapter? See the Quick Reference entries on pages xxxvii–xxxviii.

Important Before you can use the practice files in this chapter, you need to install them from the book's companion CD to their default location. See "Using the Book's CD" on page xv for more information.

Creating New Visio Diagrams in Office 2003 Files

When you're working in an Office 2003 file, such as a Word document, and you think a diagram would enhance or clarify the text, you can create that diagram directly in the file by using Visio. When you create a Visio diagram in an Office 2003 file, you use the Object command on the Insert menu to insert a blank drawing page into the file. Then you create the diagram from scratch right in the Office 2003 file. The diagram you create becomes part of the file; that is, it isn't a separate Visio drawing file. To modify the diagram, open the Office 2003 file that contains the diagram, and double-click the diagram to open it in Visio within the file. Then use the Visio shapes, menus, and drawing tools to make your changes.

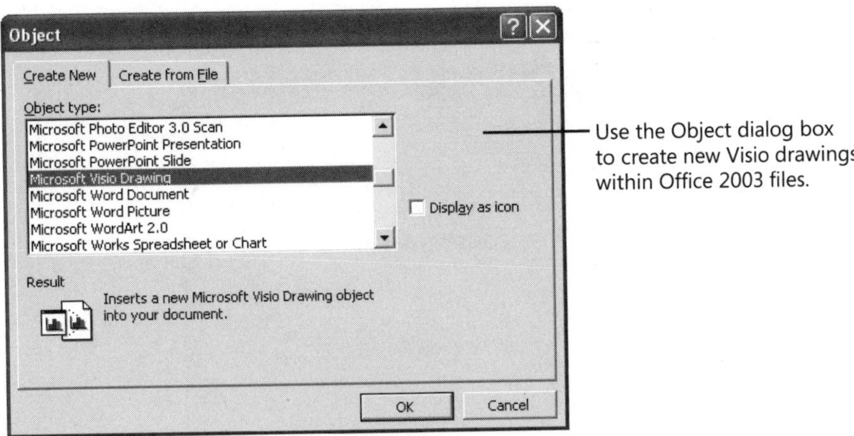

Use the Object dialog box to create new Visio drawings within Office 2003 files.

In this exercise, you create a new block diagram in a Garden Expo Schedule Proposal document, and then you modify the diagram in the document.

USE the *Proposal* file in the My Documents\Microsoft Press\Visio 2003 SBS\UsingDrawings folder.

1. Start Word. On the **File** menu, click **Open**.

   The Open dialog box displays the contents of the My Documents folder by default.

2. Double-click the **Visio 2003 SBS** folder, double-click the **UsingDrawings** folder, and then double-click **Proposal**.

   Word opens the document.

3. Select the blue placeholder text, <Insert block diagram here.>, and then press the Del key.

   Word deletes the text and places the insertion point at the beginning of the line.

4. If the insertion point appears at the end of the previous line, press the Enter key to start a new line.

5. On the **Insert** menu, click **Object** to open the **Object** dialog box.

6 On the **Create New** tab, in the **Object type** area, click **Microsoft Visio Drawing**.

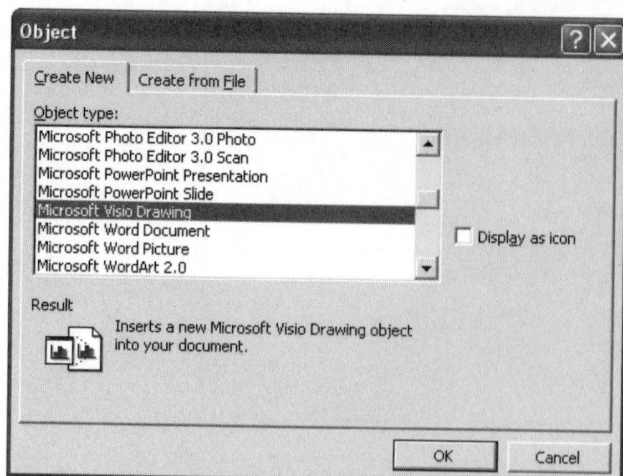

Tip When you want a Visio icon for the diagram to appear in the document instead of the diagram itself, select the Display as icon check box in the Object dialog box.

7 Click **OK**.

Visio starts, adds a blank drawing page to the document, opens the Shapes window, replaces many of the Word menus and toolbars with Visio menus and toolbars, and then opens the Choose Drawing Type dialog box.

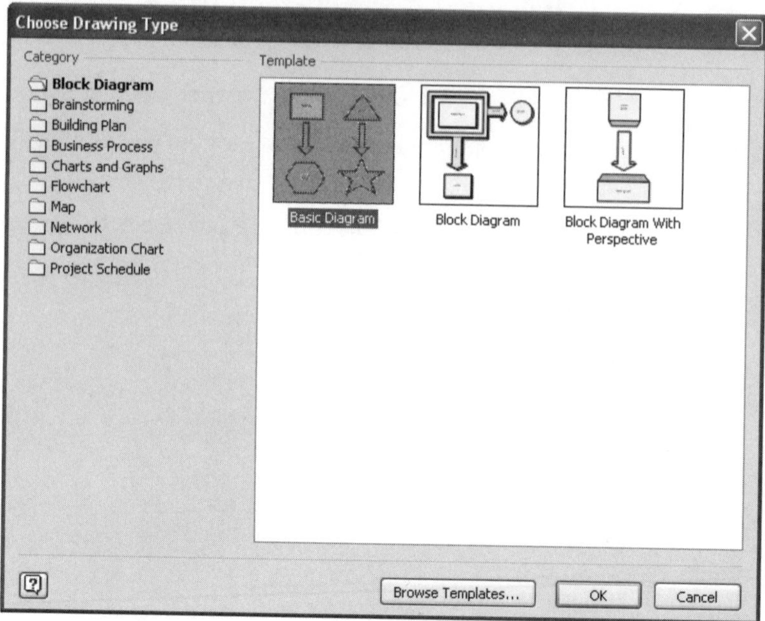

8 In the **Category** area, click **Block Diagram**, and in the **Template** area, double-click **Block Diagram**.

In the Word document, Visio opens the Block Diagram template, which opens the Blocks, Blocks Raised, Borders and Titles, and Backgrounds stencils.

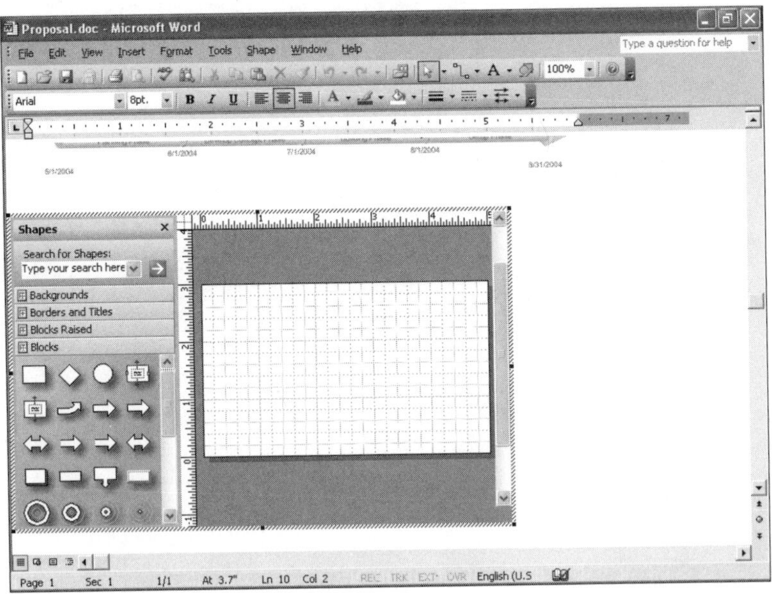

9 On the title bar of the **Blocks** stencil, click the stencil icon, point to **View**, and then click **Icons and Names**.

Visio displays the names and icons for the shapes on the stencils.

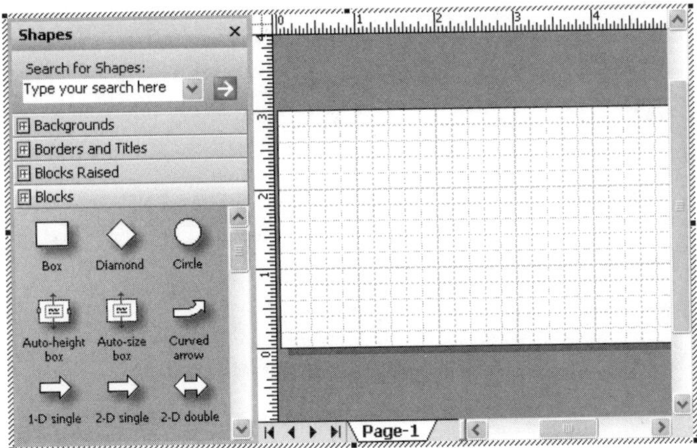

10 From the **Blocks** stencil, drag the **Arrow box** shape onto the drawing page, and position it in the upper-middle portion of the page.

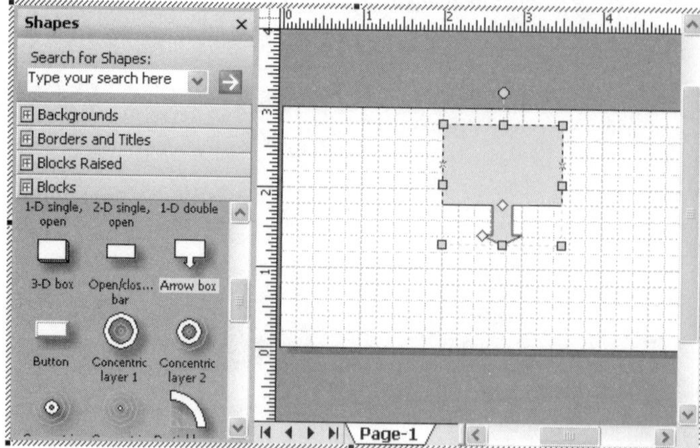

Troubleshooting You might need to scroll down the Blocks stencil to find the Arrow box shape.

11 Drag another **Arrow box** shape onto the drawing page, and position it directly below the first **Arrow box** shape.

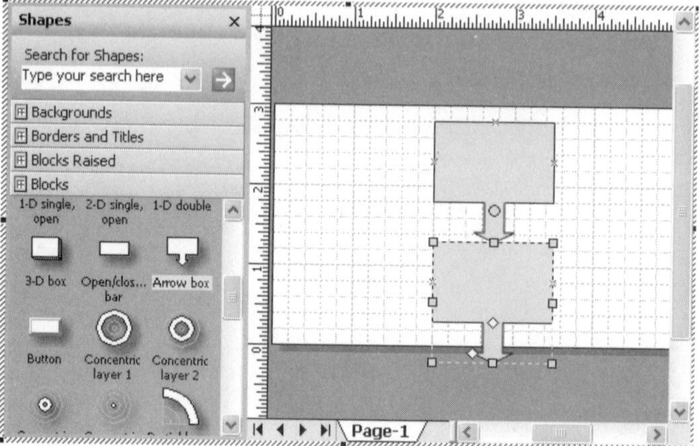

12 On the **Shape** menu, click **Center Drawing**.

Visio centers the shapes on the drawing page.

13 Select the first **Arrow box** shape, and then type Determine Scope.

14 Select the second **Arrow box** shape, and then type Create Schedule.

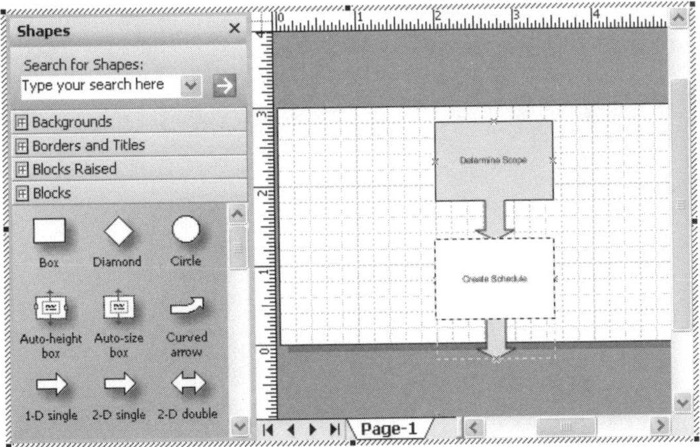

15 Click a blank area of the drawing page to deselect the **Create Schedule** shape.

16 To lengthen the drawing window so that both shapes fit on the drawing page, drag the middle, black selection handle on the black dashed drawing window (below the **Page-1** tab) down far enough to include both shapes in your diagram.

When you place the pointer over the black selection handle on the window, the pointer changes to a double-headed arrow. This visual cue indicates that Word is ready for you to lengthen the drawing window.

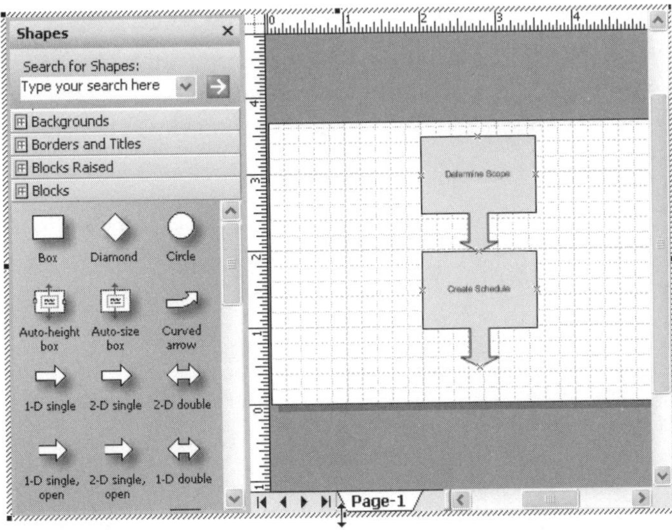

17 To close Visio and continue working in Word, click anywhere outside the Visio diagram in the Word document.

Visio closes, and Word becomes the active program again. The diagram becomes part of the Word document.

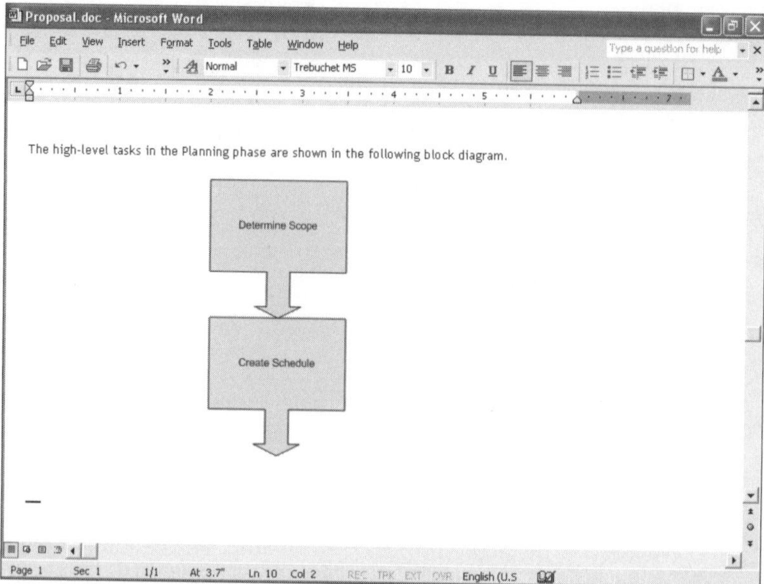

18 To modify the Visio diagram, double-click it.

Visio opens the diagram and stencils again.

19 To lengthen the drawing window again to fit a third shape under the other two, drag the middle, black selection handle on the black dashed drawing window down far enough to include one more shape in your diagram.

The length of the drawing area increases.

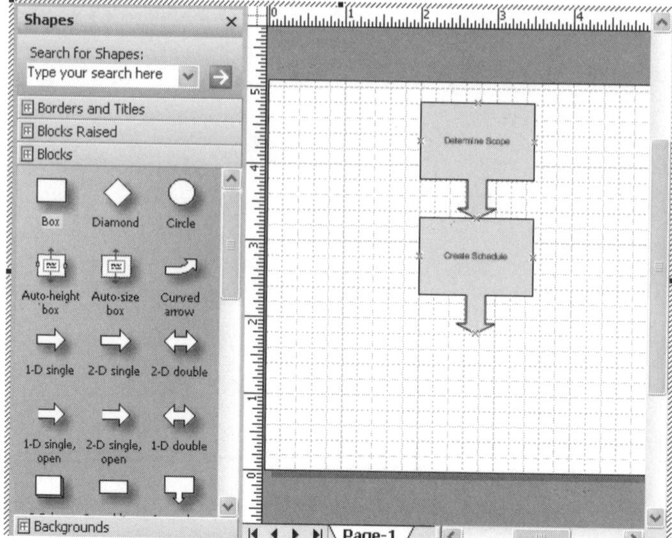

20 From the **Blocks** stencil, drag the **Box** shape onto the drawing page, and position it below the second **Arrow box** shape.

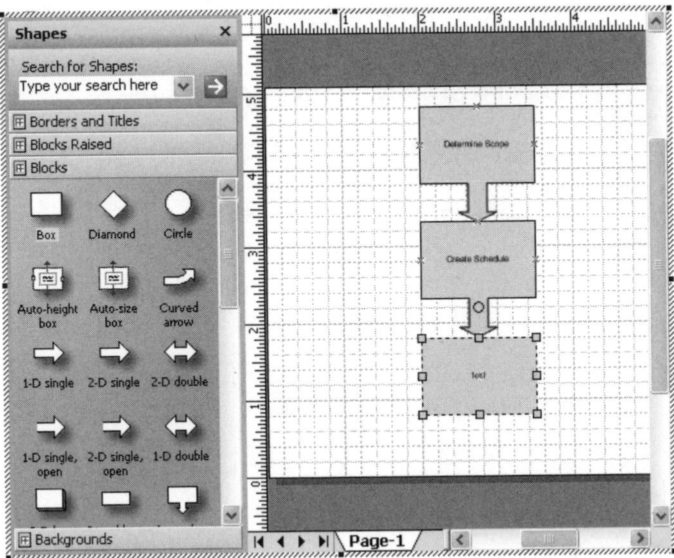

21 With the **Box** shape selected, type **Get Approval for Scope and Schedule.**

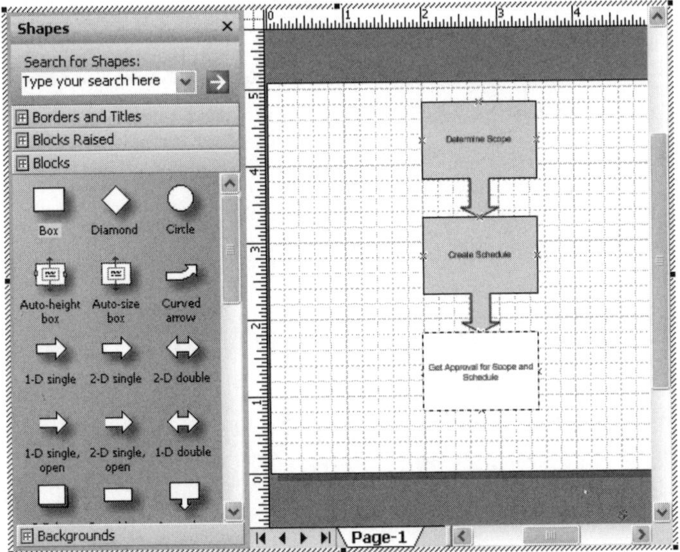

22 Click a blank area of the drawing page to deselect the **Get Approval for Scope and Schedule** shape.

23 On the **Shape** menu, click **Center Drawing**.

Visio centers the shapes on the drawing page.

24 To close Visio and continue working in Word, click anywhere outside the Visio diagram in the Word document.

Visio closes, and Word becomes the active program again. The revised diagram becomes part of your Word document.

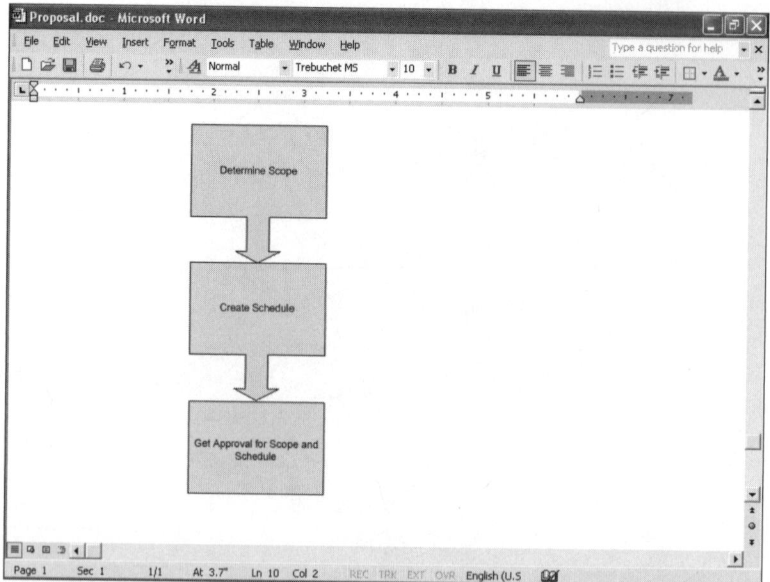

25 On the **File** menu, click **Save As** to open the **Save As** dialog box.

26 In the **File name** box, replace Proposal.doc with ProposalCreate.

27 Click the **Save** button to save the document.

28 On the **File** menu, click **Exit** to close Word and the document.

Embedding Copies of Visio Diagrams in Office 2003 Files

If you have a Visio diagram that you want to add to an Office 2003 file, you can embed a copy of the diagram into the file. When you embed a diagram in an Office 2003 file, you copy the entire diagram or pieces of it, and then paste the copy into the file. The copy of the diagram becomes part of the Office 2003 file. When you modify the embedded diagram in the Office 2003 file, you modify the copy only. Any changes you make to the copy of the diagram don't appear in the original Visio diagram because there's no link between the Office 2003 file and the Visio drawing file.

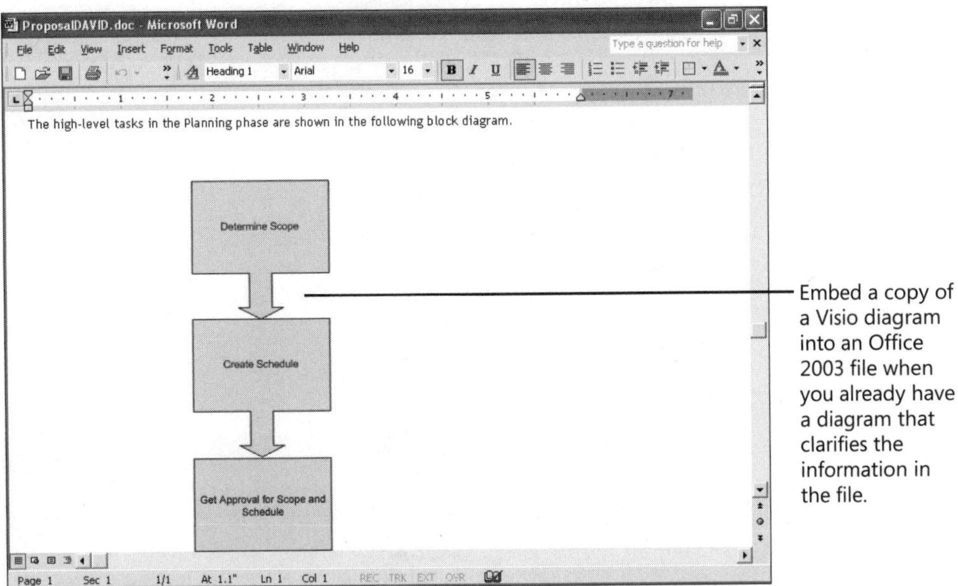

Embed a copy of a Visio diagram into an Office 2003 file when you already have a diagram that clarifies the information in the file.

In this exercise, you open a block diagram, copy it, open a Word document, and then embed the copy of the diagram into the document. Finally, you modify the copy of the diagram in the Word document.

USE the *PlanPhase* file and the Proposal file in the My Documents\Microsoft Press\Visio 2003 SBS \UsingDrawings folder.

1. Start Visio. On the **File** menu, click **Open**.

   The Open dialog box displays the contents of the My Documents folder by default.

2. Double-click the **Microsoft Press** folder, double click the **Visio 2003 SBS** folder, double-click the **UsingDrawings** folder, and then double-click **PlanPhase**.

Visio opens a block diagram and four stencils.

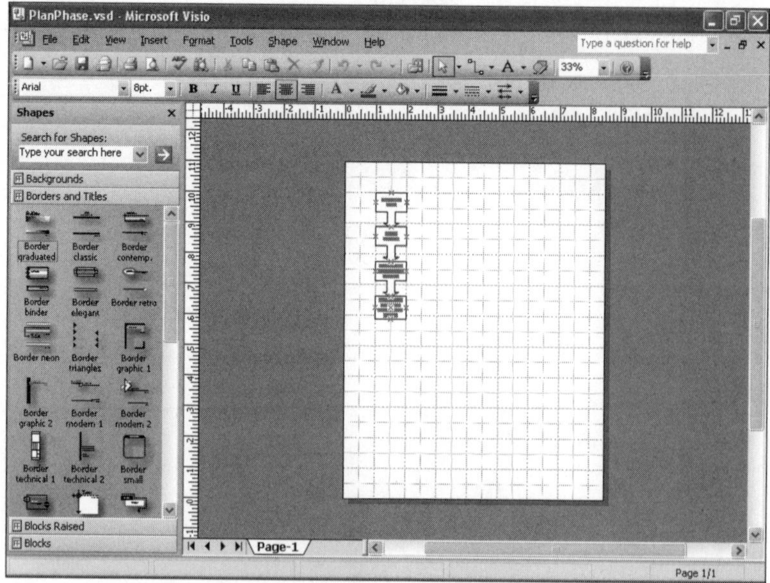

3 On the **Edit** menu, click **Select All**.

Visio selects all the shapes in the diagram.

Copy

4 On the Standard toolbar, click the **Copy** button.

Visio copies the selected shapes.

5 Start Word. On the **File** menu, click **Open**.

The Open dialog box appears.

6 Double-click the **Microsoft Press** folder, double-click the **Visio 2003 SBS** folder, double-click the **UsingDrawings** folder, and then double-click **Proposal**.

Word opens the document.

Troubleshooting If you don't see the Microsoft Press folder in the Open dialog box, navigate to the My Documents folder.

7 Select the blue placeholder text, <Insert block diagram here.>, and then press the Del key.

Word deletes the text and places the insertion point at the beginning of the line.

8 If the insertion point appears at the end of the previous line, press the Enter key to start a new line.

Paste

9 On the Standard toolbar, click the **Paste** button.

Word pastes the copy of the Visio diagram in the Word document and sizes it to fit on the page.

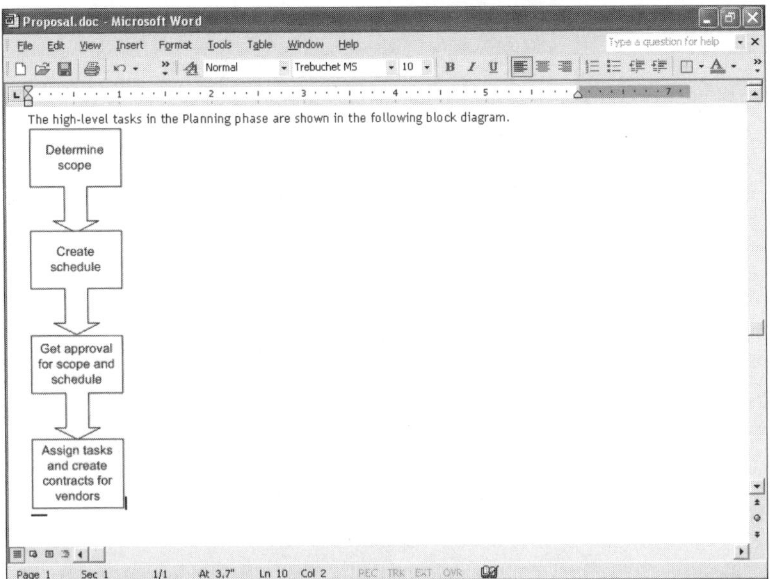

10 To modify the Visio diagram, double-click it.

Visio opens the diagram and the Shapes window, and replaces many of the Word menus and toolbars with Visio menus and toolbars.

11 To widen the drawing window so you see your diagram more clearly, drag the middle-right, black selection handle on the black dashed drawing window to the right a little.

The width of the drawing area increases.

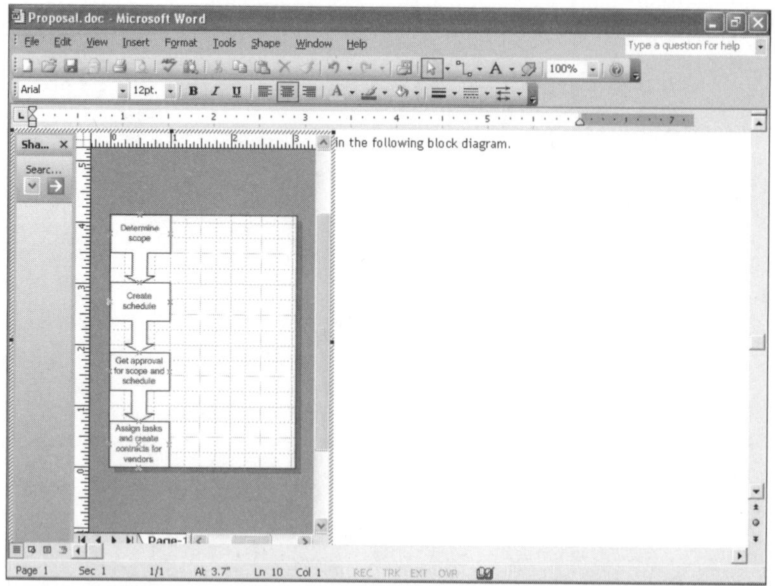

Shapes

12 On the Standard toolbar, click the **Shapes** button, point to **Block Diagram**, and then click **Blocks**.

Visio opens the Blocks stencil.

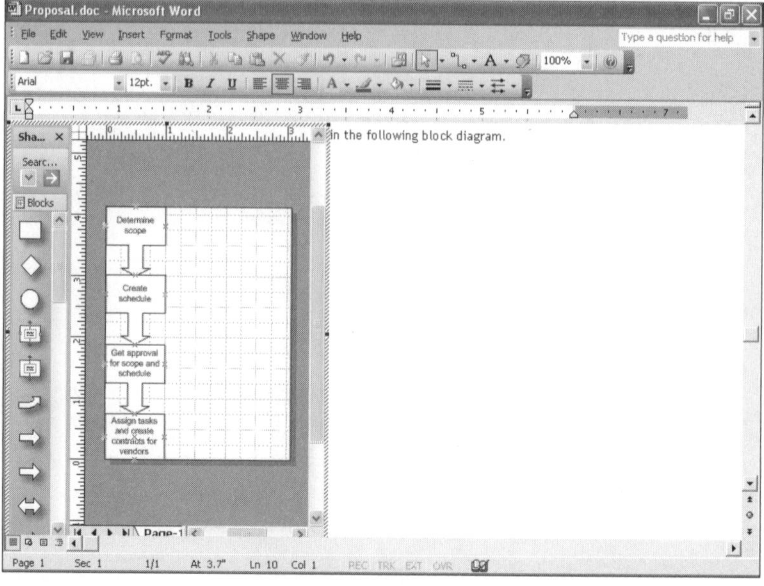

13 From the **Blocks** stencil, drag the **1-D single** shape onto the drawing page, and connect it to the right connection point on the **Determine scope** shape.

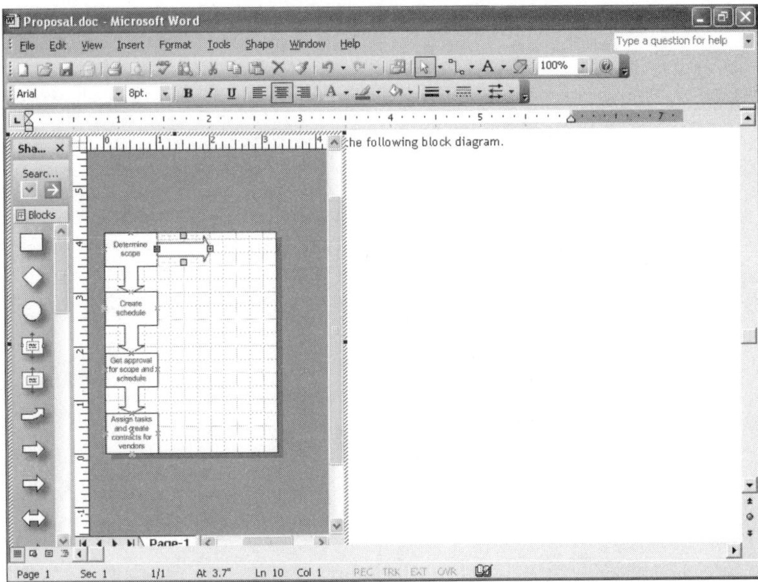

14 From the **Blocks** stencil, drag the **Box** shape anywhere on the drawing page.

15 With the **Box** shape selected, type **Determine budget**.

16 Press the Esc key to close the text block for the **Box** shape.

17 Drag a corner selection handle on the **Box** shape inward to decrease the size of the shape until it's approximately the same size as the other boxes in the diagram.

18 Move the **Box** shape and position it to the right of the **1-D single** shape so the **1-D single** shape connects to the **Box** shape.

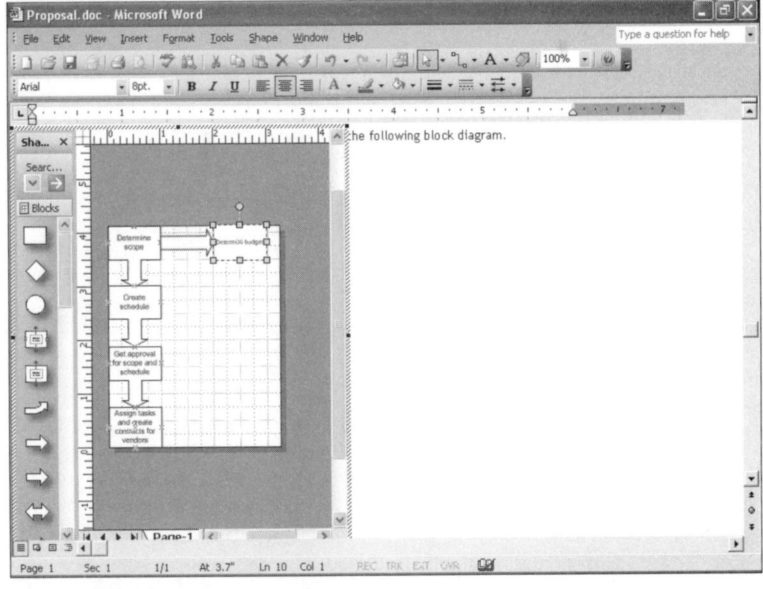

Format Painter

19 Select the **Determine scope** shape, and then on the Standard toolbar, click the **Format Painter** button.

The pointer changes to a black color and a paintbrush appears next to it to indicate that the Format Painter tool is selected. You can now copy the formatting from one shape to another.

20 Click the **Determine budget** shape to copy the formatting attributes from the **Determine scope** shape to it.

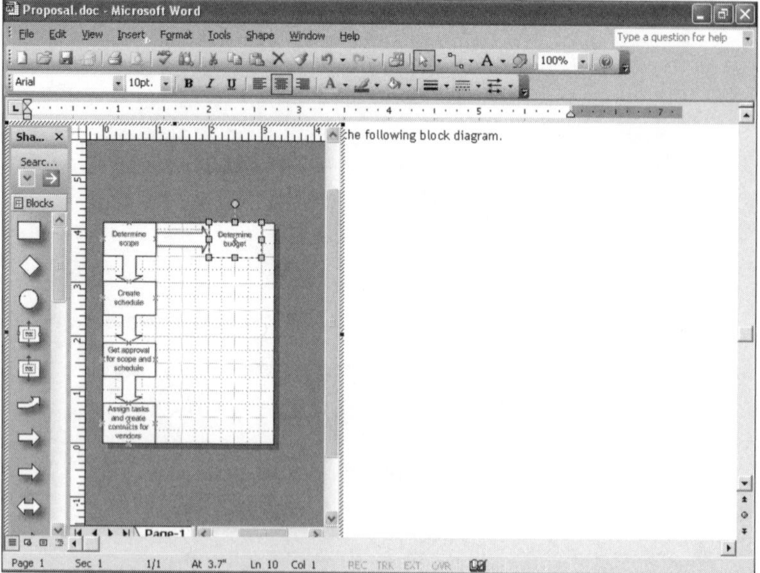

21 To close Visio and continue working in Word, click anywhere outside the Visio diagram in the Word document.

Visio closes, and Word becomes the active program again.

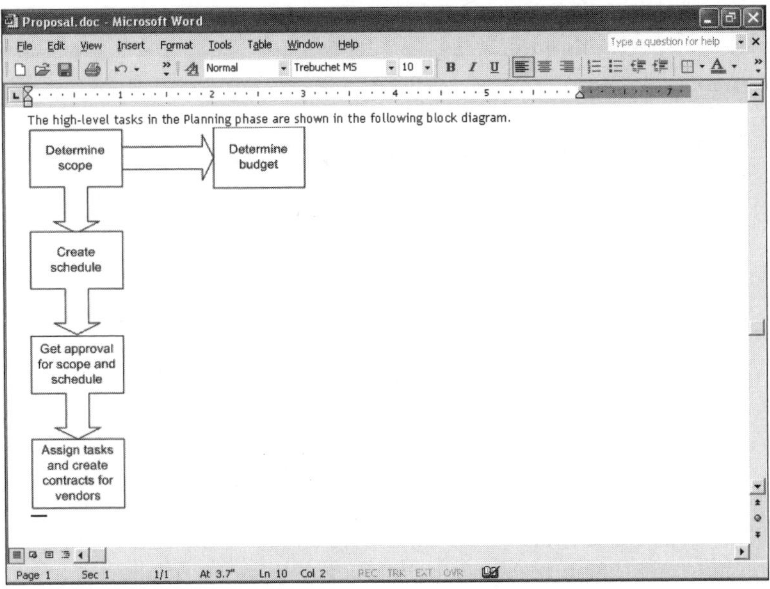

22 On the **File** menu, click **Save As** to open the **Save As** dialog box.

23 In the **File name** box, replace Proposal.doc with ProposalEmbed.

24 Click **Save** to save the document.

25 On the **File** menu, click **Exit** to close Word and the document.

26 Switch to Visio.

Notice the changes you made to the copy of the diagram in the proposal didn't affect the original Visio diagram.

27 On the **File** menu, click **Exit** to close Visio and the diagram.

Linking Visio Diagrams to Office 2003 Files

The main difference between linking a Visio diagram and embedding a copy of a Visio diagram is that a linked diagram doesn't become part of the Office 2003 file. You link a Visio diagram to a file when you want to synchronize the original diagram with the copy in the file. For example, you might link an unfinished Visio block diagram to a Word document. Then when you make changes to the Visio drawing file, those changes are reflected in the Office 2003 file, so it's always up to date.

There is another difference between linking and embedding: when you link to a Visio diagram, you link to the *entire* diagram, including the background. When you embed a copy of a Visio diagram, you can copy all or only specific pieces of it.

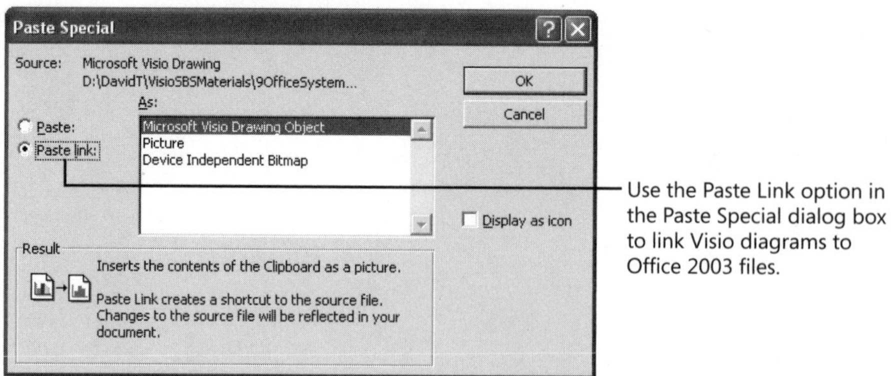

Use the Paste Link option in the Paste Special dialog box to link Visio diagrams to Office 2003 files.

In this exercise, you open a block diagram, copy the entire diagram, open a Word document, and then link the diagram to the document. Finally, you modify the Visio diagram, which updates the copy of the diagram in the Word document.

USE the *PlanPhase* file and the Proposal file in the My Documents\Microsoft Press\Visio 2003 SBS \UsingDrawings folder.

1. Start Visio. On the **File** menu, click **Open**.

   The Open dialog box displays the contents of the My Documents folder by default.

2. Double-click the **Microsoft Press** folder, double-click the **Visio 2003 SBS** folder, double-click the **UsingDrawings** folder, and then double-click **PlanPhase**.

   Visio opens a block diagram and four stencils.

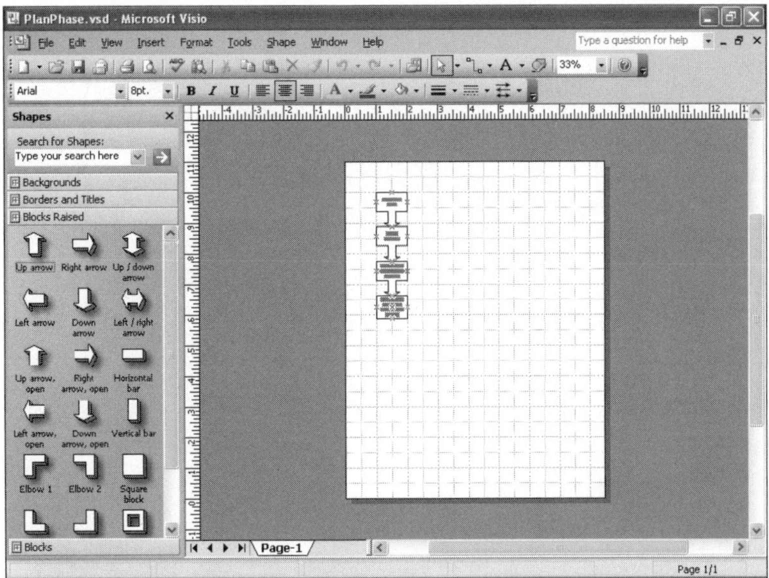

3 On the **Edit** menu, click **Copy Drawing**.

Visio copies the entire diagram.

Troubleshooting If the Copy command appears on the Edit menu instead of the Copy Drawing command, a shape on the drawing page is selected, and you will not be able to link the diagram to a file. Press the Esc key to cancel the shape selection, and then try again.

4 Start Word. On the **File** menu, click **Open**.

The Open dialog box appears.

5 Double-click the **Microsoft Press** folder, double-click the **Visio 2003 SBS** folder, double-click the **UsingDrawings** folder, and then double-click **Proposal**.

Word opens the document.

Troubleshooting If you don't see the Microsoft Press folder in the Open dialog box, navigate to the My Documents folder.

6 Select the blue placeholder text, <Insert block diagram here.>, and then press the Del key.

Word deletes the text and places the insertion point at the beginning of the line.

7 If the insertion point appears at the end of the previous line, press the Enter key to start a new line.

8 On the **Edit** menu, click **Paste Special** to open the **Paste Special** dialog box.

9 Click **Paste link**.

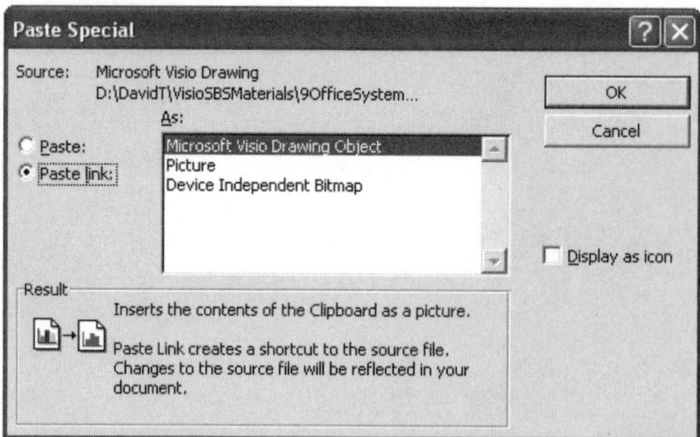

Troubleshooting To link to a diagram, you must save it first, and then link to the entire diagram. If the "Paste link" option appears dimmed, save the diagram, and then use the Copy Drawing command to copy the entire diagram.

10 In the **As** box, click **Microsoft Visio Drawing Object**, and then click **OK**.

Word links to the Visio drawing file and pastes a copy of the diagram in the Word document.

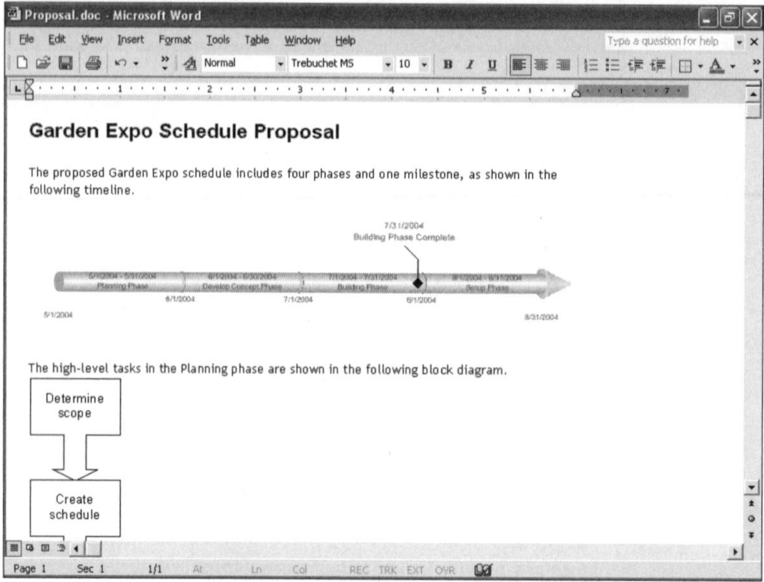

11 To modify the Visio diagram, double-click it.

The original diagram, PlanPhase, opens in a separate Visio window.

Troubleshooting When you link a Visio diagram to an Office 2003 file, you link to a drawing file with a specific name in a specific location. If you rename or move the Visio drawing file, you must update the link. To update the link, select the linked diagram within the Office 2003 file, and on the Edit menu, click Update Link. If you don't update the link before you double-click the diagram in the Office 2003 file, you'll receive an error message because Office 2003 won't be able to find the drawing file.

12 On the **Edit** menu, click **Select All**.

Visio selects all the shapes on the drawing page.

13 On the **Format** menu, click **Text** to open the **Text** dialog box.

14 On the **Font** tab, in the **General** area, in the **Color** box, select **02:** (red), and then click **OK**.

Visio changes the text color in all the shapes to red.

15 On the **File** menu, click **Save** to save the changes to the **PlanPhase** diagram.

16 On the **File** menu, click **Exit**.

The diagram closes, Visio closes, and Word becomes the active program.

17 In Word, with the diagram selected, on the **Edit** menu, click **Update Link**.

Word applies the changes to the linked diagram in the Word document.

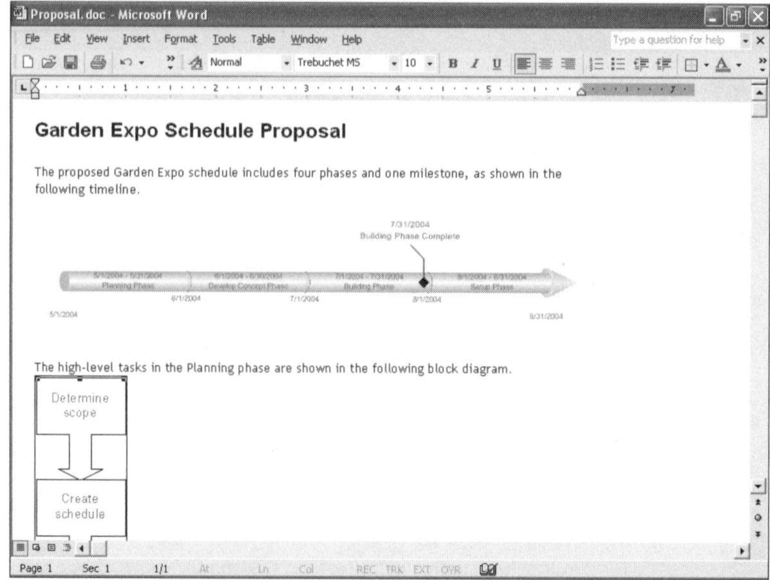

Tip Linked diagrams can be updated either automatically or manually. To specify how you want your linked diagrams in a particular Office 2003 file to be updated, open the Office 2003 file, and then on the Edit menu, click Links.

18. In Word, on the **File** menu, click **Save As** to open the **Save As** dialog box.
19. In the **File name** box, replace Proposal.doc with **ProposalLink**.
20. Click **Save** to save the document.
21. On the **File** menu, click **Exit** to close Word and the document.

Key Points

- To create a diagram directly in an Office 2003 file, on the Insert menu, click Object. The diagram you create becomes part of the Office 2003 file.
- To embed a copy of a diagram into an Office 2003 file, copy the diagram, and then paste it into the file. When you embed a copy of diagram into an Office 2003 file, the copy becomes part of the file.
- To link an entire diagram to an Office 2003 file, first make sure you save it. Next, in Visio, on the Edit menu, click Copy Drawing. Then, in Word, on the Edit menu, click Paste Special. In the Paste Special dialog box, make sure you select the Paste link option.
- When you link a Visio diagram to an Office 2003 file, you link to the Visio drawing file, so you if you move or rename the Visio drawing file, you must update the link in the Office 2003 file. To do so, select the diagram in the Office 2003 file, and then on the Edit menu, click Update Link.

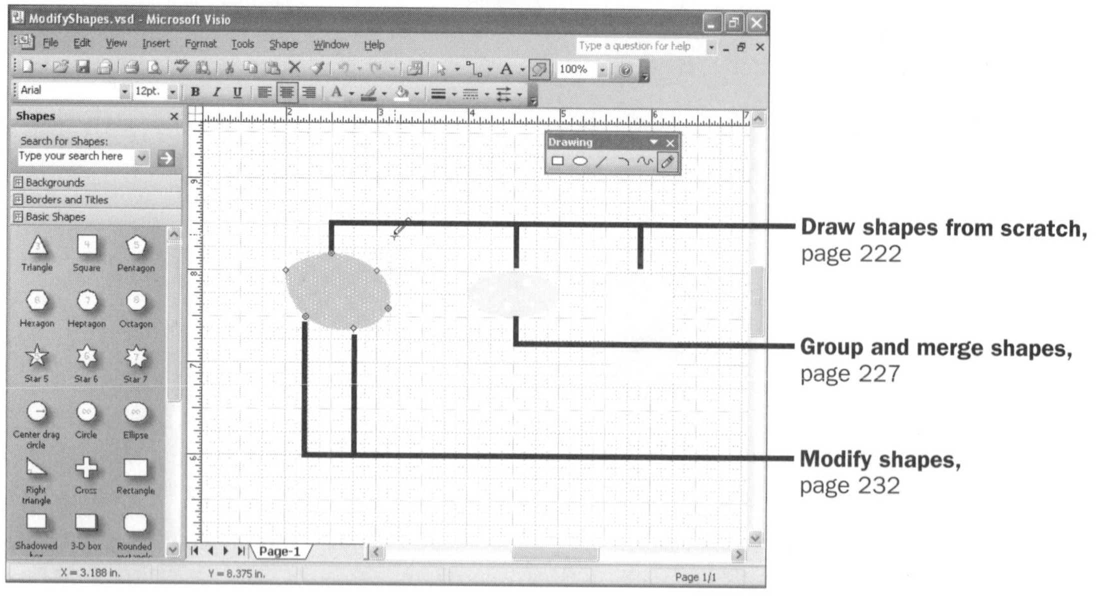

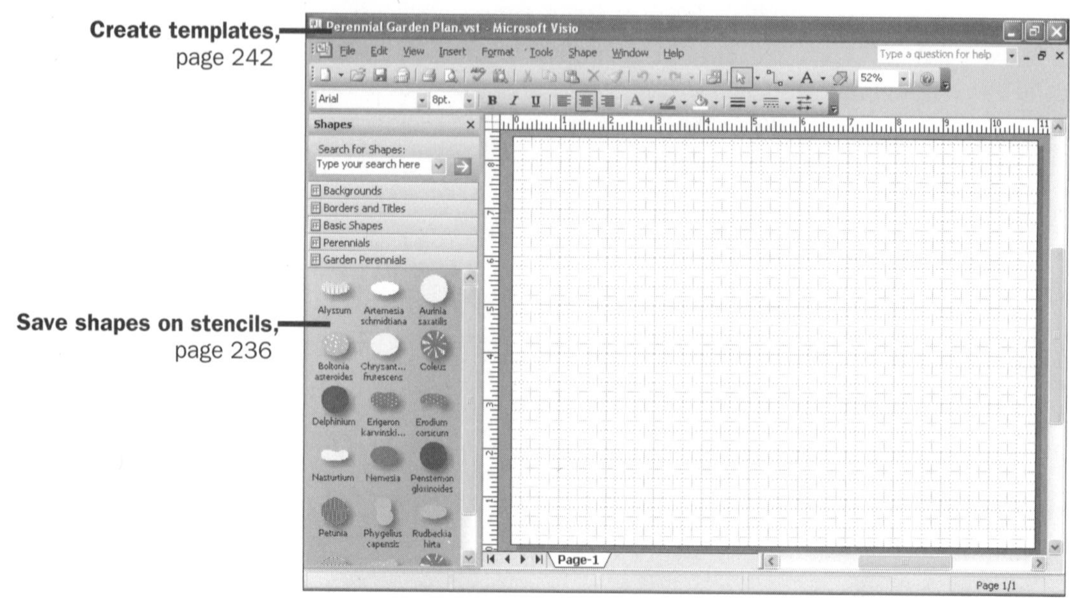

Chapter 10 at a Glance

10 Creating Shapes, Stencils, and Templates

In this chapter you will learn to:

- ✔ Draw shapes from scratch.
- ✔ Group and merge shapes.
- ✔ Modify shapes.
- ✔ Save shapes on stencils.
- ✔ Create templates.

Even though Visio includes tens of thousands of shapes, there might come a time when you need to create your own custom shapes. Perhaps you want to show special equipment or custom furniture in an office layout. Maybe you want to highlight your company's line of products in a client diagram. In any of these situations, you could create custom shapes to use in your diagrams.

With the drawing tools in Microsoft Office Visio, you can draw a shape from scratch or modify a shape that looks similar to the shape you want to create. If you want to use the shape in several diagrams, you can save it on a new or existing stencil, and then use it just like any other Visio shape. Putting your custom shapes on stencils also helps you organize and keep track of them, and you can share and send stencils through e-mail if you want to distribute your shapes to other Visio users. You can even go a step further and create your own templates to better suit the way you work.

In this chapter, you learn how to create shapes by drawing simple perennial garden shapes that the master gardener at The Garden Company can use in landscape planning diagrams. You also learn how to save the shapes on a stencil and create a template.

See Also Do you need only a quick refresher on the topics in this chapter? See the Quick Reference entries on pages xxxviii–xl.

Important Before you can use the practice files in this chapter, you need to install them from the book's companion CD to their default location. See "Using the Book's CD" on page xv for more information.

Drawing Shapes from Scratch

New in Visio 2003

The sky is the limit when it comes to creating your own shapes. You can draw anything you want with the tools on the Drawing toolbar. To display this toolbar, click the Drawing Tools button on the Standard toolbar, or right-click the toolbar area, and click Drawing on the shortcut menu. To draw a shape, just click the toolbar button for the tool you want to use, position the pointer on the drawing page, and then drag to create lines, curves, arcs, circles, and so on.

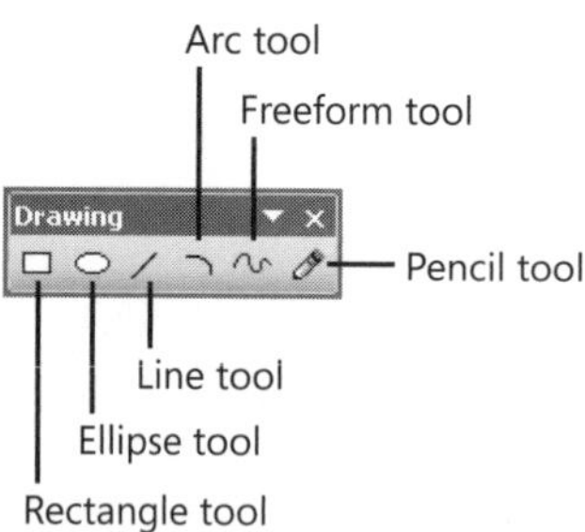

Perhaps the most frequently used drawing tool is the Pencil tool, which you can use to draw both straight lines and arcs. As you begin to draw with the Pencil tool, Visio quickly calculates the path the mouse pointer is traveling and draws a line if the path is straight or an arc if the path curves.

You can use the Line tool, Arc tool, and Freeform tool to draw different types of lines or arcs. In geometric terms, the Arc tool creates elliptical quarter-arc segments, whereas the Pencil tool draws circular arc segments. When you want to draw a continuous wavy line, you can use the Freeform tool. For example, you could use the Freeform tool to draw your signature.

Tip In some types of technical illustrations, it's important to know that the Freeform tool creates a non-uniform rational B-spline (or NURBS for short).

With the Line, Arc, Freeform, and Pencil tools, you can create either 1-D or 2-D shapes. The Ellipse and Rectangle tools, on the other hand, create only 2-D shapes. With the Ellipse tool, you can create ovals and circles, whereas the Rectangle tool creates rectangles and squares. By holding down the Shift key while drawing with the Ellipse or Rectangle tool, you create circles and squares.

When you draw a shape, it can be either a *closed shape* or an *open shape*. Shapes like rectangles or circles are closed shapes. You can fill the inside of closed shapes with colors and patterns. Lines, half-circles, or zigzag shapes are examples of open shapes. You can format the ends with arrowheads, for example, or change the line color of open shapes, but you can't fill the inside of an open shape.

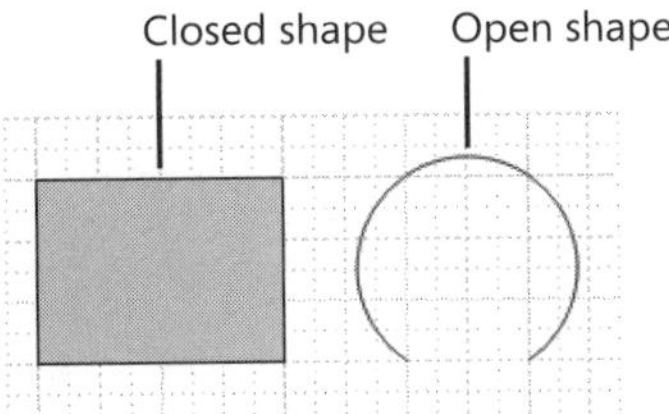

In this exercise, you use the drawing tools to create circles and ovals (closed shapes) that represent different types of perennial plants in a landscape plan. Then you fill the inside of the shapes with color.

1 Start Visio. In the Choose Drawing Type window, in the **Category** area, click **Block Diagram**. In the **Template** area, click **Basic Diagram**.

   Visio opens a blank drawing page and three stencils.

36% Zoom

2 On the Standard toolbar, click the **Zoom** down arrow, and then click **100%** to zoom in on the drawing page.

Drawing Tools

3 On the Standard toolbar, click the **Drawing Tools** button to display the Drawing toolbar.

Pencil Tool

4 On the Drawing toolbar, click the **Pencil Tool** button.

Pencil pointer

   The pointer changes to a pencil with a blue crosshair.

5 On the drawing page, point to the location where you want to create the shape.

   The blue crosshair on the Pencil tool snaps to the grid to show you where the shape will start.

6 Drag in a curving motion from left to right to create an arc about 1 inch long, and then release the mouse button.

Arc pointer

   As you drag, the pointer displays a crosshair and an arc, which indicates that you're drawing an arc rather than a line.

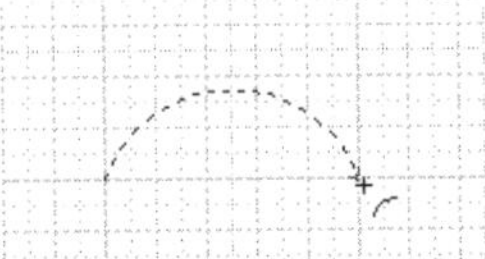

Line pointer

Troubleshooting If a line pointer appears instead of an arc pointer while you are dragging with the Pencil tool, try exaggerating your movements with the mouse—that is, move the mouse in a very circular motion until the arc pointer appears.

7. Point to the end point of the arc segment, and then drag in a downward, curving motion to draw another arc segment approximately ¾ inch long, and then release the mouse button.

   Visio creates a second arc segment connected to the first.

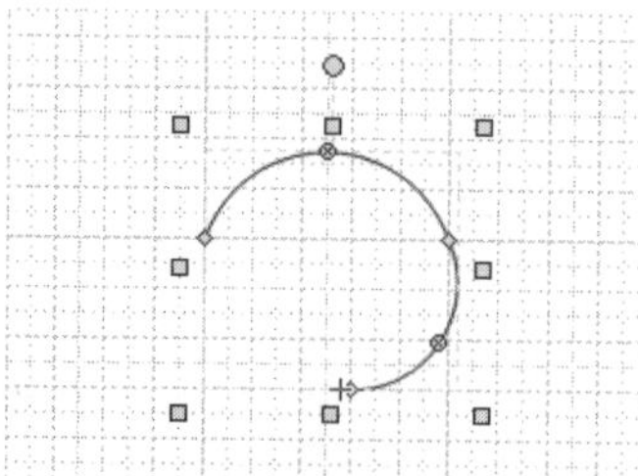

Troubleshooting Be careful not to *select* the end point of the first segment. If you select the end point, it turns magenta. To deselect the end point, click the pasteboard or a blank area of the drawing page. If you drag a selected endpoint, Visio resizes the segment instead of starting a new one. If you accidentally resize a segment, press Ctrl+Z to undo the action, and then try again.

8. Point to the end point of the second segment, drag another arc segment to the begin point of the first arc segment, and then release the mouse button.

   Visio creates a closed shape and fills the shape with a gray color.

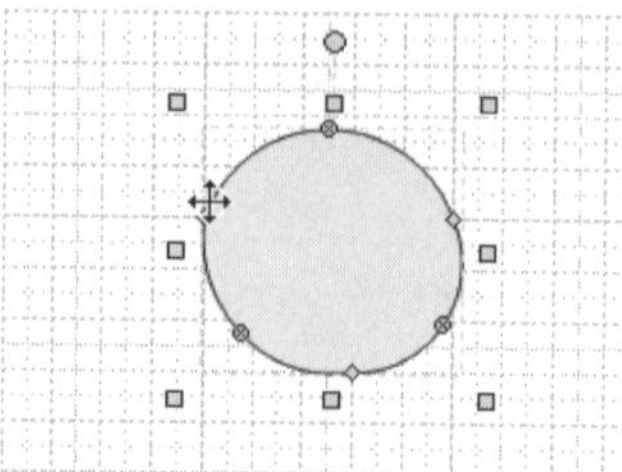

Troubleshooting If Visio doesn't fill the shape with a gray color, the shape isn't closed. Press Ctrl+Z three times to undo your last three actions, and start drawing the shape again. When you try again, make sure you start each new line segment right on the end point of the last arc segment. Make sure you end the arc segment right on the begin point of the first segment you drew to ensure you close the shape.

Ellipse Tool

9. On the Drawing toolbar, click the **Ellipse Tool** button.

Ellipse pointer

The ellipse pointer appears.

10 To the right of the shape you just drew, drag to create an ellipse approximately 1 inch wide and ½ inch tall.

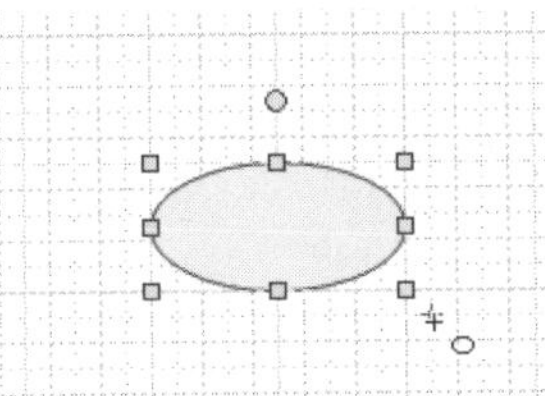

11 Click the pasteboard to deselect the ellipse.

12 To the right of the ellipse you just drew, hold down the Shift key while you drag to create a circle approximately ¾ inch in diameter.

Tip Watch the status bar as you drag to see the shape's dimensions.

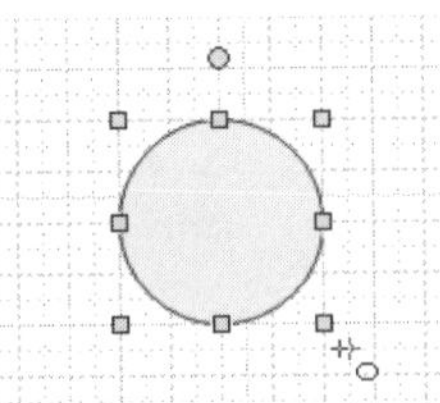

13 Place the pointer over the circle, and then hold down the Ctrl key while you drag down to create a copy of the circle. Drag downward until the copy of the circle only slightly overlaps the original circle.

The copy of the circle is selected.

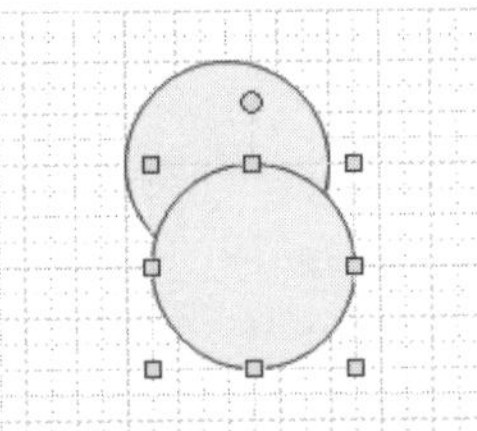

Troubleshooting If you accidentally draw a new shape instead of copying the circle, press Ctrl+Z to undo the action, and then try again. Make sure you release the mouse button before the Ctrl key when you're done copying the shape.

Fill Color

14 On the Formatting toolbar, click the **Fill Color** down arrow to display the color palette.

15 Click the light yellow color.

Visio fills the circle with the light yellow color. The circle remains selected.

Important Depending on the capabilities of your monitor and video driver, your colors might differ from those shown in this book. You can position the pointer over a color on the color palette to see a ScreenTip that tells you the name of the color.

16 Click the other circle to select it.

Visio displays the shape's selection handles.

17 On the Formatting toolbar, click the **Fill Color** down arrow, and then click **More Fill Colors**.

The Colors dialog box appears.

18 In the **Colors** dialog box, click the **Standard** tab to display a color wheel.

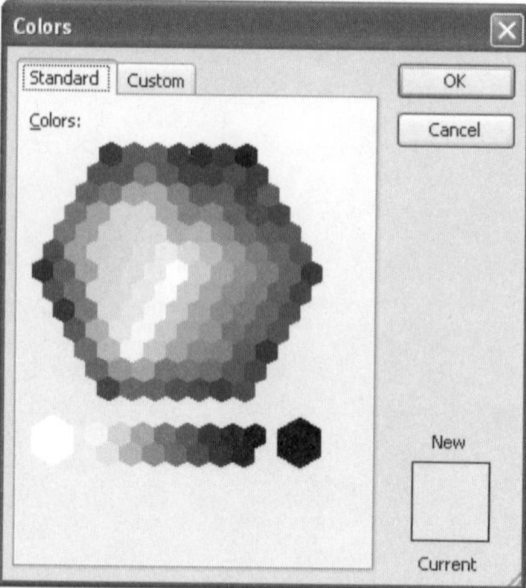

19 In the color wheel, click a shade of pink, and then click **OK**.

Visio closes the Color dialog box and fills the shape with the pink color. The circle remains selected.

20 Select the ellipse, click the **Fill Color** down arrow, and then click the light green color.

Visio fills the ellipse with the light green color. The ellipse remains selected.

21 Select the first shape you drew, click the **Fill Color** down arrow, and then click the pale blue color.

Visio fills the shape with the pale blue color. The shape remains selected.

Pointer Tool

22 On the Standard toolbar, click the **Pointer Tool** button, and then drag a selection box around all four shapes.

The shapes are selected.

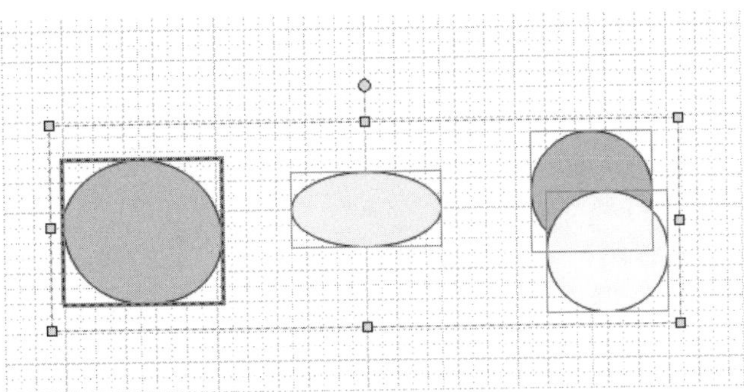

Line Color

23 On the Formatting toolbar, click the **Line Color** down arrow, and then click **No Line**.

Visio removes the black line border from the four shapes.

24 Press the Esc key to cancel the selection.

25 On the **File** menu, click **Close**.

26 When Visio prompts you to save the drawing, click **No**.

Visio closes the drawing without saving the changes.

Grouping and Merging Shapes

You can create a variety of simple shapes with the Visio drawing tools. However, you can also create complex shapes by grouping or merging two or more shapes:

- When you group two shapes, you create a third shape, the group, which contains all the original shapes and retains their formatting. You can still select and modify each of the individual shapes in the group. Use the Grouping commands on the Shape menu to create and work with groups.
- When you *merge* shapes, you combine or break up (depending on the command you use) the existing shapes to create new shapes. The original shapes are discarded. Use the Operations commands on the Shape menu to merge shapes.

Tip If you want to preserve the original shapes when merging shapes, make a copy of the shapes before merging them with other shapes.

Grouping is a great way to work with several shapes as a unit instead of individually. For example, the conference table shapes used in office layouts are groups that include table and chair shapes. When you resize a conference table group, all the tables and chairs within the group are resized. Most of the title and border shapes on the Borders and Titles stencil are groups. When you move a title or border, all the shapes in the group move at once. To create a group, select the shapes you want to group, and then on the Shape menu, point to Grouping, and then click Group. The order in which you select the shapes doesn't matter.

Each shape in a group can have unique formatting attributes; when you format one shape in a group, the rest of the shapes aren't affected. You work with the individual shapes in a group by subselecting them. To subselect a shape in a group, select the group, and then click the shape you want to work with individually. You can then format, resize, or even reshape the shape just as you would any other individual shape.

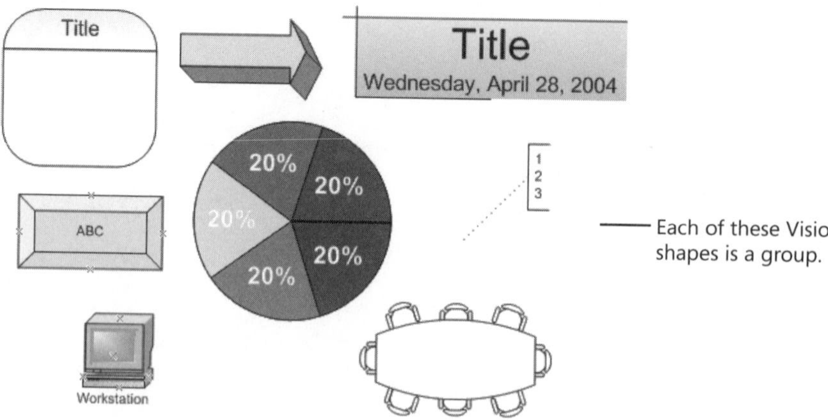

Each of these Visio shapes is a group.

New in Visio 2003

Tip You can change the behavior of groups and shapes within groups. For example, instead of resizing a shape within a group when the group is resized, you can reposition it only. To modify the settings for a group, select the group, and then on the Format menu, click Behavior. To modify the resize behavior for a shape within a group, subselect the shape, and then on the Format menu, click Behavior. You can also ungroup groups. To ungroup a group, on the Shape menu, point to Grouping, and then click Ungroup.

By contrast, merging shapes is a very different process. When you merge shapes, you create an entirely new shape; the original shapes are discarded. For example, you can merge two circles, one inside of the other, to create a single doughnut shape. Other operations split shapes apart. The following table includes some of the merge commands that you can use to create new shapes and examples of what each command does.

Operation	What It Does	Example
Union	Creates a new shape from the perimeter of two or more overlapping shapes.	
Combine	Creates a new shape from selected shapes. If the selected shapes overlap, the area where they overlap is cut out, creating a cookie-cutter effect.	
Fragment	Breaks a shape into smaller parts, or creates new shapes from intersecting lines or from 2-D shapes that overlap.	
Intersect	Creates a new shape from the area where the selected shapes overlap and removes non-overlapping areas.	
Subtract	Creates a new shape by removing the area where selections overlap from the primary selection.	

Important When merging shapes, selection order is very important. The format of the first shape you select will be applied to the new shape. For example, if you select a red shape and a green shape, in that order, and then click Intersect, the new shape will be red. Selection order does not affect groups in the same way. Each shape retains its format when you create a group.

In this exercise, you group and merge simple shapes to create more complex shapes.

OPEN the *GroupShapes* file in the My Documents\Microsoft Press\Visio 2003 SBS\CreatingShapes folder.

Ellipse Tool

1 On the Drawing toolbar, click the **Ellipse Tool** button.

2 Position the pointer over the green oval, hold down the Shift key, and drag to create a small circle approximately ¼ inch in diameter.

The circle remains selected.

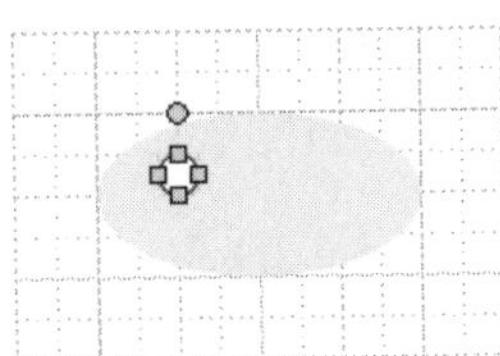

3 Press Ctrl+D three times to duplicate the circle three times.

Visio creates three new circles at even intervals, leaving the last circle selected.

Tip You can also duplicate shapes by clicking Duplicate on the Edit menu. Ctrl+D is keyboard shortcut for the Duplicate command.

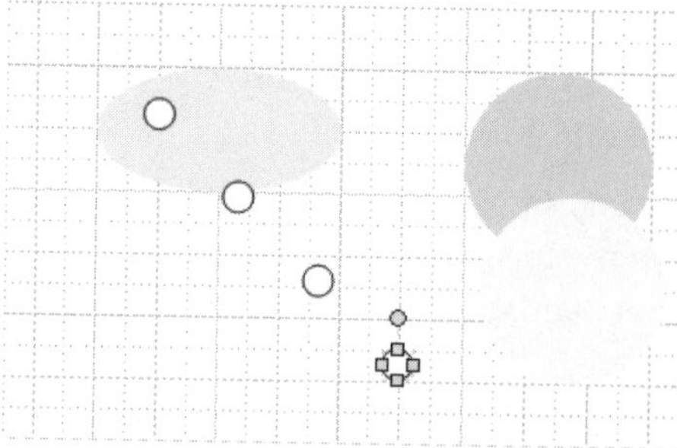

Pointer Tool

4 On the Standard toolbar, click the **Pointer Tool** button.

5 Drag each circle on top of the oval, arranging them like polka dots.

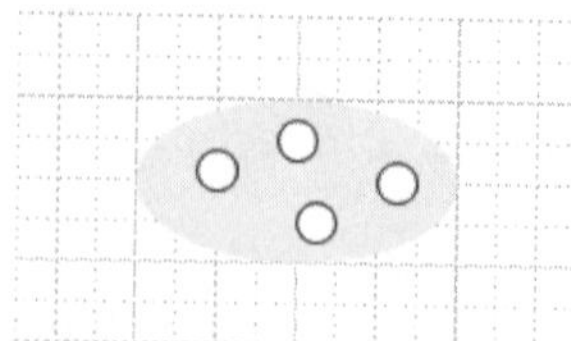

Troubleshooting If you resize a dot accidentally instead of moving it, press Ctrl+Z to undo the action, and then try again. It's often easier to move a small shape if you zoom in on the drawing page first.

6 Drag a selection box around the green oval.

Visio selects all the shapes.

7 On the **Shape** menu, point to **Grouping**, and then click **Group**.

Visio creates a group and displays the group's selection handles.

Tip Alternatively, you can use the Shift+Ctrl+G keyboard shortcut to quickly group shapes. You can also ungroup a group. To do so, select the group, and then on the Shape menu, point to Grouping, and click Ungroup. If the Ungroup command is gray (unavailable), the selected shape isn't a group.

8 Click one of the dots in the group.

Visio subselects the dot and displays the shape's selection handles.

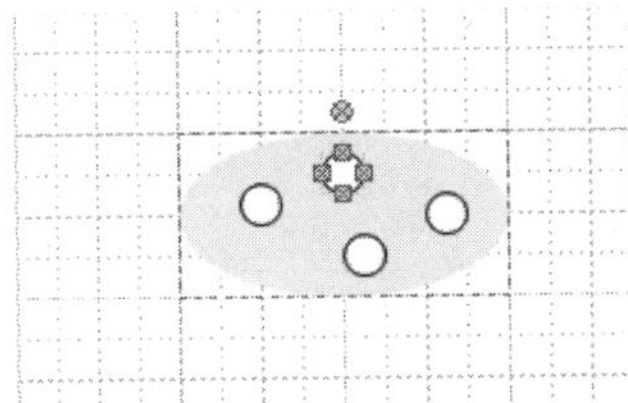

Fill Color

9 Click the **Fill Color** down arrow, and then click the light yellow color.

Visio fills only the selected dot with the light yellow color.

10 Subselect the rest of the dots, one at a time, and then click the **Fill Color** button to fill each one with a light yellow color.

Tip After you choose a color from the color palette, you don't need to open the color palette to apply that color to a shape. Just click the Fill Color button, which is loaded with the selected color.

11 Click the large yellow circle to the right of the group.

12 Hold down the Shift key, and then click the pink circle.

Visio selects both circles.

13 On the **Shape** menu, point to **Operations**, and then click **Union**.

Visio unites the two circles to create a single new shape with the same formatting as the first circle you selected.

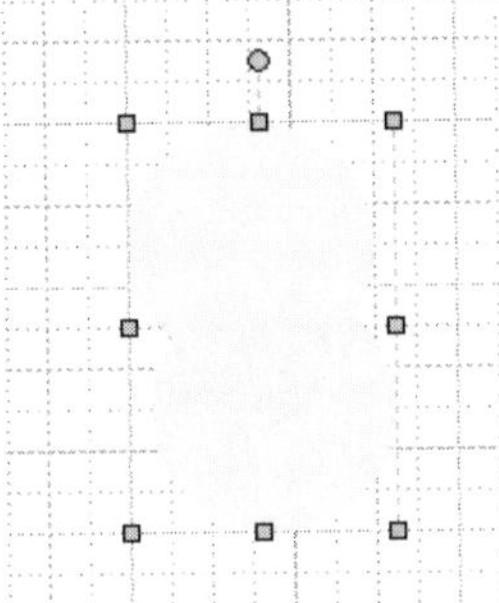

14 Click the blue, irregular shape to select it.

15 On the **Format** menu, click **Fill** to display the **Fill** dialog box.

16 In the **Fill** area, in the **Pattern** box, click the down arrow to display a list of patterns, and then click pattern **12:**.

In the Preview area, notice black dots fill the blue shape.

17 In the **Pattern color** box, click the down arrow to display a list of pattern colors, and then click color **01:** (white).

In the Preview area, notice the dots become white.

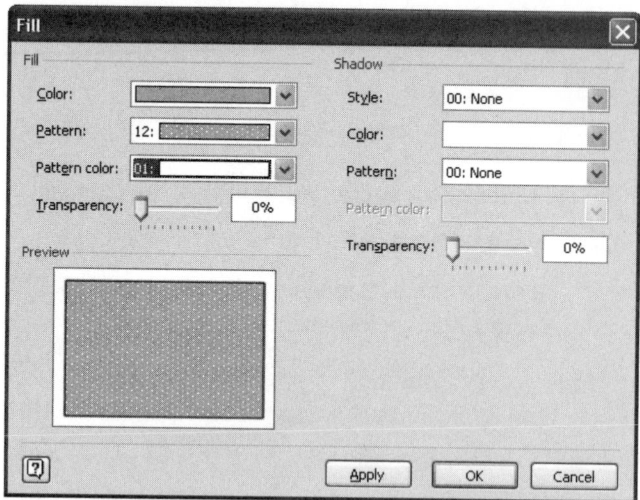

18 Click **OK** to close the **Fill** dialog box and apply the pattern to the shape.

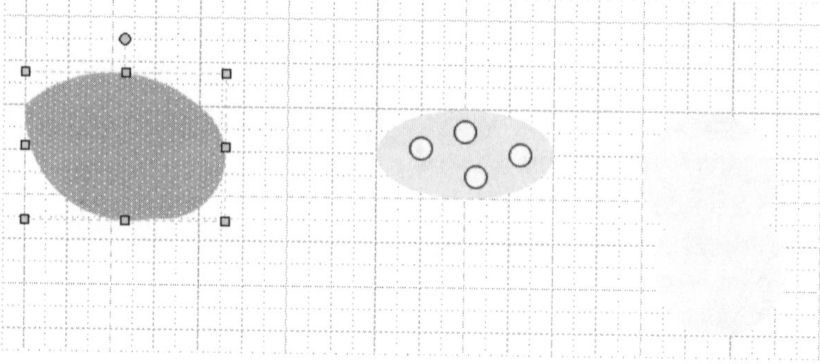

Save

19 On the Standard toolbar, click the **Save** button to save the changes to the drawing.

CLOSE the *GroupShapes* file.

Modifying Shapes

The key to creating great-looking shapes is to draw a rough version of the shape first, and then refine it. There are special handles on lines and arcs that you can use to reshape, add, move, and delete line segments. For example, if you draw a crooked line with the Pencil tool, you can edit the line segment to straighten it out and even change it to an arc. A diamond-shaped *vertex* appears where line segments are joined when you select a shape with the Pencil tool. You can delete, move, or add vertexes to reshape a shape with the Pencil tool. For example, you can delete a vertex from a square to create a triangle. A circular *control point* also appears on line segments selected with the Pencil tool. You can use a control point to change the curvature of a segment. When you move the control point down on a rolling hill shape, it becomes a sunken valley, and so on. Even if you can't draw a straight line, you can straighten a crooked line by editing the shape's vertices and control points.

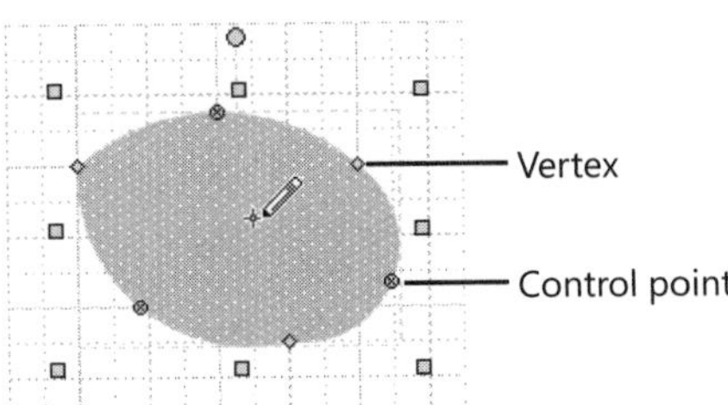

Tip Some Visio shapes are locked to prevent changes. If a shape is locked, its selection box is gray instead of green.

In this exercise, you use the Pencil tool to edit line and arc segments to refine the appearance of a plant shape that The Garden Company wants to use in its landscape plans.

OPEN the *ModifyShapes* file in the My Documents\Microsoft Press\Visio 2003 SBS\CreatingShapes folder.

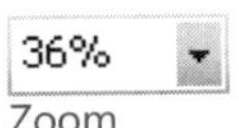

Zoom

1 On the Standard toolbar, click the **Zoom** down arrow, and then click **200%**.

Visio zooms in to 200% on the drawing page.

Pencil Tool

2 On the Drawing toolbar, click the **Pencil Tool** button.

3 Click the blue shape with the white, dotted fill pattern to select it.

Visio display the shape's vertices and control points.

New in Visio 2003

Tip In addition to moving and resizing shapes, you can use the Pointer tool to modify custom shapes. Select a shape you drew, position the pointer over the shape, and the shape's vertices and control points appear within the shape's selection box. Then drag a vertex or control point to move it. You can also drag a selection handle on the selection box to resize the shape.

4 Point to the leftmost vertex.

four-headed arrow

The pointer changes to a four-headed arrow, a selection box appears around the shape, and a ScreenTip for the vertex appears.

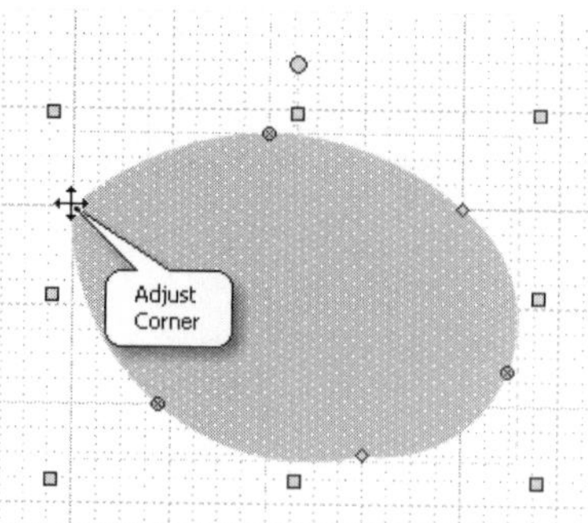

5 Click the vertex.

The vertex turns magenta.

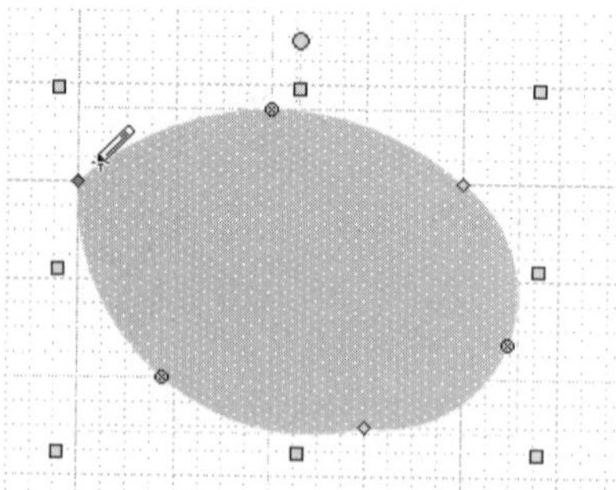

6 Drag the vertex down approximately ¼ inch.

Visio redraws the shape.

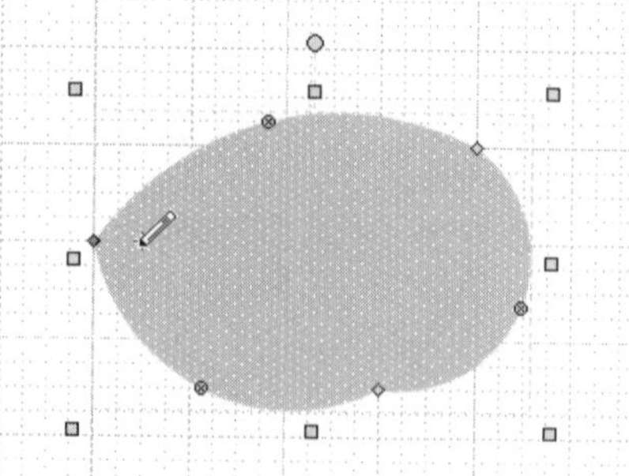

7 Click the lower-right vertex to select it.

The vertex turns magenta.

8 Press the Del key.

Visio removes the vertex and redraws the shape.

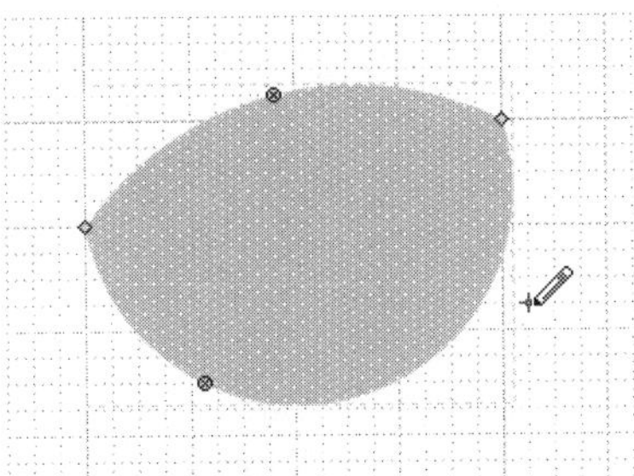

9 Click the lowest control point to select it.

The control point turns magenta.

10 Drag the control point slightly down and to the right.

Visio changes the curvature of the arc segment.

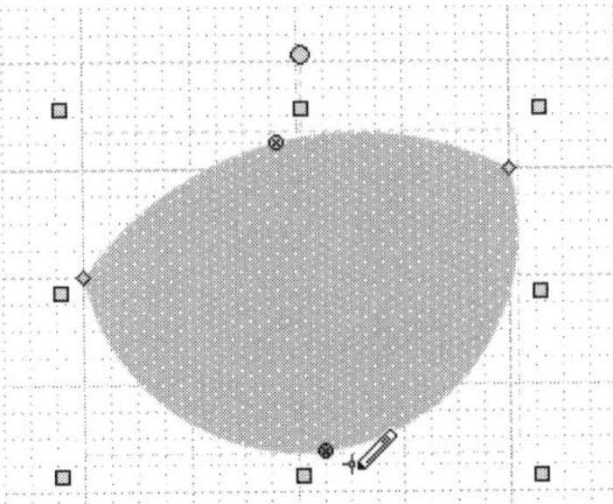

11 Hold down the Ctrl key as you click the top edge of the shape.

Visio adds a vertex.

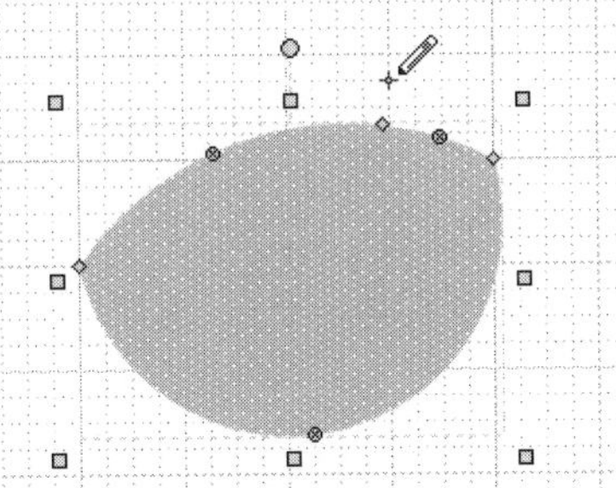

12 Drag the new vertex down and to the left approximately ¼ inch.

Visio redraws the shape.

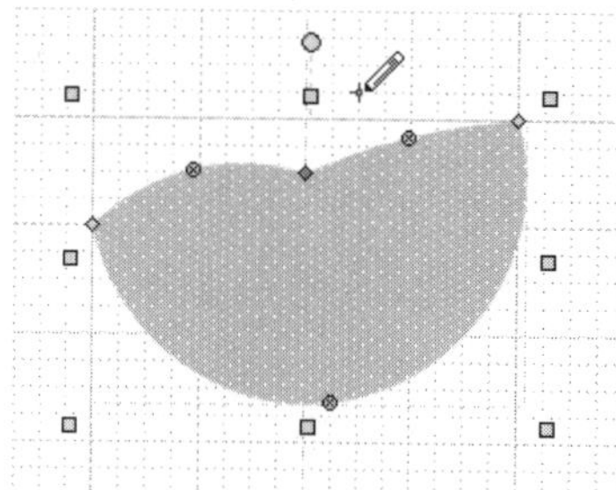

Save

13 On the Standard toolbar, click the **Save** button to save the changes to the drawing.

CLOSE the *ModifyShapes* file.

Saving Shapes on Stencils

Once in a while you might create a custom shape that you'll use only once. However, more often than not, you'll want to use your custom shapes again and again. Just as you can drag a shape from a stencil onto the drawing page to create a diagram, you can drag a custom shape from the drawing page onto a custom stencil to store it there. For example, if you customized a Visio title shape for your company's logo, you could drag it onto a custom stencil or the Favorites stencil so you could easily access it while creating any diagram. Likewise, if you use the same shapes from several different stencils over and over and you'd like to consolidate them onto a single stencil, you can add those shapes to a custom stencil or the Favorites stencil.

Shapes

New in Visio 2003

Tip You can't modify or add shapes to Visio stencils. You must create your own stencils, and then add shapes to them. You can, however, add shapes to the Favorites stencil. To open the Favorites stencil, click the Shapes button on the Standard toolbar, point to My Shapes, and then click Favorites. To add custom shapes to the stencil, drag them from the drawing page onto the stencil. When you drag the first shape onto the stencil, Visio asks you if you'd like to edit the stencil; click Yes. To quickly add Visio shapes to the Favorites stencil, right-click a Visio shape on a stencil, point to Add to My Shapes, and then click Favorites.

Saving your custom shapes on custom stencils also makes it easy to distribute your shapes to other Visio users. When you create a new stencil, Visio saves it on your computer only. However, you can share a stencil just as you share drawing files by saving the stencil in a network folder that others have access to, or by sending the stencil in an e-mail message to your colleagues.

Tip Stencils are files like Visio drawings files and templates. Stencils have a .vss file extension, which stands for *Visio stencil*. If someone sends a stencil to you, you can put it in the My Shapes folder in your My Documents folder for easy access. Then just open a Visio drawing file or template, click the Shapes button on the Standard toolbar, point to My Shapes, and click the name of the stencil to open it.

Stencils open, by default, as *read-only*—that is, a stencil can't be changed unless you specifically open it for editing. When you drag a shape onto a read-only stencil, Visio prompts you to open the stencil for editing so it can add the shape to the stencil. You can also click the stencil icon on the stencil, click Edit Stencil, and then drag the shape onto the stencil. When the stencil becomes editable, a red asterisk appears on the stencil icon on the title bar. When you create a new stencil, Visio opens the new stencil, by default, as an editable stencil; however, after you close it, it becomes read-only.

A red asterisk on a stencil icon notifies you that the stencil is editable.

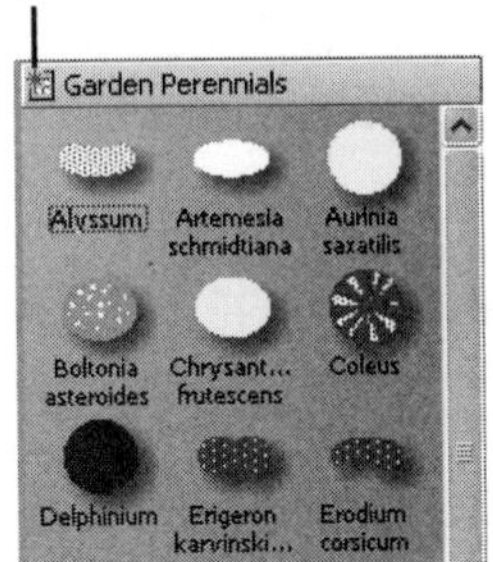

Shapes on stencils are represented by their corresponding icons and names. When you drag a new shape onto a stencil, Visio creates a shape icon and applies a default name (Master.1, for example). You can easily change the name to something more descriptive by double-clicking the default name and typing a new name.

In this exercise, you create a custom stencil, and then drag custom shapes onto it.

OPEN the *CreateStencil* file in the My Documents\Microsoft Press\Visio 2003 SBS\CreatingShapes folder.

1 On the **File** menu, point to **Shapes**, and then click **New Stencil**.

Visio opens a new stencil (named Stencil1) and docks it alongside the drawing page in the Shapes window. Notice the red asterisk that appears on the stencil icon in the stencil's title bar—this indicates that you can edit the stencil.

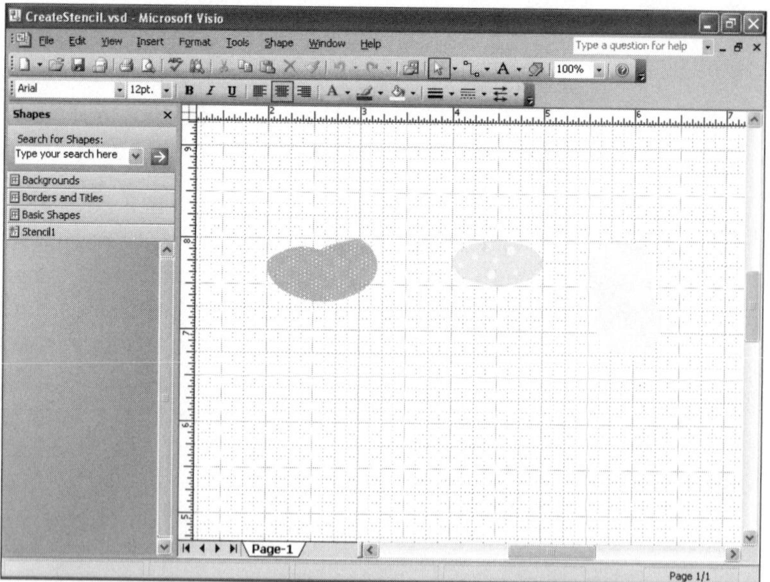

2 Drag the blue shape onto the stencil.

Visio creates a new shape (called Master.0) with a gray icon and removes the blue shape from the drawing page.

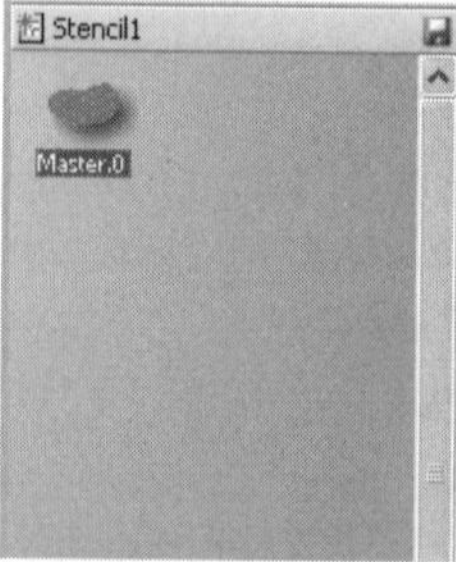

Troubleshooting When creating icons for shapes on stencils, Visio uses only 16 colors, by default. If you create a shape that isn't formatted with one of those 16 colors, Visio substitutes the closest color when it creates the stencil icon. Visio does this to save disk space—an important consideration when dealing with a lot of stencils. That's why the icon for the blue shape you just added to the stencil is gray. However, when you drag the shape onto the drawing page, it appears just the way you designed it—blue. To edit the icon for a custom shape, right-click the shape, point to Edit Master, and then click Edit Icon Image.

3 Drag the green shape onto the stencil window.

Visio creates a new shape (called Master.1) with a gray icon and removes the green shape from the drawing page.

Tip When you drag shapes from the drawing page onto a stencil, the shapes are deleted from the drawing page. If you want to retain the original shapes on the drawing page and drag a copy of them onto the stencil instead, hold down the Ctrl key while you drag the shapes onto the stencil. Make sure you release the mouse button before you release the Ctrl key when using this copying method.

4 Drag the yellow shape onto the stencil window.

Visio creates a new shape (called Master.2) with a gray icon and removes the yellow shape from the drawing page.

Tip You can also save shapes on the Favorites stencil. To open the Favorites stencil, on the File menu, point to Shapes, point to My Shapes, and then click Favorites. Before you can add shapes to the Favorites stencil, you must make it editable by clicking the stencil icon, and then clicking Edit Stencil.

5 Right-click **Master.0**, and then click **Rename Master** on the shortcut menu.

The name, Master.0, is highlighted so typing the new name replaces the old name.

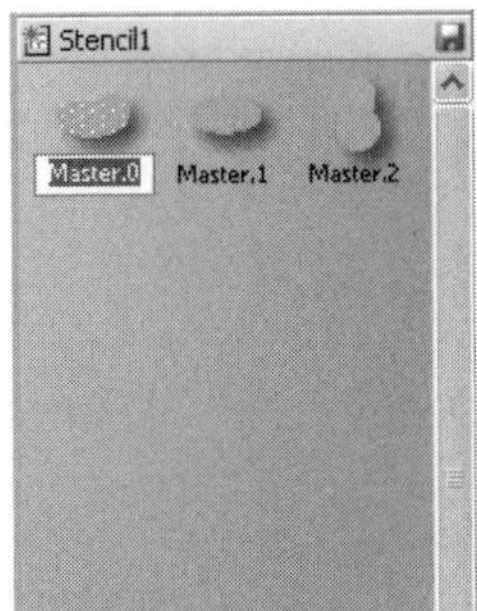

6 Type Thymus vulgaris, and press the Enter key.

Visio changes the name of the shape to Thymus vulgaris.

7 Right-click **Master.1**, and then click **Rename Master** on the shortcut menu.

8 Type Rudbeckia hirta, and then press the Enter key.

Visio changes the name of the shape to Rudbeckia hirta.

9 Double-click the shape icon name, **Master.2**.

Visio highlights the shape name.

Close Window

Troubleshooting Make sure you double-click the *text* for the shape icon and not the shape icon itself. If you double-click the shape icon, Visio opens a shape-editing window instead of selecting the shape icon name. To close the shape-editing window, click the Close Window button in the upper-right corner of the window.

10 Type Phygelius capensis, and then press the Enter key.

Visio changes the name of the shape to Phygelius capensis.

11 On the **Stencil1** title bar, click the green stencil icon.

Visio displays a menu of commands for working with the stencil.

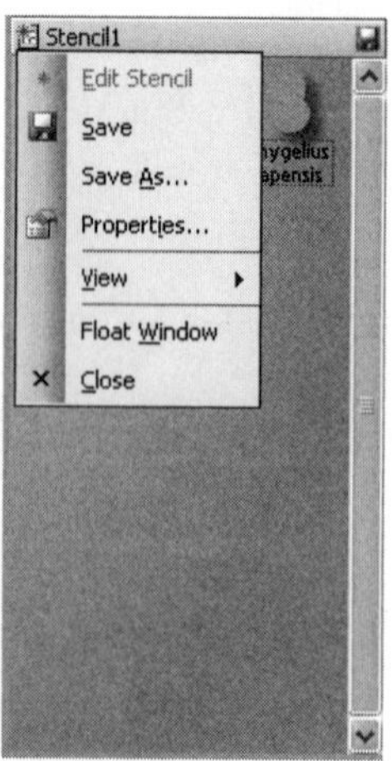

12 Click **Save**.

The Save As dialog box appears.

13 In the **File name** box, type Perennials, and then click **Save**.

Visio saves the stencil in the My Shapes folder by default, so the new stencil name, Perennials, will appear on the My Shapes submenu.

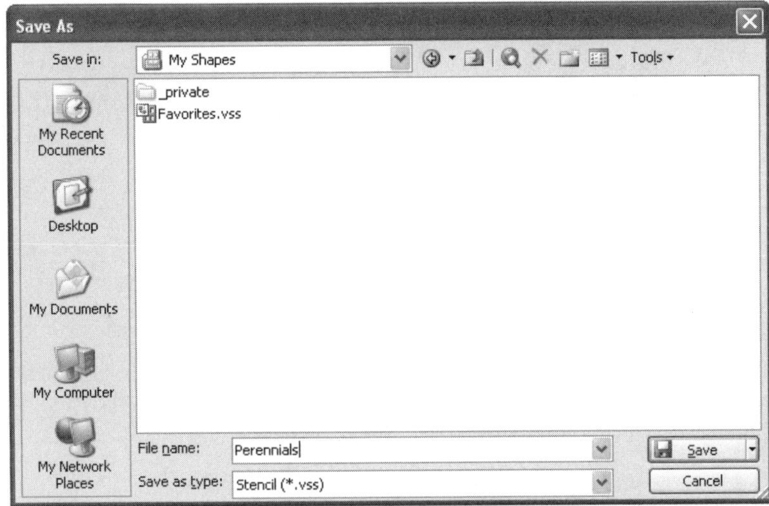

Tip Notice the default file format in the Save as type box is Stencil (*.vss). The file extension stands for *Visio stencil*.

14 From the **Perennials** stencil, drag the **Rudbeckia hirta** shape onto the drawing page.

15 From the **Perennials** stencil, drag the other two shapes—one at a time—onto the drawing page.

16 On the **Perennials** title bar, click the green stencil icon, and then click **Close**.

Visio closes the stencil.

Shapes

17 On the Standard toolbar, click the **Shapes** button, and then point to **My Shapes**.

The Perennials stencil appears on the My Shapes submenu.

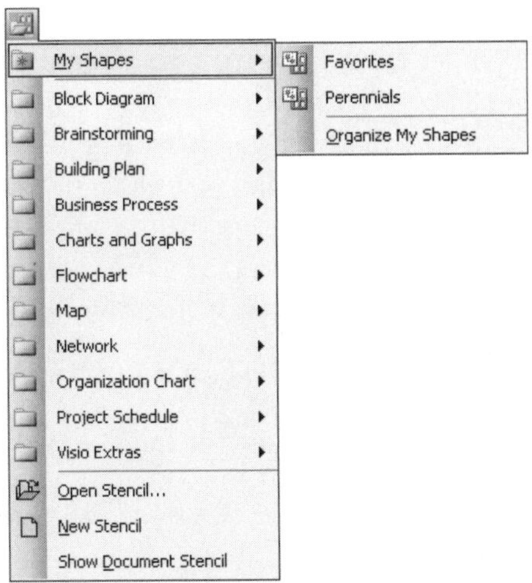

Troubleshooting If the Perennials stencil doesn't appear on the My Shapes submenu, you didn't save it in the My Shapes folder, which is where Visio looks for all stencils by default. To open a stencil in a different location, on the File menu, point to Shapes, and then click Open Stencil.

18 Click **Perennials**.

Visio opens the Perennials stencil and docks it to the left of the drawing page in the Shapes window.

Tip When you open the stencil, notice that there is no red asterisk on the stencil icon, which means that the stencil is read-only. To make a stencil editable, click the stencil icon, and then click Edit Stencil on the shortcut menu. To make the stencil read-only again, click Edit Stencil again.

19 On the **File** menu, click **Close**.

Visio prompts you to save changes to the drawing.

20 Click **No**.

Visio closes the drawing and stencils.

Creating Templates

If you frequently create a particular type of diagram that uses a unique page size or drawing scale, includes a specified number of pages, or always contains the same information, such as a corporate logo or a title bar containing file information, consider creating a custom template. For example, if you create landscape plans frequently, you can create a template that opens the drawing page at an appropriate size, opens stencils containing landscaping shapes, and includes the appropriate title and logo for your company.

You can save any of your diagrams or drawings as a Visio template, or you can revise an existing Visio template and save it with a different file name as a custom template. Then you can open your custom template to start a new diagram. For example, perhaps you always use the same four stencils, but none of the Visio templates open all four of those stencils. Every time you create a diagram, you have to go through the same tedious procedure of opening the same four stencils before you start drawing anything. Instead, you can open the four stencils for the last time, and before you draw anything, save the blank diagram as a custom template. From then on, you only need to open your custom template, and you're ready to create a diagram with shapes from those stencils.

Tip Visio templates have a .vst file extension, which stands for *Visio template*.

In addition to stencils, templates can also include the following:

- One or more drawing pages, including background pages. Each page can contain shapes, pictures, and other objects.

- Print settings that you enter in the Print Setup dialog box, such as landscape-oriented pages, a custom size, or a drawing scale.
- Styles for lines, text, and fills.
- Snap and glue options that you specify in the Snap & Glue dialog box.
- A color palette from the Color Palette dialog box.
- Window sizes and positions.

In effect, you can save all the settings you work with most often as a template so that you don't have to set them each time you start a new diagram.

In this exercise, you open a Visio template, and then revise it to create your own custom template. You change the drawing page orientation for the template, open custom stencils, and then save the file as a template.

Use the *Garden Perennials* file in the My Documents\Microsoft Press\Visio 2003 SBS\CreatingShapes for this exercise.

1 On the **File** menu, point to **New**, point to **Block Diagram**, and then click **Basic Diagram**.

Visio opens a blank drawing page and three stencils.

2 On the **File** menu, click **Page Setup**.

The Page Setup dialog box appears and displays the Print Setup tab.

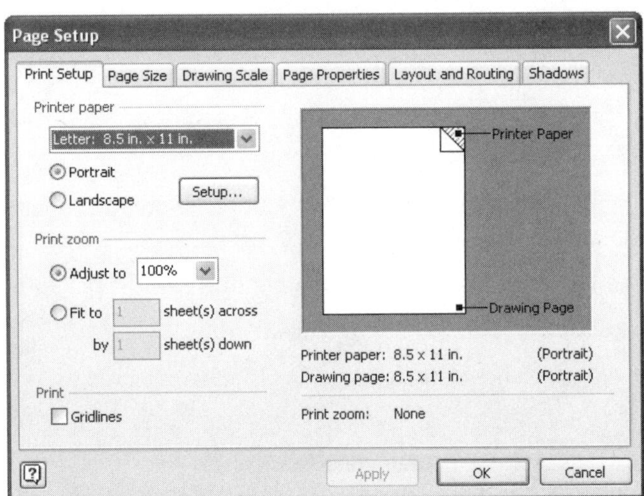

3 In the **Printer paper** area, select the **Landscape** option.

Visio updates the preview in the dialog box to show a landscape-oriented drawing page.

4 To close the **Page Setup** dialog box, click **OK**.

Visio changes the drawing page orientation so that the page is wider than tall.

Shapes

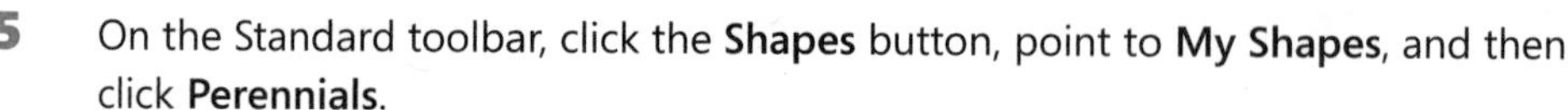

5 On the Standard toolbar, click the **Shapes** button, point to **My Shapes**, and then click **Perennials**.

Visio opens the Perennials stencil and docks it to the left of the drawing page in the Shapes window.

6 On the Standard toolbar, click the **Shapes** button, and then click **Open Stencil**.

7 In the **Look in** box, navigate to the **Microsoft Press\Visio 2003 SBS\Creating** folder, and then double-click **Garden Perennials**.

Visio opens the Garden Perennials stencil and docks it to the left of the drawing page in the Shapes window.

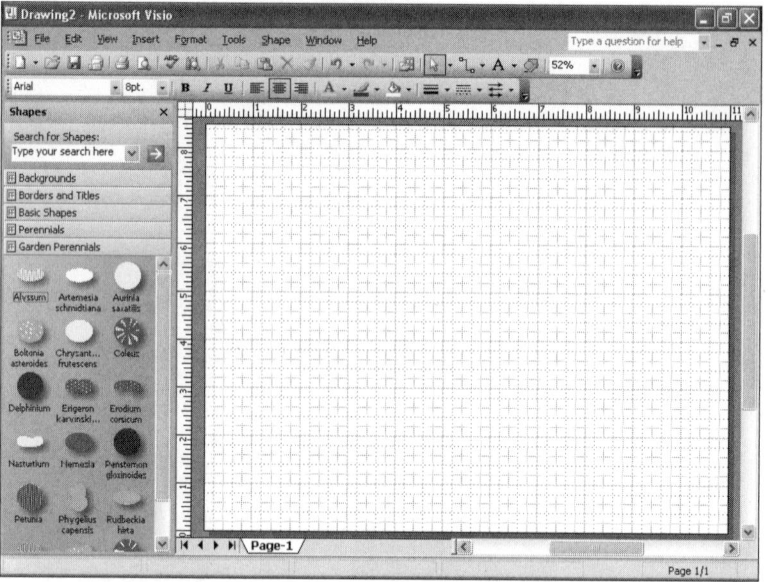

8 On the **File** menu, click **Save As** to open the **Save As** dialog box.

9 In the **Save as type** box, click the down arrow.

Visio displays a list of file types.

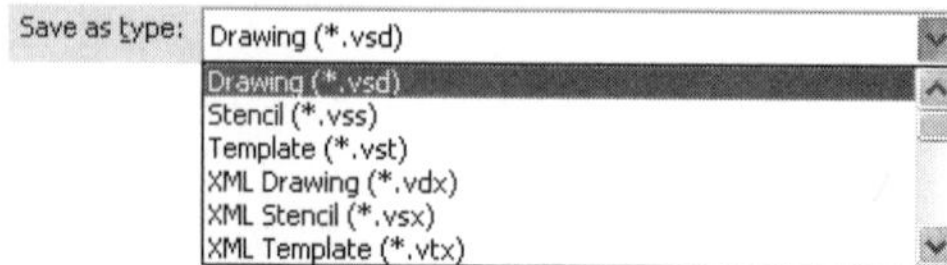

10 Click **Template (*.vst)**, which stands for *Visio template*.

11 In the **File name** box, select the existing text, and type Perennial Garden Plan.

12 Click the **Save** button.

Visio saves the new template, Perennial Garden Plan, in the My Documents folder by default.

13 On the **File** menu, click **Close**.

Visio closes the template.

14 On the **File** menu, click **Open**.

Visio displays the Open dialog box, which shows the contents of My Documents folder by default.

15 In the **Open** dialog box, double-click **Perennial Garden Plan**.

Visio opens a blank, landscape drawing page, the Perennials stencil, the Garden Perennials stencil, and three other stencils.

16 On the **File** menu, click **Exit** to close Visio.

Key Points

- To display the Drawing toolbar, click the Drawing Tools button on the Standard toolbar.
- Hold down the Shift key while dragging the Rectangle tool to create a square. Hold down the Shift key while dragging the Ellipse tool to create a circle.
- Exaggerate your mouse movements when using the Pencil tool to make sure Visio interprets the movement correctly.
- If you can't find a shape you want in the Search for Shapes box, draw your own shape from scratch or modify a similar shape.
- You can modify shapes by adding, moving, and deleting vertexes and control points with the Pencil tool or Pointer tool. Position the Pointer tool over a custom shape to display the shape's vertices and control handles.
- To create more complex shapes, group two or more individual shapes. Use the Shift+Ctrl+G keyboard shortcut to quickly group shapes.
- To modify a shape within a group, select the group, and then subselect the shape you want to modify.
- Use the Operations commands on the Shape menu to merge shapes.
- Save the shapes you want to reuse on a custom stencil or the Favorites stencil.
- To display custom stencils on the My Shapes submenu, save them in the My Shapes folder.
- To open custom stencils, click the Shapes button on the Standard toolbar.
- If you use the same custom diagram settings for many diagrams, you can create your own template based on your preferences. To save a diagram as a template, in the Save As dialog box, in the Save as type box, click Template (*.vst).

Appendix A

Visio Templates and Stencils

Microsoft Office Visio Standard 2003 includes all the templates and stencils listed in the following table.

Category	Template	Stencils Opened by the Template
Block Diagram	Basic Diagram	Basic Shapes, Borders and Titles, and Backgrounds
	Block Diagram	Blocks, Blocks Raised, Borders and Titles, and Backgrounds
	Block Diagram with Perspective	Blocks with Perspective, Borders and Titles, and Backgrounds
Brainstorming	Brainstorming Diagram	Brainstorming Shapes, Legend Shapes, Borders and Titles, and Backgrounds
Building Plan	Office Layout	Walls, Doors and Windows, Office Furniture, Office Equipment, Office Accessories, and Cubicles
Business Process	Audit Diagram	Audit Diagram Shapes, Arrow Shapes, Borders and Titles, and Backgrounds
	Basic Flowchart	Basic Flowchart Shapes, Arrow Shapes, Borders and Titles, and Backgrounds
	Cause and Effect Diagram	Cause and Effect Diagram Shapes, Arrow Shapes, Borders and Titles, and Backgrounds
	Cross Functional Flowchart	Cross Functional Flowchart Shapes Horizontal or Cross Functional Flowchart Shapes Vertical, Basic Flowchart Shapes, and Arrow Shapes
	EPC Diagram	EPC Diagram Shapes, Callouts, Arrow Shapes, Borders and Titles, and Backgrounds
	Fault Tree Analysis Diagram	Fault Tree Analysis Shapes, Arrow Shapes, Borders and Titles, and Backgrounds
	TQM Diagram	TQM Diagram Shapes, Arrow Shapes, Borders and Titles, and Backgrounds

Category	Template	Stencils Opened by the Template
	Work Flow Diagram	Work Flow Diagram Shapes, Arrow Shapes, Borders and Titles, and Backgrounds
Charts and Graphs	Charts And Graphs	Charting Shapes, Borders and Titles, and Backgrounds
	Marketing Charts And Diagrams	Marketing Diagrams, Marketing Shapes, Charting Shapes, Borders and Titles, and Backgrounds
Flowchart	Basic Flowchart	Basic Flowchart Shapes, Arrow Shapes, Borders and Titles, and Backgrounds
	Cross Functional Flowchart	Cross Functional Flowchart Shapes Horizontal or Cross Functional Flowchart Shapes Vertical, Basic Flowchart Shapes, and Arrow Shapes
Map	Directional Map	Road Shapes, Transportation Shapes, Recreation Shapes, Metro Shapes, and Landmark Shapes
	Directional Map 3D	Directional Map Shapes 3D
Network	Basic Network Diagram	Network and Peripherals, Computers and Monitors, Borders and Titles, and Backgrounds
Organization Chart	Organization Chart	Organization Chart Shapes, Borders and Titles, and Backgrounds
	Organization Chart Wizard	Organization Chart Shapes, Borders and Titles, and Backgrounds
Project Schedule	Calendar	Calendar Shapes
	Gantt Chart	Gantt Chart Shapes, Borders and Titles, and Backgrounds
	PERT Chart	PERT Chart Shapes, Borders and Titles, and Backgrounds
	Timeline	Timeline Shapes, Borders and Titles, and Backgrounds
Visio Extras		Backgrounds, Borders and Titles, Callouts, Connectors, Embellishments, and Symbols

Appendix B

Visio Shapes

Each stencil in Microsoft Office Visio Standard 2003 includes a variety of shapes that you can use to create a particular type of drawing or diagram. To help you locate the shapes at a glance, this reference shows each stencil's shapes organized by category, which corresponds to the folder in which the stencil is stored.

Block Diagram Shapes

Using the shapes on the Basic Shapes, Blocks, Blocks Raised, and Blocks with Perspective stencils, you can create simple diagrams that communicate business relationships and processes to annotate reports, presentations, proposals, and so on.

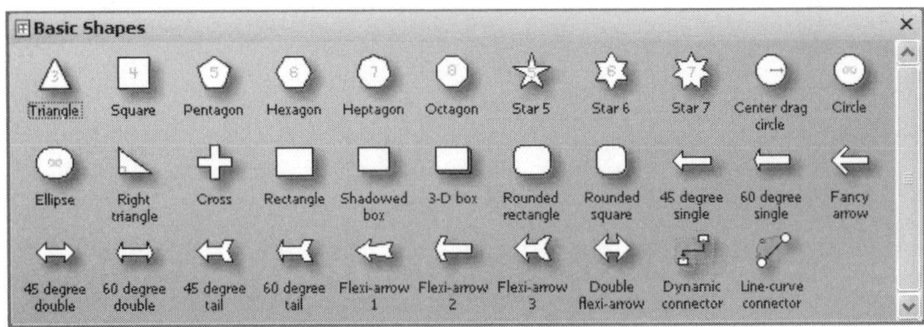

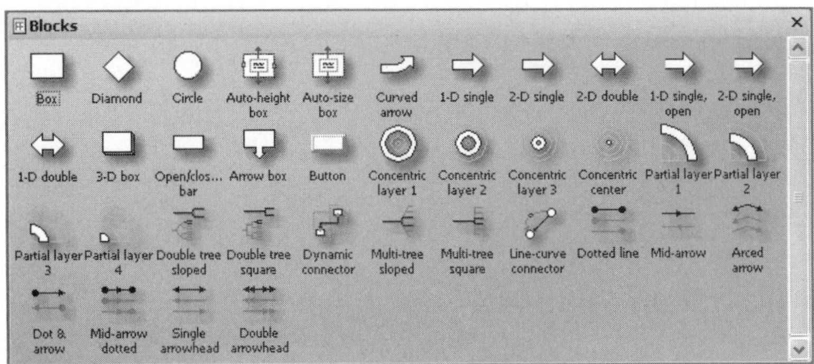

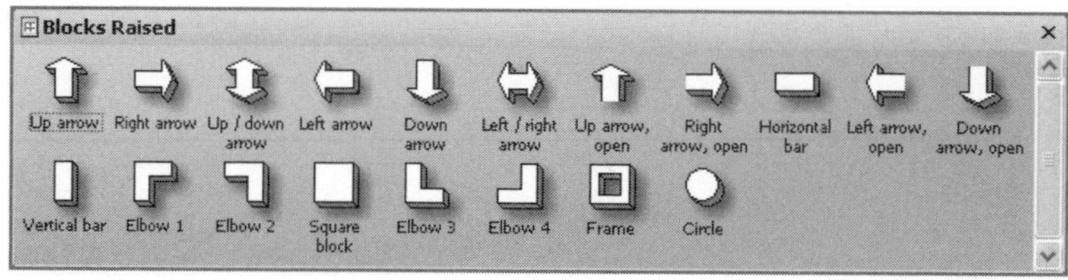

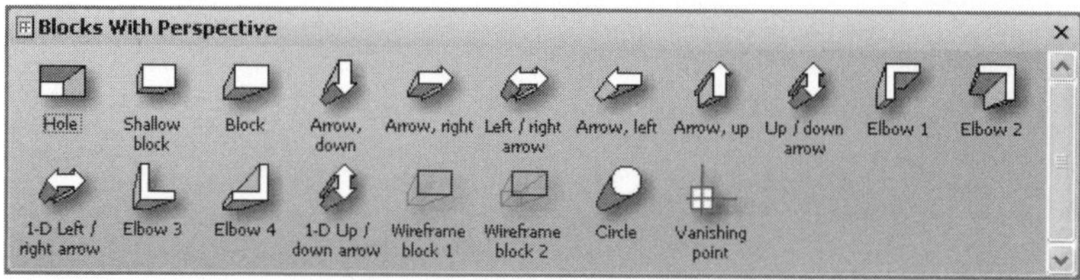

Brainstorming Shapes

Using the shapes on the Brainstorming Shapes and Legend Shapes stencils, you can create brainstorming diagrams used for planning, problem solving, and decision making.

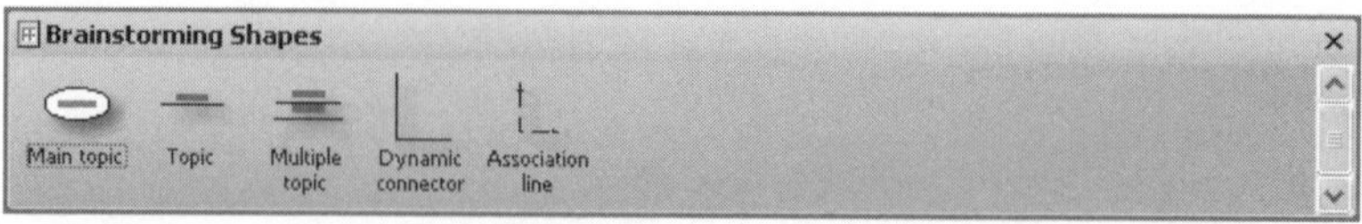

Building Plan Shapes

Using the shapes on the Cubicles, Office Accessories, Office Equipment, Office Furniture, and Walls, Doors and Windows stencils, you can create scaled buildings, home plans, and office layouts.

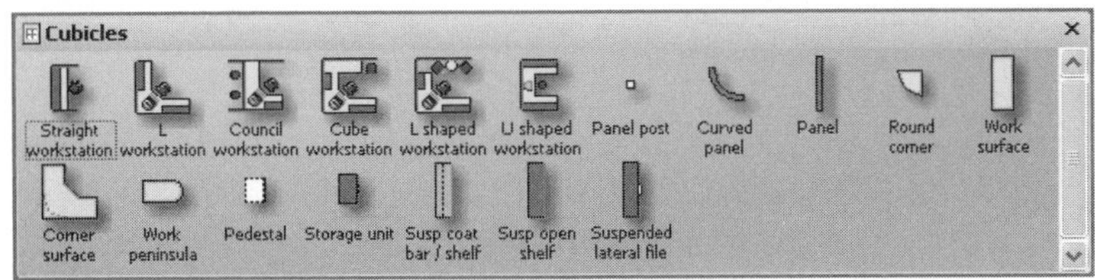
Cubicles
Straight workstation
L workstation
Council workstation
Cube workstation
L shaped workstation
U shaped workstation
Panel post
Curved panel
Panel
Round corner
Work surface
Corner surface
Work peninsula
Pedestal
Storage unit
Susp coat bar / shelf
Susp open shelf
Suspended lateral file

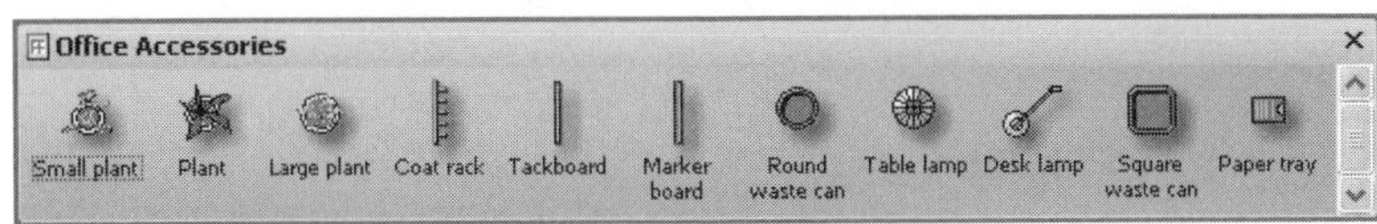
Office Accessories
Small plant
Plant
Large plant
Coat rack
Tackboard
Marker board
Round waste can
Table lamp
Desk lamp
Square waste can
Paper tray

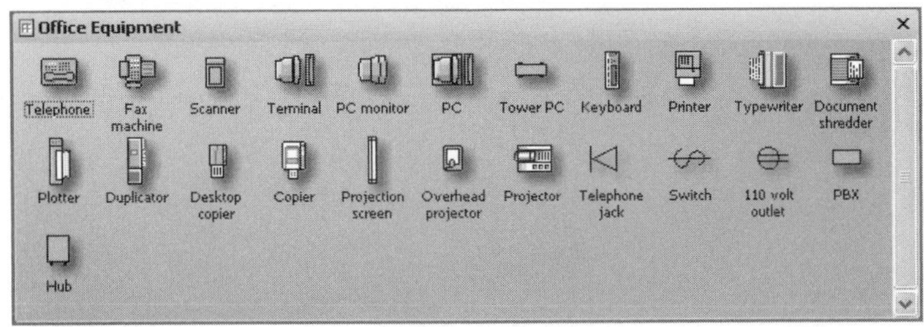
Office Equipment
Telephone
Fax machine
Scanner
Terminal
PC monitor
PC
Tower PC
Keyboard
Printer
Typewriter
Document shredder
Plotter
Duplicator
Desktop copier
Copier
Projection screen
Overhead projector
Projector
Telephone jack
Switch
110 volt outlet
PBX
Hub

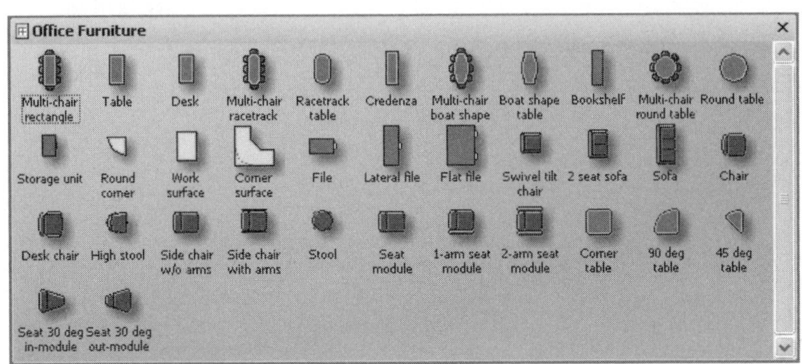
Office Furniture
Multi-chair rectangle
Table
Desk
Multi-chair racetrack
Racetrack table
Credenza
Multi-chair boat shape
Boat shape table
Bookshelf
Multi-chair round table
Round table
Storage unit
Round corner
Work surface
Corner surface
File
Lateral file
Flat file
Swivel tilt chair
2 seat sofa
Sofa
Chair
Desk chair
High stool
Side chair w/o arms
Side chair with arms
Stool
Seat module
1-arm seat module
2-arm seat module
Corner table
90 deg table
45 deg table
Seat 30 deg in-module
Seat 30 deg out-module

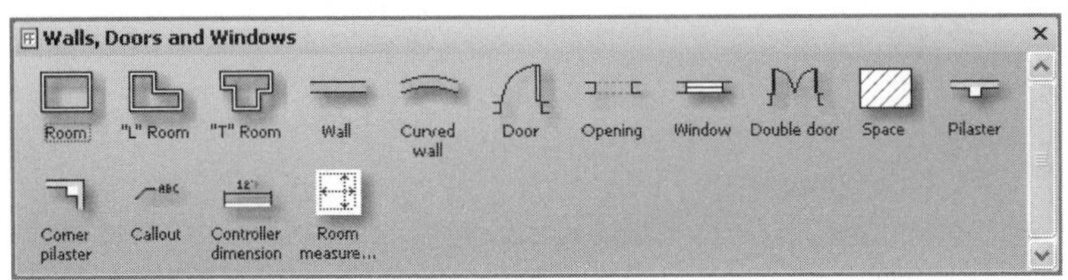
Walls, Doors and Windows
Room
"L" Room
"T" Room
Wall
Curved wall
Door
Opening
Window
Double door
Space
Pilaster
Corner pilaster
Callout
Controller dimension
Room measure...

Business Process Shapes

Using the shapes on the business process stencils, you can create general purpose and specialized flowcharts, data flow, work flow, and planning diagrams. Visio includes the following flowchart shapes: Audit Diagram Shapes stencil, Basic Flowchart Shapes stencil, Cause and Effect Diagram Shapes stencil, Cross Functional Flowchart Shapes Horizontal stencil, Cross Functional Flowchart Shapes Vertical stencil, EPC Diagram Shapes stencil, Fault Tree Analysis Shapes stencil, TQM Diagram Shapes stencil, Work Flow Diagram Shapes stencil, and Arrow Shapes stencil.

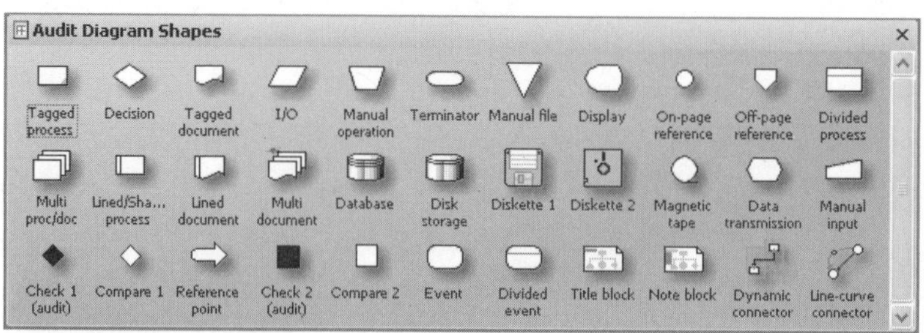

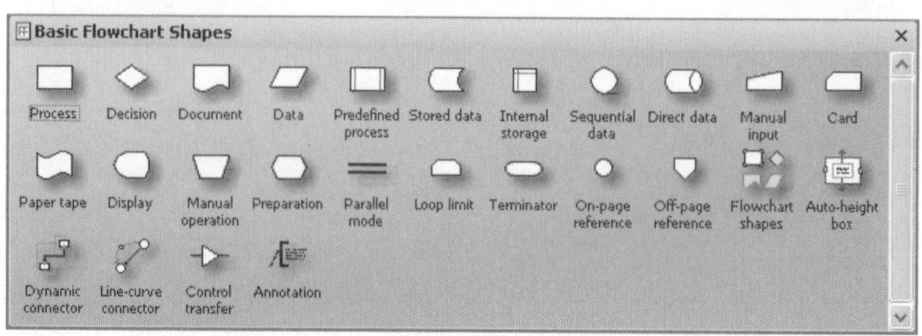

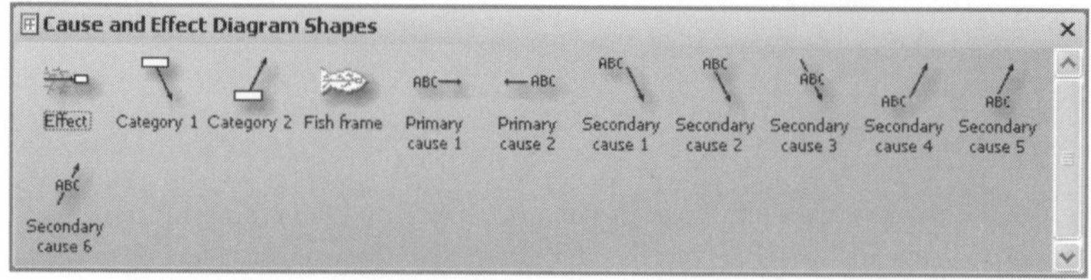

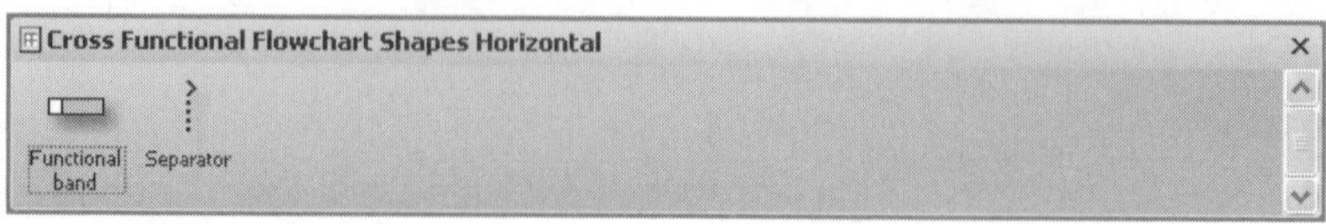

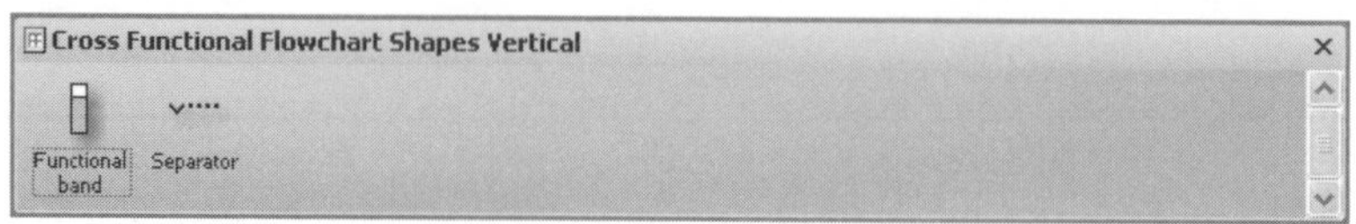

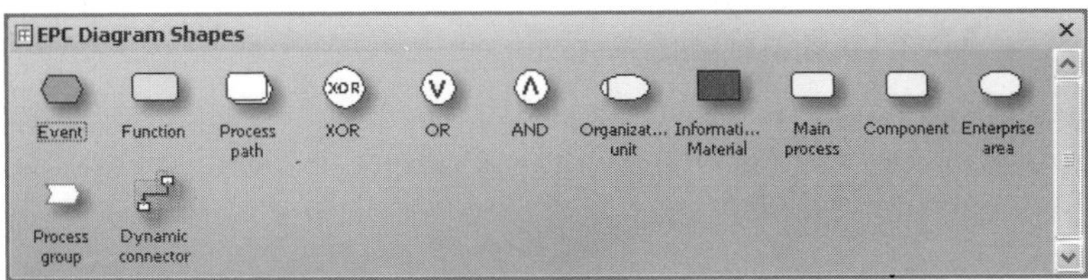
EPC Diagram Shapes
Event
Function
Process path
XOR
OR
AND
Organizat... unit
Informati... Material
Main process
Component
Enterprise area
Process group
Dynamic connector

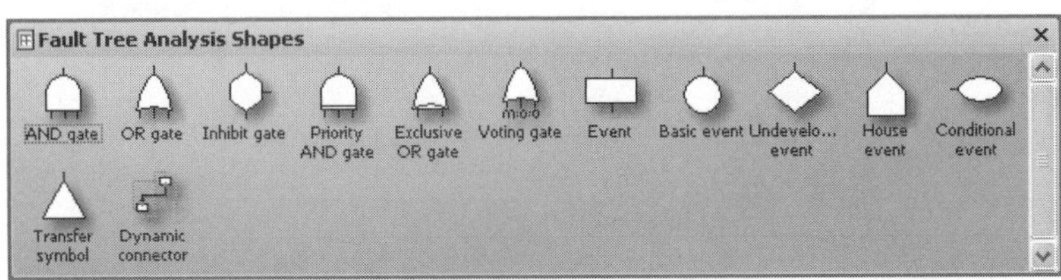
Fault Tree Analysis Shapes
AND gate
OR gate
Inhibit gate
Priority AND gate
Exclusive OR gate
Voting gate
Event
Basic event
Undevelo... event
House event
Conditional event
Transfer symbol
Dynamic connector

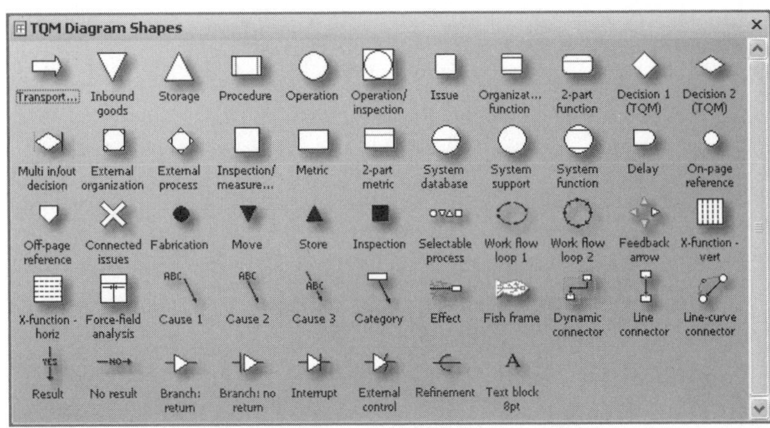
TQM Diagram Shapes
Transport...
Inbound goods
Storage
Procedure
Operation
Operation/ inspection
Issue
Organizat... function
2-part function
Decision 1 (TQM)
Decision 2 (TQM)
Multi in/out decision
External organization
External process
Inspection/ measure...
Metric
2-part metric
System database
System support
System function
Delay
On-page reference
Off-page reference
Connected issues
Fabrication
Move
Store
Inspection
Selectable process
Work flow loop 1
Work flow loop 2
Feedback arrow
X-function - vert
X-function - horiz
Force-field analysis
Cause 1
Cause 2
Cause 3
Category
Effect
Fish frame
Dynamic connector
Line connector
Line-curve connector
Result
No result
Branch: return
Branch: no return
Interrupt
External control
Refinement
Text block 8pt

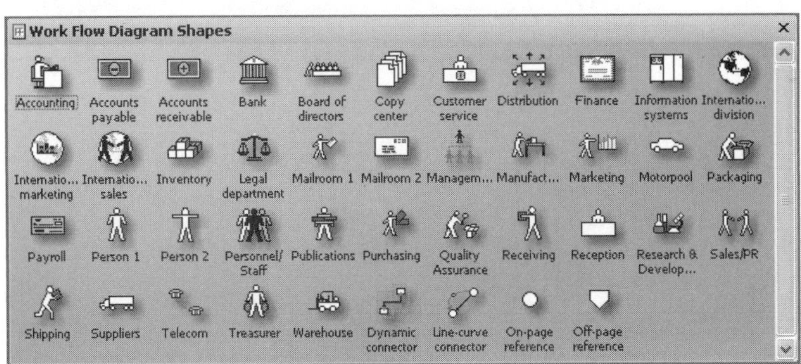
Work Flow Diagram Shapes
Accounting
Accounts payable
Accounts receivable
Bank
Board of directors
Copy center
Customer service
Distribution
Finance
Information systems
Internatio... division
Internatio... marketing
Internatio... sales
Inventory
Legal department
Mailroom 1
Mailroom 2
Managem...
Manufact...
Marketing
Motorpool
Packaging
Payroll
Person 1
Person 2
Personnel/ Staff
Publications
Purchasing
Quality Assurance
Receiving
Reception
Research & Develop...
Sales/PR
Shipping
Suppliers
Telecom
Treasurer
Warehouse
Dynamic connector
Line-curve connector
On-page reference
Off-page reference

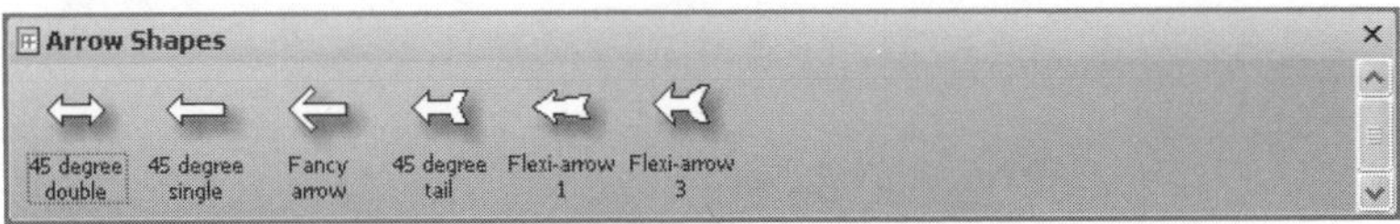
Arrow Shapes
45 degree double
45 degree single
Fancy arrow
45 degree tail
Flexi-arrow 1
Flexi-arrow 3

Charts and Graphs

Using the shapes on the Marketing Diagrams, Marketing Shapes, and Charting Shapes stencils, you can design charts, graphs, and diagrams for presentations, reports, and marketing documentation.

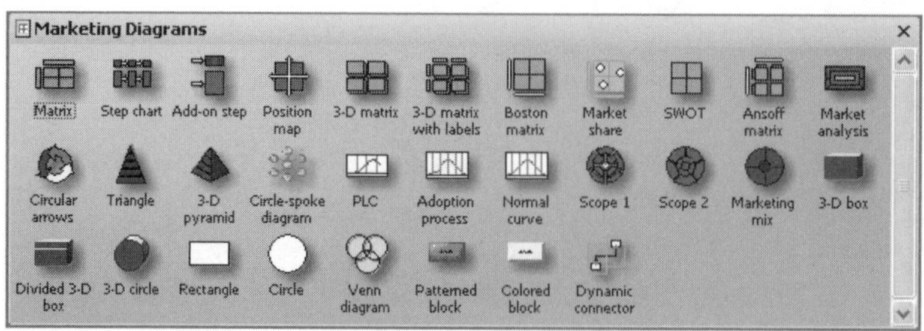

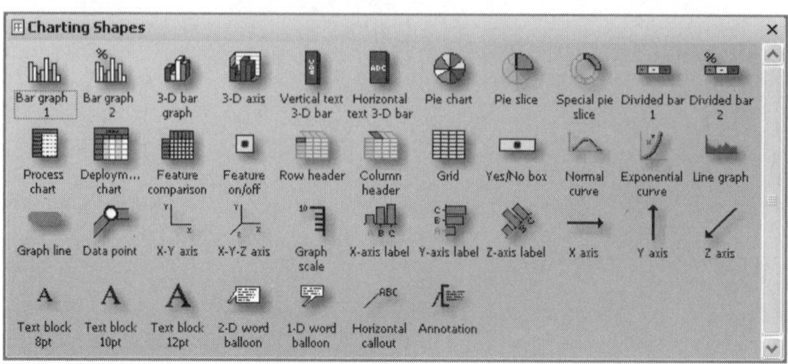

Flowchart Shapes

Using the shapes on the flowchart stencils, you can create general purpose and specialized flowcharts. Visio includes the following flowchart shapes: Basic Flowchart Shapes stencil, Cross-Functional Flowchart Shapes Horizontal stencil, Cross-Functional Flowchart Shapes Vertical stencil, and Arrow Shapes stencil.

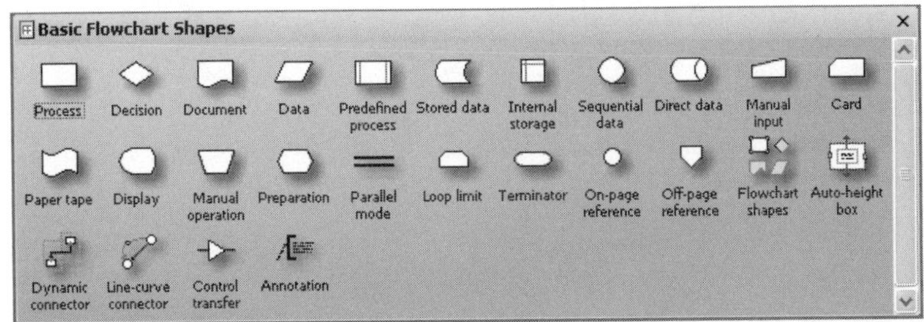

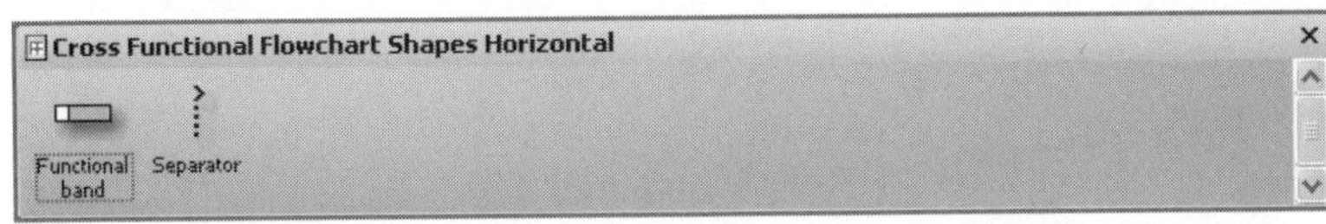

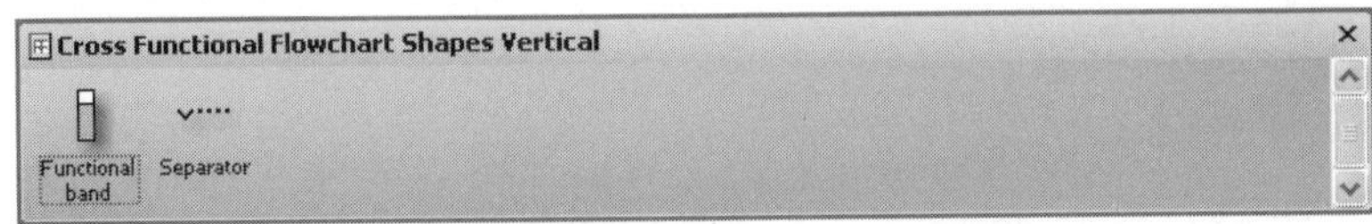

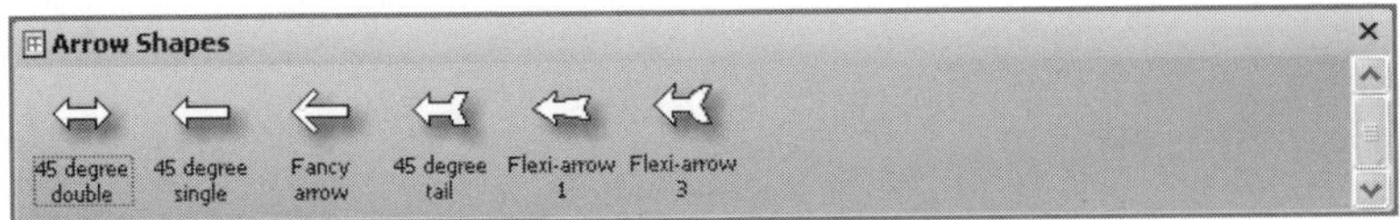

Map Shapes

Using the map shapes, you can create simple and attractive maps for invitations, Web sites, brochures, and presentations. Visio includes the following map shapes: Directional Map Shapes 3D stencil, Landmark Shapes stencil, Metro Shapes stencil, Recreation Shapes stencil, Road Shapes stencil, and Transportation Shapes stencil.

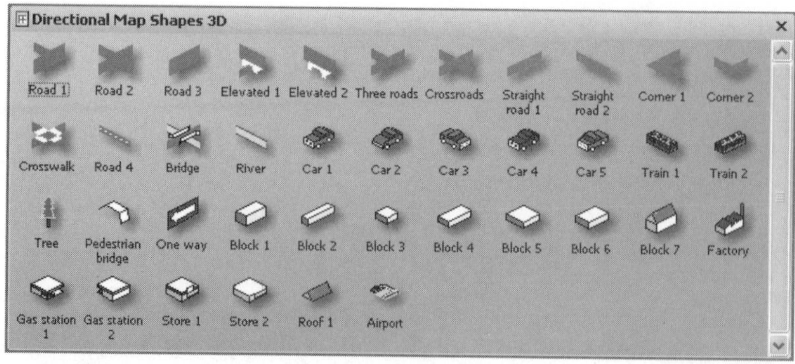
Directional Map Shapes 3D
Road 1
Road 2
Road 3
Elevated 1
Elevated 2
Three roads
Crossroads
Straight road 1
Straight road 2
Corner 1
Corner 2
Crosswalk
Road 4
Bridge
River
Car 1
Car 2
Car 3
Car 4
Car 5
Train 1
Train 2
Tree
Pedestrian bridge
One way
Block 1
Block 2
Block 3
Block 4
Block 5
Block 6
Block 7
Factory
Gas station 1
Gas station 2
Store 1
Store 2
Roof 1
Airport

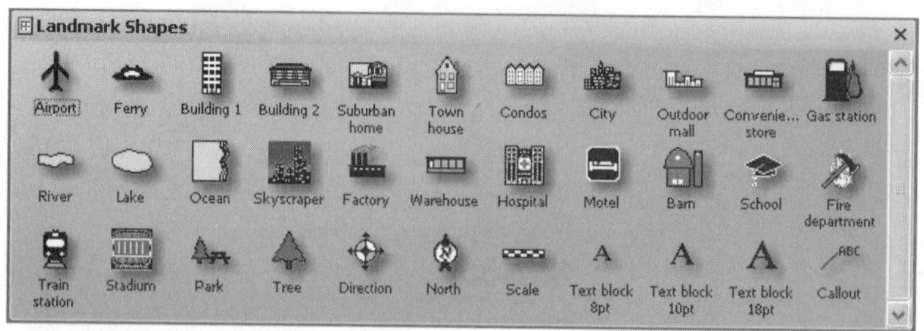
Landmark Shapes
Airport
Ferry
Building 1
Building 2
Suburban home
Town house
Condos
City
Outdoor mall
Convenie... store
Gas station
River
Lake
Ocean
Skyscraper
Factory
Warehouse
Hospital
Motel
Barn
School
Fire department
Train station
Stadium
Park
Tree
Direction
North
Scale
Text block 8pt
Text block 10pt
Text block 18pt
Callout

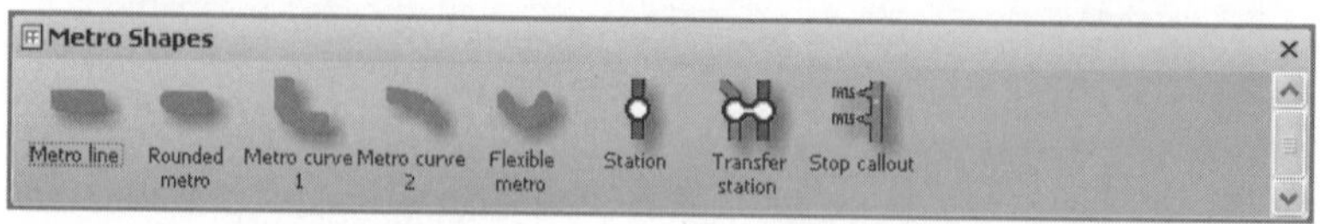
Metro Shapes
Metro line
Rounded metro
Metro curve 1
Metro curve 2
Flexible metro
Station
Transfer station
Stop callout

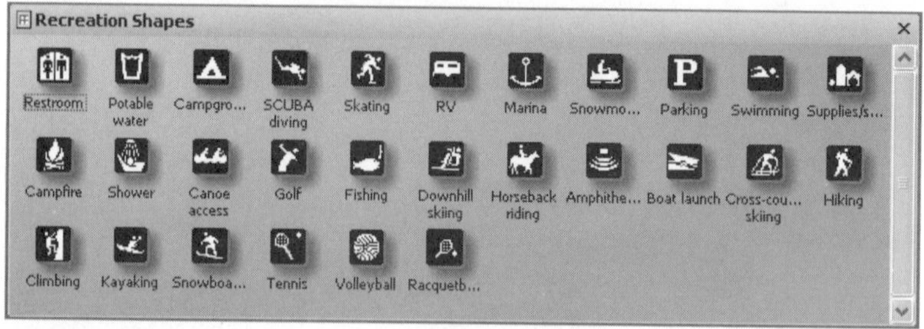
Recreation Shapes
Restroom
Potable water
Campgro...
SCUBA diving
Skating
RV
Marina
Snowmo...
Parking
Swimming
Supplies/s...
Campfire
Shower
Canoe access
Golf
Fishing
Downhill skiing
Horseback riding
Amphithe...
Boat launch
Cross-cou... skiing
Hiking
Climbing
Kayaking
Snowboa...
Tennis
Volleyball
Racquetb...

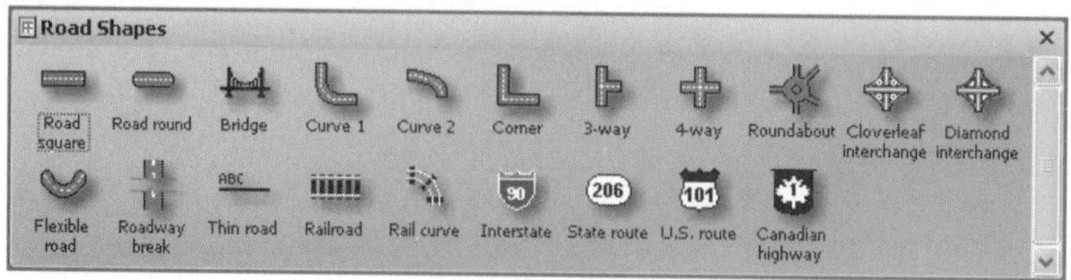
Road Shapes
Road square
Road round
Bridge
Curve 1
Curve 2
Corner
3-way
4-way
Roundabout
Cloverleaf interchange
Diamond interchange
Flexible road
Roadway break
Thin road
Railroad
Rail curve
Interstate
State route
U.S. route
Canadian highway

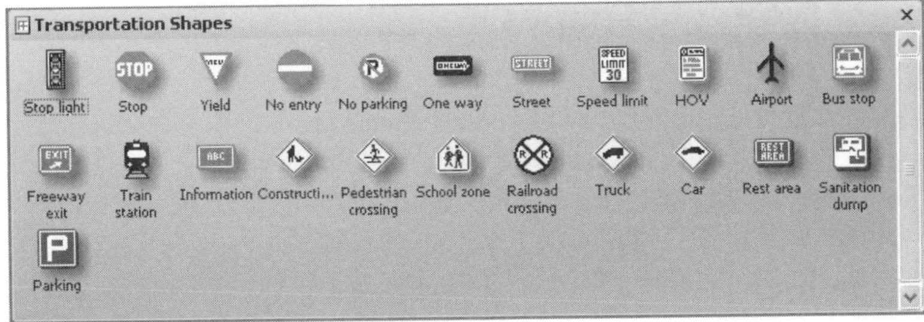

Network Shapes

Using the shapes on the Network and Peripherals and Computers and Monitors stencils, you can create high-level network diagrams for presentations and proposals.

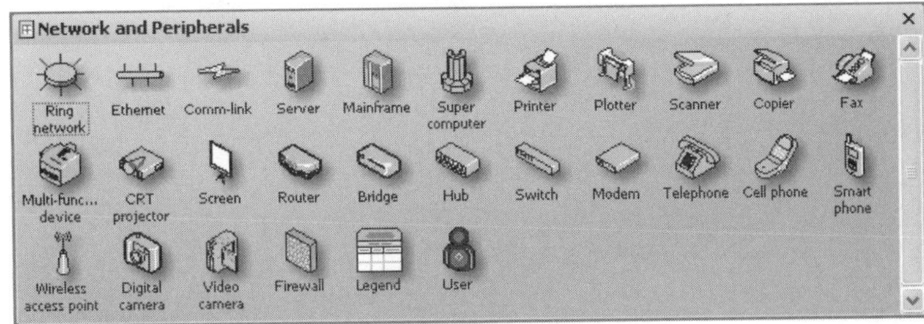

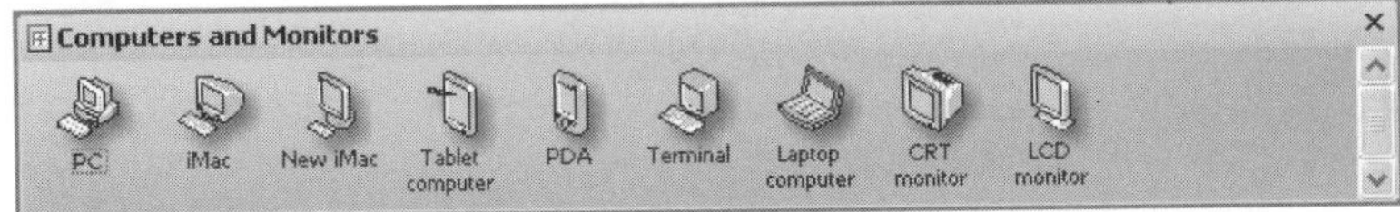

Organization Chart Shapes

Using the shapes on the Organization Chart Shapes stencil, you can show an organization's reporting hierarchy and employee-manager relationships.

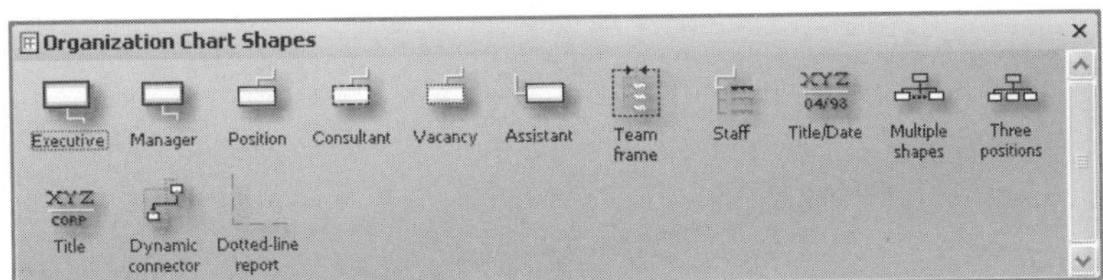

Project Schedule Shapes

Using the Calendar Shapes stencil, you can create monthly and yearly calendars. With the Gantt Chart Shapes stencil, you can show the sequence of tasks necessary for completing a project. With the PERT Chart Shapes stencil, you can use shapes that conform to the Program Evaluation and Review Technique (PERT), a project management method originally developed in the 1950s by the U.S. Navy and used today to diagram project details. With the Timeline Shapes stencil, you can show the lifespan of a project of process in a linear format that includes tasks, milestones, and intervals.

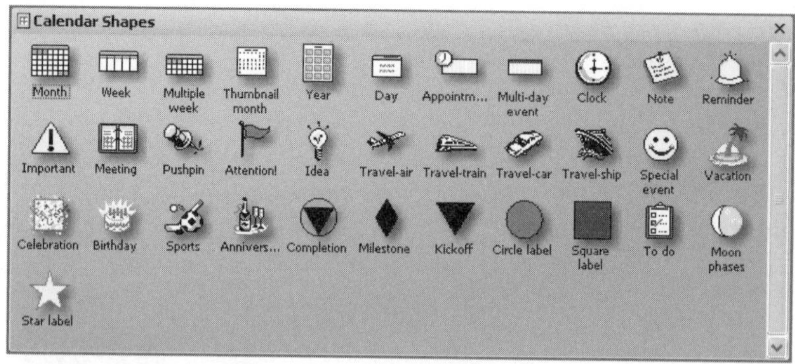

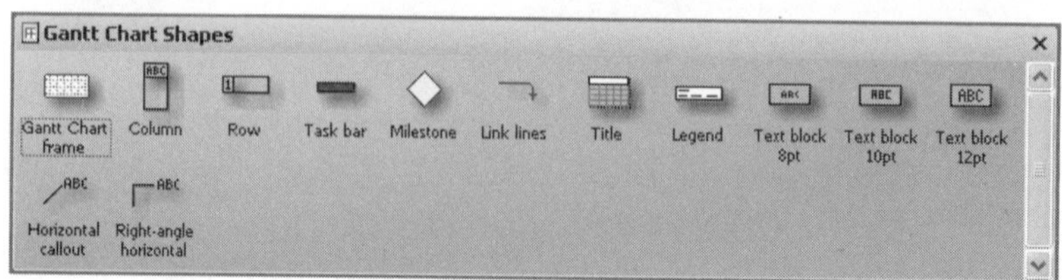

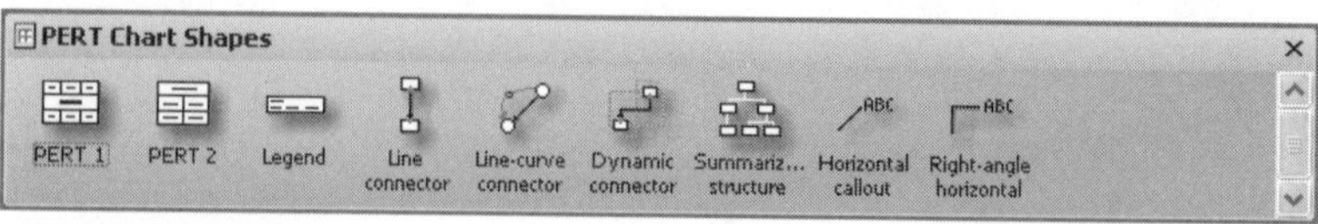

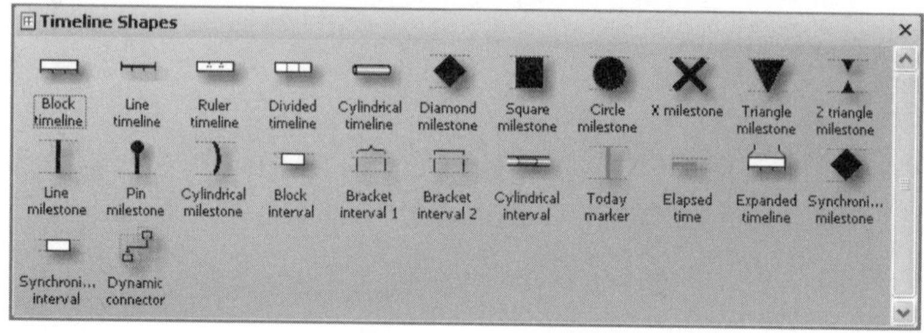

Visio Extras Shapes

Visio Extras are shapes that you can use to annotate or decorate any diagram. You can use the shapes on the Backgrounds stencil to add an attractive background to a diagram. The Borders and Titles stencil contains a variety of page border and title shapes. The Callouts stencil includes lines, arrows, and text shapes for notes. The Connectors stencil includes straight, curved, and angled connectors. The Embellishments and Symbols stencils contain ornamental shapes.

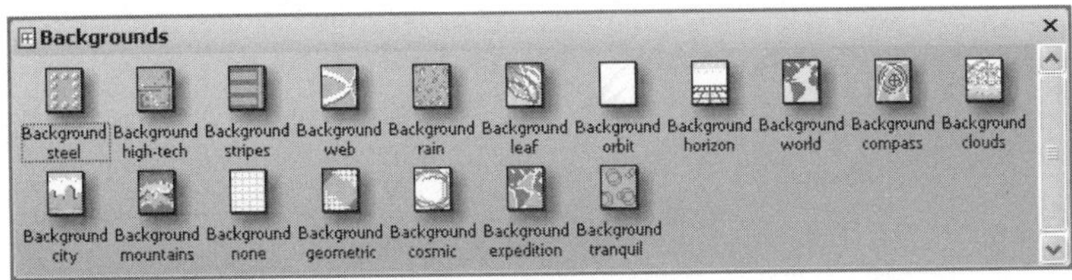

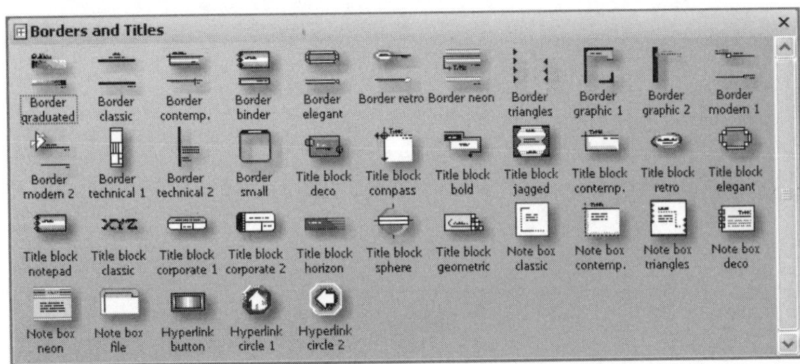

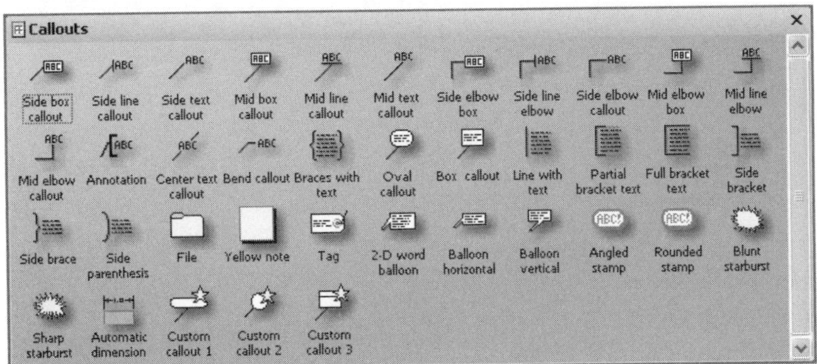

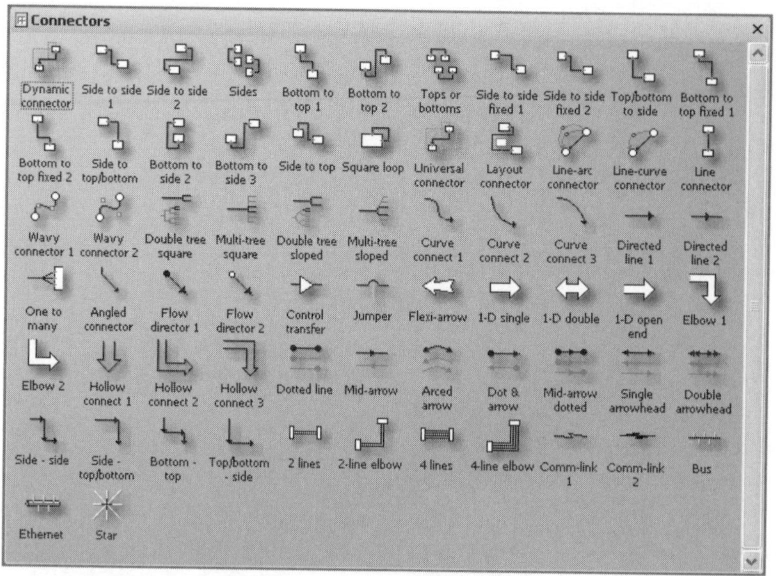
Connectors
Dynamic connector
Side to side 1
Side to side 2
Sides
Bottom to top 1
Bottom to top 2
Tops or bottoms
Side to side fixed 1
Side to side fixed 2
Top/bottom to side
Bottom to top fixed 1
Bottom to top fixed 2
Side to top/bottom
Bottom to side 2
Bottom to side 3
Side to top
Square loop
Universal connector
Layout connector
Line-arc connector
Line-curve connector
Line connector
Wavy connector 1
Wavy connector 2
Double tree square
Multi-tree square
Double tree sloped
Multi-tree sloped
Curve connect 1
Curve connect 2
Curve connect 3
Directed line 1
Directed line 2
One to many
Angled connector
Flow director 1
Flow director 2
Control transfer
Jumper
Flexi-arrow
1-D single
1-D double
1-D open end
Elbow 1
Elbow 2
Hollow connect 1
Hollow connect 2
Hollow connect 3
Dotted line
Mid-arrow
Arced arrow
Dot & arrow
Mid-arrow dotted
Single arrowhead
Double arrowhead
Side - side
Side - top/bottom
Bottom - top
Top/bottom - side
2 lines
2-line elbow
4 lines
4-line elbow
Comm-link 1
Comm-link 2
Bus
Ethernet
Star

Embellishments
Wave section
Wave corner
Braid section
Braid corner
Braid end-cap
Egyptian section
Egyptian corner
Egyptian end-cap
Greek section
Greek corner
Greek border
Cross section
Cross corner
Cross end-cap
Wave section 2
Wave corner 2
Wave corner 3
Roman section
Star section
Triangle section
Chiseled frame
Square frame
Photo frame
Art deco frame
Jewel frame
Classic frame
Fun frame
Art deco circle
Art deco tile
Wave tile
Weave tile
Zigzag tile
Op-art tile
Diamond tile
Graphic tile
Celtic ornament
Button ornament
Arc ornament
Checker section
Single line frame
Multi line frame

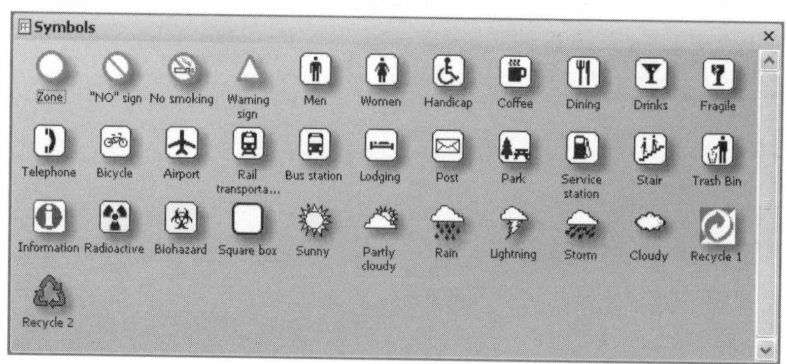
Symbols
Zone
"NO" sign
No smoking
Warning sign
Men
Women
Handicap
Coffee
Dining
Drinks
Fragile
Telephone
Bicycle
Airport
Rail transporta...
Bus station
Lodging
Post
Park
Service station
Stair
Trash Bin
Information
Radioactive
Biohazard
Square box
Sunny
Partly cloudy
Rain
Lightning
Storm
Cloudy
Recycle 1
Recycle 2

Glossary

attributes Qualities of text or shapes that you can format, including text font and color; line color, ends, weight, and pattern; and fill color, pattern, and shadow, and so on. See also *formatting*.

background page A second drawing page that appears behind the primary drawing page in a diagram and usually contains background shapes.

backbone The physical network configuration, or topology, that you can depict in a network diagram by using a shape such as the Ethernet shape on the Network and Peripherals stencil. See also *network ring*.

begin point The selection handle that appear at the start of a selected 1-D shape and is marked by ×. See also *endpoints; end point*.

closed shape A 2-D shape, such as a box, with a solid border to which you can apply a fill color and pattern. See also *open shape*.

color scheme A set of coordinated colors that you can apply to an entire diagram and its shapes by right-clicking the drawing page, and then clicking Color Schemes on the shortcut menu. Not all diagram types support the use of a color scheme. When that is the case, the command does not appear when you right-click the drawing page.

connection point A point on a shape where you can attach a connector or 1-D shape. Each connection point appears as a blue mark on a shape when the Connection Points command is selected on the View menu.

connectors 1-D shapes designed to connect other shapes. The Connectors stencil in the Visio Extras folder contains a variety of connector shapes for use in any drawing type.

control handles Yellow diamond-shaped handles that control a shape's behavior in special ways. Depending on the shape, a control handle might adjust the position of a line, reshape an arrow, or connect to other shapes. To find out what a control handle does, point to the handle to display a ScreenTip.

control point The circular handle that appears on a line or arc when you select it with the Pencil tool. You can drag a control point to change the curve of an arc or ellipse.

crop To reduce the size and cut out a portion of an imported picture. You use the Crop tool to drag one of the picture's selection handles to the desired size, and then drag the picture inside the selection box to view the portion of the picture you want to use.

custom properties Information about a shape, which appears in the Custom Properties window. For example, a shape that represents office furniture can have custom properties that identify its inventory number, owner, and location. You can enter values for a custom property and define your own custom properties for a shape.

deselect To click the pasteboard or a blank area of the drawing page, or press the Esc key so a shape's selection handles don't appear.

dock To attach a window to a side of the drawing page window. For example, stencils are docked by default in the Shapes window on the left side of the drawing window. See also *float*.

drawing file A file that contains a Visio drawing or diagram. Drawing files have a .vsd file extension.

drawing page The printable area in the Visio window that contains a drawing. Each drawing page has a size, which usually corresponds to a standard printer paper size, and other properties that you can change with the Page Setup command on the File menu.

drawing scale A measure of the relationship between real-world sizes or distances and the sizes represented in a Visio drawing. For example, an office layout might have a drawing scale of one foot of actual distance to one inch in the drawing. To set a drawing scale, click the Page Setup command on the File menu. Then, click the Drawing Scale tab.

dynamic grid The dotted line that appears on the screen when you drag a shape near another shape. The dynamic grid shows the optimal alignment. To turn on the dynamic grid, click the Snap & Glue command on the Tools menu.

embed To paste or insert an object, such as text or a group of shapes, from one program into a file created in another program. The embedded object becomes part of the file, but you can double-click it to modify it in its original program. See also *link*.

end point The selection handle that appear at the end of a selected 1-D shape and is marked by +. See also *begin point*; *endpoints*.

endpoints Either of the selection handles that appear at the beginning or end of a selected 1-D shape. The endpoint at the beginning of the shape (begin point) is marked by ¥. The endpoint at the end of the shape (end point) is marked by +. See also *begin point*; *end point*.

expanded timeline A linear graphic that represents and is synchronized with a segment of a larger timeline. See also *timeline*.

field Placeholder text that Visio uses to display dates or other information in a shape. You can insert a field into a shape with the Field command on the Insert menu.

fill The color and pattern inside a shape.

float To display and move a window anywhere within the Visio window. For example, you can drag a stencil onto the drawing page to display it in a floating window. See also *dock*.

formatting A combination of attributes that make up the appearance of a shape, diagram, or text. For example, you can format a shape to change the thickness and color of its lines, the color and pattern inside the shape, its font, and so on. See also *attributes*.

Gantt bars Bars in a Gantt chart that represent the duration of a task.

Gantt charts Diagram types you create in Visio with the Gantt Chart template that describes the discrete tasks associated with a project. In a Gantt chart, bars represent the duration of each task within a timescale that is displayed in the chart.

glue Shape behavior that causes one shape to stay connected to another, even if the shape to which it is glued moves.

grid Nonprinting horizontal and vertical lines displayed at regular intervals on the drawing page. The grid makes it easier to align shapes and position them precisely.

group A shape composed of one or more shapes. A group can also include other groups and objects from other programs. You can move and size a group as a single shape, but its members retain their original appearance and attributes. You can also subselect individual shapes in the group to modify them. See also *subselect*.

guides Visual reference lines that you can drag from the horizontal or vertical ruler onto the drawing page in order to help position and align shapes precisely. Guides do not appear on the printed page.

interval markers A shape used to designate a period of time in a diagram created with the Timeline template.

landscape orientation A printed page or drawing page that is wider than it is tall. You can change page orientation in Visio with the Page Setup command on the File menu. The orientation of the printed page and drawing page can differ. See also *portrait orientation*.

layers Named categories to which shapes are assigned in some diagram types, such as office layouts and network diagrams. You can organize shapes in your drawing by selectively viewing, editing, printing, or locking layers, and you can control whether you can snap and glue shapes on a layer.

line caps Style of a line end: round or square.

line ends Patterns, such as arrowheads, that can appear on the end of a 1-D shape.

link To create a dynamic link from one file to another so that the contents of the original file appear in the linked file. When changes are made to the original file, you can update the link so that the most recent version of the object appears in the linked file. See also *embed*.

locked A setting that limits the ways you can modify a shape. For example, this setting can prevent you from resizing a shape using a selection handle. When you select a locked shape, the shape handles appear gray.

measurement units The type of measurement system used in a drawing and displayed on the rulers. You specify the measurement units (inches, centimeters, points, miles, and so on) with the Page Setup command on the File menu.

merge To create a new shape by combining or splitting apart existing shapes using an Operations command, such as Union or Combine, on the Shape menu.

milestones A shape from the Timeline Shapes stencil that shows a significant date in a timeline.

network ring The physical configuration or topology of a network that refers to the configuration of cables, computers, and other peripherals. To create a network diagram, start with the Basic Network Diagram template. See also *backbone*.

object linking and embedding In Microsoft Windows, the ability to link or embed a shape or other object created in one program, such as Visio, into a document created in a different program, such as Word.

one-dimensional (1-D) shape A shape, such as a line, that has only one dimension and two endpoints. See also *two-dimensional shape*; *connector*; *endpoint*.

open shape A shape that does not have a continuous border, such as a line or arc. You cannot apply fill color or patterns to an open shape. See also *closed shape*.

page breaks Gray lines that appear on the drawing page when you click the Page Breaks command on the View menu. Page breaks show you where the page will break when you print a large diagram.

pan To change the view by moving the drawing page. You can use the horizontal and vertical scroll bars in the Visio window to pan a drawing, or you can use the keyboard shortcut: Hold down Shift+Ctrl as you drag with the right mouse button.

pasteboard The blue area around the drawing page, which you can use as a temporary holding area for shapes. Shapes on the pasteboard are saved with a drawing but aren't printed.

picture A graphic file created in another program that you can add to a Visio diagram. To insert a picture, click the Picture command on the Insert menu.

point-to-point connection A connection between shapes in which the endpoint of a connector stays attached to a particular point on a shape, even when the shape is moved.

portrait orientation A printed page or drawing page that is taller than it is wide. You can change page orientation in Visio with the Page Setup command on the File menu. The orientation of the printed page and drawing page can differ. See also *landscape orientation*.

primary shape The first shape you select in a multiple selection, which can affect the outcome of a command, such as the Align Shapes and Operations commands on the Shape menu.

read-only A setting that prevents you from modifying a file, such as a stencil.

report definition The settings and shape properties included in a report, which you can customize with the Reports command on the Tools menu.

rotation handle The round handle that appears above a 2-D shape. Drag it to rotate a shape.

rulers The horizontal and vertical rulers that appear on the top and side of the drawing page, which you can hide and show by clicking Rulers on the View menu. The rulers display the units of measurement specified by the Page Setup command on the File menu. See also *measurement units*.

ScreenTip Descriptive text that appears when you pause the pointer over a button on a toolbar, a shape on a stencil, handles on a shape, the rulers, and so on.

secondary shapes The shapes you select after the primary shape in a multiple selection. See also *primary shape*.

select To click a shape so that it becomes the focus of the next action. Selected shapes display handles. Selected text is highlighted.

selection handles Handles that appear on a selected shape. Visio displays different types of selection handles depending on the tool you used to select a shape.

selection box The dotted line that surrounds a shape and shows that it is selected.

selection net The dotted line that appears when you drag using the Pointer Tool. Selection nets are used to select more than one shape; anything within a selection net is selected.

shapes Objects that you drag onto the drawing page to assemble diagrams and that you create using the Visio drawing tools.

shape-to-shape connection A connection between shapes in which the endpoint of a connector stays attached to a shape at the closest point, even when you move the shape.

shortcut menu The menu that appears when you right-click an object, such as a shape, stencil, or the drawing page. Many Visio shapes have special commands that appear only on a shortcut menu.

snap The way a shape aligns itself automatically with the nearest grid line or guide.

stencils Visio files that contain shapes you can drag onto a drawing page. Stencil files have a .vss file extension.

style A set of formatting attributes, which typically include fill, line, and text attributes. To apply a style to a shape, select the shape, and then on the Format menu, click Style.

subselect To select an individual shape within a group. Select the group, and then select the individual shape. See also *group*.

task panes Panes, or windows, that open to the right of the Visio drawing page and contain task-oriented or diagram-specific information. To view task panes, on the View menu, click Task Pane.

template A Visio file that includes all of the tools, styles, settings, and shapes you need to assemble a particular type of drawing or diagram. A template opens a drawing page and, usually, stencils. Template files have a .vst file extension.

text block The text area associated with a shape that appears when you click the shape with the Text tool or Text Block tool, or select the shape and start typing. You can size a text block and move a text block in relation to its shape using the Text Block tool.

text-only shape Independent text that's not associated with a shape, but behaves like a shape. Create a text-only shape by using the Text Tool.

timelines Linear graphics that represent a specific period of time and the events that occur during that time. You create a timeline in Visio using the Timeline template.

two-dimensional (2-D) shape A shape, such as a rectangle or ellipse, that has length and width. A 2-D shape has eight selection handles and one rotation handle. See also *one-dimensional shape*.

units of measure See *measurement units*.

vertex A diamond-shaped handle that appears when you select a shape with the Pencil tool. Each vertex defines a point at the beginning or end of a line segment.

weight The thickness of a 1-D shape or the border around a 2-D shape.

zoom The degree of magnification of a drawing. A zoom of 100% displays the drawing page at the same size it will be when it is printed.

Index

Numerics

A

B

C

D

E

F

G

M

N

P

R

S

Z

What do you think of this book?
We want to hear from you!

Do you have a few minutes to participate in a brief online survey? Microsoft is interested in hearing your feedback about this publication so that we can continually improve our books and learning resources for you.

To participate in our survey, please visit:
www.microsoft.com/learning/booksurvey

And enter this book's ISBN, 0-7356-2125-X. As a thank-you to survey participants in the United States and Canada, each month we'll randomly select five respondents to win one of five $100 gift certificates from a leading online merchant.* At the conclusion of the survey, you can enter the drawing by providing your e-mail address, which will be used for prize notification *only*.

Thanks in advance for your input. Your opinion counts!

Sincerely,

Microsoft® Learning

Learn More. Go Further.

To see special offers on Microsoft Learning products for developers, IT professionals, and home and office users, visit: *www.microsoft.com/learning/booksurvey*

* No purchase necessary. Void where prohibited. Open only to residents of the 50 United States (includes District of Columbia) and Canada (void in Quebec). Sweepstakes ends 6/30/2005. For official rules, see: *www.microsoft.com/learning/booksurvey*